Urban Neighborhoods in a New Era

Urban Neighborhoods in a New Era

Revitalization Politics in the Postindustrial City

CLARENCE N. STONE AND
ROBERT P. STOKER

JOHN BETANCUR, SUSAN E. CLARKE,
MARILYN DANTICO, MARTIN HORAK,
KAREN MOSSBERGER, JULIET MUSSO,
JEFFEREY M. SELLERS, ELLEN SHIAU,
HAROLD WOLMAN, AND DONN WORGS

The University of Chicago Press
Chicago and London

The University of Chicago Press, Chicago 60637
The University of Chicago Press, Ltd., London
© 2015 by The University of Chicago
All rights reserved. Published 2015.

Printed in the United States of America

24 23 22 21 20 19 18 17 16 15   1 2 3 4 5

ISBN-13: 978-0-226-28896-3 (cloth)
ISBN-13: 978-0-226-28901-4 (paper)
ISBN-13: 978-0-226-28915-1 (e-book)

DOI: 10.7208/chicago/9780226289151.001.0001

Library of Congress Cataloging-in-Publication Data

Stone, Clarence N. (Clarence Nathan), 1935– author.
    Urban neighborhoods in a new era : revitalization politics in the post-
industrial city / Clarence N. Stone and Robert P. Stoker [and 10 others].
        pages   cm
    Includes bibliographical references and index.
    ISBN 978-0-226-28896-3 (cloth : alk. paper) — ISBN 978-0-226-28901-4
(pbk. : alk. paper) — ISBN 978-0-226-28915-1 (ebook)   1. Neighborhoods—
United States.   2. Urban renewal—United States.   I. Stoker, Robert Phillip,
1954– author.   II. Title.
    HT123S7845 2015
    307.3'362160973—dc23

                                                                    2014047165

CONTENTS

TABLES

My first venture into studying urban neighborhoods culminated in a book titled *Economic Growth and Neighborhood Discontent* (Stone 1976). It was about reshaping Atlanta from a rail-centered city to a place in a burgeoning automotive age. My Atlanta study was part of a wave of neighborhood studies, some looking internally to the features of urban neighborhoods, particularly those less well-off, and others paying special attention to the rise of neighborhood protests and, as in Atlanta, conflict between less prosperous neighborhoods and established power centers. The recurring narrative was about a largely localized neighborhood movement that scored scattered victories but was mainly positioned to wage occasional defensive battles with little capacity for affecting agendas over the long term.

In the years following World War II, the overarching consideration for city leaders, political and economic, was redevelopment. They saw remaking the central business district as their top priority. Other changes were under way, principally a black political mobilization, but city leaders had their policy eyes mainly on redevelopment—and through the federal highway and urban-renewal programs there was ample federal money to back this effort.

Whether labeled as such or not, many of these early works were studies of power. Notwithstanding the fact that nonaffluent neighborhoods did not lose all the battles, these studies described struggles between unequal contenders. The playing field was tilted heavily against less-well-off neighborhoods, and even when such neighborhoods survived, many came through this time bearing the marks of social and economic damage. Now we are in a different time, but scars from the past remain.

In contrast with accounts of the earlier era of redevelopment, this book identifies a basic shift through which relationships have become more fluid and policymaking more open-ended. Seen from a neighborhood perspective, new players, fresh issues, in some instances modified political-governmental arrangements, and a transformed context distinguish the present from earlier times. Whereas the post–World War II years accorded economic development a privileged place, the current period allows for some mixing of economic-development aims with community-based concerns. The terms of this mix are negotiable, and the line between what favors economic development and what attends to community concerns has become increasingly fuzzy. Power is less and less a showdown between clearly differentiated antagonists and more a matter of how policy issues are framed, albeit accommodations are sometimes far from amicable.

Not to be overlooked is that poverty persists, neighborhood distress remains a highly visible feature of the urban landscape, and cities are at the center of contemporary inequality. Positive-sounding initiatives abound, but rarely do urban programs live up to the high expectations and incautious rhetoric that surround their launch. Still, historian Michael Katz (2011) questions the dominance in urban scholarship of what he terms the "narrative of failure." He calls for a counternarrative while adding that the "temptation to jettison the narrative of urban failure in favor of a story based on progress and hope must be resisted" (2011, 159). In line with Katz's caution, the authors of this book see an array of incomplete steps and initiatives that have fallen short. But we also find significant accomplishments and many moves that make a difference to those who live in areas of disadvantage. While distressed neighborhoods seldom, if ever, get preferred treatment, they no longer suffer the nearly total disregard they once incurred.

Over time, understanding has grown that neighborhoods and their treatment are interwoven with other policies in the city: particularly transportation, order maintenance, and the pursuit of economic growth. There may have been a time—under Model Cities, for instance—when elite actors treated neighborhood policy as a differentiated arena to be operated separately and kept distinct from the economic-development agenda, but in the present era such policy thinking has largely faded away. Now neighborhood issues are often linked to broader city aims of growth and development, with public safety a continuing consideration as well.

Since this book identifies the emergence of a new era of neighborhood politics, perhaps not yet widely recognized, it seems in order to explain how the research unfolded and the theme for this book emerged. The present work grew out of an invitation from the Rockefeller Foundation to its Conference Center in Bellagio, Italy, to conduct a workshop on policy efforts to address distressed urban neighborhoods. The resulting Regenerating Urban Neighborhoods (RUN) project spawned by that workshop featured a two-part follow-up: a European wing and a North American wing. This book is a product of the latter, and it consists of six case studies covering Baltimore, Chicago, Denver, Los Angeles, and Phoenix in the United States and the Canadian city of Toronto. The six cities vary in size, but all are large and all are the central cities of metropolitan regions. They represent no sampling procedure but do cover a variety of political-governmental forms and socioeconomic conditions. The workshop chose to work from the ground up, with a focus on distressed neighborhoods as policy targets.

We decided on this focus not because we regarded the global economy as unimportant or systems of intergovernmental relations as inconsequential, but because we wanted to view these forces from the perspective and actions of local players. We took a cue from Arthur Stinchcombe, who cautions about a "generalizing impulse" among social scientists—an impulse, he argues, that "attaches itself most easily to the anatomy and physiology of social structures." Structures may emerge, Stinchcombe says, but the place to start is at a less abstract level with "people defining problems and trying to work their way out of them" (1978, 121).

In this study, as we sought to refine findings, we came face-to-face with the insistent reality of a shift. It grew and took shape from many particulars, cumulating into what we came to recognize as a new era for neighborhood politics. Although structural inequality remains a key feature of neighborhood politics, the new era has seen the kind of unrelenting zero-sum approach once so prevalent give way to a more contingency-filled outlook. Aiding a distressed neighborhood is no longer seen as necessarily ill-conceived redistribution; it might be part of a policy mix that yields widely shared benefits. Zero-sum calculations have by no means disappeared, but they don't necessarily crowd out other ways of thinking and acting.

The shift we found was deduced, not from a grand theory, but from viewing the perspectives and actions of local players. How did they understand neighborhood distress, what level of priority did they attach to the revitalization of neighborhoods displaying signs of decline, and what actions did they take (initiate, contend over, implement, and modify)? What lessons did they learn and act on? Our approach involved city-level studies covering (1) who the players are whose actions impinge fairly directly on neighborhood conditions; (2) which issues and policy ideas they took up; (3) through what arrangements policy decisions were made and implemented; and (4) what patterns of policy intervention took shape. Interviews, documents, and news accounts were our sources, the flow of events a guiding thread.

In looking at neighborhood distress, the Bellagio workshop defined a policy intervention by three qualifying characteristics: (1) that it be intentional and not purely incidental to some other action; (2) that it cover more than a single functional area of policy—for instance, increased policing by itself would not be sufficient; and (3) that it be distinguished from established operations by an allocation of additional resources—coordination of existing services alone would fall short. Beyond this, since a neighborhood involves people and not just space, total replacement of low- and moderate-income residents with those who were well-off was ruled out as a *revitalization* policy. For instance, we did not regard promotion of unmitigated gentrification as neighborhood regeneration. Rather, it seemed more an antineighborhood policy. A blend of some gentrification with improvement for long-term residents is on occasion a sought-after revitalization end, but rarely is it one that leaves everybody happy. Policy moves can be mixed in both motivation and consequence.

We consistently observed city actors struggling with two recurring lines of friction. One is the issue of displacement. Elite policy actors tend to favor greater displacement; neighborhood residents generally want less. The second line of friction is over physical improvement versus enhanced services. In this instance, elite actors tend to emphasize physical change, while residents often voice a need for greater services. People in distressed neighborhoods typically have a variety of community concerns, ranging from more effective policing to better schools. Residents especially favor more programs for youth, and community concerns can extend to such matters as more extensive and more accessible drug treatment. Employment and job training often rank high among community concerns, and more wide-ranging retail offerings occupy a place as well.

Physical improvement may appeal to mayors and other top officials in part because it carries the hope that a onetime expenditure fixes the problem. More grounded in immediate circumstances, residents may see physical conditions as a symptom, not an underlying cause, and cost containment is not their major concern. The two lines of friction can easily come together and heighten conflict. Seen narrowly in these terms, neighborhood policy and politics have a potential to turn into a zero-sum game in which elite actors hold the trump cards while residents in disadvantaged communities always lose. That was the typical urban-redevelopment scenario of yesteryear. Unrelenting, structural inequalities promise no other outcome.

Does the present time differ from an earlier time when broad structural forces seemed to be close to determinative? This book gives evidence of a shift toward a new, more open-ended era of neighborhood politics.

With special urging from Jefferey Sellers, the Bellagio workshop recognized from the start that it was important to avoid viewing neighborhood policy and politics as static phenomena but instead to see them as part of a trajectory. Thus, although in the workshop our main concern was the contemporary politics of neighborhood regeneration, we understood that historical background and the political legacies of cities entered the analysis. History matters.

The workshop started with a relatively simple model: socioeconomic conditions as a source of problems and challenges, along with political and policy legacies and how they are understood by current players, how policies are framed as responses to problems and challenges, and then how political-governmental arrangements filter policy solutions and yield policy outcomes. Our initial aim was to use cross-city comparisons to identify those key political-governmental arrangements in interaction with socioeconomic conditions that generated more robust policy interventions. But (apologies to Robert Burns) the best-laid plans "gang aft a-gley." We found particular differences among the six North American cities, but in many instances they were not large. Neighborhood revitalization policy was a significant presence in all six cities, but in none did it enjoy sustained standing as a matter of high priority. However, we pondered whether there was something more far-reaching at work. As research progressed, the fate of discrete policy initiatives was woven into history-informed patterns in policymaking, in the evolution of ideas about policy intersects, and in changed thinking about what could and should be brought together. The initial model was useful in organizing research but of limited value in capturing the big picture. Trajectory took on enlarged weight as a guide to interpreting findings, and feedback became part of the results considered.

The six cases pointed to a shared shift from an old to a new pattern of policy and politics. The shift was substantial enough to warrant a claim that a new era was giving rise to a discernible new politics. Of course, city policy initiatives are not an isolated phenomenon but draw from a discourse of ideas and puzzles exchanged not only among local players but also between local and national (and sometimes international) policy actors. Many historians incline toward looking at convergent forces, and that is an inclination this book shares. Issues, ideas, players, policy practices, political and governing arrangements—all tend to flow together (but not necessarily smoothly) as waves of change.

While cross-city differences remain part of RUN's overall analysis, the process of working through our cases and their wider environment gave heightened appreciation of an insight from Robert Salisbury about comparison over time. In his urban classic on "the new convergence of power," Salisbury offered: "By viewing the city historically a number of elements, particularly those which have changed, can be seen more clearly than if a more strictly contemporaneous study were made" (1964, 777). By viewing current policy for distressed neighborhoods as part of a trajectory, we could see that a cross-time framework was useful.

In the years following World War II, city leaders were caught up in a need to cope with a declining industrial order. Faced with deep-running economic change, city leaders saw themselves "in a race with time" (Lowe 1967), and in many places political and business leaders came together and created arrangements to pursue economic growth and, as much as possible, keep it uncluttered by other concerns. Nonaffluent neighborhoods were typically an afterthought or simply viewed as a source of blight. When spatially clustered social problems became increasingly hard to ignore, the response by established power centers was to keep growth policy separate and give it special standing, a pattern that can be seen in Sun Belt and Frost Belt cities alike. With the arrival of Great Society programs, community concerns were sometimes taken up, but essentially as a differentiated and distinctly secondary arena.

How did this older policy period give way to the present period of postindustrialism? What changed to lay the groundwork for a shift in practices? Postindustrialism is usually linked directly to characteristics of the world economy, specifically the rise of the information age and the ascendance of increasingly formal knowledge. In this book we look more at the offshoots of such an economy. Today's policy actors are caught between the stubbornness of inequality and a case for social inclusion (e.g., "all children can learn").

A complex postindustrial context has loosened the reins on established practices, and fresh approaches have emerged. Thus, seeing politics in the large over time can reveal things that might not be evident bit by bit. A myriad of specifics, perhaps deemed inconsequential when viewed one by one, show a pattern when aggregated. Community and social concerns have gained greater salience. Urban economists, such as Edward Glaeser (2011), stress the importance of human capital.

Yet neighborhood distress has continuity across time as an ongoing spatial expression of socioeconomic inequality. Even though the nation's racial order is undergoing change (Hochschild, Weaver, and Burch 2012), stereotyping of neighborhoods endures and has spatial impacts (Sampson 2012). Income disparities not only persist but have deepened (Hacker, Mettler, and Soss 2007). Amelioration of neighborhood distress remains, then, as a policy challenge even as social and economic changes continue to unfold. Are the policy responses to neighborhoods really so different today from what they were in the past? If so, how and why?

Although the long-standing imperative of economic growth has by no means vanished, it has been amended in a way that has implications for efforts to revitalize distressed neighborhoods. The scope and character of this amending are part of what this book explores; this book is a response to a growing but uneven recognition that economic development and community-based concerns often cannot be handily separated. Indeed, it seems that city actors cannot devote policy attention to the economic realm without engaging the social realm as well. Policy realities are intermingled. Moreover, many city leaders, while attempting to concentrate on economic growth, learned over time that public safety and neighborhood alienation are not matters that can be ignored without consequences.

What fostered a change in thinking? At one level such change can be said to come out of the transition from industrial to postindustrial society. However, *Urban Neighborhoods in a New Era* embodies no ambition to advance an encompassing theory of urban political change. Instead, it was conceived to stay close to the flow of events and how, in Stinchcombe manner, these events reflect the way things look to participants. In line with important work in American political development, this approach avoids highly abstract speculation and aims more for proximate causation. Further, the new-era shift is best seen as something that is taking hold gradually, bit by bit, and not the product of a holistic, functionally driven adaptation to a changing context. It is piecemeal, uneven, and cumulative more than punctuated. Still, over time convergence is observable, and in an overview of the decades following World War II, one can see an emerging tilt from a narrow preoccupation with land use toward greater concern with people. Consider the following as instances in which nonaffluent people began to command more attention:

· Population gain or loss became a matter about which city policymakers grew increasingly concerned, and they saw trends as derived from more than economic growth.
· Concentrated poverty emerged as a concern, and city leaders came to see it as a condition that aggravates a range of problems.
· Although street crime and disorder concentrate in poor areas, they are nevertheless city problems. And for some urban actors, the prevalence of

violence among youth became a moral concern. A worsening crack epidemic made the issue especially pressing in the latter years of the twentieth century.

· As *A Nation at Risk* (National Commission on Excellence in Education 1983) highlighted, schools assumed heightened importance in the postindustrial age and its knowledge economy. Many officials and civic leaders saw that a city's long-range economic health is linked to the performance of its education system.

As the people dimension grew through such specifics, the pursuit of economic growth was put in a different light. What had once been an urgent task of saving the city by refashioning the central business district morphed into a more complex undertaking as policy elites began to see that economic aspirations and community problems could not be neatly separated. Change came about, but not because these new themes prompted a sudden conversion from the old way of thinking. Realities gradually built awareness that a city's economic and social conditions are connected. Still, details matter in how this connection is perceived and handled. Accordingly, the policy domain of distressed neighborhoods is now populated with players and practices not prominent when downtown-centered redevelopment reigned as the distinct action priority for cities. It is the intertwining of economic development with social and community concerns that has become the terrain of the emerging politics of neighborhood revitalization. It is a terrain of struggle, conflict, and misunderstanding as well as a terrain in which positive-sum outcomes can sometimes be brought about. Bargaining and negotiation are possible but can come to a halt if distrust intrudes.

Change continues, but the past figures in through the collateral social damage that went along with massive redevelopment. A legacy of social disruption and neglect is part of the distress that many neighborhoods now confront. As Mary Pattillo observes of Chicago's experience, "the ghost of urban renewal is always present" (2007, 8).

The new neighborhood politics emerging in postindustrial cities thus partly involves a process of awakening—of discovering that a crack epidemic had to be confronted, that urban schools needed to be turned around, that severely distressed public-housing projects required attention, that concentrated poverty has far-reaching consequences, that residential disinvestment and neglect can spread and bring down adjoining areas, and that urban universities, hospitals, and medical schools could benefit from a more constructive relationship with their neighbors.

Awakening can be incomplete, and it has not brought with it ready-made and adequately supplied capacities to respond. Hence, neighborhood politics in the postindustrial city involves a scramble to assemble resources in a period of great scarcity. And a new stage of policy thinking has not precluded conflict and weltering tensions. With the winds of inequality undiminished, the particulars of pursuing the social reconstruction of cities are often contested.

The city is a place of inequalities, manifest most visibly at the neighborhood level in clusters of residential distress. This distress is most conspicuous when properties are run-down, neglected, and, in the worst cases, pocked with abandonment. Distress, however, has other manifestations— crime and social disorder, environmental hazards, inferior services, political impotence, and profound alienation. A challenge for scholars is how to frame their work so that—as put by Michael Katz—they are neither Cassandra nor Pollyanna. The "narrative of failure" is deeply entrenched but should not prevent us from seeing that social-equity gains can be real.

While inequality has a structural foundation that city policies cannot topple, local actions can mitigate many of its consequences. Much of the theoretical work related to cities and their distressed neighborhoods either greatly underplays structural inequality or comes close to structural determinism. In the concluding chapter of this book, as findings are assessed, we aim for an often-missing middle ground and offer an approach that accepts structural inequality as a reality but rejects structural determinism.

Accordingly, we find that the current period of policymaking is more penetrable by neighborhood concerns than was the case in earlier times. In part this comes from new ways of thinking about city-neighborhood connections, new actors (with different views and concerns), and a change in inclination among community-based actors (from those once firmly rooted in a history of protest to those who show a cautious willingness to bargain for community benefits).

The follow-up step then becomes one of asking what may be learned by looking at varied experiences within the present context of the postindustrial city. What factors are of consequence? We find the institutionalization of neighborhood improvement policy to be of special significance, but there are other considerations. The challenges of alliance building are worth close attention. Structural inequality is very real, but the agency of residents in distressed neighborhoods, the context within which they pursue their aims, and the intermediate arrangements, mechanisms, and policy practices employed are also quite consequential. While structural inequality continues to take a toll, the concluding chapter of this book brings together particulars that suggest a departure from an urban "narrative of failure." There is room for factors to come together in ways that advance neighborhood improvements.

A note about how this book was composed: In the conventional manner, the table of contents lists the authors for each chapter. This listing, however, misses a process in which a core group, listed on the title page of this volume, engaged in an ongoing interchange through a series of workshops, extended sessions of mealtime discussion, email exchanges, and ad hoc conversations to develop a shared understanding of this book project and how its parts fit together. Clarence N. Stone and Robert P. Stoker coordinated the final version of this shared task, but this book is thoroughly a multi-authored work. It has been a special pleasure to be part of this process.

—Clarence N. Stone

ANC	Action for Neighborhood Change
BNC	Baltimore Neighborhood Collaborative
BNIA	Baltimore Neighborhood Indicators Alliance
BUILD	Baltimoreans United in Leadership Development
CANDO	Chicago Association of Neighborhood Development Organizations
CBA	community benefits agreement
CBD	central business district
CCI	Comprehensive Community Initiative
CDBG	Community Development Block Grant
CDC	community development corporation
CDFI	community development financial institution
CED	Committee for Economic Development
CGC	Charter Government Committee
CHA	Chicago Housing Authority
CPHA	Citizens Planning and Housing Association
CRA	Community Redevelopment Agency
CRN	Chicago Rehab Network
CSP	Community Safety Plan
CWED	Community Workshop on Economic Development
DOSP	Denver Office of Strategic Partnerships
EBDI	East Baltimore Development Inc.
EZ	Empowerment Zone
FNI	Focus Neighborhood Initiative
GBC	Greater Baltimore Committee
HACLA	Housing Authority of the City of Los Angeles
HEBCAC	Historic East Baltimore Community Action Coalition
HERA	Housing and Economic Recovery Act of 2008

HNI   Healthy Neighborhoods Initiative
HOME   HOME Investment Partnerships Program
HUD   US Department of Housing and Urban Development
IAF   Industrial Areas Foundation
KEYS   Knowledge, Education, Youth, and Society
LAANE   Los Angeles Alliance for a New Economy
LAPD   Los Angeles Police Department
LISC   Local Initiatives Support Corporation
MHC   Mile High Connects
NAP   Neighborhood Action Partnership
NAT   Neighborhood Action Team
NCBR   Neighborhood, Community, and Business Revitalization
NCI   New Communities Initiative
NCP   New Communities Program
NDP   Neighborhood Development Project
NIA   Neighborhood Initiative Area / Neighborhood Improvement
          Area
NSD   Neighborhood Services Department
NSP   Neighborhood Stabilization Program
OED   Office of Economic Development
OROSW   Operation Reach Out South West
PN   priority neighborhood
PPCDC   Patterson Park Community Development Corporation
RUN   Regenerating Urban Neighborhoods
SEZ   Supplemental Empowerment Zone
SMEAC   Save Middle East Action Coalition
SNS   Strong Neighborhoods Strategy
SNTF   Strong Neighborhoods Task Force
SPAR   Social Policy Analysis and Research
TABOR   Taxpayer Bill of Rights
TAP   The Access Partnership
TAVIS   Toronto Anti-violence Intervention Strategy
TCHC   Toronto Community Housing Corporation
TIF   Tax Increment Financing
TOD   Transit-oriented development
TRF   The Reinvestment Fund
TRP   The Resurrection Project
TWO   The Woodlawn Organization
UHI   Urban Health Institute
YCF   Youth Challenge Fund

ONE

Change Afoot

MARTIN HORAK, JULIET MUSSO, ELLEN SHIAU, ROBERT P. STOKER, AND CLARENCE N. STONE

The narrative of urban change in North American cities has most often focused on the business district with its office towers, luxury hotels, convention centers, festival marketplaces, and, frequently now, sports arenas. For
many years neighborhoods bore the burden of change and received little
in return. Secondary attention to aging neighborhoods underscored their
neglect and political impotence. Except for predatory lending, housing finance sent its dollars mainly to the suburbs. Expressways ate chunks of
inner-city land and in the process often created barriers to neighborhood-
level travel, while the same multilane highways connected the business district with seemingly ever-extending suburbs. The poor, near poor, and other
nonaffluent residents of the central city were thoroughly marginalized—
displaced and disregarded, never part of the power-wielding body of in-
siders who set agendas, targeted investments, and guided the public discourse about the city's future. In light of such a past, it may be tempting
to embrace pessimism about the marginal status of distressed neighborhoods, but we see in recent trends the emergence of a different neighborhood narrative—one containing multiple possibilities, one not structurally
foreordained to end in decline and despair. Still, perils to neighborhood
well-being have by no means disappeared. The new narrative is about possibility, not an accomplished reversal of fortune.

In today's highly mobile world, why focus on urban neighborhoods,
particularly those in distress or danger of decline? The often-made claim to
be "a city of neighborhoods" suggests that, although the business district
may be the economic core, the quality of urban life is heavily residential in
character. Without neighborhoods in the picture, research provides a trun-
cated view of the city and its politics. *Urban Neighborhoods in a New Era*
aims to correct this by highlighting residential neighborhoods, not as phe-

nomena in and of themselves, but as part of a wider picture of city politics and policymaking.

Cities and their politics are not static phenomena. As conditions change, so also do motives and capacities to act. In its approach to political change, *this book focuses on distressed urban neighborhoods*. It differs from much work in urban politics in three ways:

1. Neighborhood policy, not revival of downtown, is the lens for viewing the politics of cities.
2. This neighborhood lens shows that an important shift in the political order of cities has occurred, and this shift makes some past characterizations of neighborhood politics increasingly problematic in the cities of today.
3. To better understand, and possibly improve, the political prospects of distressed neighborhoods, this book turns to a reform agenda that, while acknowledging structural inequality and its challenge, recognizes a role for political agency. It thus offers an alternative to a long-reigning narrative of urban-policy failure (cf. M. Katz 2011).

As cities have left the industrial age further and further behind, the narrow pursuit of economic development and growth as an overriding aim has been modified; the economic imperative has become less distinct and now intermingles with other considerations. We do not mean to suggest that the economic imperative has been displaced; to the contrary, growth remains a central local priority. However, economic development is no longer seen as a necessarily discrete and privileged domain. The intermingling of community-level concerns with economic development has become part of a new era in city politics. Neighborhood issues—such as fighting crime, educating children, putting youth on a constructive path into adulthood, boosting opportunities for gainful employment, and, yes, enhancing the general quality of residential life—are factors in economic growth even as economic growth itself continues to be seen as the sine qua non for city vitality.

In the new postindustrial geography, neighborhoods with market potential can readily become revitalization targets. Hence market processes are now seen as something not always tied tightly to the central business district (CBD). The new geography includes varied sites—especially those that feature anchors such as universities, medical schools, and hospitals. Access to mass transit stations has also risen in import, as has the nearby presence of parks and other recreational facilities (including those for nightlife). Desirable housing stock—whether because of its architecture, location, or both—is also a source of market potential. This is by no means to suggest that markets are always a positive force. To the contrary, many places continue to be plagued by disinvestment and its manifestation in abandoned properties, neglected upkeep, and scarce retail. A need to battle blight remains very much part of the neighborhood picture, but in some places the possibility of gentrification and its various ramifications exists too.

In a complex urban setting, all segments of the city share a common ecology. The CBD is affected in myriad direct and indirect ways by what happens in the residential areas that encircle it and vice versa. At the same time, economic growth, the fight against blight, and responsiveness to community concerns do not create a smooth fit. The mix is laden with tension, and conflict often surrounds the particulars. Community concerns often extend well beyond the narrow economic agenda that comes most readily to business elites. For their part, residents of distressed neighborhoods often emphasize public safety (especially containing violence among the young) and link this concern to a need for organized recreational activities. Prominent also are calls for maintaining adequate services, ranging from trash pickup and fixing potholes to drug treatment and aiding senior citizens who have limited family support.

Because there is nothing formulaic about the relationship between economic growth and neighborhood vitality, there is bound to be friction. In governing, policymakers are guided by neither a controlling consensus about the well-being of the city nor a technocratic calculation of the best path to follow. Instead, the concerns of distressed neighborhoods are inevitably part of a political process in which interests conflict and information is never complete. Short-term and immediate considerations often supersede broader and long-term views. Sundry motives come into play. Making a governing mesh from such fractious forces is the task of politics, and we examine this process in the belief that some versions of this mesh are better for improving neighborhood conditions than others. But before we draw any conclusions about how more hopeful trajectories of neighborhood policy might be forged and sustained, we need an understanding of what is happening at present.

We pursue this aim in multiple steps in this chapter. We first set the broad context for the six city narratives that come later in the book. This context is centered in a long-term shift from the redevelopment politics dominant in the years following World War II to the politics of today's postindustrial city. The shift involves a decline in the cohesion and concentration of policymaking power at the elite level (in Robert Salisbury's 1964 term, a "convergence of power") and the rise of more diffuse patterns of policymaking. We next discuss how the new era of neighborhood politics took shape as gradual recognition of intensifying problems set the stage for fresh thinking about the interconnections between urban problems. As a result, neighborhoods experienced modest and limited gains as subjects of policy attention. We then discuss neighborhood distress and revitalization strategies. Although it has many components, we emphasize neighborhood distress as a political problem that tests a community's capacity to engage in constructive problem solving. Finally, we sketch an analytic framework for political reform that encompasses both structural inequality and constrained political agency. The framework focuses analytic attention on the middle ground between structural determinism and free-ranging agency. Constraint derives significantly from a politics of interactions between highly unequal players: on one side is an upper stratum containing an assemblage of elite players with substantial resources, who often play a major part in agenda setting, and on the other side is a lower stratum of actors with limited resources and a history of being marginal players in urban politics.

A Major Shift

Our study of six North American cities bears evidence of an important change in the political position of distressed neighborhoods. Though far short of revolutionary proportions, change is afoot. When cities were in the early stage of transition away from the industrial era, progrowth coalitions placed economic development in a protected position, insulated it, and downplayed neighborhood problems and the collateral damage residents suffered as economic-development initiatives accelerated and amplified a socially disruptive process of change (Friedland and Palmer 1984; Logan and Molotch 1987; Dreier, Mollenkopf, and Swanstrom 2004).[1] Today, this once-entrenched policy pattern has altered. Across the six cities we have studied (our study cities are Baltimore, Chicago, Denver, Los Angeles, Phoenix, and Toronto), policy actors have come increasingly—though in some cases reluctantly—to treat economic development and neighborhood vitality as aims not easily kept separate and apart.

While the intermingling of policy domains has become an important trend across cities, significant variation in detail is also evident. Local institutions and elites differ in how they respond to issues, and the contemporary scene is now populated with a wide variety of neighborhood-related policy practices and programs. Among them are transit-oriented development (TOD), community benefits agreements (CBAs), HOPE VI and its successor modifications such as Choice Neighborhoods, and—one-time foundation favorite—Comprehensive Community Initiatives (CCIs).[2] Thus, there is room for significant city-level variation in the ways in which policymakers see and address neighborhood issues.

As cities adapted to a postindustrial economic base, new actors entered the policy process and some existing participants changed their policy aims.[3] Although efforts undertaken by local government remain a central part of the picture, private foundations have emerged as key actors in many cities, sometimes promoting initiatives that combine neighborhood revitalization issues with economic development. Such crosscutting policy actions put community-based organizations in a changed situation. As economic growth ceased to be treated as a separate arena, neighborhood-level participants could take up development issues in fresh ways. In earlier times, faced with what they regarded as a hostile agenda, neighborhood leaders mobilized to protest and resist freeways and other development projects. They are now better positioned (in some cases) to view development as an opportunity to secure community benefits. Neighborhoods still find reasons to protest, but the strategic goal has changed. Rather than seeking to protect neighborhood integrity by a go-for-broke effort to derail an intrusive economic-development agenda, neighborhoods can seek to participate in the policy process and make claims for the sake of community improvement. Bargaining for benefits is a more flexible approach than purely defensive opposition. Initiatives such as anticrime programs or TODs become opportunities for neighborhood actors to pursue a multi-faceted community improvement agenda.

Setting the Stage: Cross-Time Comparisons

In turning to a broad look at how this crucial shift in neighborhood policy and politics came about, we follow the example of Robert Salisbury (1964), who compared the politics of his time with the politics of an earlier era. Writing a half century later than Salisbury, we employ a different schema of periodization, but for the same purpose—to understand politics and policy in the contemporary city by contrasting it with politics and policy in the preceding time period. Salisbury looked back at the industrial city to highlight what was distinctive about the politics of the transition away from the industrial city. Douglas Rae covers the same cross-time comparison in what he terms the end of urbanism (2003). In work that forms an essential complement to Robert Dahl's *Who Governs?* (1981), Rae examines Mayor Richard Lee's struggle to cope with technological and economic change as New Haven's industrial base declined and its suburbs grew. He contrasts the politics of Lee's mayoralty with that of Frank Rice, mayor of New Haven a half century earlier.[4]

Salisbury, Rae, and others focus on city politics in a period of major transition. From roughly the end of World War II to the beginning of the Reagan presidency, cities went through a makeover period to adjust to industrial decline.[5] A distinct politics of transition lasted for more than thirty years. We emphasize the word "transition" because a top-level effort was mobilized with the goal of saving the city through reshaping its central business core. For an extended time urban politics was driven by this change agenda. Salisbury argued that this period experienced a "new convergence of power." For several cities it was a time in which the politics of machine versus reform gave way to the joined efforts of city hall and downtown business leadership to guide the city through redevelopment and the extensive change in land use that it brought about.

During this transition period, neighborhoods often found themselves relegated to the political sidelines. In these years the pursuit of economic growth enjoyed a protected position in the policy process, insulated from everyday politics, from community concerns, and from worries about worsening social problems. Scholarly research has consistently confirmed the marginal political status of neighborhoods during this time period.[6]

Our Salisbury-inspired aim is not to reanalyze this thoroughly researched period but to revisit it in order to set up a comparison with today's emergent postindustrial city and specifically the place of neighborhoods in the politics of this emergent city. We use the comparison to identify a latter twentieth-century shift in which distressed neighborhoods received increased local attention as places in need of revitalization. Although federal policy in the United States displayed a new level of indifference toward cities during these same years, urban neighborhoods began to gain greater local policy attention as well as, in many instances, significant philanthropic attention. This change involved no dramatic upheaval and is perhaps not widely recognized. Notwithstanding, we maintain that a basic shift in policy thinking and practice has emerged. While neighborhoods are seldom the top local priority, they can often claim positive consideration. However tentatively and incompletely, residents of urban neighborhoods have gained recognition as part of the policy puzzle that confronts cities.

Some may question this assertion. After all, structural inequality persists, and racial stereotyping and discrimination continue to shape the physical and social character of cities (Sampson 2012). In contrast with the earlier period, in which federal money heavily subsidized alterations in land use, today cities find themselves the largely neglected stepchildren of national politics. Presidential campaigns come and go with barely any mention of the urban condition. What's new, then? Although economic growth is still a local priority, it no longer occupies the highly privileged and protected position it once held. "People concerns"—police-community relations as a crime-control strategy, education and youth opportunities, workforce development and employment—have risen to a level at which economic development and a loose assemblage of community-based issues now intertwine. Cities embrace population growth (including from immigration) as an important objective. Human capital has become part of wider thinking about economic growth. The same applies to crime prevention and antiviolence campaigns. Because it is viewed as a contributor to problems in such areas as education and public safety, concentrated poverty has emerged as a condition to address. In some places youth development has gained standing as a key concern.[7]

The wider context has provided a setting in which new players entered, some old problems worsened, new concerns surfaced, and fresh thinking came easier. Gradually, decision-makers in the cities on which we focus in this book began to show an awareness that a city's economic imperative cannot stand in isolation.[8] However, the present period is not brimming with big successes, and change in terms of policy results has been modest. In the concluding chapter we find that the glass of neighborhood improvement does not measure even a metaphorical half full; a quarter full seems more appropriate. Still change has occurred and more appears possible. In our Salisbury gambit, let us turn now to past experience, the post–World War II transition away from the industrial city when redevelopment ruled supreme. Then we can contrast this to the current, postindustrial time to see more clearly the possibilities and constraints it contains. The use of a schema of periods should not be taken as an indication that order and stability are the norm; change is ongoing (Orren and Skowronek 2004). However, periodization can help us make sense of a profusion of particulars.

Transition Policy and Politics

The post–World War II transition period in North American urban politics requires some background: why would a transition occur then? A new transportation form had been in the making for some time. But although the automobile was coming into wide use during the 1920s, the arrival of the Great Depression was not a time for a concerted effort to remake the city. Many states and their localities were financially hard-pressed. World War II gave the industrial city a reprieve and put nonwar construction on hold. By the end of the war, however, the stage was set for a rapid change in the urban landscape, and central cities faced threatening new conditions of rapid suburban growth. In cities like rail-centered Atlanta and harbor-oriented Baltimore, business leaders came out of the war already planning expressways to connect downtown with an unfolding suburban future.[9] Although a few places, like business-led Charlotte, North Carolina, were able to annex for new growth, many cities were politically locked into their existing territory, limiting the strategies available to cope with industrial decline.[10]

Atlanta and Baltimore were places where business and political leaders were on good terms and could easily come together around plans for an ambitious redevelopment agenda. But many other cities had a long-standing divide between business and political leadership, which was a potential obstacle to ambitious redevelopment plans. For some cities, then, political realignment was in order. Famously, for instance, steel-town Pittsburgh saw its political boss make peace with its lead banker in order to pursue an agenda of cleanup and redevelopment. This pattern was repeated across several cities that had once been strongholds of machine politics (Teaford 1990). In some cases—Boston, for instance—the machine-versus-business struggle coincided with an ethnic-religious cleavage and was bitterly fought.[11] But even in Boston, despite its history of conflict, a changing city politics brought business and political leadership together around a redevelopment agenda.[12]

Peacemaking at the top does not preclude conflict. Redevelopment—changing an established pattern of land use—affects property owners, large and small, and businesses of all sizes, and it can disrupt residential neighborhoods. All of this and more happened in urban America of the postwar period. It was also a time in which the Great Migration added its impact, and racial change joined economic restructuring to make for a period of high turmoil. Turbulence was magnified by the fact that much of the redevelopment that led to population displacement often targeted African American communities.

The opening phase of redevelopment caught neighborhoods off guard. Their political connections from an earlier time had eroded (von Hoffman 1994; see also Salisbury 1964). The scale of expressway construction and the broad definition used to target properties designated for "slum clearance" were greater than what past experiences had encompassed. Business-led decision-makers—typically the dominant voice on planning and redevelopment bodies—had little regard for lower-income residents, particularly if residents were people of color.[13] For example, Baltimore designated a west-side neighborhood for highway construction in the 1940s. It was then left for land speculators to take over and allow decline to set in (Olson 1976, 63). For redevelopment purposes, acquisition and relocation did not come to this neighborhood until the 1960s, two decades after the community's fate had been determined by a process largely unknown to residents. Like so many others in this period, the neighborhood was African American—a population that had little political clout at that point.

Though it took time, in city after city neighborhoods mobilized, in some places more effectively than in others (Mohl 2004). Early on, many communities were simply blindsided, but that tactic had a short life. As put by one historian, after a time the implications of redevelopment "were laid bare and there was a crystallization of resistance," resistance to displacement and to the relocation spillover effects (Olson 1976, 54). High-rise public housing became the last resort of many cities, most of which faced a dire shortage of accommodations for those being uprooted (Hirsch 1983). With space for relocation housing highly confined politically, the density of projects produced elementary schools whose whole enrollment consisted entirely of children from public-housing families. Thus, the interplay of "full speed ahead" redevelopment with neighborhood political marginality laid a foundation for problems that crested at a later time.

Consider the essential elements of the politics of urban redevelopment. At its core was Salisbury's "new convergence" (1964). Two centers of power that had in many older cities been at odds with one another joined forces to pursue an aggressive agenda of remaking the center of the city. Brought together around a call to save the city, this alliance of city hall and business leadership possessed a strong capacity to act—yet was little inclined to probe conditions beyond the need to rebuild the city economy. Business consisted of major enterprises with a big stake in the CBD. Bodies like the Greater Baltimore Committee, Central Atlanta Progress, Civic Progress in St. Louis, the Vault in Boston, and the Bay Area Council in San Francisco had no small-business representation. They consisted of cohesive groupings of elites capable of acting collectively but with limited knowledge and few concerns about how their actions could have far-reaching spillover effects.

Take one of the most notorious instances, urban renewal of Washington, DC's Southwest area, which had served for many years as an entry point for poor migrants from the rural South. With federally funded "slum clearance," the area was bulldozed. The previous residents, consisting of low-income African Americans, were forced to scatter, and the operation of the gateway function was disrupted. Aggravated by inadequate relocation planning and disregard for historical networks of social support, redevelopment led to residential havoc throughout the city. Historian Blair Ruble explains: "In displacing Southwest's residents as the new Southwest took shape, planners and their construction teams threw thousands of poor African-Americans—uprooted in many cases for the second time in their lives—into relatively stable, white middle-class neighborhoods east of the Anacostia River and into stable African-American neighborhoods north of downtown" (2010, 181–82). Ruble adds that "these displaced poorest of the poor lost access to the social networks that had developed in Southwest over decades of receiving new migrants from the South" (2010, 185).

A concurrent black political mobilization was hardly a congenial companion for redevelopment.[14] Hence, the quest for economic growth faced a need for some kind of accommodation with a growing African American population. It was in the crosscurrents of these two forces for change that the politics of the time took shape. Details of the pursuit of economic growth varied from place to place, but the pursuit itself was never displaced as a high priority. In Atlanta, redevelopment was pushed heavily by the city's business elite, and they broke with the state's Jim Crow system to become "the city too busy to hate." Atlanta's biracial governing coalition gave only limited consideration to neighborhood concerns. Although for a time in the 1970s the city developed an independent but short-lived neighborhood movement with significant clout, this movement soon fell on leaner times (Stone 1989). In New Haven the pursuit of economic growth lay more with city hall, as Mayor Richard Lee played the central role in coalition building. Chicago's Richard J. Daley used his dual positions as mayor and head of the Democratic organization for Cook County to wield patronage on behalf of his centrally guided, neighborhood-unfriendly pattern of redevelopment. With its "good government" form of government protecting a Republican/business leadership resistant to social change, Oakland followed a much different path that saw the formation of an oppositional Black Panther Party, the party leadership's unsuccessful effort to push for community control, and then, after an extended period of confrontation, a degree of accommodation achieved with a moderate black mayor—but economic development remained insulated from electoral politics (Self 2003; May 1971; Douzet 2012).

Baltimore's William Donald Schaefer, as mayor, proved to be something of a political Houdini, seeming always to escape entrapment by the city's racial and neighborhood issues (C. F. Smith 1999). An admirer of Chicago's "city that works" reputation under Mayor Richard J. Daley, Schaefer employed the extraordinary power of the Baltimore mayoralty to combine multiple strategies. He was attentive to potholes and service delivery, provided a patchwork of community centers and small planning grants, and made strategic use of patronage to co-opt community leaders. To insulate his downtown strategy from popular pressures, Schaefer relied on quasi-governmental organizations and low-visibility contracting. His system came to be known as the city's "shadow government" (Stoker 1987). The city also worked out a tacit understanding with the African American community whereby the latter would control the school system but not intrude on development policy (Orr 1999). Schaefer was skilled in the art of promotion and used his version of "blarney" to tout the waterfront aquarium built during his administration. At the height of his popularity Schaefer was selected as "mayor of the year" by *Esquire*. Although Baltimore lost population and saw parts of its housing stock decay during Schaefer's mayoralty, the city focused on its Inner Harbor revival and celebrated a self-proclaimed "renaissance" (Nast, Krause, and Monk 1982); city voices claimed to have escaped a fate of urban decline. Schaefer was elected mayor four times—the fourth time (in 1983) after the city had acquired a black majority.

In the decades following the end of World War II, US cities displayed a fundamental similarity in neighborhood policy. The context was a transition from the industrial city toward a new future. Although particulars varied, the underlying reality was the powerful alliance between government and business to pursue an imperative of economic growth. In comparison to economic redevelopment efforts, neighborhood concerns were hardly even a secondary consideration.[15] Although community development efforts were undertaken in several cities, they were isolated from the high-priority growth agenda and were consistently trumped by the growth imperative. African American political mobilization was also part of the context, but not something that could push aside the economic imperative. In areas like education and law enforcement, the "good government" claim of color-blind expertise came to be replaced with a new awareness that groups had diverse interests that they had a right to voice. But economic growth was nevertheless accorded a privileged position (cf. Lindblom 1977).

Paul Peterson's *City Limits* (1981) offered a theoretical justification for privileging economic growth. Peterson employed a policy typology with developmental policy defined as "those local programs which enhance the economic position of a community in its competition with others"

(1981, 41). He defined redistributive policies as those that "benefit low-income residents but at the same time [adversely] affect the local economy." In short, Peterson saw redistribution as a negative-sum game. In his view (shared by many local officials and business leaders), any redistributive effort was constrained by a harsh economic reality—generous locally financed social policies risked the creation of an unsustainable fiscal situation in which more generous benefits would attract needy residents (increasing costs) while driving taxpayers away (reducing revenues). The implication of such a view for neighborhood policy was stark. Many local policymakers (regardless of their personal preferences) believed they could afford to do little to assist distressed neighborhoods and their residents and must be ready to sacrifice neighborhood concerns in light of the overwhelming public interest in economic development. Within the logic of the Petersonian model, local policy had to prioritize economic development or risk fiscal suicide.

During the transition period, top policymakers did in fact often deem it necessary and appropriate to marginalize neighborhood concerns to protect economic development. Hence, the Black Panthers and their allies in Oakland could not bring about community control of Oakland's port authority; neighborhoods in Baltimore could gain concessions and insist on routine services but could not alter the redevelopment agenda of the city's "shadow government"; and African American leaders in Atlanta could lay claim to some of the benefits from economic growth but made no effort to change the growth imperative itself. To Peterson, the preference for growth rested on a general consensus; hence, it was not a matter of political contention. Elites (the convergence of power) ran the show, Peterson argued, not because they exercised control, but because they had the skill and knowledge to pursue policies the populace wanted (see also Kraus 2013). Actual scenarios displayed less consensus than Peterson's model suggested, but local policy efforts fitted the model with considerable regularity.

John Logan and Harvey Molotch's (1987) "growth machine" rested on a less benign premise. Its authors contrasted the use value of property, that is, the intangible benefits of a place that is familiar and comfortable and often contains networks of mutual help, with the transaction value of property, which consists of its dollar worth in the marketplace. Logan and Molotch saw conflict, not consensus, as the basic reality underlying development policy. Under this model, the prevalence of growth machines across cities derived in part from the tactical advantages of material benefits as an organizing factor, but also from successful idea promotion (Molotch 1993).

Urban-regime analysis examined the foundation for a city's governing coalition, conceived primarily in terms of a capacity to set and pursue a priority agenda. This was a capacity that lay beyond city neighborhoods individually and even collectively because they had difficulty maintaining a coalition on the scale of the entire city, as was demonstrated in the short life of Atlanta's Citywide League of Neighborhoods (Stone 1989). Although the urban-regime literature disputed the idea that economic imperatives *determined* local policy, those studies exposed the privileged status of economic development, explaining how local leaders formed and maintained a governing coalition to promote growth while downplaying social concerns (Stone and Sanders 1987; Stone 1989; Judd and Swanstrom 1998; Dreier, Mollenkopf, and Swanstrom 2004). Demographic changes, protests, civil disorder, and African American political mobilization produced concessions on the margins, but economic development was consistently treated as the core concern. Although neighborhoods did not lose all the battles, city studies described struggles between unequal contenders. The urban playing field was tilted heavily against nonaffluent neighborhoods, and even when they survived, many were scarred by social and economic change.

While these varied studies characterized the power dynamics of city politics at the time, none emphasized the special, historical context of cities in *deep transition*, cities undergoing exceptional economic and technological change with leadership focused on the urgent challenge to resist looming decline with policies of economic growth. In the main, the various schools of thought neglected to put policy and politics into an ongoing flow of time.

The New Era Takes Shape

Even deep transitions are not necessarily visible in the flow of daily events; change is often most readily observed in retrospect (Pierson 2004). Consider how the new era of neighborhood politics took shape. Although the need for economic growth remains strong, economy-centered treatments of urban politics possess a glaring inadequacy. Cities face multiple imperatives; pursuit of economic well-being is only one. The 1980s saw a growing awareness that other considerations had claims to make. Moreover, despite an impulse toward specialization, policy domains interpenetrate one another. By emphasizing expertise, the early stage of professionalization in city government had encouraged departmental autonomy and fed an organizational tendency toward silos of activity. However, the festering social problems bequeathed by the transition period directed policymaking away from greater specialization toward consideration of interconnected and comprehensive approaches.

Seen through a neighborhood lens, the policies of the postindustrial city began to change in response to an accumulation of experiences. Still short of achieving full acceptance in policy action, a turn toward interconnection and comprehensiveness nevertheless gradually emerged, not as a sudden realization, but rather bit by bit. As the civil disorders of the 1960s so painfully demonstrated, the urban crisis had many faces. The fate of the business district was only one.

Maintaining social peace, regulating conflict, and containing violence add up to an imperative of the first rank (Shefter 1992). In a recent book Michael Katz uses the title *Why Don't American Cities Burn?* (2011); Katz reminds us that social peace is not a given. And in the urban experience subsequent to the turmoil of the 1960s, major riots erupted in Miami in the 1980s and, after the acquittal of police officers charged in the Rodney King beating, in Los Angeles in 1992; spillover disorder from the latter reached several cities, including even Canada's Toronto. Other factors intensified concern about social peace. Reaching a peak in the 1980s, the crack epidemic showed a different side of urban violence. It reverberated profoundly across the policy landscape, as many of the top police brass concluded they could not arrest their way out of the problem.

Poor neighborhoods were particularly hard-hit by the crack epidemic, and many demanded that city hall "do something." Early prevention through youth programs was one answer put forward, especially by low-income residents (Taylor 2001). At some political cost, Baltimore mayor Kurt Schmoke advocated replacing the criminalization of the drug problem with a strategy of medicalization (Beilenson and McGuire 2012).

Particularly after the Kerner Commission Report in 1968 (National Advisory Commission on Civil Disorders), police-community relations began to undergo rethinking, and by 1980 community organizing had entered the crime-prevention picture. The Chicago Alliance for Neighborhood Safety became an early supporter of such approaches (Fung 2004). It gravitated from Alinsky-style organizing toward advocacy of institutional reform, and with the Chicago Alternative Policing Strategy program, Chicago became one of the pioneering sites for efforts in community policing. The Clinton presidency initiated Department of Justice funding for community policing, and as the 1990s unfolded, community policing found its way, albeit often resisted and limited, into a majority of urban police departments (Herbert 2006).

Meanwhile, adding to the consideration of more community-oriented approaches to policing, a series of events in Boston brought about an anti-violence campaign. This effort had at its core an alliance between the police and the Ten Point Coalition, a group of African American clergy working in inner-city neighborhoods.[16] This campaign had visible success and sparked wider interest in intensive police-community partnerships; it involved using both the "carrot" of services and, for those found to be incorrigible, the "stick" of enforcement and incarceration. It operated in a setting that developed a network of cooperative relationships; the campaign worked "because criminal justice agencies, community groups, and social service agencies coordinated and combined their efforts in ways that could magnify their separate effects" (Braga and Winship 2006, 178).[17] The campaign also worked in part because its focus was youth, and it had the lofty aim of "keeping kids alive." Its backing ranged from the Boston business sector to the Catholic Church and drew on cooperation from the school system and other public agencies.

Such intensive and broad cooperation is hard to maintain, but the benefits of coordinating efforts and enlisting the community became part of the new lore about policing. Although definitions of community policing can vary, Wesley Skogan offers this crucial observation: "Community policing is defined in part by efforts to develop partnerships with community members and the civic organizations that represent many of them collectively. It requires that police engage with the public as they set priorities and develop their tactics. Effective community policing requires responsiveness to citizen input concerning both the needs of the community and the best ways by which the police can help meet those needs. It takes seriously the public's definition of its own problems" (2006, 28). Seattle's police chief amplified the point by saying that the police are "the linchpin agency in neighborhood efforts in self-improvement" (Herbert 2006, 94).[18] Behind community policing is an assumption that controlling crime is both morally worthy and a boost for economic development and that success necessitates involving the community. Ultimately, in this view, public safety is coproduced. Even so, it is well worth remembering that community-oriented policing continues to be a practice far from universally embraced.

Education reform is another strand in the story of urban-policy change. In the peak transition years, cities treated the economic imperative as something distinct from education. Concessions to black political mobilization came begrudgingly to education and were accompanied by underfunding and neglect of schools serving the poorest neighborhoods. With the racial composition of student enrollment undergoing change, civic elites let city schools fall ever deeper into neglect (Markowitz and Rosner 1996; Henig et al. 1999). Narrowing the divide between education and economic development took time. A key step was the report *A Nation at Risk* by the National Commission on Excellence in Education (1983). Although the report had little to say about urban schools or the test score gap, it did make the link between education and economic development and became part of a broad move to reform education (McDonald 2014). Today's economy is one of knowledge and information, and with the emergence of postindustrialism, academic performance and credentialing have become matters of significance at all levels of government, including for actors involved in setting citywide agendas. Education policy is a critical concern of neighborhoods and one in which the social and economic considerations converge (Bryk et al. 2010; Payne 2010).[19]

Housing provided another important domain for change. The launching of HOPE VI in 1992 signaled a turn in policy thinking. However, the program should be thought of not so much as a bold pioneering step but as a culmination point in which several strands of concern came together. In particular, HOPE VI indicated that concentrated poverty was a problem urban localities could no longer ignore. Cities were encouraged to replace troubled public-housing projects with mixed-income communities. HOPE VI has operated mainly with a short-term, location-oriented strategy and has drawn criticism for failing to replace lost units of housing for the poorest of the poor (Crowley 2009). The program's consequences are widely debated, and studies suggest that the results for residents are mixed (Popkin et al. 2004). Although many residents relocated to neighborhoods with somewhat lower poverty rates and less crime, racial segregation remained a persistent problem and families that moved from public housing into the private market (using vouchers) were more likely to experience financial difficulties (see Popkin et al. 2004). But the change in thinking was significant. Housing policy was seen in a new light; no longer simply a matter of finding quality shelter, housing was part of the larger puzzle of urban distress.

Intensifying problems set the stage for fresh thinking, and problem awareness evolved in various ways. Urban decline was unabated and population loss was substantial in several large cities. The 1990 census showed a sharp increase in concentrated poverty. William J. Wilson's *The Truly Disadvantaged* (1987) had not only anticipated this trend but also laid out its dire consequences, including connections between crime and concentrated poverty. With the crack epidemic in full swing, cities were experiencing a surge in violence. These alarming trends were closely tied to public housing, and the best-selling *There Are No Children Here* (Kotlowitz 1991) gave a human face to the struggles of people living in a large public-housing project.

Consider the immediate background of HOPE VI. Under Jack Kemp, President George H. W. Bush's HUD secretary, initial efforts to address public housing through promoting resident ownership made little progress, and in 1992, working with a bipartisan group in Congress, Kemp created the National Commission on Severely Distressed Public Housing. Later that year, after a commission report had been quickly produced, Congress enacted the program soon to become known as HOPE VI. As it took full form, it embodied a strategy of replacing high-density public housing and its concentrations of the very poor with lower density, mixed-income housing, while simultaneously encouraging intensive services for residents.[20] The pursuit of mixed-income housing was soon followed by revamped tenant eligibility rules, a blending of public and private financing, and the use of public-private partnerships. Though resident involvement was not a sustained feature, residents were extensively involved in planning some of the earliest projects (see, e.g., Engdahl 2009). In a move that tended to shortchange those least well-off, management of this new structure of housing development had a strong market orientation.[21] As put by Henry Cisneros, housing authorities were to develop skills in asset management and "use market dynamics unleashed by proven real estate management practices" (2009, 11). Some projects mixed new housing design with service features such as community centers and police substations. Community economic development was also a feature in several projects.

The idea of a comprehensive approach supported by multisector sources was by no means an innovation that HOPE VI could claim to have brought about; by the early 1990s comprehensiveness enjoyed widespread support as an abstract principle. It harked back to Model Cities and earlier. The Weed and Seed program, a Department of Justice program adopted in 1991, employed a comprehensive approach as well—in its case aimed at crime reduction and also at mobilizing resources from both the public and private sectors. The program strategy of Weed and Seed was "to remove a neighborhood area's violent and drug-related criminal elements while simultaneously providing the necessary supports for a positive infrastructure to develop."[22]

Within the foundation sector comprehensiveness had also gained wide support. One of its champions was James Rouse, a major developer and creator of the Enterprise Foundation. He was a force behind Baltimore's Sandtown-Winchester project, initially seen as a potential model for future efforts. A significant step occurred with the launching of Living Cities: The National Community Development Initiative, backed by some twenty major foundations and financial institutions.[23] It funds efforts in twenty-three cities (including all five of the US cities covered in the research for this book). Living Cities has claimed that its grants have leveraged large investment by the private sector in community building.[24] Its community-building component includes community engagement and leadership development—aims, however, often supported more in rhetoric than on the ground. The Research and Policy Committee of the Committee for Economic Development (CED) added its backing in a 1995 publication, *Rebuilding Inner-City Communities*, and in that publication called for corporate businesses to engage with the rebuilding process and join multisector partnerships: "They should exercise the same leadership in relation to inner-city community-building as they have in the past to boost downtown development or attract sports franchises" (Committee for Economic Development 1995, 51).

Publications of and about the 1990s indicate a shift that is more far-reaching than one consisting merely of programs, partnerships, and agencies. One part is a newly expressed confidence in the ability of community-based actors to launch and carry out initiatives (Grogan and Proscio 2000; von Hoffman 2003). The widely reported Dudley Street Neighborhood Initiative had gotten under way in 1985 (Medoff and Sklar 1994; Clavel 2010). John Kretzmann and John McKnight (1993) made a noteworthy impression with their call to emphasize the assets of people and their communities, not their deficits. The black middle class had grown by the latter years of the twentieth century and, as actors "in the middle," became a significant factor in efforts for neighborhood improvement (Pattillo 2007; Hyra 2008).

Significantly, David Osborne and Ted Gaebler's *Reinventing Government*, which promoted an entrepreneurial style of policymaking, was published in 1992. Similarly, Henry Cisneros saw the HOPE VI program as an instance when cities benefited "from a more entrepreneurial spirit in government": "Today's mayors are orchestrators of vast civic energies from the private and nonprofit sectors" (2009, 12). Comprehensive initiatives entailed broad, multisector forms of support. The favored approach had come to include not only listening to communities but also enlisting their organizations, the voluntary sector, and the business sector—not just as volunteers but as investors. Although not everyone was of the same mind, overall the strategy was to combine market dynamics with donor support, civil society, and the agencies of government to intervene simultaneously across multiple policy domains.[25]

For a short run many of these ideas and initiatives found a place in federal urban policy. With the Empowerment Zones and Enterprise Communities initiative, launched in 1994, the Clinton administration encouraged cities to join economic and community development. Round 1 Empowerment Zones received a flexible $100 million federal block grant along with a variety of market-oriented tools to encourage investment and economic growth. Communities in distressed neighborhoods were mobilized to develop plans integrating economic and community development efforts; plans were to be managed in a results-oriented local governance process (Rich and Stoker 2014). However, following a 1994 electoral turnover, congressional opposition altered federal urban policy to focus on market-oriented tools and stalled the Clinton administration's effort to integrate economic and community development (Stoker and Rich 2006). Years later a Government Accountability Office (GAO 2006) evaluation concluded that although Empowerment Zone neighborhoods did see improved conditions, these gains could not be definitively linked to the initiative.[26]

The Obama administration has also striven to integrate economic and community development efforts by coordinating federal grants, building neighborhood capacity, and sharing promising practices. The administration's Neighborhood Revitalization Initiative targets distressed neighborhoods with a multifaceted effort (in education, housing, public safety, health care, and economic vitality) to create Neighborhoods of Opportunity.[27] The initiative advocates "braiding" as a resource accumulation strategy, combining multiple federal funding streams and leveraging federal funds with state, local, foundation, nonprofit, and business resources (and universities are also seen as a key source of leveraged funds).

Thus far, the Obama administration's efforts have emphasized housing, health, public safety, and educational programs through the Choice Neighborhoods and Promise Neighborhoods programs. The Choice Neighborhoods program represents the continuing evolution of HOPE VI. Although the features of local plans vary, the consistent theme is to combine the redevelopment of public housing (or HUD-sponsored housing) with additional programs and services to assist low-income families. Promise Neighborhoods grants emphasize improving outcomes for children living in distressed neighborhoods through educational and integrated service initiatives. The Choice Neighborhoods and Promise Neighborhoods programs have distributed planning grants to selected local government agencies and community groups, and some initiatives have moved toward implementation. However, the administration's efforts to advance neighborhood revitalization have been constrained by austerity politics in Congress, where requests for new funding for flexible "Neighborhood Revitalization Grants" have been denied.

A Preliminary Look at Policy and Politics in the New Era

There is always a gap between the rhetoric surrounding what a new idea promises and what program implementation actually delivers; squeezed federal funding has no doubt widened that gap for urban neighborhoods. Still, the current world of neighborhood ideas is quite different from the more constricted body of ideas in circulation during the redevelopment period. What are the implications of these new ideas for neighborhood politics in the postindustrial city?

Postindustrialism is usually treated as a shift in such things as work and lifestyle. Our focus, however, is not on the concept of postindustrialism. Our concern is with what neighborhood policy and politics are like now that cities have gone through the transition from an industrial to a postindustrial socioeconomic base. Less advantaged communities paid a heavy toll for this transition. Physical reconstruction occurred without an accompanying social reconstruction. As policymakers concentrated on the CBD and its link to the suburbs, racial change posed a complex set of conditions that went largely unaddressed.

The current postindustrial period thus faces an accumulation of problems from the past, but with a fractured pattern of leadership. With no "convergent" coalition setting a policy direction, city neighborhoods are in a different time. Political relationships have become more fluid, and fragmentation prevails. Despite continuing hope for metropolitan problem solving, action on a regional scale remains limited (B. Katz and Bradley 2013; Briggs, Popkin, and Goering 2010). Policymaking is frequently ad hoc and opportunistic. In some instances, labor and environmental groups have entered the picture (Erie 2004; Pastor, Benner, and Matsuoka 2009; Meyerson 2013),[28] but citywide coalitions with a broad agenda are hard to find. At the same time that policymaking has become a much looser process, government funding has become much tighter, thereby increasing the importance of attracting private investors and donors to supplement limited public resources. As a practical matter, this means that neighborhood policy is often advanced by attaching neighborhood improvement efforts to other policy objectives.

These changes do not mean that social equity has suddenly become a high priority. Rather, they mean only that issues now mix considerations in ways that are less guarded than in the redevelopment period. Now bargaining is commonplace and more factors are weighed. Negotiation and putting together CBAs are possible but do not happen and become sustained without a political force behind them. The poor often still get the short straw (Pattillo 2007; Crowley 2009; Goetz 2003). Realizing opportunities for less advantaged groups to participate in local policymaking remains a challenge in the neighborhood politics of the present time.

Access to information is one factor, and foundations have played an important role in making relevant information available.[29] We note, for example, the formation of a philanthropy-backed National Neighborhood Indicators Alliance (in 1995). With economic-development policy and the various issues it encompasses no longer highly insulated, much ultimately depends on how well community groups and their allies are organized and linked. This is another point at which the philanthropic sector can play a facilitating role, and Denver's Piton Foundation (a local affiliate of the National Neighborhoods Alliance) is a leading example. Research suggests, however, that the philanthropic role in support of organizing and leadership development remains modest. The donor sector appears to be unevenly invested in such a role, and their efforts often seem to be more in support of individual neighborhood projects than in support of a broad approach to capacity building (Warren and Mapp 2011, 263).[30] Still, since there is no ready alternative source of support, foundations continue to be major funders of whatever organizing and capacity-building there is.

While our brief scan of the policy landscape suggests the possibility of positive prospects, reality reminds us that inequality continues as a force. Still, new policy ideas have come on the scene. The once-calamitous disregard of older neighborhoods has somewhat faded, and the possibility stands that elite policymakers may be paying more attention than in the past. Philanthropic organizations have become prominent players in the policy arenas of many of the nation's largest cities. Not only are "ed & med" institutions (universities, hospitals, and medical schools) more visible, but some show signs of increased social concern (Perry and Wiewel 2005; Rodin 2007; R. Hodges and Dubb 2012; Etienne 2012). Economic growth remains a top consideration, but its pursuit is not confined to a narrow-gauge understanding of what it involves and how to go about it. Because it is no longer treated as a distinct domain, necessarily shielded from other considerations, economic development can be linked with aims that have a neighborhood dimension. Although policy has become increasingly complex, people count, and working through the issue of how much people count and in what ways is part of the neighborhood politics of the postindustrial city, and thus our special concern in this book.[31]

Through the lens of our study of neighborhood revitalization efforts in six diverse cities, we find that urban neighborhoods have experienced modest and limited gains as subjects of policy attention. In none of the six cities has neighborhood revitalization been a defining priority, but in all it is a visible concern. The cities in our study with the highest socioeconomic distress, Baltimore and Los Angeles, are also cities in which neighborhood policy inclines heavily toward ad hoc and opportunistic intervention. Relatively well-off Phoenix has enjoyed the most systematic policy intervention, but its neighborhood program started quite small in scale and was initially justified mainly as an anticrime measure. The city best-off socioeconomically, Toronto, moved toward a systematic plan with support from the United Way, a local charity, but the failure to develop stable funding and institutional coordination for the plan brought problems in execution. All in all we find that neighborhood revitalization does not fit an unvarying "narrative of failure" but is instead filled with contingency and uncertainty.

Neighborhoods, Distress, and Revitalization

In our work, the term "neighborhood" refers to *people* and how they experience shared residential space. As Robert Sampson (2012) argues, a neighborhood is a social entity that confers advantages and disadvantages by virtue of how residents relate to one another and how they are perceived by others. Hence, a neighborhood is more than a collection of residential properties; it is a place with a social identity—a place in which there are connections among those who reside there. We see "neighborhood distress" and "neighborhood revitalization" as political terms that lie significantly in the eyes of beholders. However, it is important not to equate distress with property dilapidation and not to equate revitalization with gentrification or simply upgraded property.

Neighborhood distress is not a neatly bounded problem for which there is a set remedy. Although a strong case can be made for viewing distress as a set of interlaced and reinforcing problems, its elements are conceptually distinct and, in any given instance, may or may not be closely linked. Crime, for instance, is often associated with poverty, unemployment, and resulting disorder (Wilson 1996, 21–23), but nevertheless, crime is a separable dimension of community distress (Taub, Taylor, and Dunham 1984). Policing can lower crime rates without altering other facets of distress (Zimring 2012). Substandard schools or other forms of service provision are another factor in neighborhood distress, and although they are often closely associated with poverty, they are distinct. Improved services may leave a level of poverty unchanged. At the same time, weak service provision, particularly underperforming schools, may depress the housing market and stand as a barrier to revitalization. Connections are complex.

In addition, political distrust and disengagement among residents of lower-income areas are elements of neighborhood distress. Though political alienation is often linked closely to past experiences of neglect, broken promises, and exclusion from effective channels of representation, the condition is not irreparable. Neighborhood political disconnection can be addressed and ameliorated, without necessarily changing the economic condition of residents. For example, in their work on housing in the South Bronx, Grogan and Proscio found, despite no change in the poverty level, "an upsurge in civic participation" (2000, 28).

Far from being bounded by technical criteria, both the understanding of distress and the responses to it are contested. Differences can be quite sharp, and they reflect in part the fact that levels of distress vary. The Research and Policy Committee of the CED distinguishes neighborhoods in full distress from "threatened neighborhoods"—those not yet on, but at risk of sliding down, the slippery slope of decline. For the CED "the defining character of [fully] distressed neighborhoods is the *simultaneous* presence of *multiple* social problems: poverty and joblessness, crime and violence, family instability and welfare dependence, and depressed property values and physical blight" (Committee for Economic Development 1995, 10, italics in original). However, neighborhood distress is not merely a set of overlapping problems. The CED added a political dimension: "inner-city distress is about more than poverty or individual problems; it is about the collapse of a community's ability to cope with problems" (10).[32] We also see neighborhood distress as in part a political problem—a tangle of overlapping, intertwined, and sometimes mutually reinforcing troubles for those living in particular neighborhoods that challenge the community's capacity for constructive problem solving. Isolated social and economic improvements do not reach to the heart of the challenge. Even if limited in scope, political empowerment has an essential place.

Neighborhood revitalization efforts respond to distress; *neighborhood revitalization is about attempts to bring about improvement for those who are experiencing residentially clustered forms of distress.* However, the strategies for and consequences of revitalization efforts are matters of contention. One idea that came to be firmly embraced by policy elites is that concentrating the poor has disastrous consequences. With its aim of dispersing those with low incomes, HOPE VI drew heavily on this view. Transforming a poor neighborhood into a stable mixed-income population raises the question of whether or how to relocate a portion of the low-income population and, if relocation occurs, how to accomplish it without undue hardship or loss of community (Hyra 2011). *Residents in distressed areas tend to have a different view.* They usually seek to minimize displacement, whether from market-led gentrification or from redevelopment efforts, especially if it lacks a right of return. As a path to achieving a mixed-income neighborhood, residents generally prefer increased employment and expanded economic opportunity.

Given that a neighborhood is essentially the population living there, we do not regard simple replacement of a resident population as "revitalization." It may transform the space, but replacement can perpetuate or even greatly aggravate the distress of the once-resident population. Certainly, segregation of stigmatized groups can result in a "ghetto" and reinforce isolation. But isolation of those in distressed residential clusters comes in varied degrees and forms; concentration is not necessarily or totally the product of enforced segregation, and it may serve at least partly to create an enclave of mutual support. The gateway function continues to be important. While it may be argued that dispersing a poor population serves to decrease disadvantage, breaking up such concentrations can cause a weakening of needed social ties (Goetz 2003; Gay 2012).[33]

As will be shown in our six city studies, elements of neighborhood distress and responses to it may be joined and disjoined in various ways. Issue conflict can take many forms, as can efforts to build programmatic responses to neighborhood distress. Groups internal to a neighborhood can find themselves on opposing sides, and neighborhoods may be at odds with city hall or other funders. A recurring tension comes from the tendency of elite actors to treat property as the key to revitalization while residents call for greater attention to service needs. Some analysts might object that serving people is not a revitalization strategy, but our position is that, if neighborhoods are residential clusters of people, then steps to address their shared concerns are elements of revitalization. Thus, contention over the weight given to services versus property improvement is part of the politics of neighborhood revitalization.

Our six study cities further suggest that another key feature of revitalization strategy has to do with the scope and duration of efforts. Policy can be made up of a series of particular and disconnected initiatives, but it can also consist of a comprehensive and strategic plan of action encompassing many neighborhoods. A feature of the politics of neighborhood revitalization is, then, the extent to which a citywide vision and strategy have been given institutional embodiment. That calls for such a step are often not heeded does not make aspirations for a broad vision any less a feature of the politics of neighborhood revitalization.

Inequality and Politics in the Middle Ground

The persistence of neighborhood distress and urban poverty might, on the surface, make structural inequality appear to be the first and last word on neighborhood policy and politics. After all, in neither Canada nor the United States does the federal government offer much to turn the policy tide in a more progressive direction. Moreover, absent is a broad and vibrant movement to compensate urban residents for the history of neglect and social damage they experienced during the redevelopment period. So there is no overwhelming reason to think that an explicit agenda of social reconstruction can take hold and make fast headway against neighborhood distress. Is the urban narrative of failure to be embraced after all? We think not.

However, if ameliorating neighborhood distress is a political challenge, then efforts to enhance the positive consideration neighborhoods receive must contend with the forces of structural inequality. These forces form a prevailing wind that cannot be discounted. Nevertheless, we do not see the residents of distressed neighborhoods as passive victims of structural forces. Their agency and their bargaining power, along with those of potential allies, can be strengthened as a counterforce. Distress can become more severe or made less so. Where the marker falls is not determined by structural factors alone. Building and deploying neighborhood capacity is a task that matters, and we explore this task even further in this book's concluding chapter.

For now we sketch a framework for looking more closely at six city-level chapters that form the observational core of this book. By assuming a structure-agency framework, we examine ground that falls somewhere between structural determinism and unconstrained agency. We posit that structural forces are sufficiently attenuated in immediate impact to leave room for particular context and intermediate factors to assume a role in shaping neighborhood experiences.

A comparison of the situation today with the policy position of aging city neighborhoods of the redevelopment era indicates that significant changes have occurred. New allies within city government and on the wider civic front are observable. Policy ideas have evolved in significant ways. A concentration of power once resistant to community-level concerns has dissipated due to a wider, unfolding process of socioeconomic change, and the new governing order has shifted to a more diffuse pattern of power and a more flexible set of relationships. A diffuse power pattern does not mean a "no power" situation. However, the current power challenge for urban neighborhoods is primarily one of construction, not one of confronting and overcoming a tight-knit band of like-minded elites. For the present era, then, the power task is one of building, but building under conditions of structural inequality. Hence, a major question becomes, to what extent and in what ways can sharply unequal actors come together in a manner that addresses the concerns of the residents in distressed communities?

What is distinct about policy and politics for distressed communities is that such neighborhoods are not elite players with ample resources. Quite the contrary, they have scant resources in relation to the problems that surround them. They face the challenge that Martin Luther King often posed for the civil rights movement: "How to create a way out of no way." Perhaps overstated for effect, King's underlying point is clear.

Since inequality has a tendency to perpetuate itself, what are the grounds on which to build hope for a better future for urban neighborhoods and their current residents? This book maintains that there are such grounds, and they are to be found in more nuanced thinking about structural inequality. Consider, for example, Cathy Cohen's treatment of the politics of marginality in *The Boundaries of Blackness* (1999). Cohen centers her analysis of marginality on power. She recognizes that the actions of dominant players have a heavy impact on those who are marginal; this is what she terms "vertical power." However, she argues that the marginal should not be written off as possessing no influence or agency; even vertical power is not entirely one-way. Cohen rejects a simple dichotomy of powerful and powerless and calls for close attention to what she terms intracommunity relationships among the marginal. The latter is the horizontal dimension of power.

Elaborating, we can see that the makeup of the dominant group can also matter—it can vary in degree of concern for and responsiveness to marginal groups. A hopeful element of the emerging neighborhood politics is that newly active groups (such as foundations and the ed & med sector) are likely to be more open than corporate business has been to the concerns of marginal groups. Governing power can become less narrow in its focus.

Importantly, Cohen's view of marginality is not static. Depending on intracommunity relations, the political position of the marginal can change, and change can be intentional. It follows, then, that the dominant stratum would be less open to change when the marginal are disorganized and weak in their capacity to identify and pursue policy goals. However, as marginal groups become better organized and display greater capacity, the situation could shift. Thus, the overall impact of inequality depends on the nature of the vertical *and* horizontal relations in play.

Cohen's discussion of intracommunity relations indicates that groups can be more cohesive or less so, more inclusive or less so. Thus, neighborhoods can divide between homeowners and renters or between African Americans and Latinos. Or, by contrast, they can unify in pursuit of benefits for their common well-being. By using the word "membership," Cohen underscores the point that individuals may see and define themselves as part of a group having a common fate, or they may fail to embrace this possibility. In emphasizing the horizontal dimension, Cohen shows that "intra-community patterns of power and membership can have a significant, if not overwhelming, impact on the political histories and approaching futures of marginal groups" (1999, 36). Consequently, despite their disadvantages, marginal groups have a capacity to act, to resist subordination, and to lay claim to consideration. They do not totally control their own destinies, but they have a potential to *contribute* to outcomes.

With an emphasis on intermediate factors, Mario Luis Small's (2004) conditional approach dovetails with Cohen's analysis of the politics of marginality. "Intermediate factor" is an open-ended term, differentiating a matter more immediate to action than a broad structural force such as a market economy or a social system of racial subordination. "Intermediate" can refer to institutions but can also refer to events, that is, to experiences that leave a lasting imprint (see also Abrams 1982; W. Sewell 2005). Small's analysis suggests that despite the common condition of structural inequality, the efficacy of marginal groups varies and reflects the influence of intermediate factors such as organization, mobilization, institutionalization, and processes and experiences that can empower marginal groups.

While both Cohen and Small underscore the importance of particular and immediate context, it is important also to bear in mind the larger context, the context that has yielded a pattern of diffuse power. In talking about "intracommunity" relations, Cohen has in mind such matters as civic skills, level and scope of organization within a marginal population, their cohesion, a widely encompassing identity and sense of shared fate, communication and information sharing within the marginal population, and an enlistment of allies. This is the stuff of power—that is, the elements out of which a capacity to act collectively is forged—but the forging is constrained and not free-ranging. In Cohen's treatment of power, there are things that add weight and give leverage to marginal groups in their relationship with "movers and shakers" as policy is shaped, but the adjective "marginal" reminds us that these groups, on their own, lack the where-withal to lay a credible claim to being "movers and shakers" themselves.

A situation of diffuse power puts at center stage the question of how players come together in order to forge a capacity to act; diffusion means that much of the power struggle is about "power to." As put in Clarence Stone's *Regime Politics*: "What is at issue is not so much domination and subordination as a capacity to act and accomplish goals. The power struggle concerns, not control and resistance, but gaining and fusing a capacity to act—*power to*, not *power over*" (1989, 229, italics in original).

Fragmented Governing Power as the Postindustrial Challenge

The new era has a different mix of elite policy players from the redevelopment mix. Additionally, social and economic conditions have changed and given rise to new ideas and understandings of the city situation. With new elite players, new conditions, and new ideas and understandings, there is fertile ground for new "intermediate factors" to come into consideration. Nothing, however, is inevitable. Powerlessness can come not just from domination but also from unchecked fragmentation. The fading of one configuration of power does not mean that another of equal strength will fill the vacuum. Incapacity can succeed capacity. Or as in the case of the shift from redevelopment to the postindustrial present, limited and partial capacity can replace full-throttle capacity.

An analytical complication comes from the fact that distressed urban neighborhoods do not occupy a policy arena somehow isolated from the broad context of governing the city. Problems intertwine; policies intersect. Crosscutting policies and interaction rather than segmented coexistence form the current urban pattern.

Past social damage and neglect have left a potential agenda of social reconstruction, but little wherewithal is in sight to pursue such an agenda, *except in a piecemeal fashion.* The new elite actors from ed & med institutions and philanthropic foundations have built-in limitations as promoters of a broad and sustained agenda. Yet, in the fragmented political terrain of the contemporary city, they have significant resources and a potential to promote noteworthy initiatives. For these actors (along with local government) to make headway on many policy matters, however, they need cooperation, not resistance, from disadvantaged neighborhoods. The power to govern thus has to be forged, even when the forging occurs fragment by fragment.

The fluidity that has come with the dispersion of power in the present time period means that actors in the upper and lower strata are not locked into a zero-sum game. A positive-sum relationship is possible, but it is by no means guaranteed and often is likely to be only partial. A still-evolving middle ground, with new players, new ideas, and new intermediate arrangements, is where neighborhood policy is made, but it is terrain in which structural inequality remains a force.

For neighborhood issues the overall power question involves two phases—the transition from an old era to a new one and then the new era itself. As Small (2004) shows in his work, variations in community capacity under a general condition of structural inequality can be important. Diffuse power relations pose their own particular challenge to communities operating under a handicap of structural inequality. A study of urban neighborhoods raises multiple questions about the possibilities within a context of structural inequality. What kinds of policy efforts can be launched and sustained that address concerns held among lower-strata residents of the city? What about would-be allies of the residents of distressed neighborhoods—how unhindered are they to form such connections? Are there conditions under which unequals can form and maintain positive-sum relationships?

Even though there are new and more receptive elites on the scene, the path to coalition is not unobstructed. Ed & med institutions and philanthropic foundations are complex entities with a variety of competing impulses. New players, new ideas, and new arrangements bring important questions to the fore. The shift from more concentrated power in the redevelopment period to the more diffuse pattern of the present time introduces questions about how capacities to act are created. How does power operate when inequality is sharp, involving as it does both the holders of major institutional positions and "small-fry" actors with limited resources?

Although governing power is now fragmented, the question remains as to the extent to which fragments can be sufficiently put together to bring distressed neighborhoods more fully into the policy picture. How can their concerns be addressed by policy actions? In what scope? Power can be exercised piecemeal without encompassing a broader scale, but degree and conditions of fragmentation matter. In the concluding chapter of this book we return to these issues as we consider how the policymaking milieu affecting neighborhoods might be reshaped to enhance the expression of neighborhood concerns.

Notes

1. Services for the poor and near poor, especially among populations of color, were in decline (see Clark 1965; Markowitz and Rosner 1996). For housing, mainstream credit channels dried up, leaving the way open for predatory lending practices to take over (for an especially telling account, see Satter 2009). Racial transitions in residential areas took a turbulent and destructive form, marred by widespread incidents of violence (Seligman 2005).

2. As the insulation of economic development from popular pressures and community concerns began to break down, one version was a policy called "linked development." The idea was to require, as a condition of approval and support for development in boom areas, that the developer pay an exaction fee as compensation for losses such as those in affordable housing or as return for government assistance. Affordable housing was the usual policy link, but exaction fees were used for purposes varying from job training to open space. See Betancur and Smith 1988. Only a few cities enacted linked development as policy, but the basic idea was carried forward with the emergence of CBAs.

3. This is not to suggest that the economy was the sole driver of policy change. Racial change was interwoven with a shifting economy and was also accompanied by disquiet about crime, violence, and disorder. At the same time the destructive side of redevelopment began to evoke concerns and encouraged some actors to voice claims for social equity (Klemek 2011).

4. Another highly valuable source is Self's (2003) close examination of Oakland in the time following World War II.

5. For a treatment of this period in a national context, see Mollenkopf 1983.

6. Logan and Molotch (1987) underscored the strength of this pattern by using the concept of a powerful "growth machine" to frame their analysis of this period. Harvey Molotch's initial article on this theme was published in 1976.

7. For how youth development can intertwine with neighborhood policy, see studies of Hampton, Virginia (Sirianni 2009; Stone, Orr, and Worgs 2006).

8. Note, however, that city and national policy actions do not follow the same tides. This should not be surprising, as national politics became increasingly suburban and middle class at a time when cities had large areas of concentrated poverty. Although the distribution of the poor is now shifting to yield a more diverse suburbia, public understanding often lags behind such trends. (On shifting demography, see Weir 2011; Reckhow and Weir 2012; Ehrenhalt 2013; Kneebone and Berube 2013; Gallagher 2013.)

9. Business leaders in Atlanta as early as the 1920s recognized a need to accommodate to the automobile as the wave of future transportation. They pushed for a viaduct to create a new level for traffic flow, reducing the rail-line level to its "underground" position. Even before World War II ended, business-led leadership was looking forward to the promotion of a bond issue to build expressways. The bond election came in 1946, a decade before the enactment of the federal interstate system.

10. The major exception was the relatively undeveloped Southwest, where growth-minded business leaders were able to gain command of the region's politics before other forces became entrenched (Bridges 1997). On Charlotte, see Hanchett 1998, and for a succinct Frost Belt–Sun Belt contrast, see Bridges 2011.

11. We are using the term "machine" loosely to refer to politics largely organized

around the pursuit and distribution of patronage. For a superb treatment of variations in and the evolution of machine politics, see Erie 1988.

12. On how, in Boston, race and class replaced religious and ethnic identity as a source of cleavage in the redevelopment era, see O'Connor 1993. Note also Lukas 1984.

13. In his study of city planning, Altshuler (1965) discovered that planning bodies found race too controversial to take on openly.

14. We use the term "black political mobilization" to emphasize that the effort was wider than (and started earlier than) the civil rights movement in the South. For example, on New York, see Biondi 2003; and on Oakland, see Self 2003.

15. Toronto experienced an anti-expressway movement parallel to that in the United States, with recent immigrant Jane Jacobs reenacting her New York City role. Toronto, however, did not have the same racial dynamic characteristic of so many US cities, and city hall took a more accommodating stance toward neighborhoods at an earlier time (Klemek 2011, 224).

16. On Boston, see Berrien and Winship 2002; Kennedy 2002. On an array of innovations in community-oriented policing, see Weisburd and Braga 2006.

17. For a recent account, see Chris Smith 2011.

18. Herbert (2006) also reports significant resistance to community policing at the patrol level.

19. Though authors such as these, on the basis of considerable firsthand study, make a strong case for linking school reform with community development, the turn to test score accountability has moved reform in a different direction.

20. An informative, though perhaps excessively upbeat, source is a Brookings Institution volume, Cisneros and Engdahl 2009, containing background chapters by Henry Cisneros and Bruce Katz, both of whom were at the center of launching HOPE VI. Katz was a committee staff director when the legislation was enacted, as well as chief of staff for Cisneros, who became Clinton's HUD secretary designate and then secretary just as the program was being launched.

21. HOPE VI and companion ideas about comprehensive approaches were neither problem free nor always kind to the poor. Some cities handled relocation badly, and the very poor got the least from the program (Crowley 2009; Goetz 2003).

22. See the program's website: www.jrsa.org/program/weedseed.html.

23. The exact number and membership have varied in detail but not at all in basic profile.

24. As part of an ongoing attempt to enlist the market to advance social goals, it should also be noted that the Low Income Housing Tax Credit was enacted in 1986.

25. For a discussion of practical problems and tensions in putting these ideas into practice, see H. Rubin 2000. See also the evaluation of CCIs in Kubisch et al. 2002. Our point is not that practice smoothly followed new policy ideas but that fresh policy thinking became part of the new era.

26. The legacy of the Empowerment Zone initiative is disputed. Michael Rich and Robert Stoker (2014) show that outcomes varied locally and that the evaluations masked local successes by combining good- and poor-performing zones into a pooled analysis. They argue that effective local governance distinguished good from poor performers.

27. Though faced with an uncertain funding future, three features highlight current thinking: (1) breaking up concentrations of the poor remains a policy goal; (2) in order to receive federal funding, communities must have a Transformation Plan, that is, a comprehensive plan of neighborhood revitalization; and (3) people dis-

placed are guaranteed a right of return. The policy is elaborated in the following report: http://www.whitehouse.gov/sites/default/files/uploads/nri_report.pdf.

28. Within central cities, noxious facilities are one of the sources of neighborhood distress and therefore of contention involving environmental activism (Angotti 2008).

29. A model from the school reform arena is the Consortium on Chicago School Research (Shipps 2009).

30. In education, for example, much foundation funding has gone into private-sector areas such as charter management organizations and not into community engagement or school reforms linked to community development. On foundations and urban-school reform, see Reckhow 2013. Recent foundation interest in the concept of "collective impact" does, however, indicate an awareness that uncoordinated, individual projects hold little promise of lasting social change.

31. We are not unaware of the fact that an alternative to neighborhood revitalization is the pursuit of such regional aims as dispersing the poor. The federal Move to Opportunity program was launched in 1994 (Briggs, Popkin, and Goering 2010), and court decisions such as *Thompson v. HUD* are also part of the picture (for an analysis, see PRRAC 2005). However, regionalism is a different branch of policy study from the one we embarked on, and we see little indication that dispersion efforts are ending neighborhood distress as a problem. Moreover, deconcentrating the poor is not a policy track without limitations and difficulties of its own (Goetz 2003; Gay 2012), but on its importance in education, see Ryan 2010.

32. In the 1990s the CED estimated that 11 percent of the neighborhoods in the nation's one hundred largest cities fell into this category of full distress; 22 percent fell into the "threatened" category. Combined, the two categories accounted for one-third of big-city neighborhoods. An upbeat view might highlight the fact that two-thirds of urban neighborhoods were sound, and many of these quite prosperous. Still, one-third of city neighborhoods is a sizable problem, especially since it includes many places in which disadvantage is both concentrated and persisting (Sharkey 2013). While these figures are from the 1990s—early years of the new era—there is little reason to think that neighborhood distress has shrunk. The figures don't reflect the foreclosure calamity or the accompanying economic downturn.

33. However, in their study of Moving to Opportunity, Briggs, Popkin, and Goering (2010, 128–31) caution that social ties among those with few resources can become handicaps and limit upward mobility.

TWO

Contexts for Neighborhood Revitalization: A Comparative Overview

HAROLD WOLMAN AND MARTIN HORAK,
WITH THE ASSISTANCE OF CAMILLE A. SOLA
AND DIANA HINCAPIE

Why do cities differ in the focus, content, and tools of the neighborhood regeneration activity they pursue? Although neighborhood revitalization policies in North America are not likely to be straightforward responses to neighborhood distress, the account of the new politics of neighborhood revitalization provided in chapter 1 emphasizes socioeconomic context; specifically, the transition from an industrial to a postindustrial economy. Our investigation of local politics and policy, which we take up in detail in the chapters on individual cities that follow, is built on the conviction that local context and the way it changes over time *do* matter to neighborhood politics. The broad economic trajectory of a city and its metropolitan region, the patterns of demographic change, and the extent and concentration of neighborhood distress may affect the political articulation of neighborhood concerns, as well as the scope and focus of responses to neighborhood distress.

In this chapter, we portray the evolving local social, economic, and demographic contexts in our six study cities. We do so primarily by presenting statistical data on selected social, economic, and demographic variables. Our goal is not merely to describe individual variables. Instead, we examine how multiple social, economic, and demographic variables cluster in different patterns across our study cities to produce distinct contexts for neighborhood politics. Drawing on observations over time, we pay attention to the way in which these contexts have been changing over the last couple of decades in response to ongoing national and international processes of deindustrialization and globalization. Aggregating and interpreting the patterns across the data, we find that our study cities include three distinct types: the distressed former industrial city (Baltimore); the postindustrial boomtowns (Denver and Phoenix); and the globalized cities (Los Angeles and Toronto). Our sixth city, Chicago, is a hybrid, which has many of the traits of the globalized city, yet also harbors social distress characteristic of many older former industrial cities. It is not the purpose of this chapter to discuss the ways in which specific contexts affect the politics and policy of neighborhood regeneration—that task falls to the chapters that follow. But by identifying and characterizing different contexts in our case cities, this chapter provides a foundation for assessing the extent to which the local socioeconomic and demographic conditions, and the ways in which these conditions change over time, matter to neighborhood revitalization.

Before we present the data, a few words about scale are in order. While the case study chapters in this volume focus on politics in central cities, neither the context nor the politics of revitalization in these municipalities exists in isolation from factors that operate at broader spatial scales. Thus, for example, whether or not the broader metropolitan area in which a central city is located is economically growing or declining may have a significant impact on both the longer-term socioeconomic trajectory of the central city and on neighborhood politics.[1] Likewise, knowing the poverty rate in a particular city is of limited value if we do not establish the broader context of the national poverty rate. The national context is all the more important for us because one of our case cities—Toronto—is in a different country, where not only are national-level socioeconomic and demographic trends different from the United States, but so is the methodology for measuring certain statistical indicators.[2] In order to place cities on a comparable basis, we thus present not only the absolute value of our indicators in the various cities, but where possible, we also present the values relative to those in the larger metropolitan area and the country as a whole.

Economic Trajectories in a Postindustrial Era

In recent decades, the economic fortunes of all large North American cities, including the six that we examine in this book, have been shaped in varying ways by the shift from an industrial to a postindustrial economy. In general, cities that were more heavily dependent on manufacturing have been more adversely affected than others, yet formerly industrial cities have also varied greatly in the extent to which they have successfully restructured their economic base by replacing lost manufacturing jobs with jobs in other sectors, by integrating themselves into the global economy, or by implementing both strategies. These varying trajectories of restructuring have in turn shaped both the economic opportunities available to the poor and vulnerable residents who are at the center of our inquiry and the resources available to local policymakers.

Tables 2.1 and 2.2 trace the evolution of manufacturing employment in our cities between 1980 and 2009 at both the metropolitan and the central-city levels. A quick glance at the tables reveals a striking trend away from manufacturing in all our cities. Both the absolute number of people employed in manufacturing and the share of employment in manufacturing decreased in all our cities, at both the central-city and metropolitan scales. The decreases were steepest in the old manufacturing centers of Baltimore and Chicago. The tables also show that by 2009 the Baltimore, Denver, and Phoenix regions were almost entirely deindustrialized. In Toronto and Los Angeles declines in manufacturing employment have also been notable, but both cities retain relatively large manufacturing sectors in comparison to our other cases. It is also notable that declines were steeper in the central city than in the metropolitan region, reflecting a trend toward suburbanization of manufacturing; that said, by the 2000–2009 period, suburban

Table 2.1   Metropolitan-area manufacturing employment trends, 1980–2009

	Manufacturing employment as % of total employment, 1980	Manufacturing employment as % of total employment, 2009	Percent change in manufacturing employment, 1980–2009[a]
Baltimore	18.8	5.7	−61
Chicago	26.5	10.3	−50
Denver	14.7	5.8	−36
Los Angeles	25.8	10.3	−38
Phoenix	17.6	6.5	−9
Toronto	23[b]	13.5[c]	0[d]
United States	22.4	10.2	−35
Canada	19.2[b]	11.7[c]	−20[d]

Sources: State of the Cities Data Systems: Characteristics of Workers by Place of Work, 1980. Data for 2009 come from the OnTheMap database. Data for the United States as a whole are from Statistical Abstract of the United States, 2002, table 591 (for 1980 data); and Statistical Abstract of the United States, 2012, table 630 (for 2009). Toronto and Canadian data are for 1981 and 2006 and are from Statistics Canada census tables.

Note: Percent change in manufacturing employment from 1980 to 2009 is calculated as (total employment in manufacturing in 2009 in metro area − total employment in manufacturing in 1980 in metro area) / total employment in manufacturing in 1980 in metro area.

[a] These figures represent absolute change in the numbers employed rather than the relative share of overall employment (documented in the other columns). This is why the decreases observable across the initial columns do not correspond to the figures in this final column.

[b] Data for 1981.

[c] Data for 2006.

[d] Data for 1981–2006.

Table 2.2   City manufacturing employment trends, 1980–2009

	Manufacturing employment as % of total employment, 1980	Manufacturing employment as % of total employment, 2009	Percent change in manufacturing employment, 1980–2009[a]
Baltimore	18.9	4.5	−82
Chicago	23.2	5.5	−80
Denver	14.3	4.7	−64
Los Angeles	21.2	7.1	−66
Phoenix	19.3	4.8	−50
Toronto	24.5[b]	11.7[c]	−37[d]
United States	22.1	10.2	−35
Canada	19.2[b]	11.7[c]	−20[d]

Sources: State of the Cities Data Systems: Characteristics of Workers by Place of Work, 1980. Data for 2009 are from the OnTheMap database. Data for the United States as a whole are from *Statistical Abstract of the United States, 2002,* table 591 (for 1980) and *Statistical Abstract of the United States, 2012,* table 630 (for 2009). Toronto and Canadian data are for 1981 and 2006 and are from Statistics Canada census tables.

Note: Percent change in manufacturing employment from 1980 to 2009 is calculated as (total employment in manufacturing in 2009 in metro area − total employment in manufacturing in 1980 in metro area) / total employment in manufacturing in 1980 in metro area.

[a] These figures represent *absolute* change in the numbers employed rather than the relative share of overall employment (documented in the other columns). This is why the decreases observable across the initial columns do not correspond to the figures in this final column.

[b] Data for 1981.

[c] Data for 2006.

[d] Data for 1981–2006.

areas in a number of our cities were deindustrializing just as rapidly as central-city areas.

The move to a postindustrial economy has often had wrenching consequences, particularly for those individuals with limited education and, therefore, limited access to the better-paid niches of the postindustrial labor market. Given the paramount importance of education, both for individual access to well-paid labor opportunities and for citywide prospects for postindustrial economic development, we present data on educational attainment in our central cities in table 2.3. In general, the stronger a city's historical dependence on manufacturing (see table 2.2), the weaker the educational attainment of its population. Baltimore stands out as consistently having the lowest educational attainment between 1990 and 2010. Chicago—an old manufacturing center, like Baltimore—also had a workforce with limited education in 1990, but by 2010 it had closed the gap and had actually outpaced Los Angeles. Denver and Toronto had the strongest educational attainment overall, while Los Angeles was characterized by rather bifurcated educational attainment, with high proportions both of those with no postsecondary education and of those with a university bachelor's degree or more. It is notable that all our study cities saw significant improvement in educational attainment between 1990 and 2010.

The more dependent a city was on manufacturing, and the less well educated its workforce, the greater was the mismatch between worker skills and the human-capital needs of a postindustrial economy. The consequences of this are borne out by unemployment and labor force participation data (see table 2.4). Here we see the cities dividing into three basic groups. Unemployment has tended to be highest, and labor force participation low-

Table 2.3 Central-city educational attainment

	High school or less, 1990 (%)	High school or less, 2010 (%)	BA or better, 1990 (%)	BA or better, 2010 (%)
All US cities	51.6	42.9	23.0	28.1
Baltimore	66.8	52.6	15.5	24.2
Chicago	58.6	42.9	19.5	33.4
Denver	44.4	35.9	29.0	40.9
Los Angeles	52.2	45.2	23.0	30.7
Phoenix	46.8	45.1	19.9	24.9
Toronto	n.d.	36.2[a]	n.d.	36.2[a]

Sources: State of the Cities Data Systems; Statistics Canada census tables, 2011. Data for 2010 are from American Fact Finder 2. US numbers for 2010 are for the entire country, while 1990 numbers are for cities only.
Note: BA = university bachelor's degree; n.d. = no data. National percentages of high school education or less and of BA or better were 48.2% and 24.4%, respectively.
[a] Data include only individuals twenty-five years and older and are for 2011.

Table 2.4 City resident unemployment and labor force participation rates

	Unemployment rate, 1980 (%)	Unemployment rate, 2010 (%)	Labor force participation rate, 1980 (%)	Labor force participation rate, 2010 (%)
United States	7.1	10.8	63.8	64.4
Baltimore	10.7	14.4	57	61.4
Chicago	9.8	14.8	60.7	65.7
Denver	4.9	11.9	66.4	70.6
Los Angeles	6.8	13.0	64.6	66.6
Phoenix	5.5	11.5	66.2	65.4
Toronto	4.1[a]	9.9	70.0[a]	65.3

Sources: Data for 2010 are from American Fact Finder 2. US data for 1980 are from *Statistical Abstract of the United States, 2002.* Toronto data are from Statistics Canada census tables for 1981; and City of Toronto 2011 Labour Force Overview, http://www.toronto.ca/invest-in-toronto/labour_force _overview.htm.
Note: Labor force participation rate = labor force / population sixteen years and over. Unemployment rate = unemployed / labor force.
[a] Data for 1981.

Table 2.5   Global urban competitiveness rankings, 2011

	Chicago	Los Angeles	Toronto	Phoenix	Denver	Baltimore
Ranking	5	7	23	52	57	60

Source: Penglei 2012.

est, in the old industrial cities (Chicago and Baltimore), suggesting difficult, socially wrenching economic transformations—although the figures for Chicago indicate a less painful trajectory than do those for Baltimore. By contrast, Denver and Phoenix, which were not as historically dependent on industry and which have relatively well-educated workforces, have tended to have the lowest unemployment and highest labor force participation among the American cities. Toronto and Los Angeles are between these two extremes, but their trajectories have recently diverged, as Los Angeles has been hard-hit by recession, which Toronto weathered better than its American counterparts. Indeed, one of the most notable trends in our cities is the recent marked rise in unemployment in all the US cities in our sample.

The economic indicators we have presented so far suggest correlations between a city's historical dependence on manufacturing and the degree of difficulty it has faced in transitioning to a postindustrial economy. Does a similar pattern hold for globalization? The data in table 2.5 suggest that the postindustrial transition and globalization are not always closely related phenomena. The table ranks our study cities among the top 500 in the world in terms of their global economic competitiveness, using an index that combines a large number of global integration and competitiveness indicators.[3]

In terms of global competitiveness, our study cities divide into two groups: a "first tier" of highly globalized, internationally competitive cities (Chicago, Los Angeles, and Toronto) and a "second tier" of less globalized cities (Phoenix, Denver, and Baltimore). Notably, the first tier contains one of the two old industrial cities (Chicago), while the second tier contains the other (Baltimore), as well as the two cities that were historically least dependent on industrial development (Denver and Phoenix). It is also notable that the three first-tier cities are also the three that retained the highest percentage of industrial employment in both the central city and the metropolitan region as of the year 2009. Clearly, then, trajectories of postindustrial transformation and of economic globalization are not necessarily congruent. In order to make more sense of this disjuncture, we turn now to demographic data on our cities.

Diverse Demographic Transformations

The economic changes described above have been accompanied by corresponding demographic changes. In North America, which has long been marked by modest levels of natural domestic population increase, the economic strength of a city and its consequent attractiveness to migrants and immigrants are dominant drivers of population change. Cities that offer economic opportunities attract both internal and international migrants and grow rapidly in population as a result; conversely, cities in economic decline typically have either stagnant or declining populations. Tables 2.6 and 2.7 tell contrasting stories for our six study cities in this regard. The central cities of Baltimore and Chicago both reached the apogee of their industrial era population around 1950. Since then, however, while both cities have experienced substantial population loss, their trajectories (table 2.6) have diverged. Chicago experienced a 20 percent decline in population up to 1990, but since then, its population has largely stabilized. Baltimore's painful deindustrialization has been accompanied by a steady, continuous, and deep population decline. Toronto and Los Angeles have followed a different trajectory, with rapid population growth during the early postwar decades that has tapered off into more modest growth in recent years. Finally, Denver and Phoenix both stand out as young boomtowns with steady population growth. In the case of Phoenix this growth was extraordinarily rapid until 2008, when it tapered off with the onset of the recession.

Table 2.6 City population, 1950–2010

City	City population, 1950	City population, 1990	City population, 2010	% City population change, 1950–2010	% City population change, 1990–2010
Baltimore	940,205	736,014	620,583	−33.99	−15.68
Chicago	3,606,436	2,783,726	2,698,831	−25.17	−3.05
Denver	412,856	467,610	604,414	46.40	29.26
Los Angeles	1,957,692	3,485,398	3,797,144	93.96	8.94
Phoenix	105,442	983,403	1,449,481	1274.67	47.39
Toronto	1,117,470	2,275,771	2,615,060	134.02	14.91

Sources: State of the Cities Data Systems, 2000 (for 1990 data); *Statistical Abstract of the United States, 1950;* American Fact Finder 2 (for 2010 data); Statistics Canada census tables (for 1991 and 2011 data); City of Toronto Archives (for 1951 data).
Note: Toronto data are for 1951, 1991, and 2011. % city population change: 1950–2010 = (city population 2010 − city population 1950) / city population 1950.

Table 2.7   City population as a percentage of metropolitan-area population

City	Metro population, 1990	Metro population, 2010	City population as a % of metro, 1990	City population as a % of metro, 2010
Baltimore	2,382,508	2,714,183	30.9	22.9
Chicago	8,182,076	9,474,211	34	28.5
Denver	1,666,973	2,560,529	28.1	23.6
Los Angeles	11,273,720	12,849,383	30.9	29.6
Phoenix	2,238,480	4,211,213	43.9	34.4
Toronto	3,893,046	5,583,064	58.5	46.9

Source: State of the Cities Data Systems; American Fact Finder 2 (for 2010 data); Statistics Canada census tables.
Note: Toronto data are for 1991 and 2011.

The metropolitan-level data presented in table 2.7 in some ways reinforce the trajectories identified for central cities, but they also add some important nuances. Rates of suburban population growth outpace rates of central-city growth in all cases, such that central-city populations have shrunk over time in proportion to metropolitan populations. Indeed, even in Baltimore, where the central city is marked by long-term population decline, the metropolitan area has continued to grow. When we combine this observation with the stark differences between central-city and metropolitan poverty in Baltimore (see table 2.12), as well as the heavy concentration of minority groups in the central city (see table 2.8), a picture begins to emerge of Baltimore as a central city deeply disconnected from its own (prosperous and growing) metropolitan hinterland. Similar but less dramatic gaps in contextual profile emerge in the case of Chicago as well. It is also worth noting that Toronto, which has had only modest central-city population growth in recent years, continues to experience rapid growth in the wider metropolitan area.

The economic and social histories of our study cities are also inscribed in the ethnoracial makeup of their populations. As table 2.8 shows, Baltimore and Chicago both have very large African American populations, a legacy of African American migration to centers of industrial employment during the early half of the twentieth century. By contrast, in the other three American cities, African American populations are smaller, and the dominant ethnic minority group is Hispanic, reflecting patterns of migration and immigration to more recently growing cities. Chicago appears to be a hybrid case, however, in that it also has a large Hispanic population, reflecting its relative attractiveness to migrants in recent decades in comparison with Baltimore. Along with Toronto (see table 2.9), whose

Table 2.8 Racial composition, US cities and suburbs, 2010

City	City % white	City % black	City % Asian	City % other	City % Hispanic	Suburban % white	Suburban % black	Suburban % Asian	Suburban % other	Suburban % Hispanic
Baltimore	28.04	63.28	2.32	0.49	4.18	69.49	18.03	5.16	0.45	4.68
Chicago	31.71	32.36	5.38	0.33	28.89	64.29	10.96	5.65	0.28	17.42
Denver	52.15	9.73	3.32	0.87	31.82	70.02	3.96	3.71	0.72	19.56
Los Angeles	28.66	9.16	11.08	0.61	48.48	32.87	5.66	15.91	0.71	42.74
Phoenix	46.52	6.00	3.04	1.91	40.80	65.08	3.88	3.29	2.30	23.51

Sources: State of the Cities Data Systems; American Fact Finder 2.
Note: "Suburbs" are defined as the census metropolitan area minus the central city.

Table 2.9   Largest "visible minority" populations in Toronto, city and suburbs, 2011

	Not visible minority	All visible minority	South Asian	Chinese	Black	Filipino	Latin American
City	50.9%	49.1%	12.3%	10.8%	8.5%	5.1%	2.8%
Suburbs	54.8%	45.2%	17.5%	8.6%	6.1%	3.3%	1.6%

Source: Calculated from Statistics Canada census tables.
Notes: "Visible minority" is a category in the Canadian census that is reported separately from specific ethnoracial background. "Suburbs" are defined as the census metropolitan area minus the central city.

ethnoracial composition is very different from that of any of the American case cities and is assessed using different categories, Chicago is thus the most distinctly multiracial city among our cases.

There are also systematic correlations between ethnoracial composition and the depth of a city-suburb difference in ethnoracial makeup across the cities. The old industrial cities of Baltimore and Chicago have by far the largest gap between minority-dominated central cities and white-dominated suburbs, reflecting the historical dynamics of "white flight" and entrenched racial prejudice against African Americans.[4] By contrast, in more multiracial cities with larger populations of recent immigrants, such city-suburb differences still exist, but they tend to be much smaller. Indeed, in the globalized cities of Los Angeles and Toronto, the suburbs are nearly as ethnoracially diverse as the central city itself.

In recent decades, most of the population growth among urban minority groups in North America has been driven by immigration. As table 2.10 shows, all our cities have recently experienced growth in immigrant populations, but the percentage of foreign-born residents varies tremendously, from a modest 7.1 percent in Baltimore (2010) to nearly half, 48.6 percent, in Toronto (2011). Interestingly, while central cities have more foreign-born residents than metropolitan areas in all our cases except Baltimore, the differences across these two scales are fairly modest and have decreased over time in all cases except that of Phoenix. In other words, immigrants to our cities have settled in the suburbs almost as much as they have in the central cities.

This pattern underlines the fact that the large city-metropolitan disparities in the percentage of nonwhite residents in some of our cases (see table 2.8) are due primarily to the historical dynamics of spatial segregation between whites and African Americans. In other words, long-standing dynamics of city-suburb racial segregation persist, despite the broader immigration-driven metropolitanization of ethnoracial diversity. In addition, it is important to note that within central cities themselves,

Table 2.10 Percentage of population that is foreign born

	City % foreign born, 1990	City % foreign born, 2010	Suburbs % foreign born, 1990	Suburbs % foreign born, 2010	City/suburbs ratio, 1990	City/national ratio, 1990	City/ suburbs ratio, 2010	City/national ratio, 2010
National (US)	12.50							
Baltimore	3.20	7.1	3.88	9.9	0.83	0.256	0.72	0.567
Chicago	16.90	20.7	7.93	16.4	2.13	1.352	1.26	1.653
Denver	7.40	16.3	3.60	11.1	2.05	0.592	1.47	1.300
Los Angeles	38.40	39.1	25.89	32.3	1.48	3.072	1.21	3.131
Phoenix	8.60	20.0	6.43	11.5	1.34	0.688	1.73	1.597
Toronto[a]	n.d.	48.6	n.d.	43.6	n.d.	n.d.	1.14	2.36

Sources: State of the Cities Data Systems (for 1990 data); American Fact Finder 2 (for 2010 data); *Statistical Abstract of the United States, 2002*, table 41 (for national foreign-born population in 1990); Statistics Canada census tables.

Note: Overall US national foreign-born population (used for calculation in last column) was 19,767,000 in 1990 and 39,955,854 in 2010. Overall Canadian national foreign-born population was 6,186,950 (19.8%) in 2006. n.d. = no data.

[a] Data for 2011.

Table 2.11   Black-white segregation in US cities (racial dissimilarity indexes)

City	1990	2010
Baltimore	75.9	68.9
Chicago	87.4	82.5
Denver	67.0	54.7
Los Angeles	78.4	66.9
Phoenix	55.8	49.9

Source: Spatial Structures in the Social Sciences, Brown University, www.s4.brown .edu.
Note: Black-white racial dissimilarity indexes measure the percentage of the black population in the city that would have to move in order for each city census tract to have the same percentage of blacks in the population relative to whites. Higher numbers thus indicate greater segregation.

ethnoracial spatial segregation also exists, although it varies widely across our cases. While such within-city patterns of segregation are discussed in detail for each city in the chapters that follow, table 2.11 indicates that Chicago, Baltimore, and Los Angeles have much greater levels of black-white segregation than do Denver and Phoenix, although in the case of all five cities, segregation levels have declined modestly between 1990 and 2010.

The percentage of foreign-born residents in our cities maps quite closely onto the diverse economic trajectories and levels of global integration identified earlier. Baltimore, a distressed older industrial city with relatively low global integration, has by far the lowest percentage of foreign-born residents (table 2.10). Chicago, an old industrial city that has become highly globally integrated, has moderate numbers of foreign-born residents. Los Angeles and Toronto, both economically diverse and highly integrated global cities, have very high percentages of foreign-born residents. Finally, Denver and Phoenix, both fast-growing postindustrial boomtowns with relatively low global integration, have moderate but rapidly increasing numbers of foreign-born residents.

The Evolution and Concentration of Social Distress

The economic and demographic changes that we have described have been accompanied by the emergence of new forms and geographies of social distress in many cities. Social distress is a multifaceted phenomenon that can be measured using a variety of indicators. However, poverty rates are the most common metric, so we focus on that (table 2.12). All our central cities have poverty rates well above the national poverty rate (which was

15.3 percent for the United States in 2010). Baltimore has had the highest central-city poverty rate among our six cities in recent decades, although Chicago and Los Angeles are not far behind. By contrast, Phoenix and Denver historically had rather low central-city poverty rates, but with the recent economic downturn, their rates have increased markedly in recent years. The particularly steep increase in poverty in central Phoenix reflects the deep impact of the 2008–9 recession, but both Phoenix and Denver are also subject to broader periodic boom-and-bust cycles. Central-city poverty in Toronto has also increased markedly in recent years and appears to approach the level seen in the US cities. However, Canadian methodology for determining poverty rates is different (see note to table 2.12) and is likely to produce higher percentages than US methodology would.

Setting central-city poverty rates in their metropolitan contexts, we see that all our cities are, on average, poorer than the overall metropolitan areas in which they are situated. Yet the disparities differ greatly. In Baltimore, Chicago, and to a lesser extent Denver, the central city is much poorer than the metropolitan area as a whole. Baltimore in particular stands out here as a highly distressed central city situated in a prosperous metropolitan area. In Los Angeles, Phoenix, and Toronto, by contrast, the differences are more modest. And in Denver, with gentrification on the increase, the contrast may be declining as well. While the central-city poverty rate far exceeds the suburban poverty rate in all the six cities, in four of the cities (Baltimore,

Table 2.12   City and suburban poverty rate

City	City poverty rate, 1989	Suburban poverty rate, 1989	City poverty rate, 2010	Suburban poverty rate, 2010	City/ suburban poverty rate, 1989	City/ suburban poverty rate, 2010
Baltimore	21.9%	4.80%	25.6%	6.7%	4.53	3.80
Chicago	21.6%	6.00%	22.5%	10.0%	3.61	2.24
Denver	17.1%	6.80%	21.6%	9.7%	2.51	2.22
Los Angeles	18.9%	13.40%	21.6%	14.0%	1.41	1.54
Phoenix	14.2%	11.90%	22.5%	13.0%	1.2	1.73
Toronto	16.3%[a]	6.00%[a]	19.3%[b]	11.0%[b]	2.72[a]	1.75[b]

Sources: State of the Cities Data Systems (data for 1989); American Fact Finder 2 (data for 2010); Statistics Canada census tables.
Note: The US national poverty rate was 12.8% in 1989 and 15.3% in 2010. Poverty rate is calculated as the number of people below the poverty line from the total number of people for whom poverty status is determined. Suburban figures are calculated as the figures for the metropolitan area minus the figures for the city. The Canadian city figures show the percentage of "Low Income Families"; this is calculated using a low-income cutoff that varies geographically by cost of living.
[a] Data for 1991.
[b] Data for 2011.

Chicago, Denver, and Toronto), the *ratio* of central city to suburban poverty declined, implying a decrease in central-city relative to suburban poverty, while in Los Angeles and Phoenix the relative severity of poverty in cities compared with suburbs increased.

Turning to the concentration of poverty in specific neighborhoods (see table 2.13), we find a rather-different set of patterns emerging. In general, cities with higher overall poverty rates (table 2.12) have also had metropolitan areas with higher rates of concentrated poverty in recent decades (concentrated poverty rates for individual cities are not available, but we assume that most areas of concentrated poverty in metropolitan areas are located in central cities). However, there are striking exceptions to this trend. In 1989–90, for example, Los Angeles had an overall poverty rate close to that of Chicago and Baltimore, yet it had the lowest rate of concentrated poverty. By 2000, however, Los Angeles had the highest concentrated poverty of all the American cities. Perhaps the most notable pattern in table 2.13 involves the large magnitude of change in levels of concentrated poverty. Four of our six cities experienced a major decline in concentrated poverty between 1990 and 2000, which correlates with the broader US trend during this time, whereas two (Los Angeles and Toronto) experienced a significant rise.

When we integrate these data on poverty with data on ethnoracial composition presented earlier, some remarkable patterns are evident. For

Table 2.13 **Neighborhoods of concentrated poverty**

	Neighborhoods of concentrated poverty, 1990 (%)	Neighborhoods of concentrated poverty, 2000(%)	Concentrated poverty rate, 1990 (%)	Concentrated poverty rate, 2000 (%)	Percentage point change, 1990–2000
National (US)			15.1	10.3	−4.8
Baltimore	38	33	22.5	13.5	−9.0
Chicago	187	114	26.4	13.7	−12.8
Denver	11	2	7.6	1.5	−6.1
Los Angeles	56	137	9.0	14.9	5.9
Phoenix	27	30	15.2	10.5	−4.7
Toronto	66	120	13.9	23.0	9.1

Sources: For US metropolitan areas, Jargowsky 2003. For Toronto, United Way of Greater Toronto 2004.

Note: Concentrated poverty rate is the percentage of total people in poverty who are living in areas of concentrated poverty. US data are for metropolitan areas, whereas Toronto data are for the central city. Toronto data are for 1991 and 2001; they are for census tracts. A census tract is defined as having "concentrated poverty" if it has more than double the Canadian national average family poverty rate (12.8% in 2001).

example, city/suburban poverty rates map closely onto city/metro disparities in the percentage of nonwhite residents. Baltimore and Chicago, the
two cities with the highest city/suburban poverty disparity, are also the
two cities that concentrate racial minorities in the center (see table 2.8).
While our sample of cities is rather small, these data nonetheless provide
evidence for the continued role that the spatial and social segregation of
African Americans plays in the reproduction of social distress in American cities (see also Sampson 2012). That said, our data also suggest caution in assuming that concentration of distress among immigrant minority
groups is therefore not a significant concern. Indeed, it is remarkable that
Toronto and Los Angeles, two of the three cities with the most intensive
global economic connections and the largest immigrant populations, are
also the only ones in which concentrated poverty increased between 1990
and 2000 (table 2.13). This suggests that immigration and global integration may attenuate long-established patterns of urban sociospatial segregation, only to replace them with new patterns of segregation and inequality.

The Contextual Trajectories of Six Cities: A Brief Profile

The cities examined in this book display a variety of very different contexts for the politics and policy of neighborhood revitalization. The data
on social distress, economic trajectories, and demographic change we have
presented here display clear patterns, with variables clustering together in
complex but ordered ways, such that we can identify types of contextual
trajectories among our case cities. In this section we briefly review these
contextual types, organizing our discussion from the most to the least socially distressed.

In the data we have presented here, Baltimore stands out clearly as having the most socially distressed context for neighborhood policymaking.
As an older industrial city, Baltimore has suffered decades of economic
and population decline. It has persistently high rates of poverty and unemployment. Poverty is highly concentrated in particular neighborhoods,
even though housing is relatively inexpensive. Baltimore is situated within
a broader metropolitan area that is prosperous and growing and accentu-
ated by its proximity to Washington, DC. Yet the central city is fundamentally disconnected from this broader metropolitan context in terms of its
socioeconomic and demographic characteristics. This deep disconnect reflects, in part, a stark and enduring racial divide between a relatively affluent white population, which is now largely suburban, and a largely poor
African American population, which continues to be concentrated in the

central city. Despite the affluence of its suburbs, the Baltimore area displays rather low levels of global economic integration and receives few new immigrants. In short, Baltimore is a clear example of a distressed former industrial city.

In historical terms, Chicago's socioeconomic trajectory is in many ways similar to Baltimore's. A long-standing major industrial center with a large African American population, Chicago still displays many of the socioeconomic and demographic characteristics of an old American industrial city in the postindustrial era, including high rates of poverty and unemployment and an economic and racial gulf between the city and the suburbs. Yet in other ways Chicago is very much unlike Baltimore. It has become a highly globally integrated city with a strong postindustrial economic base, which sustains modest population growth, and has developed an increasingly diverse population base due to steady immigration. At the same time, Chicago has seen a rapid decline in concentrated poverty, despite a housing market that places a high cost burden on low-income residents. Chicago, then, is something of an unusual hybrid: an older industrial center that is reinventing itself as a global city.

Los Angeles and Toronto, for all their differences, share a broadly similar contextual trajectory. Both have histories of long-term rapid population growth, although in recent years central-city growth has slowed, and only Toronto maintains rapid growth at the metropolitan scale. Both have long had a substantial industrial base but have recently transitioned to diversified postindustrial economies. Despite their economic strength, both cities also have significant and growing concentrated poverty. In contrast in particular to Baltimore, Los Angeles and Toronto do not display the large city-suburban disparities in poverty and ethnoracial composition that mark many older American industrial centers. Toronto and Los Angeles are both highly globally integrated cities and stand out among our cases for their very large immigrant populations. High immigration has also made them multiracial cities, although Los Angeles has one dominant minority group (Hispanics), whereas Toronto does not. In short, Los Angeles and Toronto present a common type of context for neighborhood policy and politics, that of the globalized city.

Finally, Denver and Phoenix share a similar contextual trajectory. Both are younger, rapidly growing cities with low dependence on industry and a diversified postindustrial economic base. Both have historically had relatively low levels of poverty and concentrated poverty. However, both cities—especially Phoenix—were hit hard by the recession of 2008–9, which is reflected in a rapid rise in poverty and unemployment in recent years.

Both Phoenix and Denver also have rapidly growing immigrant populations, mainly composed of migrants from Mexico and Latin America. While both Denver and Phoenix display wealth gaps that disadvantage the central city relative to the broader metropolitan area, these gaps are smaller than in old industrial centers. Despite their rapid growth trajectories, neither Denver nor Phoenix is highly integrated into the global economy. They might best be characterized as postindustrial boomtowns, subject to periodic boom-and-bust cycles.

Notes

1. As of 2010, the percentage of the metropolitan-area population living in our central cities ranged from a low of 22.9 percent in Baltimore to a high of 46.9 percent in Toronto. See table 2.7.
2. These methodological differences, where they exist, are discussed in notes to the statistical tables.
3. The indicators on which these rankings are based were measured at the metropolitan scale, so some caution is necessary when comparing these results with those from the preceding central-city data. This is especially the case for Baltimore, whose central-city economic trajectory is very different from that of the surrounding metropolitan area and whose global competitiveness ranking would likely decrease if it were measured at the level of the central city alone.
4. It should be noted, however, that the demographic pattern in the Chicago region is changing, with suburbs gaining in diversity; see Hanlon, Short, and Vicino 2010.

THREE

Neighborhood Policy in Baltimore: The Postindustrial Turn

ROBERT P. STOKER, CLARENCE N. STONE, AND DONN WORGS

A onetime manufacturing hub hard-hit by deindustrialization and population loss, Baltimore underscores several aspects of the evolving politics of neighborhood policy. In the 1980s, against the grain of a rightward shift in national politics, Baltimore made a turn toward greater concern with distressed neighborhoods. After a lengthy period in which city priorities had clearly been focused on remaking downtown, the city's first popularly elected black mayor, Kurt Schmoke, ended the heavy neglect of Baltimore's poorer neighborhoods. This shift coincided with an increased presence of the city's philanthropic sector, which in the main shared Schmoke's neighborhood agenda. For its part, the once-influential, business-led Greater Baltimore Committee became less engaged in city affairs, leaving a policy vacuum partly filled by the city's ed & med sector. The centerpiece of recent action is a massive redevelopment project next to the Johns Hopkins medical campus that combines economic development with neighborhood improvements, including enhanced services for community residents. Jointly launched by the city and the university with crucial backing from the Annie E. Casey Foundation, the initiative has enjoyed support from three key sectors but has also evoked periodic protests by residents. With a long tradition of patronage politics, Baltimore's business and civic elites are wary of government-controlled initiatives. Their inclinations favor independent authorities, which have low transparency and limited space for community engagement. Overall, Baltimore's neighborhoods are sites of much policy activity, which often consists of a mix of neighborhood concerns with economic development, crime fighting, and transportation. Postindustrial Baltimore shows that, in comparison to the redevelopment period, neighborhood voices and concerns receive greater consideration but nevertheless are hampered by a highly diffuse pattern of policy leadership. As marginal players, the city's distressed neighborhoods have not gained the connections needed for a broad and sustained agenda of community revitalization. Instead, the pattern is one of ad hoc, disconnected initiatives. While several efforts have aimed to strengthen the neighborhood voice in the city, and some calls for alliance building have been sounded, many of these attempts have suffered from incomplete or lapsed backing.

In 1950 Baltimore was the nation's sixth-largest city, with a population of just under one million. By 2010 the city's population had declined by more than one-third from its 1950 peak, and its rank had fallen to twenty-first. Population loss was accompanied by residential disinvestment and abandonment. Once a regional economic dynamo, Baltimore's Inner Harbor has become an entertainment district. The city's onetime manufacturing base has faded away. The largest private employer in the state is Johns Hopkins University (including its hospital and medical school). The city's robust industrial past has given way to a modest niche in the biomedical and entertainment sectors of a postindustrial economy. Gaining an African American majority in 1980, Baltimore has remained a black-white city, its demography little altered by sparse gains in new immigration. Though part of a thriving region, Baltimore has a high level of crime and poverty. Hard-hit by the crack epidemic, Baltimore became a setting deemed appropriate for such television dramas as *Homicide* and *The Wire*. While in some ways Baltimore fits the classic portrait of the urban crisis—a city facing decline as its suburbs grow and prosper—the city's evolving reality holds complex possibilities.

What might a neighborhood lens show us about this struggling city? When we look from the bottom up, we see that decline is far from universal; the city has many thriving neighborhoods, several with a rich architectural heritage. Baltimore has a substantial ed & med sector. However, disinvestment is an ever-present danger. Neighborhood distress in Baltimore is a product of government action combined with market processes. Society in the form of racial stereotypes is a major contributing factor as well, and it mixed with the market to yield a pattern of redlining, blockbusting, and predatory lending (Pietila 2010), a body of experiences widely shared among older American cities.

In this chapter our emphasis is on what's new and in process, but with due regard to legacies from the past. Actions interwoven across policy domains form a trajectory that is well worth examining. In the past, after an initial period of destructive disregard, Baltimore's neighborhoods mobilized to defend against further displacement but found themselves unable to bring about a positive neighborhood agenda. Their efforts were contained by a politically skilled mayor and his business allies. The result was a neglect of neighborhoods, but a neglect that eventually had hard-to-ignore consequences. During the 1980s awareness of those consequences spread. By that time, several things had become evident: that a refurbished business district was insufficient to reverse the city's declining fortune, that the Greater Baltimore Committee (GBC, an association of major corporate businesses) was decreasingly engaged in the city's affairs and increasingly mindful that the city's economy had become regional in scope, that the philanthropic sector occupied an agenda-setting role largely vacated by a onetime business–city hall alliance, and that the economic fate of the city rested heavily with the ed & med sector. The emergent postindustrial era had created a new context for neighborhood policy.

In the 1980s new players and new issues entered the city's civic and political arena. There was no sudden transformation, but several events signaled the emergence of a fresh order. In this chapter we examine the key signposts along this pathway. In brief, they were (1) a broadening in the policy discourse, along with the election of Kurt Schmoke as mayor; (2) the launching of an initially touted but eventually disappointing Sandtown-Winchester community development project (followed closely by Empowerment Zone designation in selected neighborhoods); (3) the creation of East Baltimore Development Inc. (EBDI) as a large, multipart effort to revitalize an area adjoining the Johns Hopkins medical complex; and (4) the Oliver project, located adjacent to the EBDI project but initiated independently by Baltimore's IAF (Industrial Areas Foundation) affiliate, BUILD (Baltimoreans United in Leadership Development). Collectively, these developments take us through the policy shift and accompanying adjustments in political relations that constitute a new era for neighborhood politics in Baltimore.[1]

The Turnaround

Before the end of World War II, Baltimore business and political leaders had already begun planning to remake the CBD (central business district) and reshape its connection to the wider region. Expressway construction was a top priority, and black communities were prime targets for displacement. Some white working-class communities also faced the bulldozer, and others encountered disruption set loose by a lack of relocation planning and the absence of measures to counteract blockbusting (Orser 1994; Durr 2003; Pietila 2010). Although Baltimore neighborhoods were initially caught off guard, they did respond. A spate of protest organizations emerged, and the result "was a crystallization of resistance" (Olson 1976, 54). Community-based protests gained some concessions, particularly in limiting the scope of the massive plan for expressway construction (Mohl 2004). However, the CBD-focused redevelopment agenda gave rise to substantial tension with the city's older, less-affluent neighborhoods, and overall, Baltimore's policymakers displayed limited regard for the changing quality of life many of the city's neighborhoods were experiencing. Lacking a firm base of electoral support, redevelopment, for its part, required a political arrangement insulated from popular pressures. Political and business elites came together around reliance on quasi-public corporations to manage development initiatives, and this arrangement gave pursuit of economic change and growth its own protected arena.

When (following the turbulent 1960s) William Donald Schaefer became mayor in 1971, he worked closely with Baltimore's business community to use this arrangement to complete the redevelopment of the CBD and create several popular Inner Harbor attractions. Regarded by many as a highly successful mayor (he was named "America's Best Mayor" by *Esquire* magazine in 1983), Schaefer was credited with lifting city morale and engineering the "Baltimore Renaissance" (Nast, Krause, and Monk 1982). Schaefer also displayed his mastery of disarming opposition to bring protests to an end. He used federal money to create positions for co-opting strategically important community leaders, and he encouraged grassroots organizations to launch plans for which, it turned out later, there was little money to implement. Although Schaefer opened a few community centers, they fit into no larger plan of empowerment or systematic community improvement. In reality, Schaefer's actions served to demobilize the neighborhood movement and defuse militancy in the black community. The mayor also excelled in constituency service, but no matter how effective at heading off opposition, filling potholes, and picking up trash, Schaefer made short shrift of neighborhoods as a policy concern. During the Schaefer years, Matthew Crenson observed: "The big money and the big decisions are both being made at the center of the city, not in the residential communities that stretch out from the harbor along the stream valleys and over the hills to suburbia. In fact, it seems difficult to credit the commonplace claim that Baltimore is a city of strong neighborhoods when so much of the city's strength appears to be concentrated at its center" (1983, 290).

Shortly after Crenson rendered this assessment, the established order began to look less secure. Although Schaefer won reelection as mayor (in 1983) after Baltimore became a majority African American city, his leadership did not go uncontested. Notably, the formation of an IAF affiliate, BUILD, a community-based organization whose power center lies in the city's major black churches, put in motion a new and assertive force. BUILD began to address some of the persisting problems of social distress (Orr 1992), and one of its earliest successes was a 1980 campaign against redlining. Tactically, BUILD did not play down the extent to which it and Schaefer were at cross-purposes on key issues.

In November 1986 Schaefer was elected Maryland's governor and left the mayoralty. In the meantime the shine was beginning to wear off the Baltimore "renaissance." The rising philanthropic presence in the city's affairs made itself known with a far-reaching *Baltimore 2000* report from the Goldseker Foundation.[2] The report expressed concern that neighborhoods had been neglected during Baltimore's preoccupation with remaking its CBD and, in an attention-getting line, quoted an unnamed civic leader as declaring that there is "rot beneath the glitter" (C. F. Smith 1999, 262). Schaefer's departure for the state capital was soon followed by Kurt Schmoke's successful campaign to become Baltimore's first popularly elected black mayor.[3] Like the Goldseker report, his campaign emphasized a need to turn around the neglect of neighborhoods. After winning the election, Schmoke openly stated that a "rising tide" of economic development does not necessarily lift all boats. Distressed communities needed attention. Meanwhile at the national level, major foundations and corporate funders put in motion a Living Cities Project that advocated Comprehensive Community Initiatives (CCIs) as an approach to community development in highly distressed neighborhoods.[4]

In a defining move locally, Schmoke allied with James Rouse's Enterprise Foundation and BUILD (as the community-based partner) to undertake a Neighborhood Transformation Initiative in the city's Sandtown-Winchester community. As an area of great need, Sandtown-Winchester (usually shortened to Sandtown) seemed especially appropriate for a comprehensive approach. Because the initiative fit the CCI model so closely, Sandtown received national attention. Many observers saw it as the future of community development, but difficulties arose from the outset.[5]

The project encompassed housing, education, job training, economic development, community policing, and the building of community pride and spirit. Housing, however, occupied a central place, and various efforts yielded 1,600 new and renovated units (Walsh 1997, 16). Despite various gains, the project suffered tensions concerning the issue of community engagement. BUILD felt marginalized and was never able to launch the organizing effort it believed to be fundamental to the initiative's success (McDougall 1993, 153). One analyst observed that the Sandtown initiative "was particularly burdened by the tension between its commitment to community participation and the need to produce real change" (Walsh 1997, 17). Both Rouse and Schmoke were eager to show fast results and pushed in that direction, reinforced by a need for additional resources. Funders wanted quick demonstrations of success and tight control from the top. Community engagement was also complicated by the formation of multiple entities to carry out Sandtown's agenda.[6] After an initial period of setting ambitious goals, yet another complication surfaced: "post-planning let down set in when residents realized how little funding was available to implement their lofty vision" (Walsh 1997, 17).

Sandtown-Winchester signaled an important shift in neighborhood politics by placing emphasis on the plight of distressed neighborhoods, but national celebration of the initiative notwithstanding, locally it proved disappointing. Although it produced housing and other particular gains, the initiative failed to be a catalyst for a broader revitalization. Falling short of the high expectations that surrounded its launch, the initiative failed to attract much in the way of private investment. Many local players saw the lack of market appeal as its weak link.

Awakening to Neighborhoods in Distress

Although Sandtown proved a disappointment, Schmoke's mayoralty was not a one-note song. Sandtown was the initiative that attracted national attention, but Schmoke's efforts extended over a wide domain. Baltimore pursued and won (in 1994) a federal Empowerment Zone (EZ) award of a $100 million block grant plus a variety of tax incentives. Consistent with federal requirements, the zone targeted a limited number of distressed neighborhoods within the city. The city's EZ program worked with local foundations and nonprofits to accomplish goals in areas such as job creation, workforce development, and housing (Rich and Stoker 2010). To attract participation from business, civic, and foundation elites, a quasi-public corporation, Empower Baltimore Management Corporation, served as the primary entity that established local priorities and programs.[7] Citizen participation and community capacity were enhanced by the creation of an advisory council and six village centers (community-based nonprofit corporations) that implemented workforce development and family-support programs and produced community-level land-use and public-safety plans.

Although a large portion of Sandtown was included in Baltimore's EZ, community activists purposefully separated EZ community participation from the ongoing Sandtown-Winchester project.[8] As community activists saw it, the Sandtown project had evolved into too much of a professionalized intervention of the Enterprise Foundation. Indeed, a report on "lessons-learned" in Sandtown highlighted difficulties the initiative encountered in the relationship between the foundation and the community (Brown, Butler, and Hamilton 2001). Neighborhood activists in Sandtown wanted the EZ initiative to be managed by the community. Accordingly, the community did organize a village center. Although the EZ provided an opportunity for a community-driven intervention, the village center that served Sandtown proved to be highly troubled (Rich and Stoker 2014). Mired in financial scandals and with unstable leadership, the village center eventually lost the financial support of Baltimore's EZ initiative and was closed before the local EZ initiative ended.

As indicated by the Goldseker report, Baltimore's newly developed philanthropic sector joined the chorus of neighborhood concerns. For his part, Schmoke took several steps to confront the city's crack epidemic, a crisis that peaked around the time he became mayor (Beilenson and McGuire 2012). Drug dealing had a hold on the younger generation, and street violence was running at a high level. Many neighborhoods were asking for city intervention, but resources were limited. A smaller version of a comprehensive, community-based approach in Baltimore was the one initially developed by the Boyd Booth Concerned Citizens. Its centerpiece was nuisance abatement (especially against drug houses). It was launched in the early 1990s, roughly concurrent with Sandtown, and was subsequently folded into Operation Reach Out South West (OROSW), bringing together several neighborhoods with a foundation created by Bon Secours Hospital to pursue community development in the area around the hospital (Artigiani 1996; Blumenberg, Blom, and Artigiani 1998).[9] Although the initiative has been sustained over time, it has never received the scope of funding and extent of public exposure that Sandtown-Winchester enjoyed. In a related public-safety effort, Schmoke embraced community policing, and his commissioner supported the use of federal Justice Department funds to treat neighborhood organizing as an extension of his policing strategy. Key nonprofits were valuable links in the overall approach.

On another front, Schmoke confronted the city's troubled public-housing program. Though inadequate funding of upkeep and maintenance was a contributing factor, project deterioration was widely viewed as stemming from a heavy concentration of poverty.[10] Coming into office, Schmoke appointed a task force on high-rise public housing, which was shortly followed by the creation of the National Commission on Severely Distressed Public Housing and the subsequent creation of the HOPE VI program. Under this latter program Baltimore took down six public-housing projects. However, it should be noted that the city's relocation effort was not tightly administered and kept poor records. As in several cities, the goal of deconcentrating the poor came largely at the expense of the poorest of the poor.

In 1997 the Schmoke administration launched an overdue comprehensive planning process. Although this process was not complete when Schmoke decided not to seek reelection in 1999, it did lay out some significant markers. One proposal was building capacity among the city's neighborhoods, and another was to reject treating neighborhoods in cookie-cutter fashion. On the latter, the draft plan set forth the principle that different neighborhoods represent different challenges and that policy prescriptions should vary accordingly. A fourfold classification scheme was proposed. Neighborhoods with a high level of homeownership and strong property values (and thus in no need of special attention) were at the top. By contrast, "redevelopment neighborhoods"—severely distressed neighborhoods in the bottom category—were marked for drastic remaking when an appropriate opportunity opened. Policy elites concluded that revitalizing redevelopment neighborhoods would require an extraordinary intervention and the kinds of resources that could come only from cross-sector mobilization (including investors) to bring together the city's resources on a scale sufficient to create new market conditions. Between these extremes were neighborhoods at risk of decline, termed "stabilization neighborhoods" and "reinvestment neighborhoods," known collectively as neighborhoods "in the middle," that were targeted for improvement and stabilization.

Uneven Action on Multiple Fronts

In 1999 neighborhood activists took the lead in organizing a two-day Neighborhood Congress. Under the sponsorship of a long-standing civic entity, the Citizens Planning and Housing Association (CPHA), an estimated 750 residents widely representative of all segments of the city ad-opted a four-point agenda focused mainly on a need for improved services in such areas as education and drug treatment. Despite initial enthusiasm, the special effort at neighborhood mobilization soon withered away. As official sponsor of the Neighborhood Congress, CPHA declined to offer continuing sponsorship and reportedly saw the congress as a rival rather than an ally.

Further, the transition from Schmoke to newly elected mayor Martin O'Malley was disappointing to advocates of a robust neighborhood pol-icy. The aim of strengthening capacity in the city's vulnerable neighbor-hoods was lost in the mayoral changeover. Although O'Malley's campaign had centered on crime reduction, his transition team developed plans in multiple areas and included a neighborhood committee, which recom-mended creation of a department of neighborhood affairs. However, the follow-through was a letdown. An office of neighborhoods was formed, but O'Malley saw it as a constituency-service entity, not as a policy body. In addition, on the city council and as a mayoral candidate, O'Malley was a critic of community policing. He pursued an aggressive enforcement pol-icy instead, dismissing Schmoke's police commissioner and replacing him with a deputy commissioner from New York City who was experienced in Mayor Giuliani's zero-tolerance approach to policing. (O'Malley's suc-cessor, Sheila Dixon, quietly restored the basic principles of community policing.)

Beyond city hall an important development was an increasingly large role played by Baltimore's philanthropic sector in neighborhood policy-making. Foundations promoted closer and more informed attention to neighborhood conditions by backing the creation of the Baltimore Neigh-borhood Indicators Alliance (BNIA). Beginning in 1998 with two years of study and development, BNIA is presently housed at the University of Bal-timore and is affiliated with the National Neighborhood Indicators Part-nership of the Urban Institute. Its steering committee was formed out of a gathering brought together by the Annie E. Casey Foundation and the As-sociation of Baltimore Area Grantmakers and includes representatives from state and city agencies, local foundations, nonprofits, and area universities.

Reflecting growing concerns about neighborhoods in the middle, the Goldseker Foundation provided support for the Healthy Neighborhoods Initiative (HNI), a program to prevent decline in less severely distressed neighborhoods. HNI rested on a multilayered rationale (Boehlke 2001). One layer was the importance of nurturing market appeal. Another was that limited resources made a triage approach attractive. Yet another was a need to bolster and retain the city's middle class. HNI targets neighborhoods that might otherwise experience disinvestment; the aim is to make them attractive places for middle-income families to live by promoting a "market orientation" rather than a "deficit orientation." Though covering multiple communities within the city (initially seven, now fourteen), HNI is a modest initiative that provides limited funding for neighborhood improvements.[11]

Other foundation initiatives reflected a similar challenge of achieving a healthy economic and racial mix in the city's population. The Abell Foundation underwrote a study by David Rusk, *Baltimore Unbound: A Strategy for Regional Renewal* (1996).[12] In it Rusk called for an end to CCIs and gave a dismal forecast of "shattered dreams" as the likely outcome of Baltimore's EZ program. Rusk rejected the idea of ameliorating the problems of the poor through expanded services and proposed instead to disperse poor people throughout the region: "Helping poor people leave bad neighborhoods is the most effective antipoverty program" (146).[13]

With foundation support, considerable sweat equity, and, at a later time, federal earmarks by Senator Barbara Mikulski, the Patterson Park community (near the waterfront and containing a sizable park) was stabilizing itself after a period of decline. In 1996 the Patterson Park Community Development Corporation (PPCDC) was established to oversee a neighborhood improvement program.[14] Neighborhood leaders sought to overcome blight while preserving affordable housing. PPCDC also attracted new residents with foundation-funded free tuition at a local Catholic school and "home value guarantees" that compensated buyers (when they sold) if home values declined.[15] Leaders in the turnaround of Patterson Park published a widely respected booklet on community stabilization and "sustainable neighborhoods"; it was their version of "neighborhoods in the middle" (Pollock and Rutkowski 1998).

Despite action taking place on multiple fronts, the emergence of neighborhood concerns in Baltimore did not proceed smoothly. Three "nondecisions" indicated weakness in the local inclination to pursue a neighborhood agenda. The inability of the Neighborhood Congress to sustain its existence was one. O'Malley's failure to create a policy-oriented department of neighborhood affairs was a second. And the third occurred in 2003 when a nascent effort to institutionalize a community-development alliance fell apart. After preliminary discussion among representatives of government agencies, nonprofits, and the philanthropic sector, some foundation officers voiced the view that donors would not go further than the modest Baltimore Neighborhood Collaborative (BNC). Anything more ambitious, they suggested, would call for donors to sacrifice too much individual independence.

On the other hand, Baltimore's neighborhoods demonstrated a significant level of activity. BUILD had become a mainstay (even though coalition averse) of the city's political and civic scene. And notwithstanding their unwillingness to go very far in acting collectively, local foundations had emerged as players quite willing to engage neighborhood revitalization as a worthy purpose. The civic landscape had become populated with a variety of entities, ranging from the long-standing CPHA to the newly formed BNIA and BNC, through which foundations could sponsor initiatives and lend support for addressing neighborhood concerns.[16] Meanwhile, business in the collective form of GBC had retreated from its once high level of engagement as the city's ed & med sector emerged as a rising presence (Hanson et al. 2006; Strom 2008).

Current Neighborhood Policy

No overarching neighborhood policy is evident in Baltimore. Despite several ongoing initiatives, it is clear that remedying neighborhood distress is not a paramount priority. Even when experiencing substantial levels of distress, neighborhoods struggle to gain and keep the attention of policymakers. Moreover, neighborhood policy is significantly intersected by other policy concerns—namely, economic development, public safety, and transportation.[17] The attention addressed to neighborhood improvement often reflects its intersection with other domains. Neighborhood policy also blends public and private resources (city government agencies work in partnership with foundations and local nonprofits), and as postindustrial growth centers, ed & med institutions offer special promise as triggers of investment and as supportive partners. Although new possibilities have opened for neighborhood improvement, the politics of neighborhood revitalization remains a source of significant friction.

East Baltimore Redevelopment

The East Baltimore redevelopment initiative illustrates the evolving character of the city's neighborhood narrative. In it one can see with great clarity that a new dynamic has replaced the old politics of insulated development in pursuit of economic growth. This new dynamic has a rough-and-tumble side, but the lesson gleaned from accumulating experience is that policy action often calls for attention to both community-based social concerns and market forces, with government as a crucial backup source of support and investment.

East Baltimore neighborhoods are among the city's most distressed. The redevelopment project is located on an eighty-eight-acre tract of land just north of the Johns Hopkins medical complex. This long-standing African American community underwent a change from a residential area tied to industrial employment to a place of increasing poverty and housing abandonment. The redevelopment project entails the demolition of hundreds of structures, relocation of many families, and calls for new mixed-income housing, job training, biotech laboratories, office space, a new school, and an early-childhood center, along with significant social supports for the dislocated residents.[18] At its core the redevelopment plan aimed to attract commercial biomedical investment. Market-rate housing was to be constructed and sold to the workers at the new biomedical facilities. Retail development was expected to follow apace. Existing residents were promised improved housing (including a generous relocation allowance), enhanced services, and job opportunities. Local businesses were to enjoy contracting opportunities with preferences for minority- and women-owned firms.

The institutional center of this effort is a quasi-public corporation, EBDI (East Baltimore Development Inc.). With Baltimore's history of relying on such partnership organizations for development purposes (Stoker 1987), it is not surprising that EBDI provides only token representation for the community.[19] Then mayor O'Malley and leaders from Johns Hopkins and the philanthropic sector (especially the Annie E. Casey Foundation) were its core architects. EBDI's evolution highlights defining features of the new neighborhood politics. After Sandtown-Winchester proved disappointing, CCI, as a concept, faded from neighborhood policy discourse in Baltimore. However, although CCI was not prominent in local discourse, the East Baltimore redevelopment project reflects the comprehensive logic of pursuing multiple, overlapping aims.

Discussions of redevelopment adjacent to the Johns Hopkins medical complex date back to at least the early 1990s when the university, the city government, and community leaders came together to form the Historic East Baltimore Community Action Coalition (HEBCAC). The organization was originally envisioned as a means to coordinate the revitalization of the community through social services and housing rehabilitation. HEBCAC also became one of the village centers in the city's EZ program. Beginning in 1994, HEBCAC pursued a strategy of housing demolition and strategic rehabilitation in scattered sites in the area. However, after six years and substantial commitments of federal resources, little progress was evident—

only forty-seven homes had been rehabilitated, with significant cost over-runs, while the number of abandoned properties in the area had doubled. Ultimately, many of Baltimore's governmental and foundation elites, including Mayor O'Malley in a leading role, concluded that HEBCAC's efforts had failed. Given the area's depth of distress, elites concluded that a neighborhood-run community development corporation like HEBCAC could not manage programs of sufficient scale to revitalize the neighborhood and attract investment.[20] After significant cross-sector negotiations, a new entity, EBDI, was formed to bring elite actors together to manage the redevelopment process.

Throughout its various stages, EBDI has had a friction-laden relationship with the East Baltimore community.[21] Numerous early sessions with residents revealed strong resistance, reflecting a history of distrust of Johns Hopkins—particularly its property acquisition practices. Subsequently, another community organization, the Save Middle East Action Coalition (SMEAC), emerged as a voice of community concerns ("Middle East" refers to the cluster of East Baltimore neighborhoods surrounding the Johns Hopkins medical complex). Relations among the various players are complicated. As a neighborhood organization that arose to resist EBDI, SMEAC was nevertheless a beneficiary of the Casey Foundation's support.[22] Casey looked with favor on the idea of residents having an independent voice in the process.

Fueled by frustration over their exclusion from the initial planning process, forced relocation, and the manner in which the project was being implemented, SMEAC mobilized significant community-based opposition. SMEAC activists spoke out, protested, and leveraged their influence with the media and other allies. Their efforts paid off with changes to the project: enhanced relocation benefits (an increase from the "market value" of the homes to an amount that would enable the purchase of a comparable home in a stable neighborhood); significant changes to the demolition protocol to make it more ecofriendly; and establishment of the "house for a house" program by which residents in the second phase of the project were given the opportunity to relocate in the neighborhood rather than resettling elsewhere (however, tensions over the details of the housing program continue).

Although the redevelopment effort has assembled a large tract of land, relocated many families, and undertaken significant infrastructure improvements, development of the biotechnology park has not gone as expected. The original plan called for construction of five private biotech buildings, totaling 1.7 million square feet of lab and office space to house biotech

firms. However, at this stage, only one of the five originally proposed biotech centers has been constructed. Meanwhile, as part of a shift in development plans, construction has begun on a building to house the state
Department of Health and Mental Hygiene's Public Health Laboratory.

The jobs created by the new biotechnology firms were expected to stimulate demand for market-rate housing, to increase employment opportunities for residents, and to encourage retail development. However, these
initial high expectations have not been met. The lack of progress has led
EBDI leaders to adjust their strategy. While biotech ambitions remain, one
former board member acknowledged: "It's not going to be a biotech park"
because of the inability to attract investors (Simmons and Jacobson 2011).

Project leaders circulated a draft of a new master plan in the summer of
2011. The updated plan scaled back biotech facilities, proposed construction of a hotel (subsequently receiving subsidized support from the state),
placed greater emphasis on retail and neighborhood amenities, and highlighted the new school.[23] The plan, together with the public statements
from Johns Hopkins officials and others at EBDI, suggests that the quality
of neighborhood amenities (particularly the community's new school) is
now a key element of the strategy to attract people to live in the area. Although the promise of a high-performance school was part of what made
EBDI palatable to the community,[24] it is also part of an overall strategy that
some residents fear is overly concerned to make East Baltimore attractive to
middle-class families.

East Baltimore residents shut down a meeting at which the new draft
master plan was presented and charged that they had again been excluded
from the planning process. As a former president of SMEAC, noted: "They
[EBDI] keep saying, 'This is for you, this is for the residents.' . . . But who in
the world is speaking for the community? This is a new plan. Nobody ever
knew anything about a hotel, a park or this whole thing. We're not part of
the partnership. We're not included" (quoted in Simmons 2011b).

EBDI has come under a variety of criticisms. In a series of unfavorable
newspaper articles, questions were raised about the rate of progress and the
lack of transparency regarding EBDI's financing (Jacobson and Simmons
2011). Remaining residents continue to complain about the relocation process and the sluggish pace of housing construction. Recent protests have
centered on slow job growth, the lack of construction jobs for East Baltimore residents, and insufficient inclusion of minority contractors.[25] The
project's current economic-inclusion plan promises expanded contracting
opportunities for minority- and women-owned businesses and puts in
place a third party to monitor performance and compliance with the con-

tracting policy and goals (Schachtel 2011). In addition, questions about the uses of public funds have emerged following news accounts that described the level of public investment (over $200 million, thus far) and the minimal, if any, reporting requirements and oversight. The issuance of $78 million in Tax Increment Financing (TIF) bonds was particularly controversial in part because the sale was initiated by EBDI without the knowledge of the mayor or the city council (Jacobson and Simmons 2011).

Notwithstanding claims from EBDI's leadership insisting that the project is "on track to achieve its goals" (e.g., Nelson and Shea 2010), the redevelopment strategy has been significantly altered over time. What began with an emphasis on the fruits of economic development has increasingly morphed into a thoroughly multifaceted combination of developmental and social programs. Of special note, given soft market conditions for biomedical investment, the effort to revitalize the neighborhood has more and more become a project driven by public investment. Just as Sandtown taught that the market could not be left out of the revitalization picture, EBDI shows that, even when courted directly, the market is no guarantor of progress. Public funding is often a needed backstop.

The EBDI partnership is only one part of the ongoing relationship between the Johns Hopkins medical complex and the East Baltimore community. As far back as the 1960s, the university was developing "a plan for improving the health, social and economic climate for East Baltimore residents" (Urban Health Institute 2010, 2). However, the plans were suspended after the 1968 rioting.[26] Planning for a community health initiative resumed in the 1970s but was stymied by conflict over demands for community control. In the late 1990s, with the inauguration of a new president at Johns Hopkins, a small group of faculty (from Medicine, Nursing, and Public Health) went to the president to argue that the university's fate was intertwined with that of the community. They argued that the university needed to become more deeply engaged.

Beginning in 1999, a two-year planning and consultation process yielded a new entity, the Urban Health Institute (UHI). Housed in, funded through, and ultimately controlled by Johns Hopkins, UHI "was conceptualized as a partnership between Johns Hopkins Institutions, the East Baltimore community, government and business" (Urban Health Institute 2010, 4).[27] UHI initially defined its special target as the five zip codes that surround the university's medical campus, and for this area (recently extended to seven zips codes) it is currently putting into place TAP (The Access Partnership)—an initiative to provide the full range of health care to uninsured and underinsured residents in this catchment area.[28] UHI has also played a key supporting role in establishing East Baltimore's early-childhood center. [29]

Even without TAP, the East Baltimore redevelopment project has gravitated toward comprehensiveness. However, it is important to remember that its earliest planning did not start out that way.[30] The project was transformed to focus more on residents' concerns when, as a condition for their participation, the Casey Foundation insisted on a "paradigm shift" away from what its officers viewed as a narrow concern with economic development and toward a vision in which "the living conditions and outcomes for low-income East Baltimore families became the primary objective."[31] Community-based protests have at various stages pushed toward a more comprehensive effort with enhanced community benefits (including "responsible relocation" for displaced residents, job readiness services, job training, and employment opportunities), but among the elite actors the mayor's office has not been in the foreground.[32] Nongovernmental players have been the major source for bringing community concerns into the process.

Riding Piggyback

The Oliver community, which adjoins the East Baltimore redevelopment project, is the location of yet another ongoing neighborhood revitalization effort. The Oliver project was generated and led by a community organization, the IAF-affiliated BUILD. Although East Baltimore and Oliver each had distinct origins and early on followed different paths of development, their revitalization efforts have been linked because Oliver is adjacent to the East Baltimore project. Backers of both have come to count on the economic vitality of the Johns Hopkins medical complex to attract private investment and enhance the area's appeal as a residential community.

Oliver set out on its own path toward revitalization and has since won significant concessions from government officials and support from foundations. BUILD initiated the project but struggled to win support from the city's political leaders. However, in 2002 a highly publicized tragedy attracted media attention to Oliver when an arson fire killed the parents and five children in the Dawson family. The family was attacked in retaliation for their continuing complaints about drug trafficking in their neighborhood. The incident not only dominated the local media but also made national news.

BUILD had initiated its efforts in Oliver by creating an after-school program and a crime-control effort. In a parallel development, the clergy in the virtually all-black neighborhood began raising money among parishioners to redevelop housing, specifically affordable housing for residents and others of low and moderate income. At first city hall displayed little interest in Oliver, and the Department of Housing and Community Development regarded the neighborhood as not yet ready for redevelopment. However, with the Dawson family tragedy as the backdrop, BUILD's rejoinder was that "low-income neighborhoods had suffered for years because they were a low priority at City Hall" (Gettleman 2002). Ministers accused Mayor O'Malley of refusing to work with them to combat drug-related violence.

As an organization with a substantial institutional and popular base along with years of experience on the Baltimore scene, BUILD was positioned to bring pressure to bear and to keep the development issue alive. Thus, BUILD could not be simply ignored or waited out when the Dawson family arson put the neighborhood in the spotlight. At the same time, BUILD leaders knew that, by itself, pressure on a resource-poor city hall was not likely to yield very much. Furthermore, BUILD had the Sandtown project as an instructive example of how an initially celebrated effort had proved disappointing in its inability to stimulate revitalization beyond the bounds of the housing it produced. Reflecting past lessons, BUILD concluded that transformation of the Oliver neighborhood required redevelopment on a scale that was well beyond the resources available to the city, even when enhanced by foundation support. Thus, the adjoining East Baltimore project was seen as an opportunity to infuse Oliver's plan with market appeal and to press city elites to expand the benefits of the massive investment of public resources that EBDI was consuming.

To craft and implement a market strategy for the redevelopment of Oliver, BUILD partnered with The Reinvestment Fund (TRF), a nonprofit whose primary mission is to promote and finance development projects in low-income communities.[33] Initially operating in Philadelphia, TRF devised a strategy for redeveloping distressed neighborhoods that was grounded in an analysis of market data. To implement this strategy a partnership came together among BUILD, TRF, and the Rouse Company Foundation, headed by Tony Deering—former CEO of the Rouse Company and an EBDI board member. The Rouse Company Foundation contributed $1 million to the project. Together the partners created a new entity to manage the project, TRF Development Partners—Baltimore, which is governed by a board that includes three members from BUILD, three members from TRF, and Deering.

Funding for the project reflects BUILD's capacity to raise $10 million—with over $1 million coming directly from church members. The remainder came from foundation partners (including the Casey Foundation) and other donors and supporters. The $10 million is being leveraged through the Low-Income Housing Tax Credit to attain $120 million in financing. In addition, BUILD used its political clout to garner contributions from the city, state, and federal governments using techniques that were at times collaborative and at other times confrontational. One notable example involved the formation of an Affordable Housing Trust Fund. In 2005, shortly after the city announced plans to build a new city-owned convention center hotel, BUILD and other community advocates questioned why the city was able to find over $300 million for a new hotel but had not been able to find $50 million for a fund for affordable housing. Opposition to the hotel by a BUILD-led coalition threatened to derail the project. Subsequently, BUILD negotiated the establishment of a $59 million Affordable Housing Trust Fund, and the Oliver project has thus far received $2 million from the fund.[34] In addition to city funds, Mayor Dixon (who followed O'Malley in that office) also committed to turning over 155 housing units owned by the city. Federal and state officials also pitched in; Senator Mikulski diverted a portion of funds earmarked for EBDI to Oliver ($600,000), and a total of $10 million in state funds has been promised for development costs and assistance to homebuyers.

There are also ongoing efforts to catalyze redevelopment to the west of the Oliver community. The Station North community has long been designated an "Arts District" in an attempt by the city to attract the "creative class" (artists, performers, and arts-related businesses). In addition, the Central Baltimore Partnership is promoting redevelopment in ten neighborhoods and a commercial corridor northwest of Oliver that is anchored to the north by the Johns Hopkins University Homewood campus (the main campus) and to the south by the Maryland Institute College of Art, the University of Baltimore, and Penn Station (which makes the area a viable location for transit-oriented development and a potential residential space for commuters to Washington, DC).[35] In an attempt to tap into the activity in this community, BUILD and TRF initiated efforts to develop housing for low- and moderate-income artists.

As the Oliver project commenced, a conscious decision was made to begin housing construction within the part of the neighborhood closest to the EBDI footprint. This is consistent with TRF's established strategy of beginning their efforts on the perimeter of a target area. They point out that with Sandtown the vision was essentially to invest in the "worst spot" in the worst area. By contrast, the Oliver strategy is to begin in the "best spot"—the location with the greatest promise of catalyzing market activity.

Preston Place is a complex of 150 (sale and rental) units currently in the second phase of development in Oliver. By early 2013, 64 homes had been completed and occupied, and the development project, in conjunction with demolition of unsound housing by the city, had substantially reduced the number of vacant properties.

Once the Oliver project was under way, its advocates aggressively connected it to the East Baltimore redevelopment project. Promotional materials for the new housing emphasize proximity to EBDI and the Johns Hopkins medical complex. Moreover, Johns Hopkins employees who buy in Oliver are eligible for $17,000 grants that the university has made available to employees who purchase homes in the EBDI target area. Now multiple players have come to link Oliver and East Baltimore. As noted earlier, a portion of federal funds initially earmarked for EBDI was redirected to Oliver. EBDI partners like the Casey Foundation and, of course, Deering and the Rouse Company Foundation are key participants in Oliver's revitalization project. Recently, BUILD/TRF successfully collaborated with EBDI to garner funding under the Neighborhood Stabilization Program to redevelop properties on a thoroughfare that connects the two communities.

While Oliver demonstrates that a well-organized group can seize the initiative in neighborhood revitalization, it also shows the limitation of such an approach. Learning from shortcomings exposed in Sandtown, BUILD has employed its political muscle to tap the market potential that comes from Oliver's proximity to EBDI. The strategy is of necessity opportunistic. There is no larger citywide strategy or plan on which to draw. If BUILD did not have significant resources that it could mobilize and political clout to attract support, Oliver would not have become a revitalization target. Further, if Oliver were an anchorless neighborhood surrounded only by other declining neighborhoods, BUILD would not have been able to leverage the support that Oliver now enjoys.

Neighborhood Politics in Baltimore

What do the details of Baltimore's neighborhood policy trajectory tell us about the new politics of neighborhood revitalization? While there is much neighborhood activity, remedying neighborhood distress is not an overriding policy priority in and of itself. Struggle and contention mix with islands of cooperation and collaboration. Significantly, other policy concerns intersect and influence neighborhood policymaking, ranging from economic development, housing, and transportation to control of crime and violence. Neighborhood problems sometimes command attention because they intersect with these other concerns. Practices such as community benefits agreements and transit-oriented development are also direct testimony to this point.

Neighborhood policymaking is ad hoc, perhaps best described as improvisations shaped by the pursuit of resources. Those with resources have openings accordingly. Although scattered community development efforts abound, they don't cumulate or build policy momentum. As characterized by Timothy Armbruster, head of the Goldseker Foundation, neighborhood policy amounts to little more than an "opportunistic, deal-driven" approach to community development, and in his eyes such an approach is a poor substitute for "a strong mayoral vision" (2011). Armbruster's statement echoes a 2010 transition committee report accompanying the entrance to office of the current mayor, Stephanie Rawlings-Blake; this report called for the incoming city administration to "establish a clear and centralized Neighborhood Revitalization Agenda."[36] The report lamented a past lack of "vision" and called for the mayor to establish a comprehensive community development effort "which could be translated into key goals and objectives with measurable outcomes" (Carey et al. 2010, 30). However, city hall has yet to put forward such a plan.

Though personal inclinations of mayors make a difference, an endemic weakness is also at work in Baltimore. With its sizable population of poverty-stricken residents, the city has a high level of neighborhood distress and limited revenue capacity. As during the O'Malley administration with EBDI, the mayor can undertake a significant initiative but has to find allied resources. Given Baltimore's marginal standing as a global city, with limited and erratic intergovernmental support, resources are always sparse. Schmoke's mayoralty had perhaps the greatest amount of neighborhood policy activity. Much of his time as mayor overlapped with the Clinton presidency and saw resources forthcoming for the EZ, money to support community policing, the HOPE VI program, and a variety of HUD grants to which Schmoke, as a favored mayor, had access. But there was no broad federal urban strategy and no stable and substantial source of money on the scale of the redevelopment era of urban renewal and expressway building.[37] Succeeding mayors have had even less federal funding to work with. Moreover, as Baltimore struggles to find a solid position in the postindustrial world, the city confronts the fact that collective business engagement in the city has waned.

With manufacturing in decline, the city's ed & med institutions—its universities, medical schools, and hospitals—have grown in importance and have come to see their relationship to a changing city as a challenge. Ed &

med institutions have two characteristics that alleviate scarcity in investment capital. First, they have significant resources to invest because (unlike Baltimore's traditional manufacturing base) they have enjoyed growth and expansion. Second, in contrast to other potential investors, these bodies have less capital mobility (they are identified with and often committed to operating in particular locations). As the president of Johns Hopkins told the board of the Baltimore Development Corporation: "You can't sequester our institutions from the community. . . . All of these things impact very directly the survival of our institutions. The reality is that we have billions of dollars invested in Baltimore City and we cannot, like some other institutions that have left the city, we cannot willy-nilly leave the city. We are here."[38] Further, distressed neighborhoods adjacent to ed & med institutions are attractive redevelopment targets, particularly since these institutions hold promise of becoming sources of jobs for employees with varied educational backgrounds and skill levels (Bartik and Erickcek 2008).

At the same time ed & med institutions are driven by multiple concerns, not a simple "bottom line." Therefore, as Baltimore faces a disinvestment carryover from deindustrialization, ed & med institutions, as shown in the experience of Johns Hopkins, find that they can neither simply court the market nor occupy themselves with providing services. They can benefit from a community development approach that takes into account market forces, but they also encounter a need to work out an accommodation with residents in their surrounding neighborhoods. This contributes to ad hoc policymaking because there is no pat formula to follow and many competing considerations come into play. And as EBDI illustrates, an accommodation is no easy matter to achieve, especially against a distrust-filled past. There is much activity, but not the kind of convergent power that lined up behind the city's redevelopment agenda.

The new political geography of neighborhood revitalization in part reflects the locations of eds & meds, which are not concentrated in a central district but are scattered across the city, each within its own particular community. Johns Hopkins University and medical complex, the University of Maryland hospital and professional schools, Sinai Hospital, Maryland Institute College of Art, Bon Secours Hospital, and a host of smaller educational institutions and hospitals have become enmeshed in a changed demography, including patches of adjoining social disorder, while facing distrust stemming from earlier episodes of conflict and neglect. With the historic black universities of Morgan State and Coppin State as notable exceptions, much of the ed & med relationship to the community overlies a racial divide. Moreover, the strongest pull that each ed & med institution experiences is not toward some citywide concern but toward reaching an accommodation with its particular neighborhoods. Hence, the ed & med sector has no counterpart to the GBC to express a collective voice in city-wide matters.[39]

Cooperation among elite policy actors is hindered by the city's history of patronage politics (Arnold 1976; Callcott 1985; Argersinger 1988; Wong 1990). As mayor, Schaefer was a buffer between business-friendly development and the city's legacy of machine politics. Although the old-style politics with its ward-based chieftains and political clubs has long since passed into an ever-distant history, few business and civic elites see any indication that city government is capable of a long-term vision. Consequently, a self-perpetuating cycle has come into operation. Short on resources, revitalization efforts often rely upon foundation support and private investment. However, low confidence in city government makes business, civic, and foundation leaders reluctant to commit to a shared process of strategic planning. Instead, they embrace ad hoc, particularistic projects that have little potential to build confidence or strengthen capacity in city government. Meager expectations give rise to an ongoing cycle difficult to break. How, then, does Baltimore cope?

Quasi-Public Organizations in Neighborhood Politics

In a city with great needs and sparse resources, in which business and foundation leaders have limited confidence in city government, neighborhood policymaking has followed a mode of operation devised during the downtown renaissance. At its center are quasi-public corporations— autonomous nonprofits able to use select governmental powers and to draw on public money as well as private investment capital (Lyall 1982).[40] Sandtown-Winchester employed this institutional mechanism, modified it, and promoted it as a grand partnership for neighborhood revitalization. The city's EZ initiative was also implemented by an autonomous quasi-public corporation. EBDI was created in that same mold.

During the redevelopment period, quasi-public organizations were the institutional means used by business and political elites to insulate the redevelopment agenda from public scrutiny (Stoker 1987). In contrast, policymaking in the new era is not so tightly closed. Notwithstanding its status as a quasi-public corporation, EBDI has been targeted by a variety of political mobilizations and protests, some involving housing and relocation and others focused on contracting and employment opportunities. Economic inclusion was an issue even before EBDI was formally chartered.[41] Mayor O'Malley and Johns Hopkins officials signed a "Minority Inclusion Agreement" in 2002 that created targets for minority- and women-owned business contracting and specified reporting requirements. It is noteworthy that the initial economic inclusion effort focused on contracting, not employment. Significantly, an East Baltimore household survey that EBDI conducted in 2003 revealed that training and employment opportunities were the two needs most frequently cited (Schachtel 2011).

With the new era, the nature of elite players has changed. In contrast to the broad consensus among elites during the redevelopment period, elite participants now bring a variety of concerns to neighborhood policymaking. By the time the East Baltimore redevelopment initiative was fully launched, the Casey Foundation (one of the key partners) was thoroughly committed to addressing social problems and various community concerns, including employment, training, and housing. The foundation developed a "Responsible Relocation" program that coordinated relocation services and provided more generous terms for the purchase of existing housing (see Annie E. Casey Foundation 2008). Reflecting the foundation's emphasis on resident services, by 2007 EBDI had implemented the Workforce Development Pipeline in partnership with the mayor's Office of Employment Development to provide East Baltimore residents with job readiness services and employment opportunities (Schachtel 2011). All the pipeline slots made available were used by East Baltimore residents (indicating that demand for workforce development services far outstripped the supply).

Despite these various moves, economic inclusion has been a continuing source of controversy. The quasi-governmental form has not worked smoothly as a means of achieving elite-actor/community accommodation. In 2009 EBDI contracted with an independent third party to monitor progress toward achieving economic inclusion goals (Schachtel 2011, 9). However, such formal channels of reporting have not foreclosed neighborhood discontent. In December 2011, at a point when construction work had gained visibility as a potential source of jobs, the aforementioned "pop-up" protest occurred—in spite of an EBDI effort to head off such outbreaks of discontent by reporting economic inclusion figures on its website. The reports showed that EBDI was meeting its percentage goals for employing East Baltimore residents. However, using percentage figures obscured the crucial fact that, unfolding slowly, the project had generated far fewer jobs than were projected during its planning stage (Hare 2011).

Although the jobs protest had limited impact, it indicated that the policy process in Baltimore was no longer closed with the profound level of political insulation that the city's quasi-public institutions possessed during the redevelopment period. Significantly, however, it is easier for some players to penetrate Baltimore's policy game than for others. The initial focus on contracting opportunities for economic inclusion reflects the fact that the Maryland Minority Contractors Association has a strong voice in local government as a result of their organizational capacity. The need to accommodate minority contractors was anticipated and formalized even before EBDI was created. More recently, the contractors' association employed former mayor Sheila Dixon as its representative; community-based organizations seeking enhanced employment opportunities had no counterpart. In comparison to the issue of minority contracting, employment opportunities were raised later in the game, advanced by protests led by organizations lacking both experience and the staying power to work through complex administrative arrangements over the long haul.

Broadly, we see that the nature of corporate governance can hinder community engagement. Neighborhood policy operates mainly outside normal political channels in a process in which the exercise of power reflects control of resources. Governing arrangements are structured to attract and mollify investors and philanthropic elites. Although quasi-public corporations make highly consequential decisions, the politics of corporate governance limits public knowledge and constrains participation, even among elected representatives of the communities that are most directly affected by neighborhood revitalization projects.[42]

To attract and protect resource contributors, a majority on governing boards is typically composed of civic and business elites who are not accountable to the public. Because formal status as a nonprofit corporation can be used to withhold information and avoid public scrutiny, the policy process is diffuse and opaque, making it difficult for members of the public to know when and how to mobilize to influence decisions. When it does occur, mobilization is likely to focus on circumstances that reflect the corporation's specific mission in a particular neighborhood rather than pressing more general concerns. Groups hoping to promote a comprehensive vision of neighborhood revitalization lack a viable venue to voice their concerns, keeping broader questions about neighborhoods off the policy agenda.

The Missing Link

In Baltimore, there is no lack of neighborhood policy activity. Apathy and quiescence are not the problem. And the solution does not consist of hearings, charettes, focus groups, or token representation on boards dominated by civic elites; all have been employed at one time or another. Neither does community control solve the problem (even it were feasible); the process is more complicated than that (Fung 2004). An advisory body, such as the one attached to UHI at Johns Hopkins, can work if both sides recognize it as providing advice that is being listened to.[43] Although UHI traveled a bumpy road, it has achieved a working relationship with the surrounding community.

The missing link in the chain of policy representation is an institutionalized (and sustained) collective voice for distressed neighborhoods. The lack of such a voice is especially limiting to the expression of interests and concerns by the city's most distressed neighborhoods in a process in which resource constraints and the fragmentary, ad hoc policymaking centered in quasi-public corporations are the norm. Hence, the failure to continue the Neighborhood Congress, the lack of a policy-oriented department of neighborhood affairs (an O'Malley decision not revisited so far), and the unwillingness of affinity groups to give sustained support to the Community Development Alliance allow the muffling of neighborhood representation through quasi-governance to continue. On the other hand, BUILD and the Maryland Minority Contractors Association show that a sturdy organization able to bring together resources and employ politically skilled staff can have a policy impact, even on quasi-public corporations designed to be buffered from the public.

At least thus far neither political leaders nor foundation officers have shown much inclination to create a sustained voice for neighborhood concerns. In Sandtown, both the foundation sector and city hall wanted quick and measurable results, and the kind of capacity building needed to strengthen the voice of distressed neighborhoods has so far gained little traction. In the preliminary draft of the comprehensive plan during the waning years of Schmoke's mayoralty, neighborhood capacity building got brief recognition and foundation backing as a goal, but it disappeared from the final version of the comprehensive plan as finally adopted a few years into O'Malley's mayoralty. Foundations hold workshops to teach neighborhood applicants how to apply for grants—that is, how to conform to their professional standards—but they don't conduct workshops for their own staff on how to work with a population that typically has limited formal education but an abundance of local knowledge, a population that has internalized years (even generations) of neglect, exploitation, and unfulfilled promises. There is a culture gap between distressed neighborhoods and their potential allies, a gap that can be closed only slowly by following a map that is not always clearly marked.

Cautious Optimism

Looking over time, one can say that Baltimore's neighborhoods have come a long way. Gone is the near-total disregard neighborhoods suffered in the early days of expressway construction. Improvement efforts are ongoing in several of the city's distressed neighborhoods. Still, there is a high level of distrust surrounding any neighborhood project. Community engagement thus has a large obstacle to overcome, and overcoming it is not going to happen quickly. In addition, it is clear that neighborhood revitalization is not a simple matter of increasing investment in properties. Communities want and expect interventions to include attention to social needs. Residents in distressed neighborhoods see themselves and their neighbors as enveloped in a set of social conditions that need remedying.[44]

The Schaefer era's inattention to social "rot" has given way to significant concern about neighborhood distress. The police department and the school system operate with closer connection to the neighborhood level than was once the case.[45] Concentrations of poverty have become a matter of concern, though region-wide cooperation on this issue remains quite weak. Under the auspices of the Baltimore Community Foundation, the city has in place a Healthy Neighborhoods Initiative to protect at-risk communities from falling into decline. Leading ed & med institutions can and sometimes do serve as valuable partners in neighborhood revitalization efforts. Still, the combined lessons of Sandtown and EBDI offer little reason to embrace anything beyond the most cautious optimism. Major challenges have yet to be met.

The succession of protests directed at EBDI highlights the problem of weak neighborhood capacity. Although discontent manifests itself repeatedly, there is little organizational connection between the various protests. Nor is there a citywide entity to play a part in addressing these concerns, champion a response, and mobilize support to sustain it. The main philanthropic path of action has been to support individual neighborhoods with demonstrated capacity, not to take on the challenge of building capacity in areas of severe distress and promoting alignment among these areas. Neighborhood actors often perceive foundations as being uninterested in community organizing—instead favoring the less assertive aim of "community outreach." Baltimore's neighborhoods have indeed come a long way, but they still operate under multiple disadvantages. Although the philanthropic and ed & med sectors have emerged as sources of constructive social concern, their limited and particularistic interventions leave undisturbed local processes that muffle the neighborhood voice.

Notes

1. A more complete account would include, in addition to a scattering of small projects, a large Park Heights project in the city's northwest (an area that includes Sinai Hospital and Pimlico Race Course), a University of Maryland biotech initiative, and a Redline link in the region's transportation system (running through West Baltimore and giving rise to a community benefits agreement).

2. The following list shows when various philanthropic entities appeared on the city scene: Baltimore Community Foundation, launched in 1972; Goldseker Foundation, formed in 1975; Association of Baltimore Area Grantmakers, came together in 1983; Associated Black Charities, formed in 1985; Abell Foundation, fully funded in 1986; Enterprise in Baltimore Foundation, founded in 1986 (by Baltimore native James Rouse); Annie E. Casey Foundation, moved to Baltimore in 1994; Baltimore Neighborhood Collaborative (BNC), an affinity group of the Association of Baltimore Area Grantmakers, formed in 1995; Open Society Institute–Baltimore (field office for US programs), opened in 1998; and Weinberg Foundation, underwent major reorganization and refocus in 2005.

3. The interim mayor, Clarence "Du" Burns, was a close ally of Schaefer's and someone with roots in Baltimore's traditional politics. Schmoke is a Baltimore native but, in contrast to Burns, brought to his campaign a background of Ivy League degrees and a Rhodes Scholarship. He had close ties to the city's leading black clergy, who were also the backbone of BUILD.

4. CCIs have several distinctive features, including collaboration across government, business, and foundation sectors; holistic problem solving (treating interrelated problems simultaneously); strategic planning that emphasizes long-range, sustained effort; and community-based action (in which community mobilization and empowerment are key goals). See Rich and Stoker 2014, 29–30.

5. Early and largely favorable accounts of Sandtown-Winchester include Henderson 1996; Goetz 1997; Walsh 1997; Costigan 1997; Pryor *et al.* 2000.

6. To work on the initiative, Enterprise created a Neighborhood Transformation Center to house its staff and their consultants. To oversee the project, the city created its own independent nonprofit. In addition, four other entities were formed to carry out various parts of the initiative (Brown, Butler, and Hamilton 2001, 19).

7. Baltimore's EZ program was among the most effective nationally because of the local governance process the city created (Rich and Stoker 2014).

8. The area served by the Sandtown-Winchester initiative was not entirely within the EZ, in part because of federal requirements that EZ borders follow census tract boundaries.

9. *The Corner* (Simon and Burns 1997) is about a West Baltimore area included in OROSW.

10. It was during this same time period that a decision was rendered in *Thompson v. HUD* that HUD had failed to exercise its responsibility under the Fair Housing Act to prevent the central city (Baltimore in this case) from becoming a site of concentrated housing for low-income African Americans. As a consequence there is a modest program managed by the Maryland American Civil Liberties Union, funded by HUD, to move Baltimore residents from the city's housing roll to "communities of opportunity" in the surrounding suburbs. For details on the case and the settlement, see HUD 2012.

11. Recently, HNI expanded its resource base with federal assistance from the Neigh-

borhood Stabilization Program 2 under provisions of the American Recovery and Reinvestment Act of 2009. In partnership with the Baltimore Department of Housing and Community Development and several nonprofits, HNI won a federal grant of more than $26 million. These funds are being used to mitigate the consequences of foreclosures in targeted areas in twelve census tracts. Under the grant, foreclosed and abandoned housing can be acquired, rehabilitated, and resold.

12. Around the same time GBC published its "report on regionalism": *One Region, One Future* (Greater Baltimore Committee 1997).

13. For a less optimistic view of the deconcentration strategy and a more nuanced view of the problem, see the study of Move to Opportunity by Briggs, Popkin, and Goering (2010).

14. Patterson Park is now part of HNI, but it was not included in the initial set of neighborhoods.

15. Despite its early successes, PPCDC was forced into bankruptcy by the housing-finance crisis. The community, however, has been able to fend off the threat of precipitous decline.

16. BNC is an affinity group of the donor sector, and the newly formed Community Law Center is heavily supported by that sector as well.

17. Though a proposed Redline transit proposal is a state project, it enjoys priority support in Baltimore's city hall; it gave rise to Redline Community Compact signed by city and state officials and a coalition of neighborhoods on Baltimore's West Side. A University of Baltimore study commissioned by then mayor Sheila Dixon saw the design and construction of the project as generating ten thousand jobs, many at entry level (Dresser 2010).

18. While a priority, EBDI was not the only such project initiated by the city. The large Park Heights project in northwest Baltimore was started at about the same time as EBDI and, though initiated through political channels (by the then chair of the city's delegation to the state legislature), has an implementing structure, Park Heights Renaissance, parallel to EBDI.

19. The EBDI board is one indication of who has influence over the project. The board has fifteen voting members: five come from the philanthropic sector, two are public officials, two are affiliated with Johns Hopkins University, four come from the corporate sector, and the remaining two are community representatives. In addition there are three ex officio members: the two city council members representing the area plus the commissioner of Housing and Community Development, presumably representing the mayor. The complexity of the project and its financing work against transparency.

20. It should be noted, however, that there was no community-wide consensus behind the view that large-scale redevelopment was the path for the city to follow. Aside from an unheeded argument for "base communities" as an approach to revitalizing Park Heights (McDougall 1993), the leaders of the largely homegrown revitalization in Patterson Park argued against large-scale projects. In their booklet on sustainable community development, Pollock and Rutkowski (1998, 36) made the point: "Big projects are very difficult to turn around when they go in the wrong direction (and they often do)." And they added: "Any large scale plan may well miss the little things that make or break the effort—for example, trivializing the role of neighborhood-based organizations or turning a neighborhood activist into a bureaucrat." Implementation of a series of initiatives is being carried out by the Homewood Community Partners Initiative, including school improvement, public-

safety efforts, housing-code enforcement, and economic inclusion (job placement and contracting opportunities). The report (see McNeely 2012) that established the Homewood Community Partners Initiative explicitly linked the well-being of Johns Hopkins University with the health of its surrounding neighborhoods.

21. For a longer account of the East Baltimore area, see Gomez 2013.

22. It should also be noted that the Casey Foundation made close attention to a carefully designed relocation program a condition of its participation in the project, and it has funded services for displaced persons, extra funding for relocation, and follow-up surveys of those who were displaced. As an indication of the seriousness of the foundation's concern, its president also took on the chairmanship of the EBDI board's Housing Committee when the EBDI project was launched.

23. After a disappointing test score performance and complaints about order maintenance, the principal was dismissed and the school restructured to be brought under close oversight by the School of Education at Johns Hopkins University, with Morgan State University to oversee community engagement in the school. The restructuring decision occurred without public hearings.

24. Initial discussion inclined toward a charter school, but the head of the school system argued for the alternative of a "contract school," an arrangement that would provide the same autonomy as a charter school but would open enrollment only to families who live in the East Baltimore community. The status of this understanding is now somewhat unclear.

25. An organization called Baltimore Community Churches United led a march on EBDI's headquarters in which two hundred demonstrators came out to protest the lack of jobs going to East Baltimore residents. The church organization is also allied with a labor group, the Laborers' International Union of North America. The alliance, however, lacked firm ties to the city's politics. At this writing, controversy still hovers around elements of the project, including a lack of transparency in decision-making (Simmons 2012).

26. On Baltimore in the riot period, see Elfenbein, Hollowak, and Nix 2011.

27. The UHI director is answerable to the university provost and thus to the president. The UHI director is charged to work with a Community-University Collaborating Committee, and the provost regularly attends the monthly meetings of this committee. In 2009 newly inaugurated university president Ronald Daniels met with an invited group of East Baltimore community representatives in two days of facilitated briefings to reaffirm the university's commitment to community engagement and to hear the concerns of the East Baltimore community.

28. This program came about on the recommendation of Hopkins East Baltimore Community Clinic Task Force, following the closing of the Caroline Street Clinic for the Uninsured. It makes available the full services of the Johns Hopkins Hospital and Medical School. UHI was the crucial connection leading to TAP. A significant event along the way was a proposal for Johns Hopkins to do a public-health survey of East Baltimore. Triggered by a long history of community anxiety, including fears about medical use of African American residents in undisclosed experiments (Skloot 2010), the ensuing controversy was overcome only by bringing in consultants to restore dialogue (Stone 2013). In that process, residents made it known that they resented the air of "assumed advantage" and "arrogance" displayed by Johns Hopkins staff.

29. The head of UHI, Dr. Robert Blum, was cochair of the task force recommending the early-childhood center. The school and center are building adjoining facilities in the EBDI site.

30. In the early, high-confidence days of EBDI, its leadership was sure that the project would expand employment opportunities and with the aid of workforce development raise the income level of residents. Whereas neighboring Oliver focused on making housing affordable for a lower-income population, EBDI's leadership saw its community becoming mixed income in part by virtue of higher levels of earning for residents employed in the biotech industry.

31. See Annie E. Casey Foundation 2014. Later, the Harry and Jeanette Weinberg Foundation joined the coalition supporting EBDI with a $15 million, multiyear grant. According to the Weinberg Foundation's 2008 annual report, the "investment will support neighborhood residents by strengthening and expanding opportunities for children from birth to 18-years-old, workforce initiatives, and programs for older adults."

32. In the earliest days of the project, Mayor O'Malley focused on economic development. Significantly, however, even that level of city hall engagement in the project has declined. When confronted with news media questions about the cost and lack of clear accountability of the project, the current mayor, Stephanie Rawlings-Blake, offhandedly dismissed a need for an audit (Jacobson and Simmons 2011). City council members have been largely inattentive to details of the project beyond pressing for a sizable role for minority enterprises. The Maryland Minority Contractors Association monitors that aspect of EBDI, and it is now represented by former mayor Sheila Dixon. In a press release EDBI claimed that "46 percent of project contracts have gone to minority- and women-owned companies" (see also Simmons 2011a).

33. Information about TRF can be found at the organization's website: www.trfund .com.

34. The city has also built a community center, the Dawson Family Safe Haven Center, where the arson occurred.

35. The Central Baltimore Partnership is a nonprofit partnership among universities, Penn Station (Amtrak), businesses and other property owners, government agencies, and neighborhood groups and was launched by the city in 2008, with backing from the Goldseker Foundation, to revitalize a central corridor of the city. Not a developer, its purpose is described as "convener, facilitator, consultant, and advocate for its constituents" (Goldseker Foundation 2012)

36. The quotation is from the Final Report of the Mayor Rawlings-Blake Transition Team, appendix D: Community Development and Neighborhoods. See Carey et al. 2010.

37. While various Republican presidential administrations have cut sources of urban funding, they have also added to the federal urban repertoire, namely with the Justice Department's Weed and Seed program in 1991 and the Low-Income Housing Tax Credit as part of the 1986 tax reform. Such highly disjointed federal policies reinforce a local tendency toward disconnected, ad hoc initiatives. Handicapped by shrinking funding for urban programs, the Obama administration has sought to counter fragmented efforts through its policy of "braiding" (combining funding from a variety of sources).

38. Quoted in Wenger 2012.

39. The heads of the city's higher-education institutions did meet together recently, but as of this writing, they have formed no association or coalition for citywide planning and action.

40. On the use of public-private partnerships in development matters, see Squires 1989; Erie, Kogan, and MacKenzie 2011. We use the term "quasi-governmental organiza-

tion" rather than "public-private partnership" because the point of such organizations in Baltimore is often not to join government in partnership with the private and nonprofit sectors but to create an alternative action channel that is largely independent of city government.

41. The Casey Foundation sponsored a report on economic inclusion efforts related to EBDI (see Schachtel 2011). Ongoing research sponsored by the foundation suggests that economic inclusion remains a point of contention in the East Baltimore redevelopment effort.

42. A former director of SMEAC and continuing critic of redevelopment in East Baltimore said in a *Baltimore Sun* column that EBDI fails on multiple grounds, that it is lacking "community participation, transparency, objective government oversight, and consistency in its rhetoric and actions" (Gomez 2012).

43. The consensus process developed in Hampton, Virginia, provides a concrete guide to such a process (Sirianni 2009; Stone and Worgs 2004). In Baltimore's EZ, the advisory council was an effective community voice in zone decision-making in part because elites who controlled Empower Baltimore Management Corporation took community participation seriously (see Rich and Stoker 2014).

44. There is a telling parallel in a study of crime-prevention strategies in Baltimore that shows a clear class and racial divide between better-off residents, who prefer patrolling and "victim prevention" strategies, and lower-income, African American communities, where the preference runs heavily to "social-problem reduction" strategies, particularly youth programs and drug-treatment services (Taylor 2001, 290). These preferences are an unmistakable echo of the Neighborhood Congress.

45. For instance, when Andres Alonso became head of the city' school system, he brought in an experienced community organizer, Michel Sarbanes, as one of his principal lieutenants.

FOUR

Standing in Two Worlds: Neighborhood Policy, the Civic Arena, and Ward-Based Politics in Chicago

JOHN BETANCUR, KAREN MOSSBERGER,
AND YUE ZHANG

Chicago is a former industrial city that has been transformed into a global center of advanced services. The city's neighborhood policy is fragmented, reflecting the diffusion of power that follows from the delegation of neighborhood policy primarily to the wards, where contending approaches clash as multiple parties strive to advance their interests. Gentrification mixes with continuing areas of distress within a highly polarized political economy. In partnership with city government, the city's large and active foundation sector is promoting and financing neighborhood revitalization projects in several distressed neighborhoods, especially through the sizeable New Communities Program (NCP). However, local politics, particularly the power of aldermen, situates neighborhood policy action in two very different worlds. While foundations strive for professionalism, aldermen value political loyalty and the opportunity to deliver favors. The new era of neighborhood policy has not swept away the established patterns of local politics; rather, the professional orientation of foundations has been layered on top of ward-based politics, creating a context for neighborhood politics that is an uneasy combination of the old and the new. Neighborhood groups are caught between these worlds, sometimes not pleased with either. Although many of Chicago's foundation-funded efforts are significant in scope, they fall short as instruments of institutionalized policymaking. The ambitious NCP, for instance, is operated outside city government, and it has a termination date. Even with foundation support, resources for neighborhood revitalization are scarce, and multiple obstacles stand in the way of building and maintaining a vibrant infrastructure of neighborhood policy. The continuing influence of ward politics, intracommu-

nity tensions and conflicts, and a persisting grassroots wariness of top-level actors make a challenging mix.

As Chicago completes the transition from its industrial past and seeks to secure its future as a global center of commerce, a new politics of neighborhood revitalization is taking hold. The earlier era of conflict with downtown redevelopment has faded, and now many community-based groups engage in efforts to build affordable housing or to deliver services rather than protest. To the extent that neighborhood revitalization is on the citywide agenda today, it is largely through the initiative of foundations, through Comprehensive Community Initiatives that combine human-service needs with economic-development projects in low-income communities. There is a lack of consensus, however, within some communities over the path of development because of gentrification. And the electoral politics and patronage that have long characterized neighborhood policy in Chicago now operate alongside rather than being displaced by the "civic arena" of nongovernmental actors (Ferman 1996). As a result, neighborhood revitalization projects must stand in two very different worlds—the professionalized world of foundations as well as the rough-and-tumble world of the city's ward-based politics.

Neighborhood improvement projects have a long history in Chicago's low-income communities. Well-known interventions include Jane Addams's settlement house and Saul Alinsky's working-class neighborhood organizing. Over the years, these efforts have assumed many different forms and produced approaches as diverse as homeowner associations, civil rights organizations, and ethnically controlled and oriented campaigns as well as union halls and poor people's organizations that were the forerunners of groups still actively engaged in today's neighborhood revitalization efforts. Contemporary neighborhood policy in Chicago is formulated and implemented by public-private partnerships, where foundations play an important role. The most recent example is the NCP, which is supported by the John D. and Catherine T. MacArthur Foundation and is a large-scale comprehensive community-building initiative undertaken in sixteen of Chicago's seventy-seven community areas (MacArthur Foundation 2010).[1] Starting with three five-year demonstration projects in the late 1990s, the initiative grew in 2003 into a ten-year, $47 million project.

In this chapter we establish the trajectory of Chicago's neighborhood policymaking by identifying three periods: traditional machine politics, in which neighborhood concerns were marginalized to pursue downtown redevelopment; the Harold Washington mayoralty, in which short-lived reforms signaled a change in emphasis; and the public-private partnerships of recent years, in which the new politics of neighborhood revitalization has emerged. We first review citywide trends affecting neighborhood revitalization and then focus on two of the neighborhoods that have active initiatives as part of the NCP.

The Electoral and Civic Arenas

Chicago does not have a centrally defined neighborhood policy or department. Responsibility for neighborhood policy is scattered across various departments and special districts, including the Chicago Park District and the Chicago Housing Authority (CHA). However, city government is often not where neighborhood policy is conceived. Neighborhood revitalization is a composite of multiple interventions and designs initiated or carried out by numerous parties, including nonprofits and foundations, as well as private-sector developers, banks, churches and faith-based organizations, universities, and aldermen. Neighborhood policy is for the most part fragmented, often ad hoc, multidirectional, and certainly multisourced.

A significant cause of fragmentation is the delegation of neighborhood policy primarily to the wards, where contending approaches to neighborhood policy clash as multiple parties strive to advance their interests. Describing the early 1990s, Barbara Ferman (1996) argued that neighborhood policymaking in Chicago was dominated by the electoral arena, where politicians held power and neighborhood policy was defined by competition, conflict, and distributive politics. Ferman (1996, 110) depicted this issueless exchange politics as an "under-developed policy-making structure," where decisions were based on bargaining over material benefits rather than evidence, expertise, or participation. She contrasted Chicago with Pittsburgh, where strong civic organizations and foundations produced a more collaborative environment for neighborhood policy, focused on rational planning and policy innovation.

We argue that a blended model of neighborhood policymaking is emerging among government institutions, foundations, and private interests in Chicago; it is a model in which the civic arena has become more important. However, the civic arena coexists with ward politics. Aldermen have considerable discretion over decisions and interventions within their wards, especially those related to land use, zoning changes, permits, and distribution of public funds earmarked for community projects and community development. The city budget gives each alderman nearly $2 million annually for "discretionary projects" that are not subject to city council approval. Aldermen have significant control of Community Development Block Grants (CDBGs) and other public grants coming to organizations in their wards. Tax Increment Financing (TIF) districts have proliferated, and although Mayor Richard M. Daley often directed funds to areas outside the area in which they were collected (Joravsky and Dumke 2009), aldermen have significant control of TIF spending in their wards.[2]

Aldermen exercise both formal and informal sources of power. City departments often consult aldermen on issues affecting their wards. Individual aldermen enjoy a special veto power over ward decisions, known as aldermanic prerogative; if an alderman wants to initiate or block city council or city government actions within his or her own ward, other city council members defer. However, it should be noted that aldermanic prerogative is not absolute. The mayor can supersede aldermanic ward-specific power over economic-development efforts and other citywide issues, and mayors have done so on several occasions.[3] But the power of aldermen within their wards has generally been maintained in Chicago in recent years.

Within the neighborhood policy domain, this practice leads to competition and logrolling in neighborhood policy rather than a coordinated effort to set citywide goals across aldermanic boundaries and communities. Cross-boundary collaborations are rare because they are left up to the mayor's office or to special districts and because aldermen see no electoral benefit in working with neighboring wards. Thus, the tradition of exchange politics is deeply embedded in Chicago (Ferman 1996; Simpson 2001). Many aldermen use their power to reward supporters and punish adversaries, to grow their political contributions, to control their wards tightly, and, ultimately, to secure reelection.

Revitalization efforts are further complicated by the mismatch between neighborhood boundaries and ward boundaries. While some communities are included within the jurisdiction of a single ward, most are divided into multiple wards, encouraging competition or inaction rather than collaboration. Since aldermen are primarily interested in providing resources and services to areas within their jurisdictional boundaries, communities divided by ward boundaries suffer. For example, the segmentation along ward boundaries and the manipulation of local resources by aldermen have constrained development in some African American communities on the South and West Sides of the city. Another example is the failed effort to establish a historic district in Bronzeville, in contrast with the successful historic designation in Pilsen, which is contained within a single ward (Zhang 2011).

The frequent failure of the ward system to represent the residents' needs, especially in poor and working-class communities, encouraged the development of alternative forms of organization (Ferman 1996, 36). In particular, Chicago has a long-standing tradition of community organizing, which helped drive national movements, such as the civil rights struggles, the initiative against redlining leading to the Community Reinvestment Act, and the establishment of community development corporations (CDCs).

Another feature of the policy environment in Chicago, however, is a strong foundation sector with an interest in neighborhood issues. More than one hundred foundations are listed as members of the Donors Forum in Chicago, including both internationally prominent organizations and small family foundations.[4] Foundations provide resources for neighborhood programs in an era when federal funding is scarce and city budgets are tight (Koschinsky and Swanstrom 2001). In addition to local philanthropies, national foundations such as the MacArthur and Joyce Foundations have also funded neighborhood initiatives.

Although foundations are key actors in the civic arena in Chicago, other nongovernmental entities also affect the city's neighborhood revitalization efforts. Private-sector initiatives have major impacts on neighborhoods through investment decisions, project partnerships, or gentrifying interventions. Ed & med institutions play individual roles in many neighborhoods. For instance, the University of Chicago has been involved in the city's Empowerment Zone (EZ) and the NCP in South Side neighborhoods and has played other roles on its own. Universities have also contributed through institutions such as the Mid-South Commission (which included the University of Chicago and the Illinois Institute of Technology), the University of Illinois at Chicago's Great Cities Institute Neighborhood Initiative, the Policy Research Action Group consortium of various universities, and Loyola University's Rogers Park initiative. Universities have also played a role as developers in Chicago, buying up property and displacing low-income communities—for example, around the University of Illinois at Chicago and the University of Chicago.

Neighborhood Policy

Machine politics evolved as a way to counter informally the fragmented authority of the ward system, to ensure control of city hall by Cook County's Democratic Party, and to increase the power of the mayor under a city charter initially characterized by a weak mayoralty and a strong council. Richard J. Daley's control over the Democratic Party machine (1955–77) was supplemented by a change in state law that gave the mayor the power to draft the budget, enhancing mayoral power while retaining the ward system and a fifty-member council (Simpson 2001). Under this arrangement, the Richard J. Daley era was a period of neglect and conflict for neighborhoods, with a focus on downtown development (Bennett 2010).

The absence of an explicit city hall neighborhood policy meant that with no dedicated funding stream for neighborhoods, benefits were negotiated and contingent upon ward politics (Ferman 1996). Poor neighborhoods were often excluded from funding, which was used to shore up machine support in the white ethnic neighborhoods. The CDBG program, which began at the close of the Richard J. Daley administration, was quickly absorbed into the machine as a source of patronage (Ferman 1996).

Patterns of segregation and concentrated poverty were institutionalized through public-housing development, with the result that "from 1955 to 1971, the CHA built 10,256 apartments, and *all but sixty-three were in black neighborhoods*" (Simpson 2001, 153, italics in original). The 1969 *Gautreaux v. Chicago Housing Authority* decision to desegregate Chicago's public housing resulted in the withholding of federal funds and, through HOPE VI, led to the large-scale demolition and redevelopment of public housing in later decades (Simpson 2001, 145).

During this early period, neighborhoods surrounding the rim of downtown underwent drastic changes without resident consultations. This was a period of neighborhood protest and resistance, often rooted in Alinsky's methods of community organizing. It was in Chicago that Saul Alinsky and the Industrial Areas Foundation established their community-organizing strategy of "rubbing raw the sores of discontent" (Simpson 2001, 70). This style of grassroots organizing often won concessions, but it placed community groups in conflict with the political machine, especially aldermen, who saw them as political rivals.

Alinsky's methods were applied in many communities; his Citizen's Action Program included more than sixty organizations in the early 1970s and battled air pollution, expressway development, and the dearth of mortgage lending in low-income communities (Ferman 1996). Other Chicago neighborhood and housing groups rallied against community redlining, securing legislation that later influenced the Community Reinvestment Act of 1977 (Ferman 1996; Pogge 1992). Community development groups organized into citywide networks such as the Community Workshop on Economic Development (CWED), Chicago Association of Neighborhood Development Organizations (CANDO), and the Chicago Rehab Network (CRN), which significantly advanced their policy capacity and their ability to influence city affairs and the fate of neighborhoods. For example, CWED played a major role in the drafting of Mayor Harold Washington's policy platform and in the development of the city's EZ proposal, which originated with planning by community-based organizations (Gills 1991).

Neighborhood Policy at the Forefront in the Washington Era

Harold Washington's mayoral administration (1983–87) represented a clear break with machine politics, especially in the area of neighborhood policy. Mayor Washington attempted to make fairness a hallmark of his administration in several significant ways. He ended patronage by placing a limit on political appointees and supported the court-sanctioned Shakman decrees, which set limits on patronage hiring. He also signed an executive order providing freedom of information throughout the departments of his government, enabling citizens to get the same information that public officials had access to and thus providing more transparency in governance.

Mayor Washington also increased the number of community organizations certified as nonprofit delegate agencies eligible to receive CDBG funds. A peer review process was instituted throughout the city's various development and service departments to certify nonprofit delegate agencies. The number of eligible agencies increased from 40 in 1983 to more than 125 by the time of Washington's death in 1987 (Gills 1991). Washington also put $15 million more on the streets by reducing the number of patronage employees holding CDBG-funded jobs in the city (Gills 1991). Moreover, he instituted a series of rotating town hall meetings where department heads, commissioners, and deputies made regular reports to the community.

Washington's reforms were not fully institutionalized because of his short tenure and the resistance that he faced in battling the majority block of twenty-nine opposition aldermen during most of his time in office.[5] However, for the first and only time in the city's history, efforts were made to link neighborhood and downtown development to neighborhood priorities, to include the priorities of the neighborhoods in the development plan of the city, and to share the budget with them. Neighborhood concerns were institutionalized briefly through the city's short-lived Department of Neighborhoods. Although originally created in the Byrne administration (Ferman 1996, 89), this department gained real meaning during the Washington years. However, the change was not lasting; "the city Council gutted the department's budget and forced the resignation of its head" (Kretzmann 1991, 214–15).

Although some of Washington's reforms had only a brief run, his time in office had lasting implications for the relationship between the city and community groups by absorbing some community activists into city bureaucracies and by cutting city hall's share of CDBG funds, distributing this and other funding to neighborhood organizations for community development and service delivery (Gills 1991, 54). The availability of funding reinforced a shift from advocacy to service delivery that was taking place among community organizations nationally as well as locally. These local changes complemented national trends that moderated the tendency for community-based organizations to engage in confrontation and protest.

Nationally, the terrain of neighborhood revitalization was changing, with the emergence of nonprofit organizations that were supported by foundations as well as by some federal programs and that engaged in housing and local economic development. These organizations were less confrontational and more professionalized than the community organizations of the 1960s; they operated under business models and worked with lenders to attract capital to poor communities (Betancur, Bennett, and Wright 1991; Halpern 1995; Pierce and Steinbach 1987).

By the time Washington took office, Chicago had become an important center for CDCs. New institutions were created to support their growth and that of other community-based organizations. Chicago's South Shore Bank, which was established in 1980 as the first and largest community development bank in the nation (MacArthur Foundation 2011), fostered a large network of nonprofit housing providers and community-based economic revitalization efforts across the South and West Sides of the city for thirty years.[6] Also in 1980, the first chapter of the Local Initiatives Support Corporation (LISC) outside the national headquarters in New York was established in Chicago to promote community development. Chicago LISC, founded with support from the MacArthur Foundation (LISC 2011; MacArthur Foundation 2011), today lists 140 community partners and has supported the construction of twenty-eight thousand housing units.[7]

Public-Private Partnerships

When Richard M. Daley was elected mayor in 1989, he continued many of Washington's reforms for a time. However, by the mid-1990s Daley had recrafted institutional arrangements, giving aldermen even greater control of their wards while retaining his power to initiate large-scale development projects and determine citywide policy. The old Democratic machine had been weakened by this time so that Daley's authority rested more on his personal power than on the party itself (Simpson 2001, 247). The Daley administration strengthened the aldermen in order to gain their support for governing.

The Richard M. Daley administration has been characterized as the "New Chicago Machine," which "retains some aspects of the past" (Simpson 2001, 247), such as ward politics, while changing or adding others. Indeed, Daley instituted a number of management reforms to streamline city government (Simpson 2001, 260). One theme was to cultivate public-private partnerships and pursue greater privatization (Bennett 2010, 100). Daley's agenda focused on positioning Chicago as a global city in the wake of Chicago's manufacturing decline, particularly by remaking the downtown through public-works projects such as Millennium Park, again through public-private partnerships and with the help of corporate and foundation donors. The Daley administration was adept at seizing opportunities when they arose (Bennett 2010, 100) and sought to promote Chicago as an innovator by being actively involved in national and international organizations of mayors and by developing a reputation in areas such as "green" or sustainable development

Cooperation with foundations to advance public-private partnerships was an opportunity that the Daley administration seized upon as well. While no explicit neighborhood policy was created, the Daley administration did implement reforms that have had a large impact on neighborhoods. These include the Plan for the Transformation of Public Housing, restructuring of the Chicago public schools, and the institution of community policing, the Chicago Alternative Policing Strategy (CAPS). The Plan for the Transformation of Public Housing was undertaken with support from the MacArthur Foundation and other philanthropic actors; indeed, it may have generated new relationships between city hall and foundations.

The housing plan, which began implementation in 2000, is the largest housing-demolition and relocation project in the country, involving the rehabilitation or replacement of twenty-five thousand public-housing units and private-sector management of property and social services (Bennett 2010; Hyra 2008; Pattillo 2007). Residents who are subject to relocation are given vouchers to find new accommodations or are resettled in newly built, mixed-income communities (composed of one-third each of public, affordable, and market-rate housing). Some public-housing residents have been dropped from the system because of new requirements for drug-free households and for participation in training programs or employment for adult members of households and because of the exclusion of households with felons, among other requirements.

A number of factors contributed to these changes, including the legacy of segregation and lawsuits surrounding the CHA; the mismanagement and deterioration of public housing that led to a federal takeover of the CHA between 1995 and 1999; and the federal HOPE VI program, which encouraged the deconcentration of poverty through scattered-site housing and the shift to vouchers.[8] The scale of the CHA plan meant that it had spillover effects beyond the public-housing residents, at times reshaping entire neighborhoods.[9] The public-housing reforms may also have been a turning point for increasing collaboration between the city, the private sector, and foundations on social and developmental initiatives in Chicago neighborhoods.

The MacArthur Foundation contributed $50 million toward the Plan for Transformation and helped to create a fund at the Chicago Community Trust (a philanthropic organization) to pool resources across foundations for the effort (Fanton 2006). The foundation later hired as a vice-president the mayor's former chief of staff, who had helped design the Plan for Transformation. Planning for public housing took place during the late 1990s, around the same time as the demonstration projects funded by the MacArthur Foundation that developed into the NCP. The leadership of the MacArthur Foundation, including its new president, Jonathan Fanton, saw these interventions as a way to achieve greater focus and impact for its Chicago community development programs. By the time the initial demonstration projects were expanded into sixteen communities in 2003, working relationships had been established to help pave the way for closer collaboration between the city and the NCP partners.

Although the MacArthur Foundation is a prominent funder of neighborhood programs in Chicago, including current efforts addressing the foreclosure crisis, it is far from the only foundation working with city government. The Joyce Foundation has supported ex-offender reentry programs, and there was a special task force on the issue in the office of the mayor during the Richard M. Daley administration. The Joyce, Spencer, Wood, and other foundations have been involved in education reforms. The Chicago Community Trust and a coalition of forty foundations worked with the city to facilitate funding for nonprofits and low-income neighborhoods from the economic stimulus funds and to promote transparency and accountability for results from stimulus spending.

Comprehensive Community Initiatives

A recurring theme for neighborhood policy in the United States has been the attempt to take a coordinated and comprehensive approach in the battle against urban poverty. Programs such as the Ford Foundation's Gray Areas in the 1950s and the federal Model Cities programs in the 1960s have wrestled with the issue of how to address comprehensively the multiple social problems affecting poor neighborhoods. During the 1990s, some CDCs began to advocate an approach that combined housing and economic development with social-policy issues in programs known as Comprehensive Community Initiatives (CCIs) (Carmon 1997; Coulton 1998). Prominent examples include the Comprehensive Community Revitalization Program, which was formed in the South Bronx in 1993 from a partnership of six area CDCs, and the Sandtown-Winchester partnership in Baltimore, which involved the city and the Enterprise Foundation, among other partners (Kubisch et al. 2002; Wright 2001, 39–40). These initiatives define beneficial neighborhood change as increased community capacity, improved access to services, and improved quality of life within the community (Carmon 1997; Kubisch et al. 2010). While there is recognition of the need for larger systemic change, the emphasis is on generating strategies from within the neighborhood, building social capacity as well as individual and organizational capacity. During the Richard M. Daley era, Chicago had two CCIs: the EZ program and the foundation-sponsored New Communities Initiative (NCI), which grew into the NCP.

Empowerment in Chicago

The local EZ planning process demonstrates the gains made by neighborhood organizations during the Washington era that carried over into the early days of the Richard M. Daley administration. Chicago was one of six cities selected by the federal government for an urban EZ in December 1994. The EZ program was the Clinton administration's main urban policy and response to the civil unrest in Los Angeles in 1992. EZ designation provided a $100 million block grant, as well as tax incentives and priority consideration for other federal grants. The EZs were conceived of as a way to leverage private investment in urban areas hit hard by persistent poverty. However, the Clinton administration's EZ program also included funding to address social problems, provisions encouraging the reinvention of government processes, and requirements for local strategic planning that included participation from residents and other community stakeholders (Gills and White 1998; Mossberger 1999).

Chicago had one of the most effective EZ planning processes, respondents said. The planning effort consisted of more than one hundred meetings and was led by grassroots organizations brought together by CWED.

As democratic and empowering as the planning process was, however, once Chicago received the designation, patronage politics took over and EZ funding was controlled by the city council. One former member of the EZ Coordinating Council remarked that new claimants flocked in for the funding, and "some people acted as if there was no process prior to that point." Conflicts over funding were driven by competition among the aldermen to capture federal dollars and by divisions that began to emerge between neighborhood groups encouraged by city hall's politics of patronage and disregard for the EZ proposal development process. In the end, the cluster plans developed by the neighborhoods were largely discounted. The community-driven governance process and the proposed trust fund were abandoned (see Gills and White 1998, 1997). As a result, the EZ lost its comprehensive approach and intent, becoming merely another source of patronage funds used for discrete projects. Reflecting on this experience, one former coordinating council member said:

> I don't think the model worked. . . . What ended up happening was that there was a promise at the beginning that [the] community would really be involved in the creation of the governance of this type of program and, in the end, that wasn't the case. It set up a lot of false expectations, a lot of disappointed people. Some people would say, "I have never seen 100 million dollars go so little, not so far." Yet, there were positives. . . . You got these groups in the neighborhoods to talk to each other on a regular basis that didn't, health groups talking to youth groups, business groups talking to community organizing groups; it brought people together and formed a common bond for the betterment of the communities.[10]

When the EZ program drew to a close (in 2005) the Chicago zone did not compare favorably to the experience of other EZs. Indeed, federal program evaluations reported little economic impact in the Chicago zone (GAO 2006; HUD 2001). Although there was a modest reduction of poverty and unemployment in the zone, it is unclear whether this was because of improvements for residents or gentrification. The initial promise of the EZ was eventually lost in the retreat to ward politics.

The New Communities Program

The NCI was the preliminary demonstration of the NCP. The program took shape at the City Futures Forum sponsored by Chicago LISC in the mid-1990s, through a series of public panel discussions and a research project examining the past and imagining the future of community work. Influenced by the experience of nonprofits in the South Bronx, LISC sought to expand neighborhood revitalization beyond discrete and uncoordinated neighborhood-based interventions. Concluding that community organizations did not do as good a job as developers, the discussions advocated that community-based organizations should be connectors between the inside and the outside, dedicated to bringing an array of services to the community. Similarly, they concluded that development work (e.g., housing) should be carried out by a few large production organizations or private concerns to increase their scale and impact. Thus, the initial thinking was to have a few large not-for-profit or for-profit developers along with a coalition of community-based organizations working on numerous initiatives to improve neighborhood life and attract investment.

The NCI was a pilot project to carry out these ideas, launched in three low-income communities with traditions of community-based engagement and established organizations that could act as lead agencies. Beginning with a planning process, the NCI was carried out from 1998 through 2002 with support from the MacArthur Foundation in the communities of South Chicago,[11] Pilsen, and West Haven (on the near West Side). In 2003 the initiative was expanded to sixteen communities and fourteen plans[12] (including an additional round of funding in the three pilot areas), and the NCI was renamed the New Communities Program.

Sponsored by the McArthur Foundation and managed by LISC, the NCP in Chicago has designated lead agencies to work with other community organizations in the implementation of locally-developed plans. According to the program's website, "The New Communities Program is a long-term initiative . . . to support comprehensive community development. . . . The 10-year effort seeks to rejuvenate challenged communities, bolster those in danger of losing ground, and preserve the diversity of areas in the path of gentrification." In this sense, although the intervention is an "effort to offer the same (or a similar) program of interventions dispersed at multiple sites," plans and priorities vary between communities according to need, community capacity, and local choice. LISC's website defines the goal of NCP as "trigger[ing] large-scale improvements, mesh[ing] with market forces," adding that "NCP is designed to strengthen communities from within—through planning, organizing and human development. The comprehensive approach helps broaden opportunities for local residents through better education, broader job choices, safer streets, new economic opportunities and stronger personal finances." This strengthened community is better equipped to take advantage of larger market forces by

- attracting retail and housing development to areas that have experienced little new construction;
- achieving economic balance in neighborhoods where working-class residents fear displacement by higher-income newcomers; and
- creating stronger connections to metropolitan-wide business, employment, and educational opportunities.

The communities involved in the NCP vary significantly in level of distress. Logan Square and Chicago Lawn hover near the average poverty level for the city as a whole, but they have diverse populations and are undergoing significant changes. Gentrification is occurring in Logan Square and the Latino population is rapidly expanding in Chicago Lawn. Other NCP neighborhoods, like Oakland and Washington Park, are among those with the highest levels of poverty, exceeding 50 percent of the population; and the rest are somewhere "in between." All the NCP areas have poverty levels above the 19.6 percent average for the city, although they account for only half of the thirty-three high-poverty areas. NCP neighborhoods and the organizations representing them are overwhelmingly African American or Latino.

LISC selected participant communities principally on the basis of need and the existence of neighborhood institutions capable of steering and implementing the quality-of-life plan emerging from the process. In some cases, however, communities were selected for strategic reasons, to make sure that different ethnic groups and geographies in the city were represented. Even with selection criteria based on capacity, the experience and resources of the lead agencies differed across neighborhoods. As one respondent observed: "if you look at the NCP organizations, the lead agencies, you have everything from BRC [Bickerdike Redevelopment Corporation] that is 40 years old to Teamwork Englewood that is really an organization that was created to be the lead agency for the NCP in Englewood."

Goals and activities for the NCP were generated through a multistep process in which LISC played an active part. The first phase in each neighborhood consisted of a participatory planning process including various agencies and nonprofits. Consultants took notes and drafted plans that were then reviewed and adjusted. Final plans were unveiled in May 2005 during a downtown ceremony attended by five hundred community representatives and other partners, including Mayor Richard M. Daley.

The intermediary model is a prominent feature of the NCP and is central to understanding its strategy for coordination across policy domains as well as across the sixteen community areas. On one level, the lead agency coordinates the project and collaboration across groups within the neighborhood, acting as an intermediary within its community and often between its community and the outside. The MacArthur Foundation is the granting agency, but it is LISC that works directly with the lead agencies. On another level, LISC acts as the overall coordinator for the project, managing funds and synchronizing efforts across the project neighborhoods. LISC also seeks to build relationships with city agencies and private concerns, which helps to counteract the functional and political fragmentation that Chicago's neighborhoods ordinarily face. Mayoral support for the NCP during the Daley administration paved the way for cooperation with city departments. During the first five years of the project, LISC provided technical assistance, funding, and training and also intervened to manage conflicts in some neighborhoods. In a few cases LISC helped to build new community organizations, changed the lead agency, or intervened to encourage particular lead agency boards to replace directors or to open up to others in the community.

A distinctive element of the NCP is the effort to develop capacity beyond the design and implementation of neighborhood programs by engaging community-based organizations in a larger project to promote systemic changes in the way neighborhoods participate in local policymaking. As Robert Chaskin and Mikael Karlstrom (2012, iii) observed in their evaluation of the program: "Most CCIs have pursued neighborhood-level activities rather than promoting changes in the policies and systems that shape neighborhoods' broader prospects for success." By contrast, as part of the NCP, LISC was encouraged by the MacArthur Foundation to create an "initiative wide policy platform" to "leverage the potential combined influence of the NCP neighborhoods."

Focusing on systemic change reflects the belief that NCP neighborhoods face similar political and institutional challenges that "provide an opportunity for collective planning and for shaping a cross-community change agenda" (Chaskin and Karlstrom 2012, ES 9). Beyond this, in contrast with most other CCIs, the broad scope of the NCP, which targets numerous neighborhoods citywide, created the opportunity to develop the "collective influence of NCP neighborhoods acting on behalf of a sizeable constituency around policy or systems-level issues." However, collective action of this sort is unlikely to take place without "dedicated capacity to pursue it" (Chaskin and Karlstrom 2012, ES 9). Even with efforts by LISC to develop trust and build relationships to facilitate collective action across neighborhoods, much remains to be accomplished: "in spite of an explicit recognition of the ways in which local communities are embedded in larger systems and of how the decisions and actions of policy, market, and institutional actors beyond the neighborhood often have significant impact on community opportunities and outcomes, the lion's share of investment and energy still focuses inward, toward community-level activity and the development of projects and programs in response to particular community needs and priorities" (Chaskin and Karlstrom 2012, 77).

The strategies and role of the lead agency have varied across the communities, in terms of their ability to mobilize other organizations and to promote collaborative efforts. While the program prioritizes collaboration, the level of collaboration has varied across participating communities (Greenberg et al. 2010). In some cases the lead agency has carried out the bulk of the plan; in others, work has been distributed among nonprofits and private concerns. Some community groups have been uneasy with LISC's leadership, seeing it as too top-down.

Programs are eligible for funding only if they are related to the quality-of-life plan. Some plans included new projects developed by organizations to reflect the concerns and priorities that emerged during the planning process, but generally there was a large coincidence between existing programs that local organizations and institutions brought to the table and what was written into the plans. This reflects the practice of many neighborhood organizations to ensure program continuity by recasting their projects in new languages and community initiatives on an ongoing basis. The ability of the NCP to embrace existing programs can also be seen as an indication of strength, demonstrating the flexibility of the framework and its openness to agendas coming from the community and its organizations.

As intended with comprehensive initiatives, NCP activities span a number of policy domains, with the most funding expended for economic and workforce development programs, education, and social services (Greenberg et al. 2010). Respondents generally felt that plans and activities were based on local priorities: "Some themes that were promoted through the NCP are proof that they [LISC and MacArthur Foundation] had some ideas of the way they wanted things for consistency, you know, that all of our plans were sustainable. In terms of how we were structured, I don't think that they necessarily dictated to say, 'Here is how you are going to be structured.'"

Set for a ten-year period, the intervention appears to be receiving some level of continuing support. The original grant from the MacArthur Foundation was $47 million, an amount spread across sixteen community areas and fourteen lead agencies. The MacArthur funding has supported two staff positions in each lead agency as well as small seed grants. These grants have generally ranged between $25,000 and $50,000 (Greenberg et al. 2010). The seed grants, and the MacArthur funding overall, are intended to leverage other funding (interviews; Greenberg et al. 2010), attracting public and private investments. According to the midterm program evaluation, some large projects, totaling about $400 million, were built in the NCP neighborhoods by other foundations, but only 42 percent of the small seed grants generated additional funding (Greenberg et al. 2010). Still, interview respondents felt that the seed grants were important for bringing resources to the table quickly, enabling some immediate successes.

NCP Neighborhoods

This section explores the NCP in two neighborhoods—Pilsen and Woodlawn. We briefly review the legacy of other revitalization efforts in these communities, as well as the way in which the current NCP initiative fits into that history. Given Chicago's size and the diversity of its neighborhoods, these cases are not necessarily representative of neighborhood policy overall or of the NCP itself. Both neighborhoods have experienced pressures from gentrification (which is not the case in all low-income Chicago neighborhoods), and both have a long history of community organizing. Neither neighborhood has a substantial amount of public housing. Redevelopment has been the result of university efforts or the real estate market rather than the public-housing reforms. Pilsen and Woodlawn were also part of the EZ.

Pilsen (Lower West Side)

Settled in the mid-1800s and housing workers of the South Loop railroad yards, the stockyards, and nearby light industries, Pilsen has been a traditional port of entry for immigrants. With a population of 39,144 Latinos in 2000 (88.9 percent of the community's total population), it has been a gateway for Mexican Americans since the 1960s. Considered by respondents to be one of the communities with the most organizations in Chicago, it was among the three initial pilot neighborhoods of the NCI (the forerunner of the NCP). Only three miles from downtown, Pilsen is near the confluence of major highway and public-transportation systems. Its location has been a major challenge since the 1970s, as the city and private developers advanced plan after plan to redevelop the neighborhood. During the 1960s, the University of Illinois at Chicago was built on land adjacent to the neighborhood, and the resulting displacement encouraged resistance to development for many years afterward.

Prior to the NCP, Pilsen was part of the Pilsen/Little Village EZ Cluster, and that experience affected expectations about how neighborhood policy works in the city. One participant described it as an extension of the patronage system. Although EZ planning had brought local organizations together temporarily, breaking their traditional factionalism, upon implementation they went back to their feuds and competition for resources.

The lead agency for the NCP in Pilsen is The Resurrection Project (TRP), established by six Catholic churches in 1990. TRP has been a prominent nonprofit housing developer and manager in the neighborhood, although it has undertaken other programs as well. The current NCP plan lists twenty-three participating community-based organizations, twelve committees, and other local and outside institutions. Yet the bulk of program is carried out by a few large local nonprofits, including the lead agency.

Among the projects highlighted in the NCP plan are business district development (including a village center called El Zocalo), employment, family and youth support, affordable housing, and education, especially high school completion and college preparation. The aim of the NCP in Pilsen is "to create the cornerstone of a new, mixed income, predominantly Mexican community with strong cultural identity, faith and values that will be 'vibrant, colorful, folkloric, beautiful' and serve as the cultural center of the Mexican population in the Midwest" (New Communities Program 2005).

The Pilsen NCP website describes attitudes toward development in Pilsen in the following way: "There's a small cadre of anti-development types, but most leaders now take a more nuanced approach, welcoming compatible investment while insisting developers crank affordability into their plans" (McCarron 2007). Yet, we found in interviews that gentrification continues to be a divisive issue in Pilsen. While some community leaders we interviewed were advocates of high-income development and the benefits they felt it would bring to the community, others were opponents. The lead agency of the NCP has adopted the position that gentrification cannot be stopped and that the best that can be done is to promote a mixed-income community. Organizations opposed to development have suggested that the NCP has failed to confront the rising rents and tax assessments that threaten low-income residents.[13] Moreover, there is a feeling among some organizations that city policy pays too little attention to the needs of low-income residents. Of former mayor Richard M. Daley, one community leader who spoke out about the closing of neighborhood health clinics said, "His only preoccupation is with how a global city should look like, and certainly, it is not a city that has these undesirables in it. It is all about aesthetics and middle- to upper-class development. The poor do not fit in his city."

An important factor is that Pilsen's alderman is prodevelopment (Zhang 2011), and some groups expressed fear that opposition to gentrification would exclude them from funding and access to the alderman. In Pilsen (as in the other neighborhoods), respondents observed that the local alderman controls infrastructure, zoning, and brick-and-mortar projects and that anyone seeking support from city hall had to go through him.

Woodlawn

Woodlawn has experienced deep conflicts over the direction of the NCP, with a subsequent reorganization that has broadened participation. Through the NCP, the Woodlawn Children's Promise Community was developed, and recently it received a federal planning grant and a $300,000 grant from the Ford Foundation.[14] Modeled on the Harlem Children's Zone, the Woodlawn Children's Promise Community takes a comprehensive approach to education, involving parents and supporting families. Both the broader participation in the NCP and the Children's Promise initiative are perceived as positive developments, according to interviews; yet there is uncertainty among some respondents about whether these programs will lead to improvements for current residents or open the door wider to gentrification.

Woodlawn is located along the lake, adjacent to Hyde Park and the University of Chicago. It features two of the city's largest stretches of parkland: Washington Park, which was designed by Frederick Law Olmstead, and Jackson Park, which was the site of the 1893 Columbian Exposition. Eight miles south of downtown, Woodlawn is well connected to the city and region by Lakeshore Drive, the Dan Ryan Expressway, and the Chicago Transit Authority. Yet in 2000 Woodlawn had a household poverty rate of nearly 40 percent. Dramatic racial turnover occurred in the 1950s, and today, 95 percent of the population is African American. Decades of population loss left more than 1,700 vacant lots in the neighborhood, although there has been some redevelopment in recent years (LISC and Woodlawn Preservation and Investment Corporation 2005).

Woodlawn has a long history of community organizing and a sometimes-contentious relationship with the University of Chicago. Following the urban renewal of Hyde Park in the early 1960s, the university planned the development of a mile-long South Campus between Sixtieth and Sixty-First Streets in Woodlawn, with further expansion to follow. In response, speaking on behalf of many local churches, civic associations, and businesses, the Temporary Woodlawn Organization (later The Woodlawn Organization, or TWO) was formed with the support of Saul Alinsky to confront the university. By gaining a seat on the city's planning board TWO temporarily stopped the university's expansion plans. The organization continued its oppositional tactics to mobilize residents on other issues—for example, against abusive landlords and business owners. Participating in the Freedom Rides and the civil rights movement, community leaders built a local base and a national reputation that allowed them to take on powerful opponents, including city hall. The efforts of TWO, however, did not halt the neighborhood's decline, and Woodlawn subsequently lost over two-thirds of its 1960 population[15] and housing units.

Over the years, both TWO and the pastor of the Apostolic Church, Bishop Brazier,[16] gained political influence and engaged in housing and other development within the neighborhood. In the late 1960s TWO received a large grant from the federal Office of Economic Opportunity to develop a high-rise residential rental building of 502 units, Woodlawn Gardens. Then, in 1972, it created the Woodlawn Community Development Corporation to pursue further real estate development and management in Woodlawn, consummating its move from advocacy and opposition to development. In 1996 the Chicago Transit Authority tore down the last leg and station of the elevated train in Woodlawn, forfeiting millions of dollars in federal funds because of the opposition, led by Bishop Brazier, to a nearly completed extension. Then, working with developers, Brazier started to build middle-class housing along Sixty-Third Street, adjacent to his church. This broke Woodlawn into a gentrifying area north of Sixty-Third and the rest of the community south of it. Nearly forty years after halting its incursion into Woodlawn, the University of Chicago ended up incorporating the north side of Woodlawn into the South Campus expansion.

According to interviews that we conducted with residents and participants, the University of Chicago, Apostolic Church, and TWO pressed for NCP designation, and Woodlawn was among the early pilot neighborhoods. The initial quality-of-life plan reflected the priorities and vision of the organizations that had initiated the NCP. This alienated other community forces to the point that LISC put pressure on the Woodlawn NCP to open up the process to include other players during the second round of planning. The initial lead agency, Woodlawn Preservation and Investment Corporation, was removed. The program is now run by a board that includes Woodlawn Community and Neighbors Inc., which was seen by some respondents as closer to the "pulse of the community" and as representing the needs of current residents. Still, interviewees indicated that some groups had not been invited to participate in the formulation of the second plan, or elected not to join in, because of perceptions that the university, TWO, and the Apostolic Church continued to dominate the process. Changes in the NCP leadership have not entirely alleviated neighborhood distrust, especially since the university continues to play a major role. According to the head of a local community-based organization: "[The attitude among some was] 'Oh no, you are not going to get me to sign on this and they do what they want to do.' That is the way it has been played in this community. They get you at a community meeting and then they do what they want to do. . . . [But] the individuals that were originally at the table making plans are not the same bodies that are at the table now. . . . Recently, they started to identify more community residents to be part of the board." The NCP plans reflect strategies for mixed-income housing and development of retail south of Sixty-Third Street. Education, youth, health, and workforce development are other priorities, along with improvement of communications among local institutions, organizations, and residents. Woodlawn's plan includes a University of Chicago charter school and the development of retail and a student residence on the north side of the neighborhood bordering the university.

In the early years of the initiative, the best-funded priorities were tied to the initial leadership, and the development agenda had the full support of the aldermanic office. Having the resources, the University of Chicago focused primarily on its South Campus expansion and then on the local schools through faculty-driven initiatives that attracted significant national funding. Under the leadership of the Apostolic Church, the first of three phases of new housing development along Sixty-Third Street was completed, with two more to follow—all of them on land freed up by the earlier demolition of Chicago Transit Authority's Green Line. Construction problems in the first phase slowed the work, and the recent economic recession halted it altogether; retail development to follow completion of this housing came to a halt as well. Some respondents saw this as a blessing, given that the project implied gentrification was likely to advance south of Sixty-Third Street.

These same respondents argued that the programs of most interest to community residents concerned safety, health, affordable housing, and education. The neighborhood has considerable gang activity, and the return of large numbers of ex-convicts presents needs that some have argued are not sufficiently dealt with in Woodlawn's NCP. Mixed-income housing is prioritized in the plans, but affordable housing takes significant nonmarket resources that are not currently available; interviewees spoke of the uphill struggle to fund new affordable housing in the community. And while health was identified as a priority in the plan, the health program is staffed by an unpaid volunteer counting on meager resources for its implementation.

There is consensus in favor of the Woodlawn Children's Promise Community. One local organizer said that "everybody agreed that the schools and the children in the community are the most important priority." But there are worries that "once there are excellent schools, the community would gentrify because all those rich people would now come to Woodlawn to get stuff free off the back of these poor kids. . . . It is my mission not to let that happen." Still, there seems to be some cautious hope, given recent developments. According to one community organizer: "The school initiative is so young that we do not know how it is going to play out. The willingness of the groups to come together and trust each other in a way that they can support each other doing things together for the community rather than separately is something that is happening in this process, for me, anyway." The Woodlawn NCP has thus had serious problems with community conflict and governance, but it has taken some tentative steps to improve collaboration within the community. The experience in Woodlawn, however, points to some larger issues for CCIs. Since CCIs often depend upon leveraging of resources, this can privilege projects that generate revenues, such as development, over other needs. As some have suggested, university expansion, real estate development, and gentrification will be the most likely result in Woodlawn in the absence of funding for priorities such as affordable housing and services.

Astride Two Worlds

Chicago's emergence as a global city has left some neighborhoods and residents behind, and the economic crisis hit low-income neighborhoods hardest through foreclosures and unemployment.[17] Since the 1980s and the Reagan administration's cuts in federal funding, the support of foundations and corporations has become more critical for community development and neighborhood programs nationally (Koschinsky and Swanstrom 2001; Saegert 2006). In the current atmosphere of heightened government austerity, resources outside city government may become even more important for social programs and low-income neighborhoods. The politics of neighborhood revitalization in Chicago reflects these trends. In recent years, foundations have been especially important influences on neighborhood policy as key partners with city government in promoting and financing CCIs.

As a neighborhood improvement strategy, the CCI is one important sign of change in the nature of neighborhood politics. In past decades, as Chicago was making its transition into the postindustrial age, city hall focused attention on revitalizing the central business district. Neighborhoods mobilized to protect themselves from intrusive developmental initiatives and to promote an alternative policy agenda rooted in social concerns. By contrast, CCIs represent a significant break with the past: rather than separating economic-development and social-policy concerns, CCIs seek reconciliation and symbiosis between them. But the results have varied across neighborhoods (Greenberg et al. 2010), and in some communities, as demonstrated in our case studies, development and gentrification issues still create tension.

Community-based actors also have changed. Many community organizations, though steeped in the tradition of Alinsky-style confrontation and protest, have been transformed into service-oriented nonprofits (often in the form of CDCs). Despite continuing anxieties about gentrification in Chicago, many community-based groups are now more inclined to accept mixed-income housing and business development as necessary components of neighborhood improvement. This shift likely reflects, at least in part, a need for community-based organizations to appeal to foundations and other funders for support.

Despite the apparent changes in neighborhood politics, the continuing importance of Chicago's tradition of ward politics to neighborhood policy-making is clear. Aldermen control key resources that can advance or impede a neighborhood revitalization agenda. This has two important consequences. First, communities that are within a single alderman's ward are more likely than others to be favored with ward-controlled resources. Second, the resources controlled by the aldermen can be an important source of CCI financing (which emphasizes leveraging), especially when interventions strive to create synergy between economic-development initiatives and other neighborhood improvement efforts. As a result, distressed neighborhoods are caught between two worlds. They must simultaneously appeal to the foundation world, which values the capacity to plan and execute local initiatives, and to the machine world, which values political connections. Poor neighborhoods, in particular, face a policy environment where they must seek resources from many public and private actors, and there is a high level of interdependence with policies made at other scales.

NCP experience in Chicago highlights some of the issues that are likely to face other CCIs, given heavy dependence upon nongovernmental actors. Although NCP efforts have been comprehensive in terms of cutting across policy domains, the resources available are relatively modest, consisting essentially of some additional staff and monies for seed grants. Comprehensive initiatives like the EZ and many foundation and federal efforts rely on the notion of leveraging investment (Kubisch et al. 2010). This approach privileges certain types of programs (those that may have happened anyway and those that can attract market investment). In Woodlawn, for example, the practice of leveraging advantages programs that already have some resources behind them, such as middle-income housing or university development. As Mary Pattillo (2007) has so eloquently argued, low-income residents often have inadequate resources to intervene on anything resembling an equal basis. Because the comprehensive services of the Harlem Children's Zone have captured the attention of federal agencies and national foundations, there may be an opening to shift the balance toward education, however, in Woodlawn.

In a cross-national review of neighborhood revitalization, Carmon (1997) concluded that there is a need to join the comprehensive approach of the 1960s to public-private partnerships that will bring multiple resources to the table—much as in the NCP model. This emphasizes market-led investment, but with a role for nonmarket actors to provide affordable housing and to ensure mixed-income development rather than displacement. Carmon raises the concern, however, that greater income disparities in the United States make mixed-income development more problematic than in other developed countries. The smaller role of government, she concludes, may also make such goals more difficult to achieve, as even public-private partnerships are largely driven by quick market returns.

Although foundations have made neighborhood issues more visible on Chicago's policy agenda, there is still no overall policy for revitalization of low-income neighborhoods, and the sustainability of current efforts is uncertain. This difficulty highlights some more fundamental concerns regarding foundation-led CCIs as a neighborhood revitalization strategy. Foundation activity in neighborhood policy often results in a collection of experiments of limited scope and of short duration (see Brown and Fiester 2007), restricted to a few targeted neighborhoods and sectors. The NCP has a broad reach for a comprehensive initiative, involving sixteen communities. Still, our interviews indicate that because resources are scarce, there are debates over targeting, about the neighborhoods that are left out, or over the decisions made to fund some groups rather than others. The ten-year period of the NCP is unusually long, but questions remain about scale, reach, resource availability, and how healthy communities can be sustained in the longer term. As one philanthropic observer indicated, it is not clear who the policy audience is for the NCP—that is, who will take responsibility for continuing comprehensive programs after the funding from the MacArthur Foundation has lapsed.

The problems that lie ahead include how to move from an experiment to a more general policy of neighborhood revitalization, encompassing the entire city, and how to produce development without displacement. In city government, the ability to forge an effective and equitable neighborhood policy has been hampered by fragmentation and the tradition of rewarding friends and punishing enemies that is embedded in the ward system. Delegating much of neighborhood policy to this level and to aldermen suppresses the potential for meaningful change across neighborhoods. Politics-as-usual in Chicago has squandered past opportunities and has undermined confidence in the public sector, as the local EZ program demonstrated. With the election of a new mayor, it remains to be seen whether the picture will change for low-income neighborhoods. The Emanuel administration has taken steps toward making the budget and programs like TIF more transparent. But the city's recent budget cuts are carving deeply into public programs in low-income communities.

In the past, critical junctures in neighborhood policy—for example, during the Washington era—made possible gains by community-based organizations and low-income residents that have been fragile and easily subject to reversal. Neighborhoods and cities are dependent upon broader forces, such as labor markets, and upon the policies and resources of other levels of government (Hyra 2008). One community leader described this multilevel interdependence and uncertainty: "Nonprofits are not decision-makers," he said. "The policies come from above. All we can do is our best to stretch or adjust them to help people, to maximize benefit. We are only part of a large system." Programs such as the NCP contribute what some neighborhood respondents called "concrete" or "practical" interventions— the small policy changes and narrow gains that Thompson (2006) has observed are the result of other mobilizations of the poor. Residents and community-based organizations are unable to address the structural inequalities that shape opportunities within poor communities (Carmon 1997). Such inequalities demand attention beyond the neighborhoods or local levels. Nevertheless, respondents indicate why neighborhood initiatives have survived in different forms over the decades in Chicago. Despite all the limitations that such programs face, there is still a belief, as put by one community activist, that even small gains are important and "What we do at the neighborhood level is real to the ultimate beneficiaries."

Notes

The authors wish to thank Douglas Gills for his contribution to the early conversations about this chapter.

1. Chicago was officially divided into seventy-five community areas in the 1920s. Two additional communities added much later brought the number to seventy-seven.
2. Personal interview with Professor Rachel Weber about her research on TIF.
3. There are several cases in which Mayor Richard M. Daley overrode the decisions of the local aldermen (e.g., the Children's Museum in Grant Park and the sidewalk café of the Congress Plaza Hotel, both downtown). See http://articles.chicagotribune.com/ 2009-07-27/news/0907260248_1_alderman-congress-plaza-hotel-sidewalk-cafe.
4. As of October 2012, 182 organizations were listed as members at http://www .donorsforum.org/ISSIFiles/members_online/members/member_listdf.asp?action= search&ok=N&pn=1&CID=12189&DID=27166&af=DF.
5. Although reelected to a second term, Harold Washington died in 1987 and was replaced by Acting Mayor Eugene Sawyer, who continued most of Washington's policies until the election of Richard M. Daley.
6. The bank, later known as ShoreBank, failed in August 2010 but was purchased by a consortium that included banks and the Ford Foundation. It is now operating under the name Urban Partnership Bank (Yerak 2010).
7. See http://www.newcommunities.org/whoweare/liscchicago.asp, accessed March 13, 2011.
8. The Plan for the Transformation of Public Housing is still in progress. Implementation has been affected by the housing crisis, and there have been mixed reviews of the program, which focus on the reconcentration of residents in nearby poor black neighborhoods or destabilization of other ones. A recent meta-analysis of program evaluations (Vale and Graves 2010) can be found at http://web.mit.edu/dusp/dusp _extension_unsec/people/faculty/ljv/vale_macarthur_2010.pdf. An excellent history and qualitative account can be found in Pattillo 2007.
9. A major effect was the overnight decline in poverty rates in areas such as the Near North and Bronzeville following the demolition of public housing and the development of mixed-income communities.
10. Unless otherwise noted, quotations are from confidential personal interviews conducted by the authors between 2008 and 2011.
11. Originally, Woodlawn was designated as one of the pilot neighborhoods, but it was replaced by South Chicago.
12. The Bronzeville plan includes the communities of North Kenwood–Oakland, Grand Boulevard, and Douglas.
13. The Latino population has been declining steadily in the gentrifying East End of the community; in the period 2000–2010, the overall population declined, with Latinos going from 88.9 to 82.4 percent in the decade and the white population increasing from 8.1 to 12.4 percent (A. Williams 2011).
14. http://www.fordfound.org/grants/grantdetails?grantid=10255.
15. Woodlawn's population went from nearly 90,000 in 1960 to 27,000 in 2000.

16. Bishop Brazier was the longtime pastor of the Apostolic Church, which became one of the largest and most influential institutions on the South Side. Bishop Brazier had a close relationship with Mayor Richard M. Daley, and he and Rev. Leon Finney, executive director of TWO, exercised considerable power in Woodlawn. On Finney and his management of low-income housing properties, see Hyra 2008. Finney is currently being investigated by federal housing authorities for overbilling and other financial issues (Olivo 2012).

17. See, for example, the discussion of foreclosures in Chicago's high-poverty neighborhoods in Glanton, Mullen, and Glanton 2011.

FIVE

Professionalized Government: Institutionalizing the New Politics in Phoenix

MARILYN DANTICO AND JAMES SVARA

Phoenix is a story of unregulated fast growth, accompanied by embedded and emerging problems. Phoenix is the largest council-manager city in the United States, and it illustrates how political and professional leadership can interact positively to develop a consistent focus on the problems of neighborhood distress. As the influence of the "Phoenix 40" (a group representing the largest and most influential businesses in the region) declined, the move from at-large to district elections for council members and the election of Mayor Terry Goddard in 1984 paved the way for a policy shift toward neighborhood improvement. However, the city's professionalized management team played a very large role in establishing, implementing, and institutionalizing the city's neighborhood policy. A crucial decision was the creation of a robust Neighborhood Services Department to provide policy leadership and coordinate the activities of other parts of city government that contribute to neighborhood well-being. Once electoral politics moved beyond old dogmas to recognize a need to respond to accumulated distress in parts of the city, a more open-ended approach to problem solving became possible. This approach was enriched by professional knowledge and an abundance of fresh ideas, including an emphasis on enhanced community participation. Although resources have become increasingly constrained, Phoenix has stressed a comprehensive approach to neighborhood revitalization and shown adaptability. In contrast with an earlier time when a minimum-services approach prevailed, Phoenix's current neighborhood program shows how wide-ranging revitalization efforts can become. As annexed areas have aged and experienced foreclosures, the city has recently moved beyond its initial focus on small target areas to take on a much larger area of distress. Among this book's six case study cities, Phoenix has advanced furthest in providing a stable institutional foundation for strategic action in the city's distressed neighborhoods.

As a young city that experienced phenomenal growth during the second half of the twentieth century, Phoenix has a population of just under 1.5 million. The decade following 1950 saw a stunning expansion of the city; in area, it increased by a factor of ten, and the population increased by a factor of four. Moreover, the rate of growth for the remainder of the century was also impressive. The area covered by the city expanded by about a third in the 1970s, 1980s, and 1990s, and the population grew at nearly the same rate ("slowing" to about 25 percent growth in the 1990s). Annexation was a major factor throughout the city's expansion. Phoenix now covers a land area larger than that of sprawling Los Angeles and more than twice that of Chicago.

Phoenix lacks the large pockets of concentrated poverty that are found in many older cities. Even after the recent mortgage crisis, which hit the city hard, 60 percent of Phoenix households were owner occupied. Yet its present-day diversity gives it a political character quite different from the past and also different in tone from much of the rest of Arizona. More than a fifth of its population is foreign born, and 37 percent speak a language other than English at home. The Hispanic population has now reached 41 percent, nearly as large as the non-Hispanic white population. Despite the city's significant level of affluence compared with many older cities, the population in poverty, which was about one in six, has risen to a post-mortgage-crisis level of nearly one in five.

As recently as 1980 Phoenix was still a conservative city, distrustful of intrusive government—local or federal. Phoenix voters supported Republican candidates for president by large margins as recently as 1976 and 1980. Maricopa County—the home county for Phoenix—continues to do so. The city did not have a housing code until the late 1980s, and many leaders considered one to be politically infeasible; voters rejected enacting housing codes in 1963 and in 1966. A housing code and its enforcement finally became part of the city's policy tool kit when a neighborhood department was created and community revitalization became an enduring city goal. Because of extensive annexation with little inclination toward regulation, much of the housing in Phoenix falls short of today's code standards. Present housing-code enforcement policies aim to protect "neighborhoods from blighting and deteriorating conditions that have a negative impact on area property values and encourage social disorder and crime" (City of Phoenix, Neighborhood Services Department 2006). The Neighborhood Services Department responds to complaints from residents to identify and correct code violations; proactive, priority enforcement is provided in neighborhoods targeted for revitalization.

For many years the conservative orientation of the city's political leadership inclined Phoenix to be skeptical of federal assistance, "wary of 'over-reliance' on federal aid and any consequent erosion of 'local control'" (Hall 1983, 74). However, more recently the city has made extensive use of federal assistance to finance its neighborhood initiatives. Before the Community Development Block Grant (CDBG) program in the 1970s, public housing was limited in Phoenix, and the city obtained only one Neighborhood Development Project (NDP) grant, along with small water and sewer grants from HUD. The NDP grant focused on redevelopment of a low-income, minority-concentrated neighborhood between the central business district and the airport: "a substantial proportion of these funds was used for clearance, demolition, and relocation activity" related to expansion of the airport (Hall 1983, 77). CDBG funds did allow the city to make a small but slow start on housing upgrades and rehabilitation. Phoenix's turn in the 1980s toward more openness to federal resources and greater concern for distressed neighborhoods is best understood as part of a complicated political history that marries strong, professionalized management capacity with eventual acceptance of diversity by the city's changing political leadership.

Political Development

Although Phoenix adopted council-manager government in 1914, the city continued to struggle with corruption and patronage politics until after World War II, when a business-led Charter Revision Committee launched a textbook "good government" reform movement. The new system of governance featured nonpartisan, at-large elections and a city manager with full administrative powers. This change was backed by business leaders who insisted on respect for professionalism in government. Business and civic elites organized the Charter Government Committee (CGC), which dominated city elections into the 1970s. Barry Goldwater was part of the initial city council slate and typified the business-minded members and nominees of the CGC. The organization's immediate task was to end corruption and break the close link between city politics and vice. In pursuit of that aim CGC insisted on close adherence to nonpartisanship. As with many Sun Belt cities of that time, the policy goal was to create a business-friendly local government backed by an active and tightly organized group of growth-minded corporate executives and a set of arrangements that made it difficult for any alternative coalition to compete effectively (Bridges 1997; Trounstine 2008). As put in one retrospective on the CGC: "Growth was their mantra" (Nilsen 2011).

Over time, the "growth *uber alles*" agenda began to wear thin, and in 1975 an incumbent council member, Margaret Hance, broke away from the political establishment. She brought into power a new majority, still dedicated to economic development but also eager to protect the area's quality of life. Under Mayor Hance (1976–1983), the Phoenix Mountain Preserve was established to protect some mountainous areas from development. Hance also embraced privatization, using contracting for city services as a means to control the growth and influence of organized labor.

When the CGC proved to be no longer able to control access to city offices, new forms of business leadership mobilized. A new elite group of top business leaders formed the Phoenix 40 (currently operating as Greater Phoenix Leadership) and maintains a staff and website.[1] One study on the original Phoenix 40 reports that members represented twenty-five of the thirty largest and most important enterprises in the metropolitan region (McLaughlin 1975). However, the Phoenix 40 proved unable to dominate city elections as the CGC had. Indicative of the depth of political change, the established political order in Phoenix was challenged again in 1982 when Terry Goddard led a successful battle to change council elections from at-large to districts (the Phoenix 40 unsuccessfully opposed the change.)

As an activist with Democratic Party ties, Goddard followed this initial foray into electoral politics with a successful bid to become the first mayor under the new system. Elected to his first of four terms in 1984, he served until 1990, when he resigned to run for governor. Goddard and the first district-based council inherited a government that had moved decisively into contracting under Hance's leadership. There were council members who were strong advocates of further expanding contracting for municipal services, but Goddard—who illustrated the potential for council-manager mayors to provide effective leadership (Svara 2008)—and several members of the council under the district system found no convincing arguments to expand the city's privatization program. (Organized labor supported the move of council elections to districts.) Although the city never abandoned contracting, using contracting as a weapon against public employees ceased. Goddard's first city council included a former president of the Phoenix Fire Fighters union.

The shift to district-based council elections had several important consequences. One result was that representation became more diverse. Goddard was joined by the first Latino council member elected in over a decade. The next ten years saw the replacement of all the council members
who had been elected at-large, and who had been considered unbeatable
before the inauguration of districts (Laake 1990; Mushkatel et al. 1984).
Goddard was part of a new wave of change-minded citizens seeking reform
in electoral practices and representation. While the initial targets were state
and national representation, community mobilization efforts connected to
the Great Society programs had opened other doors to people interested in
increased participation in local affairs (see, e.g., Karnig 1976; Karnig and
Welch 1980).

Not all of the changes that occurred under the district system were so
dramatic, but most of the changes received positive reviews. There is a consensus that district representation improved access to city hall, that neighborhoods had more influence, and that the city was quicker to respond to
mundane problems (Horstman 1989). People of color, Democrats, and organized labor were more influential in elections under the district system.
The support of these groups became important to candidates, and office-
holders began to represent a more diverse set of concerns.

Beyond this, with the inauguration of district elections, council members received funds for offices and for professional staff support. Historically, members of the city council did not have private office space, and
their ability to respond to citizens was limited. District elections were accompanied by the installation of a computerized complaint-monitoring
system that permitted council members and their staff to track complaints
and evaluate response time. This single change helped level the playing
field in that council members now have a way to make independent evaluations of city service provision in their districts. While the city manager and
the public-service bureaucracy hold significant power, the city's political
system has become more balanced.

The new council and mayor brought into office a very different outlook from their predecessors. For example, Goddard secured approval for
an Arts Commission and sponsored one of the country's most generous
percent-for-arts ordinances. He oversaw passage of history-making bond
issues in support of the arts and pushed the city to develop a geographic
information system (GIS). More importantly for the purposes of the present research, in creating districts, Phoenix inaugurated a political system
in which neighborhoods began to matter. Goddard's agenda focused on
neighborhoods, and he argued that you cannot have a strong city without

both a strong downtown and strong neighborhoods. In Goddard's view, "we wanted to maintain balance between strong neighborhoods around the city and a strong downtown."[2] However, despite Goddard's rhetoric, there was little direct connection between the emerging neighborhood strategy and the downtown strategy during the 1980s.

Goddard did enhance neighborhood planning and encouraged use of an urban-village concept that had been popularized in the 1970s. Village planning groups were organized and their views were funneled into the city decision process (Weschler, Cayer, and Ronan 1984, 102). This represented a major push to incorporate citizens into the policy process. However, the influence of these planning efforts was limited because village and city council district boundaries did not overlap. Although the grandest ideas pushed by urban villagers (live-work-play in a single community) are not in widespread evidence, the village planning process drew participants from a wide range of the population and encouraged city staff to incorporate neighborhood concerns into citywide initiatives.

Professionalism in City Government

The shift to district-based city council elections did not undermine the professionalism of Phoenix city government. To the contrary, Phoenix has become a city noted for management excellence. Since the inauguration of districts, Phoenix has shared the Bertelsmann Prize for the best-run city in the world with Christchurch, New Zealand (1993); has been named the best-run city in the country by *Governing Magazine* (1990); by 2006 had received a Government Finance Officers Association Distinguished Budget Award for seventeen consecutive years; by 2007 had received an International City Management Association Award for Local Government Performance six years in a row; and, along with five other cities, has been named an "All American City" five times (three of these five awards were received after the city switched to district elections).[3] While there are literally dozens of other awards posted on the Phoenix website, the "All American City" award is notable because it recognizes the city's community-driven projects (Bommersbach 2009).

Early on, Phoenix displayed features characteristic of the "reinventing government" movement (such as "customer satisfaction") and was cited extensively by authors propounding this approach (Osborne and Gaebler 1992; Osborne and Plastrik 1997). Phoenix uses local planning committees, records in excess of seven hundred neighborhood associations, and conducts citizen attitude surveys (the city has conducted thirteen citywide citizen attitude surveys since 1985). The surveys are instructive; for example, although residents consistently rate Phoenix as a good place to live, a recent survey found a concern about police conduct. In line with other predominantly minority urban areas, residents are beginning to worry, a quarter disagreeing with the statement "The Phoenix Police Department treats all residents with respect" and 30 percent disagreeing with the statement "The Phoenix Police Department treats all residents fairly regardless of race" (Behavioral Research Center 2010, 5). This finding is noteworthy because earlier in the year a Phoenix police officer, in response to an intruder call, mistakenly detained a helpful neighbor; that neighbor was a member of the city council, and while the immediate neighborhood is disproportionately Anglo, the council member is African American. The incident was kept alive for quite some time by the press and no doubt prompted inclusion of some focused questions in the 2010 survey.

Phoenix's city manager has broad authority. Some observers expected Goddard to remove the incumbent manager and inaugurate a wholesale rebuilding of the city's administration when he became mayor. However, Goddard noted that the city manager at the time, Marvin Andrews, was the ideal city manager; he appeared to be conservative when he served conservative mayor-councils because policies were conservative. However, with changes at the top of the political structure, Andrews continued as he had before—that is, he worked diligently to implement council policy directives, and he happily worked in the background leaving mayors free to develop a strong public profile. Andrews served as city manager for thirteen years. In 1986 *City and State Magazine* named him the best city manager in the United States; the International City Management Association and the National Academy of Public Administration also recognized him with major awards. In short, Phoenix had developed a highly regarded management structure, with a reputation for nonpartisanship that endured when elections brought a change in policy direction.

Neighborhoods

Under Mayor Goddard and City Manager Andrews, the Neighborhood Services Department (NSD) was created in 1992. Goddard reports having gotten the idea for such a department during a visit to Chicago, during the mayoralty of Harold Washington, when neighborhood services occupied a prominent and highly visible place in the city hall agenda. Phoenix's department received a broad mandate—do what needs to be done—and considerable latitude. With council support, responsibility for implementation was given to the city manager. Prior to the 1980s, there had been little input from neighborhoods. The transition to the district electoral system, the mayor's and the council's interest in neighborhood concerns, the focus on village planning, the end of the Phoenix 40's electoral influence, and the rise of labor unions came together to bring neighborhoods into more prominence. Though neighborhood groups had grown in importance and become more of a force throughout the 1980s, they were typically reactive, responding to issues that others put on the agenda.

In the late 1980s, in a notable policy shift, the city finally began housing-code enforcement. Phoenix had done little prior to that time, as code enforcement went against long-held values, and it was, and is, expensive. Furthermore, in a young city, the problem of housing decay was a new concern. Still, there was increasing public awareness that conditions were changing. "'New' cities also deteriorate," proclaimed an editorial in the *Phoenix Gazette* in 1986 (April 30); the paper ran articles on a failed county government weatherization program and the spread of deterioration to the point that 22 percent of the housing in Phoenix was blighted (May 7, 1986).

Initially, the council did not support code enforcement. However, the emerging problems of housing deterioration brought a shift in attitudes. As a case in point, the then councilman John Nelson, who represented the Maryvale community, was a conservative who at first was concerned about intrusive government interfering with property rights. However, when Maryvale started to deteriorate—seemingly all at once—he became an advocate for stronger housing-code enforcement. NSD staff cast code enforcement under the rubric of safety and public health, and a council that had approved early efforts with mixed feelings became supporters of a more intense enforcement effort. NSD became one of the fastest-growing units in city government.

At the same time, the city had undertaken an ambitious downtown redevelopment effort that included a spate of new construction projects, including a new civic center, a new city hall, a baseball stadium, and more. However, the hopes for downtown commercial revitalization were frustrated. The collapse in the real estate market in the early 1990s removed the optimism and investment capital that were plentiful during the 1980s. Square One, a block in the heart of downtown that was targeted in the 1980s for redevelopment, never overcame legal and economic obstacles. It was cleared for a parking lot in 1992. Sustained downtown development did not come until fifteen years later with the opening of a light-rail system and the creation of a new campus for Arizona State University, a new branch of the University of Arizona medical school (in a location that adjoined one of the target neighborhoods in this study), and biotech research facilities.

The local political climate shifted further toward neighborhood concerns in the 1990s. Goddard argued that his administration had been an exception to the norm: "Phoenicians have traditionally chosen a mayor that essentially keeps the lid on for the business community. They [Phoenix mayors] don't rock the boat, they don't cause a tremendous amount of waves and they don't really do much, if anything."[4] Large-scale development projects were at a standstill because of the economy. At the same time, the focus of attention in neighborhood associations changed. Competing candidates for the mayor's office in a special election in 1994 offered only modest proposals; with no big projects in the works, public safety emerged as a key neighborhood concern. Skip Rimsza, who enjoyed the support of the business community, defeated a neighborhood activist aligned with Goddard in the special election. Rimsza served as mayor until 2004, when term limits brought his time in office to an end.

Neighborhood Initiatives

With neighborhood concerns institutionalized in city government through the NSD, during the 1990s a new initiative emerged from city staff that focused on distressed neighborhoods and offered a proactive approach to deal with crime. In 1993 Maryann Ustick was recruited to Phoenix's NSD from Virginia Beach, Virginia, whose neighborhood programs were considered to be a model. Ustick pushed for targeted and comprehensive efforts to turn around struggling neighborhoods and developed a rationale for targeting neighborhood revitalization efforts. Working from the base of designated redevelopment areas, NSD sent staff to meet with neighborhood leaders, identify neighborhood needs and goals, and create mechanisms for communication between the neighborhoods and the city. The staff conducted a needs-based analysis and argued for making a long-term commitment to selected distressed neighborhoods. They also convinced the council that it would be easier to see progress if small areas were targeted. At the same time, the city created a fund for loans to cover the cost of home improvements required by code enforcement.

A targeted community revitalization strategy began to emerge, designated as the Neighborhood Initiative Area (NIA) program. The NIA program was approved by the city council in 1993 (though work in some neighborhoods had begun earlier). The program was designed to focus resources in a limited number of areas to provide concentrated and comprehensive neighborhood revitalization components, which included housing-code enforcement, blight abatement, housing rehabilitation and reconstruction, infill, neighborhood economic development, infrastructure improvements, community-based policing, neighborhood capacity building, and youth programs. The NIA program sought to have a substantial and sustained impact on both quality of life and physical conditions. The major source of funding was CDBG allocations, but federal housing programs and other federal grants (such as Weed and Seed) have also played a part. Federal funds have been augmented by resources from the city, other levels of government, nonprofit organizations, and the private sector.

In the NIA program the NSD employed a variety of programs, some targeted at youth and crime reduction, but revitalization efforts also included physical improvements and economic development to attract private reinvestment and increase the positive feelings of the residents about their financial and emotional investment in the neighborhood. Efforts in each neighborhood thus included blight elimination to remove unsafe buildings, which were seen as discouraging new investment and attracting criminal activity. Reluctance to turn to government gave way to housing rehabilitation and promotion of infill to stabilize ownership and increase property values. Under the banner of partnership with the residents, the city and neighborhood organizations joined with the private and nonprofit sectors to address a wide variety of needs.

Each NIA has an interdepartmental team, headed by a staff member employed by the program.[5] This team is empowered to "make things happen" and prevent breakdowns in cooperation across functional areas, and with the spending flexibility that the NIA program provides, the teams have become a resource with which individual city departments cooperate and from which they seek help. This practice has strengthened incentives for interdepartmental cooperation, and over time the scope of activity has broadened to include, and even initiate, activities close to but outside the officially designated neighborhoods.

There are cities where narrowly targeted neighborhood improvement programs would have resulted in fierce competition for resources. However, that was not the case in Phoenix when the NIA effort began. Rather, at first some council members were reluctant to admit that neighborhoods in their districts needed targeted improvement efforts. This mentality enhanced the operational autonomy of the NSD staff; city staffers were able to target resources to increase the likelihood that improvements would be clearly evident.

The NSD selected six neighborhoods for concentrated revitalization activities. To select NIAs, NSD staff reviewed data that included (but were not necessarily limited to) existing commitments and staff assigned to the area, other resources to leverage in the area, neighborhood organizational capacity and activity level, geographic spread, need, potential for success, ongoing funding commitments, and owner-occupancy rates. Staffers acknowledged that some science and a good deal of art were used in the selection process. However, the idea from the beginning was to develop a plan with the area residents so they could help define "success." Staff explained to the council that these were long-term commitments to targeted neighborhoods.

Two NIA communities, Garfield and South Phoenix Village, are discussed in detail below. In keeping with the city staff's long-term commitment, these neighborhoods were targeted by a series of interventions over time. Both were designated as NIAs. The census tracts composing the South Phoenix Village and Garfield NIAs had CDBG-defined poverty rates of over 50 percent. Later, these same areas were designated as Neighborhood Redevelopment Areas, which provided the city with additional tools to encourage revitalization. Most recently, both neighborhoods were targeted to receive Neighborhood Stabilization Program funds in response to the serious foreclosure problems that plagued Phoenix with the onset of the Great Recession.

Although both neighborhoods are distressed, Garfield has superior market appeal because it adjoins downtown and is more likely to attract investment. Although Garfield was not fully integrated into downtown planning, the effort to improve the neighborhood and reduce crime was undertaken in part so that the neighborhood's distress would not threaten downtown development. By contrast, South Phoenix Village is three miles southeast of downtown; the neighborhood's primary appeal is its proximity to the river and the mountains. Recent decades have seen the city undertake efforts to enhance these natural assets.

The two neighborhoods selected for in-depth analysis are poorer than the other NIAs. Garfield has an exceptionally high proportion of Latinos, and the African American population is higher in South Phoenix Village than it is elsewhere in the city. Like other NIAs, the designated areas are relatively small.

City officials initiated the various revitalization efforts by holding community meetings. All property owners in the designated area were notified by mail of the initial meeting. At these meetings, community stakeholders identified priority issues and goals for reaching their collective vision of how the neighborhood should be revitalized. Meetings continued on a monthly basis to discuss these issues and goals and refine them into a strategy. As the strategy developed, city staff members worked with the residents and other interested parties to offer a package of funding resources and programs to address neighborhood problems.

As part of the development of the NIA strategies, the city evaluated land use and commercial and residential property conditions. City staff visited businesses in the neighborhoods to assess their needs for security, physical rehabilitation or upgrading of their buildings, and financing or technical assistance for ongoing operations. Once this information was gathered, city staff members from the Community and Economic Development Department and the NSD met with interested businesses to explain the available resources and how to access these resources. City staff members worked with business owners to identify barriers to investment in the neighborhoods, including security, blighting influences, obsolete infrastructure, outdated platting, and environmental contamination.

In each of the NIAs, a unique redevelopment or revitalization strategy was created and approved by the city council. Annual implementation strategies and funding recommendations for CDBG and HOME funds are developed in partnership with neighborhood organizations. The city staff regards the rehabilitation of owner-occupied properties in the NIAs as the most essential component of neighborhood revitalization. In their view rehabilitation efforts stabilize and increase homeownership, foster neighborhood pride, remove blight, augment improvements to the neighborhood's infrastructure, and strengthen the capacity of neighborhood organizations. The approach taken is based on the premise that once revitalization efforts begin to yield visible improvements, private investment returns to the neighborhood, residents take better care of their properties, and housing values increase.

Garfield

The Garfield NIA covers one square mile and is bounded by an interstate highway to the north. By any reasonable standard, Garfield is one of the most distressed neighborhoods in Phoenix. According to 1990 figures cited in Garfield's neighborhood plan (City of Phoenix, Planning Department, 1992), approximately eight thousand people resided in Garfield, 88 percent of whom were low or moderate income (low income is defined as 50 percent or less of the Maricopa County median household income; moderate income is between 50 percent and 80 percent of the county's median income). Although there was some sound and affordable housing in the area, the quality of housing stock generally declined between 1970 and 1990. A windshield survey of housing in Garfield conducted by the Planning Department estimated that more than one-fourth of the existing housing was in need of major repair. In 1990 housing vacancy rates were higher in Garfield (17.6 percent) than was true citywide (12.3 percent). The proportion of owner-occupied housing in Garfield was only 30.0 percent, compared with a then citywide rate of 51.2 percent. Social and economic distress was also evident in Garfield. Compared with citywide proportions, people residing in Garfield were more likely to be unemployed and to receive some form of public assistance. Demographically, the area was approximately 78 percent Hispanic, 3 percent African American, and 5 percent Native American.

The Garfield neighborhood was known for drug and violent gang activity. Prior to NIA designation, public safety was a serious concern. Goddard reported that when he was mayor, the police had told him that he needed to either tear the neighborhood down or make a serious effort to clean it up. With the issue of the future of Garfield put before him by the police, Goddard and city administrators were also pressured by neighborhood residents. Some in the Latino community had lived in the neighborhood for generations. They and others, many of whom had spent their entire lives in Garfield, wanted their neighborhood preserved for its residents.

Subsequent to NIA designation, a redevelopment plan for Garfield was approved by the city council in 1999. Garfield's designation as an official Neighborhood Redevelopment Area allowed the city to use the power of eminent domain, which facilitated blight elimination and land assembly for commercial development. A special Garfield focus was on strategic acquisition of vacant lots for new single-family housing. The neighborhood's vision was for Garfield to become a stable, multicultural, mixed-income community with convenient shopping and retail services. This was to be accomplished by enhancing homeownership, restoring historic structures, making property improvements, cleaning up the neighborhood, and reducing crime (City of Phoenix 1999).

For the first decade of revitalization work in Garfield, there was little economic activity close to the target area. However, the expanding economic activity downtown associated with university and research development along the western border of Garfield, which is adjacent to downtown, and the light-rail line that passes two blocks from the southern border of the neighborhood may change this situation. These developments came late to Garfield and were not in place as an initial prompt for action.

An earlier, unsuccessful effort to locate the Arizona Cardinals football stadium where the research facilities ultimately were located could have had negative effects on Garfield. When the site was being considered, land was acquired in the event that the site would be chosen. When the stadium moved to Glendale, Arizona State University and other groups took advantage of the acquisitions. The educational and medical developments were made possible and, combined with the development of light rail, hold promise of benefit to Garfield. As economic conditions improve, it is likely that this area may face significant pressures for gentrification. It is designated as a historic neighborhood and eligible for incentives for improvement of existing residences. A longer-term goal is to see Garfield take its place on the National Register of Historic Places, an action that would trigger further incentives for rehabilitation and preservation.

Current revitalization efforts include many different elements. The downtown Arizona State University campus has opened a charter school in Garfield. Weed and Seed funding has allowed the city to keep more police officers in the neighborhood, and the crime rate in Garfield has begun to fall; perhaps more importantly, the perception of residents is that the neighborhood has become safer. The Police Department has coordinated with the Garfield neighborhood team to address crime issues in the area by conducting several "demand reduction" operations to reduce drug activity. The area has also cooperated with the city prosecutor's office, supported by federal funds, to fund a community prosecution program that assists efforts to address rental properties with crime and blight problems. AmeriCorps volunteers worked in the neighborhood and assisted the development of the community-based Garfield Organization. Housing code enforcement is now a major goal. The neighborhood has a center providing information on various programs, including qualifying for the federal Earned Income Tax Credit program. Park improvements and youth programs are also part of the Garfield improvement strategy.

Through a combination of code enforcement, rehabilitation of existing structures, and new housing construction, the condition of housing has been substantially improved. At present it is estimated that only about 10 percent of Garfield properties are in need of substantial repair (Dantico, Guhathakurta, and Mushkatel 2007). In 2005 a major grocery store (Ranch Market) and a restaurant that cater to the Hispanic community were opened on the eastern boundary of Garfield in a remodeled former Kmart store. More than three hundred Garfield residents have new jobs, and more than $8.5 million in leveraged private investment has gone into the project.

Although 2015 is the expected completion date for the Garfield NIA program, some activities are already winding down. The city initially announced that its efforts in Garfield were being scaled back, and staff would be moved elsewhere. With fresh approaches in the offing, no new NIA neighborhoods have been identified for the period 2010–15 (City of Phoenix 2010, 71–73). However, more recently, in response to the foreclosure crisis, the city has targeted Garfield for the Neighborhood Stabilization Program, using program funds to bring vacant or foreclosed property back on the market and to demolish blighted structures.

Meanwhile, elements of revitalization success have brought new challenges. Garfield faces a future with increased prospects of outside investment to provide housing opportunities for persons who work in the downtown area or elsewhere in the region and commute via the new light-rail system. Historic-preservation efforts have been expanded, which can make property improvements more complicated and expensive because of requirements to maintain the original appearance and use appropriate materials. These changes could threaten the cohesion of the neighborhood and bring in large numbers of people who may not be committed to preserving its character as an affordable residential area with a strong Latino orientation. On the other hand, gaining historic-district status would prevent redevelopment and replacement of existing houses with larger ones and, perhaps more importantly, give the city more authority and a larger, more expansive toolbox from which to draw.

South Phoenix Village

South Phoenix Village was designated as an NIA in 1999. Prior to the launching of the NIA program, revitalization efforts were first stimulated when the Southwest Leadership Foundation purchased Key's Market in 1989. This drug and crime haven was converted into the KEYS (Knowledge, Education, Youth, and Society) Community Center. The center provides preschool and after-school programs, a youth development program for at-risk and adjudicated young people aged fourteen to twenty-one, GED prep, classes in computer literacy, job readiness and life skills training, and social services.

Bounded by the Salt River on the north, South Phoenix Village is somewhat isolated from downtown. Land in the community is used for a mixture of residential, commercial, and industrial activities, with a substantial proportion being vacant; detrimental land uses include outdoor storage of junked cars and appliances (City of Phoenix, Planning Department 2001).

NIA designation formalized the city's commitment to preserving the neighborhood while also working to upgrade it, particularly in terms of enforcing appropriate land use, eliminating blight, and improving the housing stock. At the time of NIA designation, 1990 census figures showed that approximately 4,200 people lived in South Phoenix Village. In comparison to citywide statistics, the village showed signs of distress. Four of five households were low or moderate income, and the unemployment rate was over 20 percent. Land use in the area (according to a 1988 survey) was majority residential, with approximately one-fifth of land in the area used for commercial or industrial purposes and one-fourth vacant (City of Phoenix, Planning Department 2001).

Lacking the locational advantages of Garfield, South Phoenix Village posed a different set of challenges. For many years the area fell well outside the bounds of incorporation. When many of the older houses were built, there were no operational building codes. The neighborhood is adjacent to the area in which the first subdivision constructed by black residents was built in the late 1940s. In a 1994 housing survey, the problems in the South Phoenix NIA were much more severe than in other areas surveyed, with three-quarters of the housing units in need of major repairs (compared with 23 percent of the units in all census tracts surveyed) and with only 3 percent of the dwellings meeting city standards. As was the case in Garfield, a combination of code enforcement, rehabilitation of existing structures, and new housing construction has contributed to housing improvement in South Phoenix Village. In a follow-up study in 2004, only 7 percent of the area's housing units needed substantial repairs (compared with 5 percent of the full sample), and the proportion of units that met code requirements had jumped to 33 percent. Nevertheless, the 2008 economic downturn put most plans for new construction on hold.

South Phoenix Village is a small NIA, about a square mile, and city planning has extended to a wider area to make use of some assets from nature. Close to the NIA is the Rio Salado Restoration Habitat. For decades, the riverbed, which was dry most of the year, was an illegal garbage dump that physically and psychologically separated South Phoenix Village from the rest of the city. Beginning in 2001 as a combined effort involving the city, the US Army Corps of Engineers, and the Audubon Society, this project has cleaned up the river, restored natural habitat, and added trails for hiking and biking. Construction is complete and today there is a multiuse pedestrian trail adjacent to South Phoenix Village. The long-range plan is to connect the Rio Salado Restoration Habitat to South Mountain Park.

The NIA program was developed and sold as a program in which small areas would see progress, and visible progress would encourage ongoing improvements and continued city support. While the program was generally popular with the council, there was concern that residents would be unable to afford repairs to their units and that proactive code enforcement would undermine efforts to increase the proportion of residents who owned their homes. City staff responded to this concern by making low- or no-interest loans available to residents; the loans were forgivable over time if owners continued to occupy the units. Originally, federal funds were used for this purpose, but eventually, alternative sources were identified. According to former city manager Frank Fairbanks, the city has spent hundreds of millions of dollars in South Phoenix Village. In an interview, he said that South Phoenix Village "has probably cost more money than everywhere else combined." In that same interview, he gave Councilman Cody Williams credit for pushing for private-sector engagement in South Phoenix Village. There is a wide consensus that this involvement was helpful, as was the nearby Matthew Henson HOPE VI redevelopment project.

Initially, the city put a "public safety" face on all its efforts, especially those aimed at improving housing conditions. From the early 1990s into the 2000s (and likely even now) there was tension because some saw distinctions between the rights of property owners and neighborhood improvement interests; where some saw the city involved in encouraging (even requiring) property maintenance, others saw the city using Gestapo-like tactics on property owners. Recognizing that courts are expensive and not generally a good strategy for gaining compliance in civil cases, the city encouraged strategies likely to secure voluntary compliance. Staff argued that it was appropriate to make repairs because owners wanted to be seen as "good citizens" or sometimes because "it's futile to object." In the city extreme antigovernment sentiments have declined over time. And in the past five years efforts have evolved to the point where the courts can be used when necessary. Judges have become educated about the issues; there are neighborhood prosecutors, and neighbors are often willing to attend court hearings to support compliance efforts.

A redevelopment plan for part of South Phoenix Village was first adopted in 1989, even before NIA designation. However, in 2000 the redevelopment area was expanded to make its borders the same as the NIA. The redevelopment plan's central tenets were to stabilize existing viable residential areas and to reclaim declining areas by removing structurally substandard buildings and other blighting influences; to rationalize land uses in terms of lot size, platting, and buffers; to encourage redevelopment through land assembly and disposition; to create suitable and affordable housing; to provide adequate public facilities and infrastructure; and to bring back a sense of neighborhood and community.

The hope is to encourage large-scale infill housing and commercial development that will enhance property values in the NIA and offer job opportunities. Recent economic conditions have not been favorable for expanded development. For now, efforts rely heavily on demolition to remove some of the remaining problems, but without a strong economic upturn for the city, the market is proving to be a weak support for further revitalization. The recent planning move to include the Rio Salado Restoration Habitat is an indication that small revitalization areas can be handicapped by their size if not accompanied by a broader city strategy of revitalization.[6] Distance from the city center can be a disadvantage, whereas proximity to the center carries not only an advantage but also a gentrification threat.

Challenges to Revitalizing Neighborhoods

In a number of ways progress in Garfield and South Phoenix Village has been compromised. First, the incredible climb in the housing market prior to 2007 conspired to undercut some of the successes. As Garfield looked more interesting to potential buyers and the book value of houses climbed, some residents took the profit from housing appreciation and ran, while other residents refinanced in order to have cash and now find themselves owing more than their homes are worth. Jerome Miller, former head of the NIA program, reported that the city urged property owners to be cautious, and he refused to waive restrictions on borrowing more money on top of the loans that would be "forgiven" by the city if residents remained in their homes. Some residents borrowed enough money to pay off the city loan and have cash as well. Miller noted that the city was buying some homes in Garfield and South Phoenix Village for the second time.

Second, finding resources to finance neighborhood revitalization has been a continuing challenge. Total NIA program funds have grown over recent years from $29.7 million in fiscal year (FY) 2004–5 to $105.4 million in FY 2010–11. Money from the city's general fund has remained almost constant; $12.4 million in FY 2004–5 and $11.0 million in FY 2010–11. However, CDBG funds have more than doubled, moving from $13.9 million in FY 2004–5 to $30.2 million in FY 2010–11. The most significant increase in support is the result of state and federal grants, which grew from $1.8 million in FY 2004–5 to $59.1 million in FY 2010–11. Any change in federal priorities is likely to severely impact the NIA program.

Finally, Phoenix is under severe financial stress. The state legislature is unlikely to move to enhance revenue streams by increasing taxes, but without additional revenue the picture is worse than bleak. The state faces a huge revenue shortfall. In addition to measures already implemented (such as eliminating all-day kindergarten), programs like the NIA are likely to experience continuing budgetary pressures.

The state and the city continue to be plagued by the housing crisis, high unemployment, and responses to Arizona's anti-immigration measures. The state was expected to end 2010 with a record number of home foreclosures; this was the third consecutive year in which foreclosures in the area set national records. From January through November 2010, nearly 66,000 owners lost their homes to foreclosure. With the crash, home prices declined 50 percent from their peak in 2007. Two-thirds of the state's foreclosures occurred in Phoenix. Estimates claimed that as many as 80,000 area homes shifted to rentals occupied by the people who used to own them.[7]

Phoenix is essentially a poster child for what went wrong with the housing market. In one year alone the median home price in Phoenix declined 18 percent, a one-year price change as great as any experienced in a metropolitan area (Anderson, Konig, and Dempsey 2011). When data are examined by zip code, neither South Phoenix Village nor Garfield found itself with the lowest median home prices; this dubious distinction is held by neighborhoods on the west side of Phoenix. Both Garfield and South Phoenix Village are, however, among the neighborhoods with the highest proportion of sales that are foreclosure sales.

Institutionalizing Neighborhood Improvement Efforts

Phoenix illustrates how council-manager governments operate, and how the structure of government can make a difference in local policymaking. Neighborhood revitalization in Phoenix bears the influence of the city's socioeconomic and political setting, but the workings of the policy are very much a product of the city's professional staff and the mode they developed for working with neighborhood groups. Although something of an outlier among large American cities in terms of the scope of the policy role played by professional managers, Phoenix highlights the extent to which savvy career administrators can make major contributions to neighborhood policy, even in places undergoing political and demographic change.[8]

In Phoenix, the NIA program by no means encompasses the total neighborhood revitalization effort. HOPE VI, Weed and Seed initiatives other than the one in Garfield, and the Rio Salado Restoration are all programs under way in non-NIA communities. Although the original focus on

NIA projects is now giving way, the program offers a valuable insight into the Phoenix story. The neighborhood cases show that a crucial element of neighborhood revitalization in Phoenix has been the ongoing and consistent effort of the city's administrative staff to direct resources to the areas where they are acutely needed. Although Phoenix has not identified new NIAs, the city is committed to those currently in existence.

However, even as the NIA program was winding down, Garfield and South Phoenix continued to be targeted by new initiatives, bringing new resources and tools into the mix. Finally, when federal resources became available to respond to the foreclosure crisis, city staff opportunistically and consistently targeted housing in Garfield and South Phoenix Village for local interventions financed by stimulus funds. The onetime wariness about federal programs is little in evidence in Phoenix today, and the measured moves made by city administrators played a large part in that shift. Phoenix experienced a remarkable turnaround from its earlier unwillingness to adopt a housing code to a willingness to employ comprehensive, multipronged efforts to revitalize distressed neighborhoods. And the shift has proved durable.

Greg Stanton, who was elected mayor in November 2011, has acted on campaign promises and expanded his commitment to transparency and neighborhood policy. Shortly after his inauguration, he created a "Neighborhood Advisory Committee," whose twenty-nine members are to provide counsel to the mayor on neighborhood issues. In announcing committee appointments, the mayor wrote, "Phoenix is only as strong as each of its neighborhoods, so it is vitally important to stay directly connected with neighborhood leaders and their ideas and concerns."[9]

With its powerful administrative arm, city government has thus institutionalized a neighborhood revitalization policy that has sustained its focus over time. Phoenix has a neighborhood department that has extensive interaction with its constituency base, in-depth management experience in neighborhood programs and their funding, and a widely accepted approach of targeting specific areas to facilitate comprehensive efforts that are sustained over time. The original six NIAs have been succeeded by another generation of initiatives, employing the same strategy of targeting areas and addressing multiple concerns, including housing improvement, public safety, economic development, youth services, and other social-policy efforts. The initial concentration of effort in a small area heightens the chances of making a visible difference. Of course, it was the absence of vast areas of concentrated poverty and distress that made such targeting feasible in Phoenix.

Today, given the continued aging of early housing developments and new problems arising, small scale has become less appropriate. With the neighborhood program now firmly established, the strategy of small projects of intense treatment has given way to one of intervention commensurate with the scale of connected problems. South Phoenix Village has come in for some rethinking, but the clear break from the original strategy is the large, multipart project in west Phoenix. The city's fifty-two-square-mile West Phoenix Revitalization Area—though markedly different from the NIAs—is a tribute to the respect the earlier program has garnered. The West Phoenix Revitalization Area is a council initiative supported by bond funds. The program has a citizen steering committee, and city staffers have a "coach," just as NIA interdepartmental staff groups had coaches.

Phoenix has learned that money is necessary but not sufficient to support revitalization; neighborhood involvement is imperative, as is interdepartmental cooperation. The route Phoenix has traveled in reaching this stage is worth examination. Professionalized city management is a key feature of the governing process. Under business protection against any return to ward politics and its reliance on patronage, professional city management gained strength and developed a capacity that was both autonomous and robust. As the professionalism of the city's administrative arm was developed, it proved not to be a captive of its business sponsors. However, political realities do set limits on administrative autonomy. City elections were at the center of the shift in policy direction.[10] The city's growing diversity and the emergence of a new generation of political activists formed an essential foundation for change.

The shift in policy was not revolutionary. The turn from a narrow, business-oriented policy of growth to an increased acceptance of government-led problem solving was incremental. Crime reduction, for instance, was prominent in developing a case for neighborhood revitalization. Property rights were handled gingerly. The launch of the NIA program was deliberately small in scale and backed by a promise of showing results. In general, NIA staff members kept the program's profile low and stressed that it was being funded with federal money—even though substantial service contributions came from various city departments. When some council members pressed staff to say how much money was devoted to the NIA in their district, they were told that no pot of money was designated for any given area. Hence, no pressure built to distribute NIA funds among council districts.

The dampening effect of an economic "bust" of the kind that Phoenix has suffered reminds us that a shift in electoral balance, even when combined with a strong management capacity, still has to cope with a sometimes-fickle and always-unpredictable market. Even with its conservative past, Phoenix has found a way to combine economic development with social concerns. But in pursuing such a path, the city is not freed from market constraints. The contrast between Garfield and South Phoenix Village reminds us of the large role played by the market.

Although Phoenix was initially resistant even to having a housing code, by the 1980s the buildup of unaddressed problems opened the way to new thinking among an increasingly diverse populace. The city's "old politics" of immediate solutions (expressway construction, annexation, and total clearance for a distressed neighborhood) was revealed to be inadequate for a maturing, postindustrial city and its problems. With professional planners and managers in place, the stage was set for longer-term consideration of the causes and consequences of neighborhood problems. Once electoral politics moved beyond the old dogmas, a more open-ended approach to problem solving became possible and was enriched by professional knowledge. An abundance of fresh program ideas was soon circulating. For Phoenix it was the city's professional staff who fed this stream; resources, not ideology, were (and remain) the primary constraint.

Power is less concentrated in Phoenix than it was in the days when the CGC controlled access to electoral office. Although business has suffered some significant defeats, such as its unsuccessful opposition to district elections, and the city's policy agenda has evolved far beyond the minimum-services stance the business sector once championed, Phoenix business has hardly become powerless; it is part of an array of interests that make up the political order of Phoenix and its surrounding region. The remarkable feature of Phoenix politics is that a policy of neighborhood revitalization has an institutional center that gains focus and draws energy from the city's NSD. The fragmentation of effort and diffusion of energy characteristic of neighborhood policy in many other places are counteracted to a substantial degree by a department embedded in a highly regarded municipal government. Unlike Chicago's neighborhoods, those in Phoenix are not forced to navigate between two distinct political worlds. Unlike neighborhoods in Baltimore, those in Phoenix have an ongoing center of support—professional staff, technical assistance, ideas, information, institutional memory, and more—to which they can turn and draw inspiration.

Notes

1. See http://www.gplinc.org/about/our-history.aspx.
2. Terry Goddard, personal interview on September 27, 2011.
3. See http://phoenix.gov/awards/index.html.

4.   This quotation and others in this chapter with no published reference are from confidential personal interviews conducted by the authors.

5.   NIA had full-time staff members as a program of NSD. NIA staff worked in "teams" that often included members from other governmental departments. Team members from departments other than NSD were not reassigned, but their work assignments were rewritten to include support for an NIA team as a part of their "normal work assignment." In this way multiple departments had a stake in NIA projects. NSD is now so much a part of Phoenix's municipal culture that when another department plans neighborhood-related action, it will typically contact NSD for suggestions, recommendations, and support.

6.   In this case, the city's Water Services Department provided a complementary effort by accelerating implementation of the restoration project in support of the aim to revitalize the South Phoenix NIA. In short, there was a cross-department understanding that the two efforts were linked, leading to policy coordination.

7.   Bob Christie, "Arizona Sets Another Foreclosure Record in 2010," December 31, 2010, www.victoriaadvocate.com/news/2010/dec/31/bc-az-foreclosures-arizona1st -ld_writethru.

8.   To place Phoenix in comparative perspective in terms of the policy role played by professional administrators, see Mouritzen and Svara 2002.

9.   Mayor Stanton quoted in Cone Sexton 2012. See also Bui 2012.

10. The switch to district elections opened the way for a surge in participation. The first district-election campaign saw 120 candidates for city council.

SIX

City Fragmentation and Neighborhood Connections: The Political Dynamics of Community Revitalization in Los Angeles

ELLEN SHIAU, JULIET MUSSO,
AND JEFFEREY M. SELLERS

Los Angeles is a global city with widespread pockets of severe distress. Neighborhood policies reflect the city's hyperfragmented polity and diffuse power distribution. More than most other cities, Los Angeles lacks a main current of revitalization. Rather, multiple strands exist largely independently of one another, as actors, relationships, and revitalization strategies vary significantly across neighborhoods. However, there are some strong, shared, citywide experiences, such as the city's role as an immigration gateway. Moreover, major outbreaks of civil violence in 1965 and 1992 were traumatic for all segments of the city. Additional perturbation came when the city faced a secession movement, which resulted in city charter reforms that strengthened the mayor's office and created a neighborhood council system, while decentralizing planning decisions. Although the city has undergone a broadened understanding of the aims of development, neighborhood revitalization initiatives remain widely disconnected. As home to LAANE (Los Angeles Alliance for a New Economy), an organization that has spearheaded coalitions of labor, community organizations, and environmentalists around a large and historic community benefits agreement, Los Angeles is a place of significant innovation—fed in part by increasingly politicized immigrant communities. Yet no citywide neighborhood vision has emerged, and there is much reason for each neighborhood to mobilize its own network of players. The thinly resourced system of Neighborhood Councils has failed to become a force and is more a channel for homeowner interests than for the concerns of residents in distressed communities. With fragmentation unchecked, substantial citywide forms of collaboration have yet to gather momentum.

Neighborhood politics in Los Angeles takes place within a highly fragmented setting where policy is hotly contested and at times shaped by outbreaks of violence. Los Angeles does not have a broad-based neighborhood revitalization policy that integrates efforts across policy domains, invests significant resources in communities, and targets distressed neighborhoods. Instead, efforts to address neighborhood distress most often arise in ad hoc fashion in response to particular opportunities or in reaction to community outrage. Historically, these efforts have emphasized market-driven approaches such as infrastructure development, business investment, and lending programs. The scarcity of citywide and multisectoral neighborhood initiatives reflects the city's institutional, geographic, and social fragmentation. In neighborhood matters, the city council is a major player, where norms of deference empower individual council members. Political action thus requires the resources and capacity to mobilize constituencies to gain the attention of the local council member.

At the same time, as a primary port of entry for immigrants, Los Angeles has experienced significant demographic changes over the past four decades. During its transition to the postindustrial age, the city simultaneously shifted from being predominately white with highly segregated pockets of African Americans and Latinos to its current status, where Latinos are the largest single ethnic group and (in 2005) were instrumental in electing the city's first Latino mayor since 1872. These population dynamics have created a complex politics of race and class, with some neighborhoods experiencing significant tension as they change. However, the city also has experienced a new wave of social movements as immigrants have been mobilized by labor and community organizers working to include broader social aims in development policies.

Although business and developer interests have historically dominated policymaking in Los Angeles, with a weakening of its growth regime the city has experienced a rise in grassroots innovations in neighborhood policy. Community actors have sometimes been successful in mobilizing and capitalizing upon opportunities to advance their interests and address their concerns. A recent factor on the scene is the citywide neighborhood council system. In the late 1990s, residential pressure and the threat of secession led to the initiation of a neighborhood council system that has increased the residential voice but has so far done little to advance the interests of the disadvantaged (the system tends to focus on issues surrounding local land use and traffic, issues dear to middle-class homeowners). Nevertheless, the neighborhood councils have broadened participation in community-oriented activities and helped to further local and regional political networks that may serve as resources for future mobilizations.

Community benefits agreements (CBAs) are a development in neighborhood policymaking in Los Angeles that has contributed to neighborhood gains. CBAs attained national prominence in May 2001 when the Los Angeles Alliance for a New Economy (LAANE) led a coalition of community, environmental, and union organizations in negotiating a very large and historic agreement with the Anschutz Entertainment Group during its construction of L.A. Live, a $2.5 billion entertainment complex in the Staples Center area. The movement toward CBAs as a community development tool has shifted community mobilization beyond a defensive stance to encompass efforts to pursue and negotiate direct community gains from development activities. While neighborhood councils and especially CBAs have enhanced the likelihood that communities gain from development activities, these initiatives have limitations: neighborhood councils have not integrated neighborhood interests broadly or served as a venue for facilitating neighborhood revitalization; and in Los Angeles most CBAs are connected to high-profile projects in parts of the city with market appeal. Thus, because of the lack of a more comprehensive social-investment strategy, selected neighborhoods have experienced gains while others are left wanting.

In the absence of a more strategic approach to neighborhood improvement or more inclusive avenues for community representation, neighborhood revitalization in Los Angeles is likely to continue to involve fragmented, ad hoc, and often reactive initiatives that vary from neighborhood to neighborhood. However, within neighborhoods, local actors are more likely to take advantage of the opportunities that do occur to influence government action and private investment, with varying approaches, actors, alliances, and levels of community capacity. Such a finding indicates that there is not one characteristic pattern of neighborhood politics but *many* patterns across Los Angeles.

Geographic, Economic, and Social Fragmentation

As the second-most populous US city, Los Angeles had an estimated 2010 population of 3.79 million spread across some 470 square miles in more than a hundred distinct communities. The sheer scale of the city contributes to its fragmented character. The territory of the central city (less than that of Phoenix but double that of Chicago) extends irregularly into the northern expanses of the San Fernando Valley, west to Venice Beach, and south to the Port of Los Angeles, which is attached to the city by a narrow strip. The city and its surrounding metropolitan area lack the central-city/ periphery development pattern that is associated with industrial era cities such as Baltimore and Chicago. The origins of economic fragmentation trace to early twentieth-century patterns of industrial and residential location, which—buttressed by zoning, transit networks, and other policies— placed key facilities for manufacturing and such activities as film production in a variety of locations around the region (Hise 2002; Fogelson 1967). The city is part of an urbanized metropolitan region of 18 million people that is a major hub in the global economy.

Early growth in Los Angeles was shaped by a tightly knit coalition of powerful local businessmen who were responsible for attaining state infrastructure investment that fostered rapid economic development (Erie 2004). However, by the late twentieth century, several factors contributed to a weakening of this growth coalition. Globalization and economic restructuring have fragmented the elite power base and enhanced opportunities for community resistance and influence (Purcell 2000; Saito 2012). The economy of the central city and its close surrounds fractured into a variety of subregional and local industrial concentrations. The region developed strong internationally networked service and commercial sectors, and the role of manufacturing enterprises diminished in relative terms. Globalization, reinforced by the growing importance of international economic ties among immigrant-run firms, drew the strategic attention of business actors toward the Pacific Rim and away from coalition building within the region (Purcell 2000).

Patterns of disinvestment have occurred not only in historically African American neighborhoods in the southern center of the city but also in parts of East Los Angeles, neighborhoods adjacent to the Port of Los Angeles, and formerly industrial parts of the San Fernando Valley. As immigration intensified in the late twentieth century, many African American residents moved west and south into communities outside the city, and historically African American communities in South Los Angeles and the northeastern San Fernando Valley transitioned into predominantly Latino communities. Severe segregation (evident as early as 1965) has increased, including racial segregation of local schools (Ethington, Frey, and Myers 2001; Orfield, Siegel-Hawley, and Kucsera 2011). Moreover, contrary to the national pattern, concentrated poverty in the city has doubled in recent decades.

The result of these population dynamics is a city with complex spatial patterns of class, race, and ethnicity—and attendant social and racial tension. In particular, communities with proportionally higher Latino and African American populations are likely to experience significant distress. The 1965 Watts and 1992 South Los Angeles outbreaks of civil disorder show how deeply anger runs in some of the city's distressed communities. Despite the public investment that followed the 1965 Watts uprising, the conditions of Watts and many other South Los Angeles neighborhoods did not change significantly. Community frustration about neighborhood conditions flared again with the acquittal of four white Los Angeles Police Department (LAPD) officers in the videotaped beating of black motorist Rodney King in 1992. Following the 1992 collapse of civil order, city officials implemented a number of neighborhood policies to address distress in South Los Angeles. However, these policies had limited impact, and South Los Angeles remains one of the most distressed areas of the city.

Residential resistance to city politics has not been isolated to lower-income communities. While ultimately unsuccessful, the push toward secession catalyzed reform of the city charter and the creation of a citywide neighborhood council movement that further fragmented the politics around local land use and development. Thus, the city's urban form, rapid population change, and socioeconomic segregation isolate communities, supporting development of geographically diffuse political identities, a strong sense of competition for city resources, and continuing conflict over development.

Institutional Fragmentation

The formal institutional structure of Los Angeles exhibits significant fragmentation, with power shared among the city's relatively weak mayor, a fifteen-member city council elected through a nonpartisan ballot, and more than 240 mayoral-appointed city commissioners who govern city departments (Box and Musso 2004). This form of government dates to Progressive era charter reforms that sought to decentralize governance to prevent patronage politics and partisanship (Sonenshein 2004, 2006). In a city that has grown to almost 4 million, however, a fifteen-member council with districts the size of many cities can no longer be considered decentralized governance. Rather, council districts operate as fiefdoms in a political context dominated by regional interest groups, such as unions and chambers of commerce.

City council members historically have shaped land use and facilitated service delivery within their large and often-diverse districts, wielding substantial, if not unilateral, influence over a wide range of issues. In a massive city lacking the substructure of boroughs or other integrated service areas, services are poorly coordinated, and lack of communication within the city administrative apparatus is commonplace. Los Angeles has more than thirty service departments—from police to parks and recreation—headed by departmental general managers appointed by the mayor but vulnerable to removal by a two-thirds vote of the city council. City government's fragmentation is magnified by the broader institutional context of local government in California. Education is provided by the massive Los Angeles Unified School District, which contains not only the City of Los Angeles but numerous other cities and unincorporated communities in Los Angeles County. Public assistance, health, mental health, and other social services are primarily the purview of county government.

In the 1990s residential dissatisfaction fueled several reform measures. In 1993 a ballot initiative limited the tenure of the mayor and city council to two four-year terms (term limits subsequently were extended to twelve years for the city council). This was followed in short order by the emergence of the secession movement in the San Fernando Valley, Hollywood, and Harbor communities. In response, city officials initiated a charter reform process that spanned almost two years, ultimately producing the first major reform of the city's charter in decades. Although secession failed at the polls, the city's neighborhood council system, which emerged from charter reform, provides new venues for residential engagement and mobilization.

Among the most important agencies engaged in neighborhood policy are the Planning Department, the federally funded Housing Authority of the City of Los Angeles (HACLA), and the Community Redevelopment Agency (CRA), each of which has distinct governing arrangements and unique funding sources. The Planning Department is overseen by a relatively powerful decision-making commission and receives funding from the city's general fund. It has the responsibility of preparing, maintaining, and implementing the city's General Plan and thirty-five community plans, which guide housing, land use, transportation, and open-space decisions. The city's 9,300 public-housing units are owned and managed by HACLA.

Until recently the Goliath of neighborhood development was the CRA, which administered more than thirty redevelopment areas throughout the city. Relative to other city agencies, the CRA was resource rich by virtue of its access to locally generated resources in the form of Tax Increment Financing to be used within redevelopment project areas designated by the CRA board, mayor, and city council.[1] Although state redevelopment laws required evidence of blight, the definition was sufficiently broad that project areas experienced considerable variation in levels of distress. Historically an engine for economic growth, the CRA helped finance a number of large-scale projects, such as the massive Staples Center and L.A. Live complex that have made the southern edge of downtown Los Angeles a tourist destination.

The recent repeal of state community redevelopment policy has changed the local institutional landscape and contributed to uncertainty in neighborhood policymaking. In 2011 the California legislature and Governor Jerry Brown eliminated the state's four hundred redevelopment agencies as part of a deal to balance the state's budget. The Los Angeles City Council voted not to absorb the CRA. Instead, it created a new Economic Development Department and an accompanying nonprofit corporation to consolidate development services and spur new investment. While the role of the new department in neighborhood revitalization remains to be seen, initial discussions suggest that it may prioritize assisting distressed communities over traditional large-scale redevelopment projects.

Political Transitions and Neighborhood Policy

In Los Angeles neighborhood policy has followed a trajectory dominated by periods of economic development—often centered on big infrastructure projects rather than community-level priorities—interrupted by crises that brought greater attention to neighborhoods. During the post–World War II era, policymaking evolved from advocating large-scale development projects that mainly ignored and displaced local communities to a more disjointed and episodic approach in which the city pursued economic development with occasional periods of appeasement in response to episodes of community protest. Notable in this regard are the city's responses to the civil unrest of 1965 and 1992, the advent of bargaining for CBAs beginning in the 1990s, and the 1999 charter reform that instituted a neighborhood advisory council system.

As was true of many American cities participating in federal urban redevelopment programs, post–World War II policies centered on massive downtown redevelopment projects that involved residential displacement. The heavy cost paid by neighborhoods to advance the redevelopment agenda is exemplified by the 1960s redevelopment of the Bunker Hill neighborhood to create today's downtown Los Angeles and the 1950s redevelopment of Chavez Ravine into Dodger Stadium, projects that drastically reshaped the areas at the cost of substantial community displacement. During this period, the city consistently marginalized lower-income neighborhoods, failing to provide adequate public services while using a heavy-handed policing style that led to continued animosity between communities and the LAPD.

The hostility toward the LAPD in South Los Angeles neighborhoods both preceding and following the severe outbreak of civil disorder in Watts in 1965 has been credited with mobilizing the African American community to form an alliance with the Westside that ultimately propelled Mayor Tom Bradley, the city's first and only African American mayor, to victory in 1973 (Sonenshein 1994; Siegel 1997). Following the 1965 civil disturbances, the city invested in Watts, constructing a shopping center, the Martin Luther King Jr./Drew Medical Center, and the Alain Leroy Locke High School. Nevertheless, private disinvestment in the community continued over the ensuing decades, and both King/Drew hospital and Locke High School have struggled in the face of persistent poverty and crime.

Evolving Electoral Coalitions and Unrest in the Bradley Years

The election of Mayor Tom Bradley in 1973 was facilitated by the growing political mobilization of minority groups and signaled a shift toward a more progressive and multiracial style of governing (Sonenshein 1994). The Bradley administration channeled federal money into social programs, created greater opportunities for minorities through administrative appointments and city affirmative-action programs, and sought to attain greater civilian control over the police. However, the administration's focus on downtown redevelopment "cemented" its alliance with downtown business and labor interests, alienating poor, minority neighborhoods (Sonenshein 1994). As Josh Sides describes Bradley's policy: "In his unswerving commitment to make Los Angeles a 'World Class City,' Bradley diverted resources toward downtown redevelopment and away from projects aimed at expanding the affordable housing stock in the city or improving infrastructure in blighted neighborhoods" (2003, 194).

The 1992 civil disorder marked the unraveling of the Bradley regime. The six days of violence that occurred might have catalyzed a citywide public intervention to address community distress, but instead the city developed several discrete private-sector initiatives. For example, the "Rebuild LA" program, first headed by former baseball commissioner and US Olympic Committee chair Peter Ueberroth, ultimately brought together

$389 million in largely private-sector investments in manufacturing and retail. Nonetheless, the program was criticized for its failure to counter widespread disinvestment in distressed South Los Angeles neighborhoods (Modarres 1999).

Privatization and Community Mobilization during the Riordan Administration

With Bradley's electoral coalition in some disarray, the well-organized and wealthy Richard Riordan was elected mayor in 1993 on a platform that stressed a tough, probusiness approach to reform city government (Sonenshein 1994). Soon after his election Mayor Riordan confronted the devastating 1994 Northridge earthquake and the secession movement. The city continued a largely private-sector response to these crises. For example, in response to the 1992 breakdown in civil order, the city won a Supplemental Empowerment Zone (SEZ) designation through the federal Empowerment Zone (EZ) program, which provided about $435 million in grants and loan guarantees for a nineteen-square-mile area (J. Rubin and Stankiewicz 2001). The city implemented the SEZ through a largely private-sector approach, creating the Los Angeles Community Development Bank to facilitate business lending. Experiencing operating difficulties and lacking any significant social-service or human-capital effort, the bank did little to sustain community development and was phased out in 2003 (Modarres 1999; J. Rubin and Stankiewicz 2001).

Riordan also created a nonprofit organization, the Los Angeles Neighborhood Initiative, in 1994, utilizing funds from the Federal Transit Administration's Livable Communities Program to support redevelopment in a thirty-month demonstration project in eight transit-dependent neighborhoods. Since 1994, the organization has assisted twenty-one neighborhoods through a community improvement approach.[2] A second Riordan program was the 1997 Targeted Neighborhood Initiative, financed largely by federal Community Development Block Grant (CDBG) funding. This initiative provided $3 million to each of twelve neighborhoods for programs in which community members worked with city agencies to allocate funding to streetscape, sidewalk, lighting, and façade improvements. The program eventually was expanded to include fourteen additional neighborhoods, but many projects were discontinued in 2007 due to reduced CDBG funding.

During the Riordan era, some movement occurred toward a more proactive public-safety approach when in 1997 the city council's Ad Hoc Committee on Gangs and Juvenile Justice established the L.A. Bridges anti-gang program following the 1995 gang-related shooting death of a three-year-old girl. The L.A. Bridges program provided after-school activities for youth, case management services, and gang intervention activities at twenty-seven school sites. Mayor Riordan caused significant controversy by announcing the program's closure in 2000, citing a city controller audit that found the program to be poorly managed and lacking accountability measures. The city council unanimously overrode the proposed closure.

While neighborhood policy during the Riordan administration primarily was oriented toward private-sector development, neighborhood councils and CBAs signaled that neighborhood policy was changing. The charter reform of 1999, which increased the engagement of residential interests in city policy, also modestly strengthened the powers of the mayor vis-à-vis the city council by giving the mayor more authority over departmental and commission appointments. As sweeteners to induce voter support for reform, the charter contained provisions to decentralize planning and increase the neighborhood voice. The charter enacted decentralized Area Planning Commissions to localize land-use review and created a system of neighborhood councils to serve in an advisory role on policymaking, budgeting, and service delivery. The city also created a Department of Neighborhood Empowerment charged with supporting neighborhood council operations.

Following a prolonged planning and implementation process, the city established a system of neighborhood councils (now numbering around ninety), which are self-governing elected boards that represent communities with populations of, on average, thirty-eight thousand people. While neighborhood councils do not have an explicit community revitalization agenda, in concept the councils provide forums for community engagement and advocate for and inform neighborhood revitalization activities. Many neighborhood councils have joined citywide and regional alliances that promote information sharing and can serve as sources of mobilization and advocacy on regional and citywide issues. The councils can submit community impact statements that support their positions on proposed city council ordinances (during 2010 and 2011, 123 such impact statements were submitted). In addition, neighborhood councils are encouraged to provide the mayor with advisory input in the development of the city budget.

After more than a decade in operation, the effect of the neighborhood council system remains unclear. It is significant that some two thousand volunteers serve on community boards, and many others became engaged with committees and community projects. Some of the councils work earnestly to promote a sense of community, support local organizations, and facilitate community improvement. However, the system has not served as a source of mobilization around social-policy concerns. Rather, mobilization has tended to be more reactive to pocketbook issues, such as a proposed 18 percent water-rate increase and a measure to require solar power that was perceived as a union giveaway (Musso and Weare 2009). In many communities, the councils serve to channel community opposition to "undesirable" land uses, including low-income housing. This orientation is not surprising, as the system tends to be dominated by higher-income and white homeowners and to vastly underrepresent Latino communities (Musso et al. 2011). Characterizing neighborhood councils as uniformly "NIMBYistic" may be an exaggeration, but the dominance of homeowners in the system fragments policymaking and limits the substantive representation of distressed communities.

Concurrent with the largely middle-class secession movement of the late 1990s and the formation of the neighborhood councils, Los Angeles experienced a surge of community and labor organizing that politicized recent Latino and Asian American immigrants around issues such as wages, transportation, and community development (Nicholls and Beaumont 2004; Gottlieb et al. 2006; Milkman 2006; Brodkin 2007; Pastor, Benner, and Matsuoka 2009). New regional social-movement organizations, such as LAANE, helped organize progressive coalitions that achieved some important gains, including the adoption of a living-wage ordinance in 1997. While much of the agenda was regional, the progressive movement also was responsible for a pioneering CBA in 2001 that exacted community benefits from real estate developers redeveloping the downtown Figueroa Corridor surrounding the Staples Center arena.

CBAs are legally enforceable contracts signed between developers or cities and community coalitions to ensure that developers remain accountable and that community members have a role and share in the benefits of redevelopment (Gross 2005). Negotiated between community leaders and developers, each CBA is unique and geared to the project area and may include provisions for employment opportunities, affordable-housing requirements, environmental mitigation, historic- or neighborhood-character preservation measures, and community amenities services. In exchange for these benefits, community stakeholders—who potentially can stall or block projects—agree to support the project throughout the development process, including the procurement of government approvals and subsidies.

A coalition of community-based organizations, labor unions, and clergy, with the help of LAANE, negotiated a CBA in 1999 related to the construction of the Hollywood and Highland shopping and entertainment complex, where the Academy Awards have been held since 2002. However, the landmark CBA that gained national attention was signed in 2001 between the Anschutz Entertainment Group and a coalition of community and labor organizations spearheaded by LAANE concerning the development of L.A. Live, which is a $2.5 billion sports and entertainment complex surrounding the Staples Center in downtown Los Angeles.[3] The agreement—the largest of its kind at the time—required the Anschutz Entertainment Group to include affordable housing, a living wage, local hiring, parks, environmental mitigation, and parking and other amenities in the four-million-square-foot project, which received substantial public subsidies.

CBAs have been touted as a "new model for civic engagement" for low-income communities (Saito 2012). CBAs in Los Angeles reflect the efforts and accomplishments of an impressive progressive coalition of community, labor, environmental, and faith-based groups. Energized by the politicization of Latino and Asian immigrants to the Los Angeles region, the surge of community and labor organizing in the 1990s helped create the progressive political infrastructure necessary to contend with development forces and capitalize on the opportunities that arise with large-scale development projects (Pastor, Benner, and Matsuoka 2010; Soja 2010; Saito 2012). The strong involvement of labor in progressive community coalitions may be one reason why CBAs have been particularly successful in Los Angeles compared with other cities, such as New York (Saito 2012).

While signaling a shift in policy ideas and actors in the postindustrial era, CBAs are not without limitations. Reliance on developer-driven neighborhood revitalization can exacerbate inequalities by concentrating resources in locations with market advantages—to the neglect of other city neighborhoods. As noted by others, CBAs tend to be successful in project areas with a robust development climate that can attract substantial public subsidies (Wolf-Powers 2010). In this way CBAs are subject to the same vulnerability as urban development: projects that receive the most city attention and resources tend to be high-profile developments with significant market potential. A city insider described these types of projects that generate city interest as the "glossy, giant projects" for which elected officials can claim credit, leaving distressed neighborhoods in other parts of the city less able to use CBAs.

Another risk is that as CBAs are institutionalized they will become a tool primarily to facilitate real estate development rather than to further justice aims. As an example, the CBA established for the Atlantic Yards redevelopment project in Brooklyn in 2005 drew criticism when developer Forest City Ratner provided financial support to three of the eight nonprofit organizations that signed the agreement, ignoring the more than fifty community groups united in opposition (Been 2010; Robbins 2012). The CBA strategy can be successful only when community members can unite around objectives rather than face limited gains that pit them against one another. For example, the 2008 CBA process in the Los Angeles neighborhood of Pacoima generated some conflict when development of a former industrial site was framed as a choice between bringing jobs (by supporting the construction of a Costco Warehouse) or bringing community amenities (by supporting the construction of a family-oriented community plaza surrounded by smaller retail stores). In reality, community members sought both, but they could not be supported by a single CBA.

Toward Neighborhood Policy under Hahn and Villaraigosa

Term limits required Mayor Riordan to leave office in 2001, and Democratic mayor Jim Hahn took office, serving a single term and losing a bid for reelection to Antonio Villaraigosa in 2005. The election of Villaraigosa resulted in a shift to social and youth-related policies, some of which have a neighborhood focus. For example, after an unsuccessful bid to assume responsibility for the Los Angeles Unified School District, the Villaraigosa administration put into place the Mayor's Partnership for Schools, which involved mayoral control of several underperforming schools. Other initiatives include the Housing That Works plan, which created a capital plan and production targets for affordable housing; the Gang Reduction and Youth Development program, which retooled the L.A. Bridges program to provide funds to geographically defined areas for gang prevention, intervention, and community reentry programs; and the South Los Angeles 5-Year Strategic Plan, which was developed in partnership with several city council members and aimed to coordinate the existing activities and programs of fifteen city agencies to address socioeconomic disparities in South Los Angeles.

Under both Hahn and Villaraigosa, there was a noticeable shift in emphasis away from business development to affordable housing, an indication of increased attention to social issues. At the same time, the approach to neighborhood revitalization remained largely ad hoc. For example, the Hahn administration established the Affordable Housing Trust Fund to address the financing gap in affordable-housing developments. The trust fund was promised $100 million but has rarely been fully funded. According to a city official, the trust fund in some ways "took the politics out" of affordable housing by providing clear criteria for allocation of housing funds through a competitive process. This was a laissez-faire approach to neighborhood improvement in that the trust fund does little to coordinate city departments involved in housing and development. Recognizing the trust fund's limitations, the Villaraigosa administration attempted to develop a strategic housing plan—Housing That Works—to coordinate activities among the Housing Department, Planning Department, HACLA, CRA, and the Los Angeles Homeless Services Authority.

Both the Hahn and the Villaraigosa administrations also sought more neighborhood-oriented policing practices. Mayor Hahn's replacement of Police Chief Bernard Parks with Chief William Bratton, who served as chief from 2002 to 2009, arguably was Hahn's most significant "neighborhood policy," albeit in a nontraditional sense. The celebrated police chief—the former New York Police commissioner—changed the nature of policing in Los Angeles by establishing more collaborative community relations in several distressed neighborhoods. Villaraigosa subsequently revamped the city's gang prevention approach in 2008 by transforming the L.A. Bridges program into the Gang Reduction and Youth Development Initiative, a program that targets resources to twelve geographically defined zones. Developed in consultation with gang reduction experts, the program coordinates services and intensifies resources within spatially defined areas in a more holistic approach to gang reduction that stresses prevention and not just suppression strategies. The initiative has an annual general fund budget of, on average, approximately $17 million for gang prevention and for intervention and reentry services provided by community-based organizations. In its first year, private donors funded the initiative's Summer Night Light program, which extended park hours and provided alternative activities for youth.

In sum, in Los Angeles the trajectory of neighborhood policy at the city level has shifted modestly but noticeably toward greater attention to neighborhood concerns and the social dimensions of city policy with the establishment of the city's neighborhood council system and increased focus on social issues around policing and housing. Still, these do not constitute a comprehensive approach to neighborhood improvement, and city investments continue to emphasize large-scale infrastructure projects, such as redevelopment of the downtown Figueroa Corridor near the University of Southern California's main campus and the development of a biomedical research corridor near USC's Health Sciences campus in northeast Los Angeles. At the same time, community organizations have experienced more success in resisting negative impacts than they did in the redevelopment era, organizing local residents to fight residential displacement and negotiating CBAs.

Despite charter reform that aimed to provide the mayor with more oversight over city departments, city council members continue to wield the greatest influence over their districts; several respondents described city council districts as "individual fiefdoms." The district level is where policy initiatives must be vetted and neighborhood stakeholders can exert influence, but even here the influence of community stakeholders is often limited relative to well-funded downtown lobbyists. A further destabilizing force is term limits. In 2001 the city replaced its mayor along with more than half the city council. The shifting patterns of mayoral and council influence, along with the fragmented sociopolitical character of the city, contribute to the fluid and often opportunistic patterns of neighborhood politics. As one city official explained, "the bottom line is there is no strategic plan for community revitalization and for the city." Instead, city policies and programs occur in an ad hoc way and as a response to the fluctuating influence of city council offices, the mayor, department managers, and, sometimes, strong community advocacy.

However, opportunities for change exist. The recent demise of California's CRAs has spurred conversations about the direction of redevelopment in the city. A 2012 report commissioned by the Los Angeles City Council highlighted the city's shortcomings: its disjointed, reactive economic-development approach, which is highly influenced by individual council districts; its narrow focus on property-based redevelopment; and its need to institutionalize the prioritization of economic development in the city's underserved neighborhoods.[4] In the meantime, in the absence of a coherent, citywide approach to neighborhood revitalization, greater attention to the divergent patterns of redevelopment and community involvement across neighborhoods provides important insights into neighborhood politics in Los Angeles.

Neighborhood Connections and Neighborhood Revitalization

The hyperfragmentation of Los Angeles has consequences for the representation of neighborhood interests in the policymaking process (Lejano and Taufen Wessells 2006). The city's sociopolitical fragmentation, dis-

persal of power, and council-member control contribute to widely varying neighborhood revitalization strategies and patterns of neighborhood
political action. In this section, we illustrate these divergent patterns in
three economically distressed communities: the development of grassroots
nonprofit networks in Boyle Heights; the emergence of philanthropic and
public-private partnerships in Pacoima; and much more tenuous and contested community-city relationships in Watts.

Community Capacity in Boyle Heights

Boyle Heights is situated just east of downtown Los Angeles across the Los
Angeles River. This proximity to downtown and the lack of racially restrictive land covenants in the past have been a draw through several waves of
in-migration: first, working-class Jews; later, the braceros in the midcen-
tury; and currently, Mexicans and Central Americans. Today, Boyle Heights
has a population of about 93 percent Latino/Hispanic, many of whom are
multigenerational residents, with the most common country of origin being Mexico. The community has a long history of community organizing
in response to neighborhood concerns, such as freeway construction, the
proposed construction of a state prison and a toxic-waste incinerator, and
the destruction of affordable housing.

Boyle Heights developed organizational capacity through its deep history of community organizing and strong city council representation dat-
ing to the election of Edward Roybal in 1949 (the first Mexican American
to win a council seat since 1887). Area social-movement organizations
have included the Community Service Organization (most well known for
training labor leaders Cesar Chavez and Dolores Huerta), the student-led
Chicano rights movement in the late 1960s, and the influential Mothers
of East Los Angeles, which was formed by members of a Catholic church
in 1985 to oppose the siting of a state prison and toxic-waste incinerator
in the community. This history of grassroots organizing has resulted in a
diverse network of groups that range from social-action organizations to
homeowners' associations.

The most pressing community concern during the study period was the
construction of the Metro Gold Line and community development related
to the construction of four new Metro stops. Gold Line subway extension
construction began in 2004, and the extension became operational in late
2009. While revitalization was not the primary intent of the $900 million
project (a mix of federal, state, and local funds), the extension has had
significant implications for the community. Metro owns several adjacent

sites that have been slated for mixed-use development with affordable-housing components, in keeping with the national movement toward transit-oriented development (TOD) and greater attention to community concerns.

With the assistance of the Los Angeles Housing Department, private developers plan to build approximately five hundred affordable-housing units on transit authority–owned land. One station will include the construction of a full-service grocery store, which Boyle Heights currently lacks. Moreover, station construction has been accompanied by redevelopment of the Pico Gardens and Aliso Village public-housing project. However, TOD also has created pressures that have brought policy differences within the community into sharp relief.

Given the proximity of Boyle Heights to downtown Los Angeles and the recent subway extension, the neighborhood is facing gentrification pressures. Although this investment can be economically beneficial for members of the community, the changing nature of the neighborhood has led to competing visions and new cleavages and alignments among community-based organizations. According to one nonprofit administrator, "the separating and dividing issue is on affordable housing and renters versus owners."[5] Thus, despite their strength and effectiveness in influencing local decision-making, community organizations sometimes work at cross-purposes, and social action encounters divisions around issues related to gentrification, class, and immigration status. The result is significant controversy over proposed redevelopment, which in turn limits the ability of the community collectively to influence the city's development agenda.

While at times in conflict, Boyle Heights' civic sector nevertheless actively represents disparate community interests in the neighborhood-level debate over community development. Moreover, Boyle Heights' active civic sector has defended the community from further marginalization and attracted resources to the community. For example, recently several organizations, such as the California Endowment and the quasi-governmental organization First 5 LA, selected Boyle Heights for targeted investments due in part to the organizational capacity of the community. In addition, a coalition of nonprofit organizations successfully obtained Boyle Heights' status as a federal Promise Neighborhood.

Philanthropic Investments in Pacoima

Pacoima, in the northeast San Fernando Valley, was a historically African American community distant from the center of Los Angeles, isolated by racially restrictive housing covenants. Over the past few decades Pacoima has become a predominantly Latino community with a population of approximately 81 percent Hispanic/Latino residents. Pacoima was a center of industrial development that supported a diverse working-class residential neighborhood. Its industrial past has left a legacy of severe environmental problems. Surrounded by three freeways and divided by a railroad line, Pacoima has been disproportionately burdened by industrial activity, with more than three hundred industrial facilities and a small airport. The community, which has several pockets of severe distress, experienced significant job losses when several manufacturing plants closed in the 1990s.

With a more intact economy and a more positive public image, for several decades Pacoima has attracted philanthropic attention that aimed to foster community organizations and support a network of collaborative initiatives oriented toward youth development and education. This nonprofit collaboration has roots reaching back to 1986 and the United Way North Angeles Region, which initiated community-building efforts in Pacoima under its Underserved Geographic Areas Project (Maida 2008). This initial investment by the United Way sowed the seeds for the development of strong relationships among nonprofit, community, and philanthropic organizations. In addition, philanthropic foundations, such as the Los Angeles Urban Funders, supported collaborative approaches to addressing neighborhood needs, which further developed the capacity of community leaders and organizations to work together.

Pacoima's strong tradition of community partnerships with external actors, such as foundations and private businesses (Gaeke and Cooper 2002), stands in contrast to the grassroots organizing tradition of Boyle Heights. Community politics in Pacoima have a quiet collaborative character within organizational networks that trace their origins to the philanthropic interventions that began in the 1980s. Consistent with Jones-Correa's (2001b) observations regarding the privatized nature of many Los Angeles community organizations, the primary players in Pacoima have been nonprofit, community-based, and philanthropic organizations and private holders of capital that have tended to operate outside city politics (Maida 2008; Hopkins 2005; Letts and McCaffrey 2003).

While racial, ethnic, and socioeconomic cleavages are not absent in Pacoima, they are not as sharply pitched or difficult to resolve as they appear to be in some other areas of Los Angeles. The demographic transition in Pacoima was relatively peaceful, and the community has not experienced the same magnitude of disinvestment as have other distressed neighborhoods. Moreover, the community's distance from downtown dampens the development and gentrification pressures that often fuel community conflict. The earlier-laid foundation for community collaboration is an important legacy that continues to have an impact.

At the same time, while they have been proactive on education and environmental issues—for example, securing US Department of Education, US Environmental Protection Agency, and Promise Neighborhood grants for innovative initiatives—organizations in Pacoima have been more reactive in the realm of development politics. This reactive tendency was evident in the case of the proposed redevelopment of the twenty-five-acre former Price Pfister plumbing manufacturing site. Emphasizing the need for jobs and fiscal benefits, Mayor Villaraigosa successfully advocated locating a Costco Warehouse at the site, which would bring $2 million in annual sales-tax revenue to the city. In response, community cleavages emerged, with some groups supporting the mayor's proposal on the basis of job creation, while others envisioning a pedestrian-friendly community plaza surrounded by retail stores rather than a "big box" development. This conflict exposed tensions in the community between economic-development and quality-of-life concerns. Ultimately, nonprofit organization leaders reached a compromise and accepted a CBA to ensure local hiring and environmental protections, among other benefits.

While capable of forming interorganizational collaborations and working with the private sector, the community has been less successful in engaging and challenging local public officials. Community members see city decision-making processes as opaque and engagement as tokenistic. One respondent observed: "The residents of Pacoima are frustrated because they feel like their opinion isn't being heard. [Elected officials] try their best to get people's input, but in the end, you don't know how far that input goes. You just don't see it being made a priority."

Pacoima has an active civic sector that defends the neighborhood against marginalization and attracts significant foundation resources. The collaborative environment in Pacoima illustrates the nature of community politics that stem from philanthropic investment in capacity building, less contentious development, and relatively harmonious race and class politics. In the presence of foundation investments, a more intersectoral and less politicized approach to community improvement has emerged. However, a lack of connections to central-city political actors, in part resulting from the community's geographic isolation, may in turn limit Pacoima's effectiveness in the political sphere.

Protests Bring Attention to Watts

Of the three neighborhood case studies, Watts is the best known, with a controversial history frequently emblematic of social problems in Los Angeles. Held in the popular press as a center of social dysfunction and distant from areas of prime investment, Watts has suffered from disinvestment and serious public-safety issues. It also has experienced the most dramatic ethnic change, transitioning from a majority white community to majority African American in the 1940s and 1950s and, more recently, experiencing a rapid dispersion of African American residents and significant in-migration of Latinos, making them now the majority group in Watts. The community—today approximately 58 percent Latino and 40 percent African American—has experienced a history of repressive policing accompanied by undesirable developments, such as freeways and several large public-housing projects.

Historical patterns of disinvestment and distrust have constrained the development of civic-sector networks in Watts, which has fewer high-capacity nonprofit and community organizations than either Boyle Heights or Pacoima. Nonetheless, a legacy of protest politics has brought attention from city lawmakers and the development of partnerships between the community and the city on issues related to public safety and public housing. Termed by some to be "urban rebellions," the widespread breakdowns of civil order in 1965 and 1992 have been defining moments in the community's history. In contrast to Pacoima, which is somewhat detached from the political realm, Watts has strong connections with public officials—such as its city council representatives, LAPD leadership, and US Congress representatives Maxine Waters and Janice Hahn. These political connections are evident in such groups as the Watts Gang Task Force, which regularly involves elected officials and high-level public administrators. According to one respondent, "it is one of the most successful groups as far as actually getting things done . . . because . . . for whatever reason, that group has huge political clout. I mean all the way up to the president of the United States. When the US attorney general came out here to view the housing developments, he wanted to go see the Watts Gang Task Force." The task force has broadened its focus from public safety to other community issues, such as the proposed redevelopment of the community's seven-hundred-unit Jordan Downs public-housing project.

The strong ties between community organizations and city officials have been a source of controversy. Some community members remain skeptical, viewing city policy actions as symbolic only rather than substantive responses to community concerns. Moreover, in comparison to Pacoima, which has developed community capacity through the support of outside nonprofits and foundations, and Boyle Heights, which has an array of community organizations developed as a result of earlier mobilizations, organizational capacity in Watts is tenuous. Difficulties exist in building broad, self-sustaining community coalitions. Relationships among community organizations are marked by mistrust and territoriality rather than collaboration and cooperation. And compared with the other two neighborhood cases, Watts is characterized by greater conflict around race and ethnicity. For example, community organizations in Watts have not effectively engaged the growing Latino community, although Latino residents now make up more than half of the Watts population.

The shortage of private investment in Watts is related to the neighborhood's distance from downtown, public-safety concerns, and the enduring stigma surrounding the community—as well as the community's history of protest politics. These factors, combined with a relatively thin organizational capacity, have led the government to assume a greater role in community development initiatives. This public-sector attention potentially could have a transformative impact, particularly through the redevelopment of public-housing projects. The improving nature of police-community relations in recent years in Watts provides one example of the potential value of city-community partnerships. At the same time, the limited development of the nonprofit sector—most strikingly among the rapidly growing Latino community in Watts—points to continuing challenges in ensuring adequate representation of diverse community interests.

Postindustrial Transitions in Neighborhood Politics

Looking at the trajectory of neighborhood politics in Los Angeles, three observations stand out. The first is that the benefits acquired by communities depend on organizational capacity at the neighborhood level. The second is that the role of city government is not only anemic overall but also highly uneven. The third is that city government has done little to strengthen the voices of neighborhoods, while foundations have striven to fill this void in some instances. Although the city created a system of neighborhood councils, it invested little in making this institution an effective and representative voice in the policy process. In the highly fragmented system of governance found in Los Angeles, the potential for a more robust effort of neighborhood revitalization remains untapped, although community networks to support it continue to grow and develop.

Despite these various limitations, progress is also evident. After years of neglecting neighborhood concerns while directing energy and resources toward downtown redevelopment, Los Angeles currently has several ongoing neighborhood improvement efforts. However, the size, geographic configuration, and volatile demographic makeup of Los Angeles, together with a fractured institutional structure, work against broad, strategic thinking about neighborhoods. Neither is there, outside government, a strong, centripetal force concerned with the city's neighborhoods. Foundations have a role, but not one that has overcome fragmentation. The city's associational life is thickly populated but clusters around no large neighborhood vision. Neighborhood "policy" is largely happenstance, ad hoc, and a matter of seizing opportunities as they come along.

The level of neighborhood distress does not guide revitalization efforts. Rather, three factors, which vary across neighborhoods, seem to be at work. The first is market potential. Among the three case study neighborhoods, this factor is most evident in Boyle Heights, which enjoys proximity to downtown and an enhanced investment potential due to TOD. Second, community capacity is an element of neighborhood improvement efforts. Neighborhoods with existing capacity, such as Boyle Heights and Pacoima, are better positioned to take advantage of opportunities that do emerge. Beyond this, efforts to enhance community capacity (such as the foundation-led efforts in Pacoima) can prepare communities to respond more effectively when opportunities do arise. Finally, the attention of political elites (perhaps reflecting anxiety about violent protests) also plays a role in targeting neighborhood improvement efforts, particularly in Watts.

The content of community revitalization in Los Angeles has varied dramatically across neighborhoods in a manner that is related to the city's significant institutional and political fragmentation. Community revitalization is also shaped by economic geography and the history of specific communities. This is not a simple story of distributive politics, which is often prominent in accounts of electoral or racial coalitions. Rather, racial and ethnic politics varies across the city in a manner that is contingent upon historical relationships with particular political and nonprofit actors and upon neighborhood geographic and demographic landscapes. Moreover, community-level differences in civic capacity and political style lead to varying patterns of involvement among community activists, private and philanthropic organizations, city officials, and various state and federal actors.

The variant patterns in Los Angeles communities raise practical questions regarding the proper mix of civic and government mobilization in neighborhood regeneration. In large, diverse cities like Los Angeles, without strong frameworks for neighborhood policy, the challenges to fostering both strong civic and strong governmental involvement vary widely across neighborhoods. Lacking neighborhood policies or institutions that integrate different policy sectors and parts of the city, Los Angeles nevertheless has offered important opportunities for community influence in addressing local problems. Community action has achieved some gains, yet it also faces limitations that appear to be at least in part a legacy of past social action. In Boyle Heights, for example, where policy initiatives have succeeded in generating economic investment, neighborhood civic organizations have split over class and particularistic interests. In Pacoima, where neighborhood actors and foundations have succeeded in bridging community divides, they have been less effective in engaging with city policy. And in Watts, city and intergovernmental actors have taken charge of neighborhood initiatives in ways that have yet to yield highly effective civic mobilization. It is noteworthy that, though LAANE is an important political phenomenon, it has no significant role in any of the three case study neighborhoods; nor have neighborhood councils mobilized residents in the interest of neighborhood improvement.

The fragmentation of the city and its political structures has thus fostered a variety of local organizational trajectories, policy priorities, and outcomes. Nonprofit and philanthropic sectors have played important roles in neighborhood revitalization, albeit in a fractured and varied manner, and have supported action that works somewhat independently of the city on narrow neighborhood revitalization aims. Unlike Chicago, for example, communities follow essentially separate tracks. Thus, in a postindustrial era, neighborhood policy—albeit limited in reach and impact—occurs through the kaleidoscopic interplay of policy initiatives, intersectoral and civil society networks, and developmental trajectories within specific neighborhoods.

When we examine Los Angeles through a neighborhood lens, what does it reveal about the new politics of neighborhood revitalization? The policy position of neighborhoods clearly has shifted over time. No longer heavily disregarded, neighborhoods now have a policy voice. Neighborhoods are, however, not a high priority, and the particulars of place matter. Those with greater organizational capacity and more market potential get more attention and additional resources, whereas communities without much of either receive limited assistance, primarily from government action. When neighborhoods have limited market appeal and little capacity, government appears to be the agent of last resort.

Although the large population, extensive geographic area, and high level of fragmentation in Los Angeles make it difficult to detect a dominant trend, the long sweep of the city's experience reveals a shift. In the redevelopment era big economic-development projects largely ignored community concerns, and harsh policing methods undermined the community's role in securing public safety. By contrast, the present time shows evidence of scattered efforts to ameliorate social problems as part of a continuing emphasis on economic growth, and a turn to community-oriented policing aims to establish a cooperative relationship with neighborhood stakeholders. While this is not a sea change in city politics, these shifts do signal a heightened appreciation of the linkages between the social and economic realms that is the foundation of the new era in neighborhood politics.

Notes

1. Tax Increment Financing allowed the CRA to retain all property taxes resulting from increased property values in the redevelopment project areas. These tax increment funds were then used to finance additional investment within the project area.
2. For a description of the programs, see http://www.lani.org/projects.htm.
3. LAANE has received support from multiple national foundations. On LAANE, see Meyerson 2013.
4. See report at http://cao.lacity.org/OEA/HR&A%20EDD-NP%20Final%20Draft%20 Report_12-31-12.pdf.
5. The authors conducted forty-eight semistructured interviews with stakeholders in Los Angeles between 2007 and 2009. Unless otherwise noted, quotations with no published reference are from confidential personal interviews conducted by the authors.

SEVEN

The New Politics in a Postindustrial City: Intersecting Policies in Denver

SUSAN E. CLARKE

Denver is a growing city that has been attractive to well-educated young people as well as Latino immigrants. The city experienced a succession of policy changes (under various mayors), eventuating in a new era linking economic development and the treatment of neighborhoods. Created by then mayor Hickenlooper in 2004, the Office of Economic Development reports to the chief executive and is well placed to set and pursue priorities. However, as crafted, this institutional link strongly favors a market orientation to neighborhood development and is not necessarily accessible to community voices. Under this institutional arrangement, the city diverted Community Development Block Grant funds to a nonprofit community development financial institution pursuing an entrepreneurial strategy at the neighborhood level. Although this initiative eventually failed, it featured the recasting of traditional neighborhood boundaries into a set of larger districts drawn to highlight investment opportunities. Concurrently, these policies are now intersected by Denver's construction of an ambitious regional public-transit system. Transportation has major development implications, including a potential to strengthen an already-robust gentrification trend, which both the philanthropic sector and the federal government have partially mitigated by grants for affordable housing and other social ends. Overall, through a varied mix of players, Denver has a development pattern consisting of intersecting policies and power shifts, with pursuit of sometimes-overlapping and multiscalar economic growth, neighborhood revitalization, and transportation goals. Scattered efforts to address community and social concerns are increasingly being transformed into more coordinated, collaborative initiatives headed by the philanthropic sector. As an important and autonomous body of actors, the philanthropic sector has a major role in defining selected areas of distress, generating information about neighborhood conditions, and funding combined efforts to address them. But this

new era includes partial and incomplete policy shifts; as a result, there is much
neighborhood-related activity but not a comprehensive strategy of neighborhood
improvement.

For several decades, Denver has been a destination for well-educated young people seeking an outdoor lifestyle and knowledge-based jobs. However, despite its growing affluence, the city is subject to boom-bust cycles. The 1990s were a boom time, with many "previously poor" neighborhoods growing in population and prosperity. However, Denver's sparkling economic growth dimmed at the turn of the century. The period from 2000 to 2010 is referred to locally as "the lost decade." The Piton Foundation (2004, 71) reported: "In just two years, from 2000–2002, Denver lost 36% of the jobs gained over the previous decade. And jobs for low-skilled residents disappeared faster than jobs for skilled workers." Although a recovery had begun by mid-decade, the subsequent national recession hit the city hard; the housing bubble and rapid growth made Denver a foreclosure hot spot.

Immigration and the growth of the Latino population are important recent demographic trends. Denver's Office of Economic Development (OED) reported in 2007 that 62 percent of the city's 96,601 foreign-born residents had arrived in the country in the last ten years, suggesting that "Denver may face unique challenges in connecting these newcomers to the economic, political, and educational mainstream" (City and County of Denver, OED 2007). Denver's 2010 population was over 600,000, an increase of more than 8 percent over the decade but a slower rate of growth (by half) than that of the surrounding metropolitan area. One-third of this new population was Latino but over half of the new growth was white. In 2010, 52.2 percent of the city's residents were white, 31.8 percent were of Hispanic origin, and 9.7 percent were African American. This represents a slight increase of whites, a slight but continuing increase of Hispanics, and a continuing decline in African American residents (Piton Foundation 2011b). In short, Denver is becoming "whiter" even as its suburbs are growing more diverse (Hubbard 2009). Within the city change is widespread, including a growing Hispanic presence in many formerly black neighborhoods and a growing white presence in many previously poor neighborhoods of color.

The poorest neighborhoods are predominantly Latino and African American: most of the Latino population lives in neighborhoods where the concentrations of poverty are greatest. Many of these neighborhoods are near the downtown, have good housing stock, and other amenities that are attractive to young, white singles and families seeking affordable housing. As more affluent people move in, they seek to "improve" the neighborhood through involvement in neighborhood associations and by making demands on city services (public safety is often a priority). Associations in these changing neighborhoods are now often led by young, white homeowners who find that "neighborhood improvement" often clashes with "mind your own business" sentiments.

Changing Policies and Power Shifts over Time

Corresponding to the election of new mayors, three turning points shaped Denver's current neighborhood policy orientation by bringing into play new ideas and new actors for neighborhood revitalization. The first was Mayor Peña's upset election in 1983, which raised the visibility of neighborhood concerns and sparked an effort to create a new policy milieu within the city. The second was Mayor Webb's reframing of the problem of neighborhood distress as an impediment to downtown development, joining but subordinating neighborhood revitalization to downtown development. Finally, Mayor Hickenlooper's 2003 election introduced a market-oriented policy paradigm that emphasized assets and entrepreneurship while reprogramming public resources to leverage private investment. Efforts by Peña and Hickenlooper are of special significance because they introduced new institutional arrangements to the policy process. Hickenlooper's election effectively marked the arrival of a new era in Denver neighborhood politics. Although his emphasis on market-oriented strategies did not result in a wholesale transition to a new policy paradigm in Denver, it destabilized the previous distributional orientation and created new political spaces for nonelected policy actors.

Three themes are interwoven into the overall narrative: (1) the scarcity of general city revenue heightens the importance of a variety of funding sources and reliance on extraordinary means for raising money—these encompass foundations and other nongovernmental bodies and regional and intergovernmental revenue streams; (2) the incidental consequences of an ambitious regional transit plan; and (3) an overall move away from the small-scale, neighborhood-based distributive allocations introduced by Peña and toward investment channeled through larger, strategic districts favored by Hickenlooper. These bigger and more complex projects are less penetrable by community groups but also have to contend with a counter-tendency to favor a distributive approach as a way of gaining support and containing opposition.

The new politics of neighborhood revitalization features Denver's current efforts to join up downtown development, construction of transportation infrastructure, and neighborhood improvement policies. Financing is in place to advance Denver's ambitious transportation agenda, which deemphasizes automobiles in favor of transit infrastructure. Efforts are under way to deconcentrate poverty in selected distressed neighborhoods (by creating mixed-income housing and commercial development) that are near downtown and the new mass transit system.

Players in City Politics

Denver considers itself a "neighborhood-oriented" city and it is characterized as such in much of the scholarly literature (Judd 1986; Galster et al. 2003; Leonard and Noel 1990). The City and County of Denver have seventy-seven officially recognized neighborhoods, which, while overall quite diverse, are characterized by cultural and socioeconomic concentrations in a rapidly changing mix.[1] A closer look, however, challenges this assumption of a neighborhood-oriented city. Although Denver has over 250 neighborhood organizations registered with the city, neighborhood activists argue that the city is primarily reactive to the "squeaky wheel" and lacks a vision for neighborhoods. As a result, neighborhood benefits depend on community capacity or influential allies; more affluent neighborhoods tend to do better.

Like most western cities, Denver is nonpartisan and hybrid "reformed" (nonpartisan but district-based elections), although there are obvious partisan dimensions to the politics. The city council has thirteen seats: two are elected citywide "at large," and eleven are by district. Elected independently on a citywide basis, the mayor is a "strong mayor" with veto power over council decisions and significant budgetary authority. In the last thirty years, one Latino and two African Americans have been elected mayor through biracial coalitions. Denver is a consolidated city-county (since 1902) and so has social-service and welfare responsibilities that many other American cities lack. Education policy, however, is controlled by an independently elected (also by district) school board with its own tax base. With the city's district-based elections, neighborhood voices are channeled primarily through council representatives.

The salient players in neighborhood politics include participants inside and outside government. Participants inside the mayor's office are especially important. New actors include the OED, now responsible for Community Development Block Grant (CDBG) allocations and neighborhood policy along with broader economic-development priorities. The growing importance of transit-oriented development (TOD) projects increases the influence of the Department of Public Works, the Regional Transportation District, and the Denver Regional Council of Government (DRCOG).

But much of the impetus for neighborhood-focused programs comes from outside government. Participants include local foundations, such as the Piton Foundation; business organizations such as the Downtown Denver Partnership and the Metro Denver Chamber of Commerce; banks; community organizations and various neighborhood coalitions and community development corporations; national foundations and locally based organizations linked to national partners.

The nonprofit sector and particularly the philanthropic sector (especially the Piton Foundation) are increasingly important to city governance; some of these organizations have ties to national nonprofits and foundations (such as the Annie E. Casey Foundation, the John D. and Catherine T. MacArthur Foundation, and the Local Initiatives Support Corporation [LISC]). Also, the ties between the city and the nonprofit sector are becoming more structured.[2] The Piton Foundation, a private operating Denver-based foundation, pursues an "embedded philanthropy" strategy that emphasizes long-term and "intimate" engagement with communities and groups.[3] Its official goals are to "develop and implement programs to improve public education, expand economic opportunities for families, and strengthen low-income neighborhoods in Denver."[4] Piton develops and operates its own programs in these three priority areas; increasingly, it also partners with other foundations and organizations in large-scale collaborative ventures. Piton generates databases on poverty and neighborhood well-being that are highly regarded and widely used in the city.

Denver's intermediary organizations are rarely structured along racial or ethnic lines, and there is an institutional lag in responding to the recent demographic shift from African American to Latino ethnic dominance. Latinos are not as well organized and not as influential as African Americans, and intermediaries are slow in taking into account the different policy agendas within the Latino community. An important exception is the NEWSED Community Development Corporation, one of Denver's influential Hispanic organizations, launched in the late 1970s to focus on neighborhood revitalization, cultural preservation, and business generation in the La Alma / Lincoln Park area in west Denver.

Neighborhood Policy and Its Funding

In Denver, as in many American cities, resource scarcity is a key constraint on neighborhood programs. Constraints on local resources from state-imposed tax and expenditure limits, outdated local tax structures, and declining federal aid are a constant backdrop for Denver's policymakers. State support of local government is modest. Property taxes are a declining source of local revenue. Sales taxes and user fees are significant and growing revenue sources (more than 50 percent of the general fund is generated by sales taxes). A highly restrictive state tax and expenditure limitation constrains the city's tax base: in 1992 Colorado voters approved a constitutional amendment, a Taxpayer Bill of Rights (TABOR), limiting both revenue and expenditure choices for local governments. Any state or local tax change that produces more revenue (after allowing for inflation and population growth) must be approved by voters.

Denver's historic boom-bust economic cycle is exacerbated by the city's reliance on sales tax.[5] Tellingly, there are numerous special authorities with independent taxing and borrowing powers (annual designation as a TABOR enterprise exempts special authorities and districts from TABOR requirements). In 2005 state voters approved a "waiver" of TABOR until 2015 if local voters approved. Denver voters approved this waiver by a 2 to 1 ratio.

In contrast, the availability of debt mechanisms enhances Denver's ability to undertake large-scale projects. Relative to other American cities, Denver enjoys an excellent credit rating in the municipal-bond market.[6] Denver is exceptional in its success in gaining voter approval for these initiatives and overcoming state limitations intended to thwart such government activity. Denver voters frequently approve general-obligation bonds (backed by taxpayers' "full faith and credit") for public projects and school financing. Tax Increment Financing (TIF) is also a significant resource for large-scale redevelopment in Denver.[7] The city is also adept at constructing single-issue multicounty tax districts in support of large cultural and athletic facilities, such as the zoo and multiple sports stadiums. A regional tax district voted to expand the light-rail transportation system (2004) to serve the Front Range metropolitan area, creating the FasTracks program. Such voter support for taxing themselves for civic improvements sets Denver apart from many other American cities.[8]

Most of Denver's neighborhood spending is funded by federal grants and foundation grants.[9] With scant city resources to support neighborhood initiatives, CDBG funds have been the primary source of public spending; however, the importance of funding sources outside government has been growing.

Competing for external resources is more evident than interneighborhood competition, but it is not clear whether neighborhoods have much voice in that process since foundations, LISC, and other nongovernmental funders target neighborhoods according to their own criteria. The federal entitlement grants currently received by the City and County of Denver from the US Department of Housing and Urban Affairs (HUD) include CDBGs, HOME Investment Partnerships Program (HOME), Housing Opportunities for People with AIDS, and Emergency Shelter Grants.[10] In 2010 the city received $9.5 million from CDBG funds. By 2012 the total for the four HUD grants in Denver was $11.5 million, with CDBG funds at $6,957,695.[11] In 2013 the four HUD grants totaled $11,072,526, with $7,170,263 in CDBG funds.

Unfortunately, given the historical importance of CDBG funds for the city's neighborhood programs, Denver is disadvantaged by the federal CDBG formula. The city's 2010 allocation of roughly $9.5 million was at the low end of national allocations. In comparison with other cities included in this study, Denver suffered the greatest loss in intergovernmental aid and federal funds. With recent cuts in CDBG funds, Denver has lost about $2.1 million, or 18 percent, of that funding in the past few years. In the past, most CDBG funds were spent on neighborhood physical revitalization: in 2007 the bulk of CDBG funds available were allocated to physical redevelopment and beautification projects. By 2011, 26.7 percent of CDBG-funded projects reported by OED were for economic development, with nearly 16 percent expended for Direct Financial Assistance to For-Profits. Now in second place, Public Facilities and Improvement accounted for 21.3 percent (HUD 2013).

Ironically, the foreclosure crisis injected some new federal resources. In July 2008 Congress passed the Housing and Economic Recovery Act of 2008 (HERA) to create initiatives and funding to help localities acquire and redevelop foreclosed properties. HERA funding in turn authorized the Neighborhood Stabilization Program (NSP) to use city CDBG funds for acquisition and rehabilitation of housing units, with a particular focus on purchasing foreclosed units and returning them to the housing market. Denver's three NSP partnerships, managed through the OED, are a complex mix of government agencies and nonprofit organizations working with $27 million in NSP funding over the three cycles.

Neighborhood Policy and Its Politics

Throughout the 1970s, Denver's employment growth was second only to Houston's, but in the early 1980s Denver faced a bust cycle triggered by the nationwide recession. The city lacked a coherent economic-development plan. Denver's politicians found themselves out of touch with the city's young electorate, many of them newcomers to the region and unappreciative of the old-guard alliance of Republicans and Democrats. A few months before the 1983 election, a huge Christmas snowfall caught the McNichols administration (William H. McNichols served as mayor from 1968 to 1983) unprepared. Denver was ripe for change.

Peña's New Coalition

An outsider to Denver politics, state legislator Federico Peña capitalized on these events, aided by a campaign team drawn from Governor Richard Lamm's and Senator Gary Hart's political organizations (Munoz and Henry 1990). Peña campaigned under a progressive banner that appealed to a broad coalition of urban liberals by stressing environmental and social issues, promising to open city hall to minorities, seeking to create jobs for the city's chronically unemployed, and reinstating long-term planning as a guide for curing Denver's economic ills. The new electoral coalition included blacks, Latinos, labor, gays, feminists, environmentalists, neighborhoods, and organizations of people with disabilities. Peña's business backers included some with large development ambitions, but younger real estate developers who specialized in historic redevelopment also supported his campaign.

Peña's upset election in 1983 marked a historic event for both Denver and the country. It was the first time that a Latino mayor won election in a major US city that lacked a Latino majority. Indeed, Latinos made up only 18 percent of Denver's residents at the time. With Peña's election, Denver began a shift to a political order more reflective of the city's changing demographic and economic character. But Peña's election was not, by itself, sufficient to produce a new politics. Fundamental to the establishment of a new urban regime is the forging of a governing coalition that can control key public and private resources necessary to advance governmental policies (Stone 1989, xi). This governing coalition did not form itself immediately or automatically.

Although expectations for reform remained high, Denver's recession created a set of reinforcing constraints and opportunities that shaped Peña's policy agenda and political regime. As an incoming Latino mayor dealing with the systemic biases facing any American mayor, Peña found it necessary to be the progrowth, fiscal conservative that could bring the business community to the table. But the business element of his governing coalition had to be forged anew. In part, this was because of Peña's outsider status but it also stemmed from the fragmentation of business elites in the face of economic downturns and restructuring trends. The fragmentation and disarray among economic elites encouraged more public discourse about the city's future and expanded opportunities for public leadership. Under Peña, the city took a lead role in development planning, a feature that distinguishes Peña's administration from those prior to and those following his time in office (Vasquez 1999).

Neighborhood organizations were part of this new dynamic. By the mid-1980s, many of Denver's neighborhood organizations had transformed themselves into nonprofit housing or economic-development corporations. Peña's election provided a window of opportunity for these neighborhood groups and their newly developed organizational capabilities. Rather than merely channeling material benefits to his electoral supporters, Peña sought to change the planning process to be more sensitive to neighborhood interests while also accommodating business interests. It can be argued that he recognized the need to change the policy environment in order to enhance the neighborhood voice. He did so by distributing the "small opportunities" available through his appointive and contracting powers, expanding neighborhood representation in planning processes, and increasing opportunities for participation in public hearings and meetings (Saiz 1993). Peña also redirected revolving-loan and neighborhood business programs to lower-income neighborhoods and reallocated program income from the Skyline urban-renewal projects (the projects that were responsible for destroying some of Denver's oldest neighborhoods during the McNichols era) to these neighborhoods.

Significantly, the Planning Department was the only agency to receive increased funding during Peña's first administration (Saiz 1993). The department used the additional funding to hire eight new planners to work with the low- and moderate-income neighborhoods surrounding downtown. In several neighborhoods the planners established task forces consisting of representatives of neighborhood organizations (including neighborhood development organizations), churches, businesses, and local developers. For the city, this provided a means for institutionalizing these neighborhood voices and drawing on their strategic knowledge in planning processes. By the end of Peña's first term, eight neighborhood plans were completed and adopted as amendments to the city's comprehensive plan. Even though the new planning process allowed local government to manage neighborhood participation to some extent (Horan 1997), the process also provided a new voice for neighborhood groups in nonelectoral arenas.

Webb Reframes Neighborhood Distress

Wellington Webb succeeded Peña (Webb served as mayor from 1991 to 2003), becoming the first African American mayor in Denver by winning the support of a multiracial electorate. The succession was not seamless: Webb had lost an earlier mayoral primary to Peña and they were not close allies. Once in office, Latino activists and voters questioned Webb's support of Latino agendas. Although Webb had the crucial backing of NEWSED, factions within the Latino community and among Latino council members generated continual unease about Webb's ability to mobilize the Latino vote. And any Webb electoral victory was contingent on keeping the Latino vote along with African American votes.

Peña was perceived as a neighborhood advocate, and Webb suffered by comparison (A. Hodges 1994). Webb came into office saddled with the myriad startup hassles of the new Denver International Airport, and he was oriented more toward megaprojects—including a new baseball stadium— than neighborhood improvements. Although both Peña and Webb relied on "deracialization" electoral strategies to reach diverse constituencies, Peña's administration is credited with giving neighborhoods a real voice in decision processes while Webb's overall record is not distinguished by support for poor and disadvantaged communities, despite his support for numerous programmatic neighborhood initiatives (George 2004).

In 1992 Webb appointed Jennifer Moulton, former executive director of Historic Denver Inc., as the first woman to serve as Denver planning director. Her professional and political networks enabled her to integrate historic-preservation interests into the larger development community. In her view, the city moved from the "planning" phase that had characterized Peña's administration into a "full-blown building" and implementation phase during the 1990s (Vasquez 1999). This encompassed several megaprojects such as the redevelopment of Lowry Air Force Base and the old Stapleton Airport site, the new Denver International Airport, the new sports stadiums, the Union Station restoration, and Central Platte Valley redevelopment, which expanded the downtown core.

Planning that did occur during Webb's administration is notable for its focus on bringing the middle and upper class back to the city by making the city—particularly the downtown area—attractive to investors and tourists. Inner-city neighborhoods were characterized by Moulton as "an intimidating moat" discouraging access to downtown. Those neighborhoods just north of the downtown—including Curtis Park, La Alma / Lincoln Park, and Five Points (the last a historic African American enclave)—were targeted with a $12 million HUD grant to be used to tear down public housing and replace it with new public housing and market-rate housing (Vasquez 1999). To Moulton, neighborhood revitalization was a necessary, if not sufficient, condition for downtown redevelopment and Denver's overall economic growth.

Indeed, in Moulton's "Downtown Agenda," Denver's role was to be "an efficient economic machine" able to transform lower-income areas into "investor quality downtown residential neighborhoods" and to attract "people with money to spend on housing" (Moulton 1999). As critics saw it, the city wielded TIF to address the "first mover" problem in these disinvested neighborhoods: TIF support for new up-market housing reduced the developer's risk and ensured that early investors would see an increase in property values (Robinson 2005, 27). In many blighted neighborhoods, low-income housing disappeared and "bleached barrios" emerged—that is, more white and fewer Latino and African American residents (Robinson 2005, 29).

In contrast to Peña's interest in changing the rules of the game to secure a voice for the neighborhoods, Webb's administration emphasized the city's economic revitalization through enhancing the investment climate for upper- and middle-class investors. But Webb also instituted the Focus Neighborhood Initiative (FNI) in 1998 in recognition of the fact that a number of areas of the city were not doing as well as others and needed extra attention. Census data on unemployment and poverty rates were used to identify the FNI neighborhoods; none had benefited from the 1990s boom period in Denver (most continue to be listed by the Piton Foundation as "persistent poverty" neighborhoods). Denver applied for Empowerment Zone designation to capture additional resources to advance FNI. However, when the city was not selected, Webb decided to allocate significant CDBG funds to the sixteen "target" FNI neighborhoods, with the expectation of substantial citizen participation.

Webb's administration marked an important turning point in Denver: neighborhood revitalization became increasingly subordinated to the downtown redevelopment goals and reliant on shrinking federal funds. To one observer, this change foretold the imminent "Los Angelization of Denver"—firmly in the grip of the growth machine (Robinson 2000).

"Stuck" in a CDBG World

In the words of an adviser to John Hickenlooper, who was elected mayor in 2003, Denver appeared "stuck" in a CDBG world. In both the Peña and the

Webb administrations, neighborhood policymaking centered on the distribution of CDBG funds. The city's definition of neighborhood problems and the solutions identified were driven by the CDBG program, targeting neighborhoods in need and distributing resources locally for small-scale efforts. The focus on distributing modest resources to a large set of neighborhoods may reflect, in part, the deracialization political strategies employed by both minority mayors (Clarke and Saiz 2002; Hermon 2004; Kraus and Swanstrom 2005). The CDBG focus that prevailed during the Peña and Webb administrations complemented the city's penchant for public investment in large-scale megaprojects and public works.

The CDBG-centered system began to unravel in 2003. The economic disarray at the turn of the century created an opening for John Hickenlooper's bid for mayor. Hickenlooper is a white businessman, in contrast to the Latino and African American mayors of the previous three decades and the current African American mayor. Much of Hickenlooper's appeal came from his self-identification as an entrepreneur and maverick: facing unemployment as a geologist during one of Denver's boom-bust energy cycles, he founded the city's first microbrewery (Wynkoop Brewery) in an area of the city known as LoDo (Lower Downtown, formerly Skid Row) on the edge of revitalization. Hickenlooper brought his entrepreneurial experience to city issues, including the need to recognize and respond not only to need but also to opportunity. He created a multiagency Development Council in 2003 to set and coordinate policy for development issues, projects, and regulations. This attempt at centralizing the locus of development policymaking was followed by institutional changes particularly important to neighborhood revitalization. While a director of Neighborhood Relations was established within the mayor's office, the most significant factors in creating a new approach involved new organizations that merged neighborhood and economic-development policymaking.

Hickenlooper brought in outsiders to direct his new entrepreneurial approach to city government and economic development. Many were from the East Coast and Midwest; the cities they had worked in previously had much more complex and sophisticated policy and financial infrastructures and professional expertise for neighborhood revitalization and economic development. The new policymakers frequently compared Denver with other cities and appeared to be focused on bringing Denver "up to speed." Not only was the CDBG distributional paradigm outdated, in their eyes, but it also prevented Denver from becoming the "Great City" it aspired to be. To neighborhood activists, these policy shifts ignored the long-standing citizen participation and voluntary action traditions that made Denver distinctive. In the competition of ideas about neighborhood investment, however, promoting the "same old, same old" CDBG approaches rarely triumphed over the symbols and discourse of entrepreneurial market strategies. Hickenlooper's reelection in 2007 with 86.3 percent of the vote accelerated the move toward entrepreneurial initiatives.

The Hickenlooper administration's approach to neighborhood revitalization was thoroughly entrepreneurial, addressing neighborhood revitalization as an opportunity for economic development. Faced with shrinking CDBG funds and concerned that Denver lagged behind other cities in adopting the tools necessary for this new policy context, an ad hoc group of Denver city officials from the city council and the mayor's office turned to Shorebank Advisory Services for consultation. Subsequently, the mayor relied on Shorebank's (2005) market analysis to justify a new paradigm for neighborhood revitalization. The Shorebank study underscored Denver's outdated and underdeveloped approaches to community development.

The paradigm shift endorsed by Shorebank and pursued by the city defined neighborhood problems in terms of the lack of gap financing and proposed community development financial institutions (CDFIs) as a policy solution. CDFIs leverage external capital (including federal funds) to provide equity and debt financing to projects that will benefit low-income people and/or projects unable to secure conventional lending. Shorebank proposed using CDBG funds for asset building and leveraging private investment in a smaller set of distressed neighborhoods. For Denver, this required reallocation of a share of CDBG funds from the traditional neighborhood targets to equity investment in select distressed areas.

Following the 2005 Shorebank study, a small group of experts in the mayor's office put out a request for quotation for a CDFI.[12] In selecting Seedco, Denver gained a private, nonprofit CDFI operated through Seedco Financial Services of New York City to work with the city on community economic development, including neighborhood commercial revitalization, affordable housing, and small-business expansion.[13] Seedco is able to loan more than the $450,000 limits set on the City of Denver. Seedco promised to leverage and invest at least $17 million in Denver to create jobs and stabilize distressed neighborhoods.

To establish the financial base for Seedco's ventures the city council approved granting $15 million of CDBG funds (over a five-year period beginning in 2007), along with $437,000 in start-up costs, to Seedco. This controversial decision was intended to "expand the pot" to leverage further external capital for investments in a few distressed neighborhoods.[14] In addition, Seedco sought to influence how other organizations operate, making them more aggressive, more entrepreneurial, and more focused.

With the city council's approval in February 2007, the city began to focus on gap-financing issues in distressed neighborhoods, using the Seedco CFDI as intermediary. A Hickenlooper policy adviser, Peter Chapman, left the mayor's office in 2007 to be executive director of Seedco. In return for the CDBG allocation, Seedco planned to invest $13 million (in approximately seventeen projects) in Denver in the first year, provide CDFI staff, and partner with other Colorado CDFIs such as the Housing and Finance Authority to create a funding pool. From this base, Seedco promised to increase assets under management to $300 million by 2009 (Denver City Council 2007b, 4). Projects were funded only if no other revenue streams or resources were available. Seedco promised performance-based contracts to allow for regular monitoring (Denver City Council 2007b, 4).

However, the Seedco venture exemplifies the risks as well as the potential of entrepreneurial strategies. Audits of Seedco indicate that expectations were not fully met. By the end of 2007, Seedco had reviewed twenty-five projects and made six loans, totaling $5 million; the claim was that these deals brought in $2.9 million in new capital (Denver City Council 2007b, 4). However, concerns about invoicing practices, record-keeping, and the handling of CDBG funds brought repeated attention from the city council. Seedco supporters claimed that these were minor incidents, while critics charged misuse of public funds (*Denver Post* 2008). After much debate, Seedco's contracts with the city were renewed yearly by split votes in the city council. By November 2009, the city had had enough and terminated the Seedco contract. Seedco had generated only sixteen loans, eleven using CDBG funds, and had created total loan capital of $5.2 million, $2.0 million of which was from CDBGs. Only forty jobs had been created. Since ninety-three jobs were promised in Seedco's last contract alone, the lack of job creation and the failure to build local capacity brought Seedco down. The city planned to reassess the use of CDFIs but still refers to the Shorebank study recommendations as justification for allowing CDFIs to support small business.

The city council's role in neighborhood revitalization was diminished by the market-oriented policy approach. Traditionally, the city council had been the champion of CDBG distributional programs, but the entrepreneurial discourse left its members in a defensive, dispirited stance. In the CDBG era, the council played a strong role in directing allocations across the board; in the entrepreneurial setting, there are fewer funds to allocate overall and the emphasis is on leveraging investments. The diminished role that the council plays in making policy decisions is often reduced to questioning OED policymakers and others making presentations and recommending actions.

To some extent, the diminished council role reflects the increasingly technical and arcane financial details of the projects being developed: the scale and complexity leave little space for council deliberation and even less consideration of neighborhood concerns. But it can also be traced to the inexperience of the council: the 2003 election of Hickenlooper also brought in ten new city council representatives (out of thirteen), thanks to term limits. One neighborhood activist described this as "unfortunate" since there was very little institutional memory and recognition of the "mutual understandings" that had characterized the informal and long-standing ties between neighborhood groups and city agencies in the past. As a result, the council was dependent on the information and analyses presented to them on new projects, with little precedent or experience to build on or refer to. In 2006 the council established the Neighborhood, Community, and Business Revitalization (NCBR) committee to address issues associated with neighborhood revitalization.

The formal institutional structure for developing and implementing neighborhood revitalization policies increasingly subsumes neighborhood concerns under the larger economic-development agenda. Although economic development is a continuing issue in Denver politics, particularly as the city struggles to escape the boom-bust energy cycles dominating the state economy, it became a more coherent and distinct priority throughout the 1980s and 1990s. It gained significant weight with the 2003 Hickenlooper election: although a very popular candidate, "Hick" was elected (over a Latino candidate, after nearly two decades of Latino and African American mayors) primarily by support in the southeastern, wealthy neighborhoods. His emphasis on entrepreneurial economic development and the competitive global economy justified his creation of a new set of development agencies accountable to the mayor's office and his elimination of the neighborhood planners who had been key links between the neighborhoods and those controlling revitalization programs.

Much of the institutional structure supporting neighborhood revitalization in Denver stemmed from federal programs and council initiatives. Denver does not lack for plans, many of them targeting neighborhood development. When Hickenlooper created the OED by Executive Order in 2004, it consolidated several agencies and departments, including the former Mayor's Office of Economic Development and International Trade,

Workforce Development, and the Housing and Neighborhood Development Services Division from the Department of Community Planning and
Development.[15] The OED is now the leading neighborhood revitalization
agency. Although the OED argues that "healthy neighborhoods are the
bedrock of a healthy city," its emphasis is more on strategic investment,
business loans and gap financing, and business development than on distributing resources to poor neighborhoods. In 2006 the OED released a
Neighborhood Revitalization Strategy, which designated the OED's Division of Neighborhood and Housing Development as the lead city agency
for neighborhood revitalization. The strategy promotes poverty deconcentration by creating mixed-income communities. Both placement of
affordable-housing sites and business investment are key means of moving
toward this goal. The need for a "new approach" to neighborhood revitalization was affirmed in the 2008 Consolidated Plan and further implemented in the 2013 plan. To the OED, neighborhoods are important as the
locus for small businesses, a significant element in Denver's economy.

While neighborhoods are still referred to by their traditional names,
they are being systematically carved up into districts that better serve the
policy emphasis on their business roles. The asset-based community development paradigm emphasizes the positive features of poor communities; distressed neighborhoods are transformed into a literal, economistic
inventory of neighborhood or locational assets potentially contributing to
wealth generation. As OED's Neighborhood Market Initiative proclaims,
"small is the new big": creating neighborhood business districts, community improvement districts, and other specialized territorial agents able to
work directly with the city has become established practice.

The promotion of these new institutions and territorial arrangements
is often challenged by members of the city council's NCBR committee, but
to date, nearly all proposed districts have been approved. In 2005 voters
approved changes in Denver's charter to give the council the ability "to
provide more flexibility among the various types of districts, including the
power to include, exclude, consolidate, and dissolve local districts" (Denver City Council 2008, 3). Denver was slow to adopt Business Improvement Districts, which must be created through a state statute and council
approval of the governing board of directors. In addition, Denver is promoting Community Improvement Districts, in which private-sector (residential, commercial, and mixed-use) actors in a specific geographic area
voluntarily tax themselves for improvements and services augmenting the
basic-level services provided by the city in that area (Denver City Council 2008, 3). The shift to market thinking has thus been accompanied by

increased use of improvement districts, which give formal expression to unequal levels of service.

Current Neighborhood Policy

Current neighborhood policy in Denver is explicitly asset based and targets a limited number of neighborhoods with redevelopment potential. The objective is to leverage opportunities emerging from TOD to create mixed-income communities. As CDBG funding declines, transportation funding increasingly shapes neighborhood revitalization projects. TOD is emerging as a new intersection of federal and nonprofit funds that influence neighborhoods. In 2004 Denver metro area voters approved a 0.4 percent increase in the sales tax (four pennies on every ten dollars) to support the construction of a regional transportation system, known as FasTracks. TOD, particularly the FasTracks system, is touted as "opening up development opportunities in neighborhoods" (City and County of Denver 2014, 13). By 2016 over fifty transit stations are expected to be completed, transforming neighborhoods throughout the metropolitan area. The current rhetoric of neighborhood policy emphasizes "transit-oriented development" and "people-oriented places" as ten different transit corridors are being built out nearly simultaneously. An eleven-member Citizen Advisory Committee approves most plans, with "participation opportunities" also scheduled.

The FasTracks project is locally initiated, financed, and directed, but as costs rise, federal funds are becoming more critical. For their part, nonprofits and foundations are providing resources to avoid the gentrification rush often associated with TOD. The Front Range Economic Strategy Center, founded by the Denver Area Labor Federation in 2002 but now a 501c3, plays a critical role in providing data and analysis related to economic justice issues. A MacArthur grant of $250,000 awarded to the city in February 2009 was steered to establish a revolving credit fund for investing in affordable-housing opportunities within half a mile of transit stations. Subsequently, a Denver nonprofit—the Urban Land Conservancy—partnered with Denver and Enterprise Community Partners to establish a $15 million Denver Transit Oriented Development Fund in 2010 to "create and preserve" affordable housing near transit lines.[16] Backed by public and private investors (including the MacArthur Foundation and Wells Fargo), it's the nation's first such fund.[17] "Essentially, the funding allows ULC to purchase properties near light-rail stations and then sell them to developers who promise to build affordable housing. In turn, the developers earn tax credits from the Colorado Housing and Finance Authority" (Hill 2013). By fall 2013 the TOD fund had made possible the acquisition of eight different sites on five different transit corridors, with 625 permanently affordable apartment homes in production.

Although FasTracks is a regional transit plan, it may prove to have the strongest influence on neighborhood revitalization. The funds for FasTracks dwarf the funding for all other neighborhood initiatives. The interagency collaboration involved provides a coherent strategy melding resources and personnel. Although the scale of the project and the regional scope mean that neighborhoods are not meaningful actors, each corridor and transit mode is organized around "stations" with clear neighborhood referents— and council representatives.[18] Many of these stations are located in the neighborhoods identified by the Piton Foundation as "persistently poor."

La Alma / Lincoln Park—One Neighborhood, Many Plans

The La Alma / Lincoln Park neighborhood exemplifies the intersection of policies and the overlay of old and new eras in neighborhood policy and politics. Denver established a Neighborhood Revitalization Plan in 2006 that emphasized strengthening underutilized assets in communities with demonstrated need. In preparing its five-year Consolidated Plan in 2008, the city called for "deconcentrating poverty, strengthening neighborhood assets by building upon them, maximizing resources, incorporating a comprehensive approach that assures collaboration among city agencies and other private and public partners, and developing exit strategies once self-sufficiency is achieved." The 2008 Consolidated Plan also reduced the number of neighborhoods targeted for revitalization. The city shifted from Webb's sixteen-neighborhood strategy to a focus on four core neighborhoods. As stated in the plan:

> Central to the strategy is a methodology for identifying target areas based on two principals [sic]—need and opportunity. Analysis of several need- and opportunity based criteria identified clusters of neighborhoods in the north, east and west of the city as ripe targets for revitalization. The target areas roughly coincide with areas where minority and ethnic populations are concentrated. All the proposed activities and projects are intended to principally benefit citizens of Denver who have extremely low-, low- and moderate-incomes, and populations that have special needs, such as elderly, persons experiencing homelessness, disabled and HIV/AIDS families and individuals. (City and County of Denver, OED 2007)

La Alma / Lincoln Park is one of the four core neighborhoods scheduled for revitalization in the 2008 Consolidated Plan. The neighborhood has been targeted by just about every city neighborhood initiative and by foundation programs (such as the Enterprise Community and Annie E. Casey Making Connections programs). It is also currently the site of a light-rail station, and another station is being developed by FasTracks in the area. One of Denver's oldest neighborhoods, La Alma / Lincoln Park is across a major interstate from the Sun Valley neighborhood, but even closer to downtown. It is a historic settlement area for Hispanic residents, who have been here since the early settlement of Denver's precursor, Auraria City. The area features the historic Santa Fe Drive Arts District but also the South Lincoln Park public-housing complex—composed of 270 units built in 1954. Two anchor projects now dominate the neighborhood, although neighborhood views on their impacts are mixed. The neighborhood is home to the Auraria Higher Education Center, housing the University of Colorado at Denver campus and the Metro State campus.

The area is a persistently poor neighborhood that is currently experiencing demographic changes. While the city overall gained 18.6 percent in population from 1990 to 2000, the neighborhood's population declined slightly (–0.06 percent). However, between 2000 and 2010 the neighborhood registered a slight gain in population. The area once had a majority of Latino residents, but by 2010 there was no majority population group. In terms of ethnic change, Lincoln Park has lost Latino and African American residents and gained white residents since 1990; this trend continued in 2010, with a 14.8 percent decline in the Latino population. In 2000, 52.5 percent of residents were Hispanic; by 2010, Hispanics were only 38 percent of the area's population.

The tensions between improvement and stability are especially strong here, as the threat of gentrification looms over the neighborhood. Many nonprofit public organizations and governmental agencies are active in La Alma / Lincoln Park, but there are continuing issues of coordinating efforts and cooperating on mutual interests. The city's 2006 neighborhood plan recognized La Alma / Lincoln Park as a mixed-use neighborhood with distinct subareas of industry, single-family housing, multifamily housing of various scales, retail, and health care. Early neighborhood goals were to preserve and expand the housing stock, increase rates of homeownership, remove nonconforming uses from the residential and industrial areas (allowing industrial expansion within existing limits), strengthen the employment base, and reconcile land use and zoning. Although many of these remain neighborhood concerns, the goals have shifted. The OED selected

La Alma / Lincoln Park for comprehensive treatment focusing on affordable housing, workforce and human-capital development, business development, and quality schools.

The City and County of Denver completed a neighborhood assessment for the La Alma / Lincoln Park neighborhood in 2006.[19] This assessment indicates that revitalizing La Alma / Lincoln Park now is seen by the city as part of its downtown development strategy. Hence, the city's consistent policy attention to the neighborhood can be attributed at least in part to its location and function as part of the downtown redevelopment plan. By 2010 La Alma / Lincoln Park was identified as an "Area of Change" in Blueprint Denver, the city's plan to integrate land use and transportation.[20] The 2010 Neighborhood Plan identified "the 10th and Osage Station Area together with the industrial land west of the Central Corridor light rail line as Areas of Change for several reasons related to latent land development potential, access to and demand for enhanced transit, proximity to downtown and Auraria Higher Education Center, opportunity to supply more housing and ability to stimulate economic development, as well as re-investment in historic resources" (City and County of Denver, OED 2007). NEWSED, a nonprofit community development corporation, is the most visible and effective neighborhood organization in the area; it has been instrumental in revitalizing businesses, assisting individuals attempting to buy their first home, and lending other support services to the community. In addition, there are seven other registered neighborhood organizations that focus on the La Alma / Lincoln Park neighborhood. However, the "neighborhood associations have lacked a credible, consistent grassroots voice to represent neighborhood concerns to the City and there has been mistrust between the neighborhood associations and City agencies" (City and County of Denver 2006, 29).

Neighborhood revitalization is complicated by the history of tension and poor relations between the neighborhood and the Auraria campus. Neighborhood activists fear that campus expansion will erode the community, and they oppose any efforts by Auraria to expand into the neighborhood. However, campus expansion is a possible consequence of the TOD now under way. Thus, the anchor developments have mobilized fear and distrust in the neighborhood. The city's 2006 assessment observes:

> Lincoln Park faces challenges related to the physical enhancement and re-development of the neighborhood. The residents, property owners and other community stakeholders have been working individually to address the neighborhood issues, and they appear to be starting to work together. There

appears to be some agreement on what issues should be priorities and what goals would best address the issues, but not on what methods would best implement the goals. There are signs of continuing transition of the neighborhood both in terms of land use and in terms of the demographics of the neighborhood. Neighborhood expectations may be unrealistic. Members of the public have indicated that they want to preserve the existing neighborhood character and support the current residents, but they also want more home ownership and affordable housing opportunities. They would like infrastructure and housing improvements, but fear loss of affordability and gentrification that would change the neighborhood demographics. (City and County of Denver 2006, 50–51)

These concerns exemplify the tensions between growth and stability that characterize neighborhood policymaking in Denver.

The Intersection of Neighborhood and Transit Policies

However, TOD and housing redevelopment are likely to challenge the desire for neighborhood stability. In 2009 a multiagency[21] $10 million grant was awarded to continue the South Lincoln Park Homes redevelopment planned around the Tenth and Osage Station as part of a nationwide effort emphasizing affordable housing, public transportation, and the environment. Redeveloping the South Lincoln Park Homes is an important element of TOD. The 270 public-housing units on 15.1 acres are owned and managed by the Denver Housing Authority.[22] As part of TOD, the Denver Housing Authority is now tearing down the existing low-rise public housing and redeveloping the site for higher-density mixed-income housing.

Not surprisingly, residents are concerned about displacement and a weak likelihood that they will be able to return to the neighborhood once they lose their present homes. During public meetings, the city emphasizes sustainability, while residents continually refer to the value of strong ties that exist within the neighborhood. In 2011 HUD awarded $22 million to the Denver Housing Authority for continued redevelopment of the South Lincoln Park Homes; the first building, an eight-story, one-hundred-unit apartment building for seniors, offers a stark contrast to the historic low-rise architecture of the area.

Other neighborhoods are in various stages of planning for improvement, with TOD and proximity to downtown as key factors in how much attention they receive from city hall. For neighborhoods, TOD is a two-edged sword: it can aid improvement but at the risk of substantial resident-displacing gentrification. The philanthropic sector is an important source for helping to mitigate rapid gentrification and in launching such social measures as the Piton Foundation's Children's Corridor—an initiative to enhance the education and well-being of children in poverty through cross-sector coordination (Piton Foundation 2011a).

Joining Policy Domains

Three turning points highlight the policy trajectory in Denver's neighborhood revitalization agendas. Mayor Peña's 1983 election raised the visibility of neighborhood distress and ensured that CDBG funds targeted neighborhood revitalization, creating a distinctive pattern of neighborhood policymaking centered on the allocation of federal resources. Mayor Webb's reframing of the problem of neighborhood distress as an impediment to downtown development joined neighborhood revitalization to economic development. Webb established a pattern that persists to this day, as neighborhood revitalization is a secondary priority to downtown redevelopment. However, Webb's change in focus retained the distributive politics of CDBG allocation established by Peña. Mayor Hickenlooper's support for Shorebank's conception of neighborhood problems as stemming from shortcomings in the financial infrastructure completed the transition initiated by Webb, while undoing Peña's distributive politics of CDBG allocation.

Overall, Denver's trajectory illustrates a shift from the "politics of competition," in which the policy agenda centers on distribution of public resources, to the "politics of construction," in which assembling resources rather than directing resources is the key public role. As described above, this shift is partial and incomplete. Hickenlooper's financial reforms shifted power from city agencies, particularly the Community Planning and Development Agency and its Housing and Neighborhood Development Services Division, to the mayor's office and to off-budget units such as Seedco. The mayor's OED became the locus of neighborhood policy formulation and implementation. The Consolidated Plan of 2008–12 argued that "a new model" for community development is needed—one that emphasizes assets rather than only needs. The language of assets, wealth generation, and leveraging marked all the policy messages coming from the Hickenlooper administration.[23] The need to assemble, package, and blend resources from multiple sources was paramount.

In a sense, turning to entrepreneurial leveraging recognized and responded to the resource scarcity constraining city choices. In Jones, Sulkin, and Larsen's (2003) terms, a new paradigm for neighborhood policy emerged from changing policy images. Joining what had been separate policy domains and using CDBG funds to leverage investment capital rather than distributing them to neighborhoods (albeit at funding levels too modest to have much discernible impact) became the new policy solution in the face of resource scarcity. This leveraging strategy also retained a place-based focus, although one targeting the economic fabric at the neighborhood level rather than a more holistic approach to "assets." Leveraged investment was directed to a smaller number of neighborhoods, including some perennially listed as the city's CDBG neighborhood targets. However, CDBG funds were no longer being distributed for graffiti cleanup, energy efficiency, and beautification.

One future prospect is that neighborhood policy reforms will continue to "churn" through the system, as in the past. It is also possible that the city will restore enough of the distributional elements of its pre-entrepreneurial policy system—potentially through council-approved TOD projects—to establish a semblance of a citywide neighborhood revitalization strategy consonant with Denver's traditional infrastructure orientation and a less-needy, "whiter" city population. As the snapshots above suggest, TOD may prove to be Denver's most significant and lasting neighborhood revitalization strategy.[24] Although it is not framed as an intentional neighborhood revitalization strategy, TOD's unintended consequences may be its lasting legacy.

Finally, the obstacles to an entrepreneurial policy path during recessionary times may have opened a new policy space for collaborative foundation and nonprofit initiatives. While individual foundation and nonprofit efforts in previous decades were modestly effective at the neighborhood level, recent collaborative efforts such as the Children's Corridor and the formation of Mile High Connects (formerly the Mile High Transit Opportunity Collaborative) reflect a maturing of the philanthropic sector and an increased capacity for collaborative, focused strategies. In May 2011, supported by a Ford Foundation Metropolitan Opportunity grant, fourteen nonprofit and philanthropic organizations, along with US Bank, announced their collaboration to ensure that the multibillion dollar investment in FasTracks infrastructure also provided equitable development, especially for impacted and low-income neighborhoods. Within a few days, the city announced its new Denver Livability Partnership, with similar goals supported by $2.9 million from a HUD Community Challenge grant and a US Department of Transportation TIGER II planning grant. Both initiatives center on equitable TOD: the focus is on affordable housing, good jobs, better education and health services, and mitigation of stark gentrification along the proposed transit lines.

Denver continues to debate how best to combine attention to neighborhood revitalization with the aim of becoming a more entrepreneurial, competitive city. A major question within that debate is how TOD will connect to other initiatives. Resource scarcities, accompanied by ongoing searches for funding, help feed continuing uncertainty, volatility, and instability in policy approach. Denver displays considerable "elite disarray" (Tarrow 1994), often centered in changes in the mayor's office but also involving nongovernmental players, particularly those in the philanthropic sector. Foundation participation brings a different perspective to bear. The ongoing evolution in the city's neighborhood agenda will draw on Denver's rich competition of ideas.

Notes

1. In 2010 "all but 10 of Denver's 77 neighborhoods have a racial/ethnic majority. In 2010, 47 were majority white, 19 were majority Hispanic, and one was majority African American" (Piton Foundation 2011b, 4).

2. The Denver Office of Strategic Partnerships (DOSP), created in January 2004 by Mayor John Hickenlooper, serves as a liaison between the city and the nonprofit sector. This includes, but is not limited to, linking government to neighborhoods. By April 2010 over 2,300 nonprofits had received resources from and 80 nonprofits had ongoing projects with the DOSP. Since January 2007 the DOSP has raised over $30 million in federal grants for city agencies and nonprofits. In 2012 the DOSP launched the Funding and Contracting Efficiency (FACE) initiative to inventory the multiple ways in which city agencies contracted with nonprofits and to highlight procedures enhancing the efficiency, effectiveness, and accessibility of funding for nonprofits. Significantly, the DOSP was able to leverage its Excel Energy franchise funds (franchise fees paid to the city by Excel) with other OED funds to provide the city's $2.5 million share in the Transit Oriented Development Fund. A fifteen-member commission appointed by the mayor of Denver governs the DOSP.

3. The Piton Foundation is a founding member of the National Neighborhood Indicators Partnership, through the Urban Institute. Piton is the partnership's affiliate in Denver. Within its Strengthening Communities (formerly Neighborhoods) initiative, Piton supports the Colorado Community Organizing Collaborative, which brings together grassroots organizations throughout Colorado.

4. Piton's goals are listed on the foundation's website: www.piton.org/piton-foundation.

5. Denver's sales tax rate is 3.62 percent, with 3.50 percent distributed to the general fund and 0.12 percent distributed to a special revenue fund that supports the city's preschool program.

6. In 2009 the general-obligation bond ratings for the City and County of Denver were upgraded to AAA from AA+ by Standard and Poor's Rating Service.

7. Since 1990 Denver and the Denver Urban Renewal Authority have created thirty-seven TIF districts.

8. The contrast with San Diego is particularly sharp (Erie, Kogan, and MacKenzie 2011).
9. Denver controls an unusual revenue source through the Skyline Fund, which receives income from loans and investments made with federal Urban Development Action Grant funds. Denver challenged HUD's efforts to recapture the income generated by the original grant; through litigation, the city wrested control of this program income and continues to invest it in CDBG-eligible neighborhoods through the OED. In 2009 the balance was over $900,000 and replenished monthly at the rate of about $10,000 from existing loans. In addition, the Campaign for Responsible Development spearheaded a campaign (in 2006) for brownfield redevelopment of the fifty-acre Gates Rubber plant in Sun Valley. In exchange for $85 million in TIF subsidies, the Gates developer (Cherokee Denver LLC) agreed to guarantee living-wage jobs, to provide affordable housing (20 percent of the one thousand rental units) in the new mixed-use development, to ensure a cleanup that exceeded state minimum standards, and to hire a union contractor committed to good wages and health care benefits for construction of the publicly financed portion of infrastructure development (Robinson 2006).

    The AEC Foundation's Making Connections initiative in support of the Gates Rubber project resulted in a series of agreements between the developer and city agencies similar to a formal CBA (eventually signed in 2006). While the Gates Rubber project is often listed as a CBA, it does not feature a legal contract between the developer and community groups, as in the Staples CBA in Los Angeles. Rather, a coalition of over fifty labor and community groups mobilized by the Front Range Economic Strategy Center prodded the city to action, garnering significant community benefits in exchange for a development agreement providing $126 million in city subsidies for the project. These linkages include jobs, facilities, affordable housing, and a neighborhood voice in the development of the Gates site, an unusually aggressive linkage program for Denver. The Denver Urban Renewal Authority announced that it would create an urban-renewal district at the site, facilitating the formation of a TIF district (not yet approved) and two other special taxing districts to generate up-front funding for remediation and infrastructure development at the Gates site. La Alma / Lincoln Park and Sun Valley would both gain from these agreements. However, by 2009 these redevelopment efforts had failed and Gates Rubber regained title to most of the site. In 2009 redevelopment of Union Station included a similar CBA to advance construction, service-sector careers, small-business development, and sustainability.
10. To date, organizations in Denver have unsuccessfully applied for Promise Neighborhood federal grants. Denver is not considered eligible for 2013 Promise Zones designation. In 2011 the Denver Regional Council of Government and its partners were awarded $4.5 million in grants by HUD, the US Environmental Protection Agency, and the US Department of Transportation for its Sustainable Communities Initiative. The Denver Regional Council of Government is the lead agency in efforts to address the regional challenges of TOD, with implementation at the level of transit corridors and specific sites. The council is credited with shaping Denver's strong reputation for regional cooperation on transit, environmental, and land-use issues.
11. The city's Revolving Loan Fund, which makes loans to low-income homeowners and businesses for revitalization efforts, is completely funded by CDBG.
12. There are other CDFIs operating in Denver, including Enterprise Partners, Denver Neighborhood Housing Fund, and Mile High Community Loan Fund, but they are primarily involved in housing, not the economic-development initiatives pursued

by Seedco. The Mile High Community Loan Fund did invest funds in the Transit Oriented Development Fund in 2009 and worked with Seedco in 2007.

13. Seedco Financial Services is a subsidiary of its parent company, Seedco, and is a CDFI that managed $178 million in assets in 2007.

14. The leverage measure is the contribution of CDBG money against what other funding sources are available.

15. In 2008 OED's budget was $74 million, 75 percent of it federally funded by HUD and the US Department of Labor. It leverages its resources at a 6:1 ratio, on average.

16. A local nonprofit, the Urban Land Conservancy, made the initial equity commitment of $1.5 million to the Transit Oriented Development Fund and is leading real estate acquisition and management and disposition of assets. The conservancy was formed in 2003 by local business leaders who understood the need for an organization that could permanently secure community assets in metropolitan Denver's urban neighborhoods. Enterprise Community Partners, a national nonprofit, assembled the initial capital and the fund began operations in early 2010. Investors in the fund include the City of Denver, MacArthur Foundation, Colorado Housing and Finance Authority, Rose Community Foundation, Mile High Community Loan Fund, Wells Fargo, US Bank, FirstBank, Enterprise Community Partners (see http://www .enterprisecommunity.com/financing-and-development/community-development -financing/denver-tod-fund#sthash.o1Ff6NQt.dpuf). The City of Denver is the largest investor, providing $2.5 million mobilized and packaged by the DOSP (see n. 2 above) as top loss investment in the fund. See http://www.urbanlandc.org/denver -transit-oriented-development-fund/.

17. Mile High Connects (MHC), founded in 2010, is a Denver-based coalition of more than twenty local and national nonprofits that also supports affordable housing, jobs, and workforce development initiatives for TOD, with the goal of developing low-income communities within walking distance of transit centers. MHC members include Reconnecting America, foundations, community lenders, nonprofit leaders, and philanthropies. With support from the Ford Foundation's Metropolitan Opportunity Initiative, MHC plays a major role in providing data and analysis on the equity and access of area transportation through its Regional Equity Atlas. As of 2013, with a grant from the National Convergence Partnership Innovation Fund, MHC established the MHC Grant Fund to award small grants (less than $25,000) for proposals enhancing integrative community along the transit line. In addition to its independent data-gathering and grant-giving roles in TOD, Mile High Connects is a partner in the Denver Transit Oriented Development Fund and seeks to make it a regional initiative. See http://www.milehighconnects.org/main.html.

18. By 2011 four members of the thirteen-member city council had strong ties to labor or community-organizing groups or both: Robin Kniech, city councilwoman at-large; Paul Lopez (District 3); President Chris Nevitt; and Susan Shepherd (District 1).

19. Numerous academic and private studies have looked at parts of La Alma / Lincoln Park, especially the residential subareas. In 1999 the Annie E. Casey Foundation prepared a profile of the neighborhood, "Transforming Denver's Near Westside," for its community-building initiative. The report is available at www.aecf.org/.

20. Blueprint Denver defines an Area of Change as a place where growth and redevelopment are either desired or under way. The city is to direct growth to those areas and (implicitly) not to others.

21. The agencies involved are HUD, the White House's Office of Urban Affairs, the US Environmental Protection Agency, and the US Department of Transportation.

22. The City and County of Denver Housing Authority is a quasi-municipal corporation governed by a nine-member board of commissioners appointed by the mayor of Denver and approved by the city council. It is actively involved with the Regional Transportation District, the city, and other groups in creating transit villages located along light-rail corridors adjacent to such Denver Housing Authority–owned developments as South Lincoln Park Homes, Sun Valley Homes, and Westridge Homes. It is also involved in partnerships shaping development along the West Line corridor of the FasTracks system. See http://www.denverhousing.org/aboutus/Pages/default.aspx.

23. Tellingly, the Denver Economic Prosperity Task Force (established in 2008) included no neighborhood topics on its agenda.

24. In July 2011, Michael Hancock, an eight-year city council member (including president) and former Urban League president, was sworn in as Denver's second African American mayor after winning 58 percent of the vote. In his inauguration speech, he declared that he wanted to complete FasTracks and to turn the twenty-two-mile corridor between Denver International Airport and downtown Denver into a "Corridor of Opportunity." During his campaign, his top-ten priorities for Denver's neighborhoods included appointing city agency directors who prioritize neighborhood input; merging five existing agencies (unnamed) to create a new Community Partnership Office to facilitate communication and collaboration among city agencies, neighborhood associations, schools, and nonprofit organizations; consulting closely with neighborhoods on matters affecting neighborhoods; implementing community policing; promoting block organizing and neighborhood watches; creating web-based platforms for city-resident communication and neighborhood information using social media, the city's website, and existing Internet resources; continuing the Neighborhood Marketplace Initiative and expanding it into new areas; and creating Community Advisory Boards for each recreation center. In late January 2012, Mayor Hancock's OED launched JumpStart12 as a strategic plan for "revving up Denver's economic engine." His goal of sustainable neighborhood development emphasized "strategic investments to develop/preserve eco-friendly affordable housing in key neighborhoods adjacent to high-transit corridors that were hardest hit by the recession" (City and County of Denver, OED 2012). His plan for 2013 also emphasized transit links but targeted only five neighborhood projects, including the Welton Corridor in Five Points and Elyria-Swanson. See City and County of Denver, OED 2013.

EIGHT

Policy Shift without Institutional Change: The Precarious Place of Neighborhood Revitalization in Toronto

MARTIN HORAK AND AARON ALEXANDER MOORE

Toronto is an affluent, globalized city. However, this aggregate prosperity masks growing sociospatial inequality, which is particularly evident in the city's neighborhoods following the redefinition of Toronto's boundaries by the provincial government. In recent years, a variety of neighborhood revitalization efforts have been launched, many of them under the umbrella of a citywide Strong Neighborhoods Strategy; nevertheless, resource shortages and the limited institutional capacity for addressing neighborhood distress have constrained progress. Like Phoenix, Toronto enjoys a highly professional and activist management structure, but Toronto's managers lack an institutional base for aggressively pursuing a neighborhood revitalization agenda. In this context, the vicissitudes of relying on philanthropy and a complex and changeable intergovernmental climate work against institutionalization of neighborhood concerns. A paradoxical picture emerges in which neighborhood revitalization is on the city's policy agenda and is linked to concerns about rising crime and violence; yet the opportunities for the political expression of neighborhood concerns remain weak because institutional and fiscal capacity are fragmented. Although Toronto's United Way has served a neighborhood advocacy role that parallels that of some foundations in the United States, a significant toll has been taken by fiscal constraints and the failure to institutionalize neighborhood policy. Other than areas with strong gentrification potential, neighborhood improvement projects are difficult to sustain, and momentum is hard to mount even in an affluent city, when efforts rest on a weak institutional base and uncertain financial commitments. As an electoral force, Toronto's stable, older, and progressive-leaning middle-class neighborhoods in the city core have largely been bystanders on the issue of revitalizing distressed communities.

With a population of over 2.5 million situated in a city-region of over 5 million, the City of Toronto is the largest municipality in Canada's largest urban area. Toronto is by most measures an affluent city. The City[1] has many wealthy and middle-class neighborhoods, enjoys steady population growth, and is a powerhouse of economic production. As Canada's dominant "global city," Toronto holds a high share of employment in postindustrial economic activities such as finance, advanced research, higher education, and cultural production, and it is the country's leading center for transnational economic connections. Yet this aggregate picture masks significant growth in sociospatial inequality since the 1980s, characterized by an increasing income gap between the largely gentrified urban core and postwar inner-suburban neighborhoods that feature growing pockets of concentrated poverty. These trends belie Toronto's image as a city of mixed-income neighborhoods, nurtured and sustained by comprehensive planning and a strong local orientation toward social-policy aims (Savitch and Kantor 2002, 108–11).

Although Toronto has little history of major neighborhood revitalization efforts targeting distressed neighborhoods, over the past few years the City has spearheaded two significant policy initiatives. The first involves the complete physical reconstruction of several public-housing complexes. The second is the citywide Strong Neighborhoods Strategy, which promotes youth programming, community capacity building, policing, and neighborhood services in thirteen "priority neighborhoods" located in Toronto's postwar inner suburbs. The ambitious Strong Neighborhoods Strategy has had some success, but it has also faced implementation problems due to a lack of sustained resources and coordination, and its future is in doubt. By contrast, the redevelopment of public-housing projects into mixed-income communities in locations that have market appeal has proceeded as planned. A comparison of these two initiatives illustrates the constraints on neighborhood revitalization in Toronto and suggests that neighborhood improvement is more likely to be realized when it is compatible with economic-development objectives.

This chapter investigates the conditions that have led to the new neighborhood focus in Toronto and examines how historically developed institutional configurations and patterns of political representation have shaped and constrained the current initiatives. What emerges is a paradoxical picture: a confluence of factors has recently driven neighborhood revitalization onto the policy agenda, yet this has occurred in a broader setting where opportunities for the political expression of neighborhood-level social concerns are very weak and where relevant institutional and fiscal capacity is fragmented. As a result, current neighborhood revitalization initiatives rest on fragile political and institutional foundations.

Historical Trajectories: 1953–1998

The present-day City of Toronto covers both the old urban core and the surrounding "inner suburbs" that were developed between the 1950s and the 1980s. This City is a rather new institutional creation. In Ontario—as in some other Canadian provinces—the boundaries, structure, powers, and financing of municipalities can be changed at will by provincial governments. The present-day City was created in 1998 by the Ontario provincial government, which—despite much local opposition—amalgamated the constituent municipalities of the two-tier Metro Toronto federation into a single City. In order to understand current dynamics of neighborhood revitalization, we must first look to the time before amalgamation, when many of the actors and policy orientations that shape and constrain current practice emerged.

Senior levels of government have long funded selected local social policies in Toronto, including affordable housing and social-support programs. Yet there is no Canadian analogue to the succession of federal programs—Model Cities, Community Development Block Grants, Empowerment Zones, HOPE VI—that have financed much neighborhood activity in the United States. The only significant intergovernmental neighborhood program in Canada, the federal Neighborhood Improvement Program, began and ended in the 1970s. Partly as a result, Toronto has little history of revitalization programming targeted toward poor neighborhoods (with a few exceptions, noted below), so we cannot speak in Toronto of a clear historical trajectory of revitalization. Instead, we must pay attention to the intersection of multiple historical trajectories of politics and policy. We will focus, on the one hand, on local social policy, including affordable housing and local social services, and, on the other hand, on neighborhood politics.

Between 1953 and 1998, the area now comprising the City of Toronto was governed by a two-tier Metropolitan system. The upper-tier Municipality of Metropolitan Toronto (or Metro) had responsibility for major roads, public transit, metropolitan planning, policing, and—after 1966—the delivery of a range of provincially mandated social services. Six lower-tier municipalities, including the old City of Toronto, managed all remaining municipal responsibilities. Until 1988, when direct elections were introduced, Metro Council was composed of indirectly elected political representatives chosen by the councils of the lower-tier municipalities. The trajectories of local social policy and neighborhood politics, and the relationship between them, developed differently in the old central City of Toronto than in the postwar suburban municipalities that also formed part of Metro. We will thus discuss trajectories in each of these geographical areas separately.

Social Policy and Neighborhood Politics in Metro's Postwar Suburbs

The lack of decent affordable housing was a significant issue in Toronto in the 1950s, and it spurred a major effort to construct public housing. Conscious of the failures of American urban renewal, provincial policymakers chose to spread public housing across Metro's newly developing postwar suburbs. The construction was led by the provincial government's Ontario Housing Corporation. The new upper-tier Metro government played a role as well, using its planning powers and control over infrastructure spending to pressure in-Metro suburbs to take on their "fair share." Between 1964 and 1975 the Ontario Housing Corporation constructed more than fifteen thousand units of public housing in Metropolitan Toronto, almost all of them on "greenfield" sites in the postwar suburbs (Rose 1980, 175). The provincial government's focus on equity also led it to pool local financing for provincially mandated social services[2] and to grant responsibility for their delivery to Metro. By 1966 Metro was responsible for delivering services such as old-age supports, welfare, and children's services. As Frances Frisken (2008) argues, by distributing public housing and equalizing social-policy capacity across the Metro area, these developments helped to prevent the kind of inner-city decline that many American cities experienced at this time.

Yet Metro's rapidly growing postwar suburbs resented and resisted the imposition of new social infrastructure and costs. Already in the 1960s, suburban resistance altered plans to distribute suburban public housing in small low-rise developments; instead, it was built in larger high-rise complexes clustered in "undesirable" areas (Frisken 2008, 94–95; PI[3]). In the 1970s, in response to pressure from suburban representatives, Metro developed the norm of not going beyond minimum provincial mandates in the delivery of social services (Frisken 2008, 172). As a result, Metro remained a vehicle for the delivery of provincially mandated social policies, dependent on provincial financing, and unable to develop significant social-policy initiatives of its own.

Metro's suburban municipalities experienced rapid property development between the 1950s and the 1980s. Maintaining low property taxes and providing a hospitable environment for developers were top priorities of the lower-tier municipal councils. Neighborhood-level organizations had little influence over policy, and neighborhood politics was dominated by ratepayers' associations. The quintessential example of these governing arrangements existed in the municipality of North York. Under the leadership of Mayor Mel Lastman from 1972 until amalgamation in 1998, North York developed close relationships with large development companies and focused on large-scale property development. Local social concerns were simply not on the policy agenda. As one longtime neighborhood social activist in North York put it, "We were pretty much invisible to [North York] City Hall before amalgamation. They didn't want to hear about us; they liked to pretend that we didn't exist" (PI). The development focus of councils in the inner suburbs, together with the Metro government's policy of sticking to minimum provincial social-policy mandates, meant that the Metro system was largely incapable of responding to the emergence of new pockets of suburban poverty in the 1980s.

Social Policy and Neighborhood Politics in the Core City of Toronto

During the Metropolitan Toronto years the core central City of Toronto, whose population held steady at about 650,000, followed very different trajectories of local social policy and neighborhood politics than the rest of Metro. Between the 1940s and the 1960s, the central city was the site of Toronto's few experiments in urban renewal. The first and largest, Regent Park, was a two-thousand-unit public-housing complex built in the late 1940s on the site of demolished nineteenth-century row housing (Frisken 2008, 68). A handful of further urban-renewal projects were realized in the 1960s. Yet absent systematic intergovernmental support, their impact on the fabric of the core was limited. Even so, as Christopher Klemek (2011) notes, in the late 1960s urban renewal and Metro's program of expressway construction became the target of a wave of vociferous criticism led by middle-class gentrifiers and their intellectual supporters, who included urban thinker Jane Jacobs. This wave crested in 1972, when a middle-class-led neighborhood "reform" movement—which Klemek (2011, 179) characterizes as an example of "New Left urbanism"—swept Toronto's local elections.

Under "reform" mayors David Crombie (1972–78) and John Sewell (1978–80), the central City of Toronto focused on harnessing its rich property tax base in order to pursue a variety of progressive policies. Some of these—such as historical preservation and the beautification of public spaces—reflected the quality-of-life concerns of the new middle class. Others involved elements of social redistribution. The City established a new affordable-housing company, CityHome, which built more than two thousand units of cooperative housing in the 1970s, with federal and provincial funding support. It established a wide variety of small-scale discretionary funding programs for local social services and amenities, which in turn nurtured a vibrant base of nonprofit organizations of all kinds. Such policies soon gave the city a reputation as a center for urban progressivism.

Yet as the city continued to gentrify and the intergovernmental social-support system was cut back, poor residents increasingly got squeezed out of the core area, and the property and amenity interests of the middle class took precedence (Magnusson 1990, 178). The city retained a range of small-scale social programming, and it regularly leveraged funding from property developers for social amenities. Yet there were also frequent conflicts between neighborhood associations dominated by middle-class homeowners and advocates for the poor. In the end, the reform movement left central Toronto a somewhat-paradoxical legacy of innovative social programming and social-service organizations, on the one hand, and vibrant neighborhood associations dominated by upper-middle-class residents, on the other.

The Rise of Sociospatial Inequality in Toronto

There is much historical truth to the image of Toronto as a city of mixed-income neighborhoods. While the city has long had some very poor neighborhoods, sociospatial inequalities were for many decades quite low. Yet, starting in the early 1980s, gentrification in the old core city was mirrored by the growth of pockets of poverty in the inner suburbs. In the 1990s this trend accelerated markedly, with poverty in the city becoming more spatially and ethnoracially concentrated.

After a severe recession in the early 1990s, Toronto reinvented itself as a hub of Canada's new postindustrial, globally integrated economy. The well-paid "knowledge workers" who flocked to the central city pushed housing prices up steadily.[4] Yet the postindustrial economic sectors that have driven inflation in housing values and rents since then employ only a minority of Toronto's residents, and the economic base for middle-income work has shrunk. As a result, Toronto has experienced significant income polarization, analogous to that experienced in other globally integrated cities (Sassen 2001, 250; United Way of Greater Toronto 2004, 15). Income polarization has been accompanied by increases in sociospatial segregation. Intergovernmental support for social housing[5] declined steadily between the late 1970s and the late 1990s (Carroll 2002), and social-welfare supports were slashed drastically by a conservative provincial government that came into power in 1995 (Ibbitson 1997). In the expensive local housing market, this contributed to the emergence of a new reality, in which the mixed-income metropolis of the popular imagination is increasingly sociospatially divided. Affluent neighborhoods are located in the old urban core, as well as along subway corridors that extend into the inner suburbs. Concentrated poverty, meanwhile, is increasingly found in parts of the inner suburbs that feature aging public housing, sparse social-service facilities and public amenities, and poor public-transit access. Between 1981 and 2001, the number of "poor" or "very poor" census tracts in the inner suburbs shot up from 16 to 108 (calculated from United Way of Greater Toronto 2004, 26, 27).[6]

In addition, sociospatial segregation is taking on an increasingly ethno-racialized dimension. Toronto has for many years been a magnet for immigrants, and since the 1970s most immigrants have come from places other than Europe. Between 2001 and 2006 alone, about 448,000 immigrants settled in the Toronto Census Metropolitan Area, 287,000 of them in the City itself (City of Toronto 2011). While many immigrants are highly skilled, there has in recent years been a growing correlation between immigrant settlement and poverty (Ley and Smith 2000, 2007). Gentrification of the core has forced many immigrants to settle in low-rent, high-rise housing in the postwar suburbs (Ley and Smith 2007). The result has been the rapid ethnoracialization of sociospatial segregation. As of 2005, only 28 percent of residents in wealthy inner-city areas were foreign-born, as opposed to 61 percent of residents in poor areas in the postwar suburbs (Hulchanski 2010, 12).

The new poverty in Toronto's inner suburbs is highly concentrated in small geographical areas, mostly in high-rise housing complexes (both public and market) built in the 1960s. One consequence is that poor areas tend to be much smaller than the boundaries of any one ward, which impedes the political representation of the needs of the poor at the municipal level. In addition, in contrast to historical patterns in Toronto, recent immigrants have by and large *not* concentrated in ethnically homogeneous neighborhoods; rather, small pockets of various ethnic groups are scattered across the city, and the population in any one poor area is usually very diverse (City of Toronto 2008b). Such settlement patterns help to account for the apparent inability of the political system to respond to rising suburban poverty concentrations in the 1980s and 1990s. Indeed, the poverty trends we have discussed here went virtually unnoticed by politicians or in broader public discourse in Toronto until 2004–5, when they suddenly exploded onto the local policy agenda following the amalgamation of Toronto.

After the 1998 Amalgamation: Institutions and Actors

By the 1990s the Metro system was in crisis. The introduction of a directly elected Metro council in 1988 exacerbated long-simmering political conflict with the lower-tier municipalities. In addition, Metro was surrounded by a rapidly growing ring of affluent outer suburbs without political or fiscal ties to Metro, which was seen as a problem by many policymakers. A lengthy debate about reform (Frisken 2008) ended in 1998, when the Conservative provincial government amalgamated the two-tier federation into one large City of Toronto, over the strenuous objections of many local actors (Horak 1998). The outer suburbs, which were a bulwark of support for the provincial government and opposed integration, remained politically separate from the new City.

The New City of Toronto

The post-1998 City of Toronto, which covers all of what used to be Metro, has a modified council-manager system of government. The nonpartisan council is composed of forty-four councilors elected in single-member wards, plus a mayor elected at-large. The new City's wards are large (the average ward population is 58,000) and often combine several dissimilar neighborhoods. While well-established homeowners' associations have at times been able to use the ward system to pursue their interests (Moore 2013), the new ward system further entrenches the long-standing disconnect between political representation and neighborhood-level social-policy concerns. Toronto's mayor has a prominent public presence and is typically the subject of high public expectations, yet in most respects the mayor remains first among equals on council. Mayors have on occasion benefited from a confluence of factors to champion their own causes, but sustained agenda-setting influence has been elusive.

Toronto's leadership structure is often criticized as being simultaneously top-heavy, in that political power is concentrated at the citywide level, and fragmented, in that there is no clear locus of authority in the large, non-partisan council (Bellamy 2005). In this context, many long-range munici-pal policy initiatives have come from the administration. The City has a vast and professionalized administration, presided over by a City manager, who is appointed by council. Its social-policy apparatus is strong and so-phisticated, built on the combined institutional capacity of the old City of Toronto and the upper-tier Metro government. The lead administrative body for neighborhood revitalization policy is the Social Development, Fi-nance and Administration Division, which is responsible for coordinating social policy. In addition, Toronto has several major special-purpose bod-ies that council controls at arm's length. One of these, the Toronto Com-munity Housing Corporation (TCHC), has also played a particularly cru-cial role in neighborhood revitalization.

While Toronto's administrative capacity is strong, the City operates in a perennial atmosphere of fiscal shortage that restricts the possibilities for new program development. Toronto is very dependent on property taxes, which in 2005 made up 43 percent of operating revenues (City of Toronto 2005a, 56). In addition, the 1998 amalgamation was accompanied by a "local services realignment" that gave the City more responsibility for fund-ing from its property tax base a range of services, including public transit, social housing, and mandated social-assistance programs. When combined with other postamalgamation costs, these new responsibilities placed fis-cal stress on the City. In addition, the City's high commercial property tax burden relative to surrounding suburban municipalities places pressure on local politicians to hold the line on tax increases in order to avoid business flight. All these factors create an environment in which new policy initia-tives that require a significant commitment of City funds rarely win council support.

Societal Actors

Most of Toronto's grassroots policy actors are not particularly well suited to participate in comprehensive neighborhood revitalization initiatives. While Toronto is home to a host of small-scale nongovernmental social-policy agencies, these are heavily concentrated in the inner city and are sparse in the postwar suburbs. In addition, community social agencies tend to focus on service provision rather than on municipal-level advocacy and policy and are "used to thinking of what we do in terms of serving people, not in terms of serving particular neighborhoods" (PI). Finally, as we saw above, emerging high-poverty areas are both geographically hyperconcentrated and ethnoracially diverse, which works against political representation of these areas through the ward system.

However, Toronto does have a major organization that has the political and the fiscal clout to put social-policy interests on the political agenda. The United Way of Greater Toronto, founded in 1956, collects donations from individuals and corporations and distributes them to its network of member organizations—a broad cross section of social-service agencies of varying size and focus. Since the early 1990s, the United Way has grown rapidly, filling some of the void left behind by the decline of government social expenditures. Between 2001 and 2009 its budget grew from $69 million to $147 million (United Way of Greater Toronto 2001, 2009). Until the 1990s, the United Way operated purely as a charitable funding agency. In the late 1990s, however, the agency began to reorient itself toward policy advocacy as well—a trajectory that would place it at the forefront of the push to develop a citywide "Strong Neighborhoods Strategy."

Market-Linked Revitalization in Regent Park

Despite more than two decades of growth in concentrated poverty in Toronto, comprehensive neighborhood revitalization remained off the citywide political agenda in the early years after amalgamation. Indeed, City government was in a state of near chaos as officials grappled with integrating seven municipal units into one while facing severe fiscal shortages (Bellamy 2005). During the two terms that Mel Lastman served as mayor (1998–2000 and 2001–3), council was dominated by politicians whose primary concern was fiscal restraint. No intergovernmental support for addressing neighborhood distress was available, and the City's political structure lacked mechanisms for the articulation of neighborhood concerns. While many City administrators in the Social Development, Finance and Administration Division believed that the problems of distressed neighborhoods called for integrated place-based policy, there was, in the words of one administrator, "zero political appetite" for this approach (PI).

Nonetheless, it was during this time that the first of Toronto's two major multineighborhood revitalization initiatives was launched, driven by TCHC. TCHC was formed in 2001 out of the merger of the Metropolitan Toronto Housing Authority, which managed provincial public-housing stock, with CityHome, the social-housing authority run by the preamalgamation City of Toronto. With 58,000 housing units in its portfolio and a $742 million (2009) budget, TCHC is the second-largest social-housing authority in North America (TCHC 2010a). TCHC's founding director, former CityHome chief Derek Ballantyne, saw the creation of an integrated social-housing entity with massive physical assets and borrowing power as an opportunity to reconstruct deteriorating public housing in Toronto (PI). But in an environment of political disinterest and fiscal shortage, any such effort would have to have minimal impact on the municipal budget. An opportunity emerged in the case of Regent Park.

Regent Park is Toronto's oldest and largest social-housing project. For decades, it has held the dubious distinction of being Toronto's poorest area. Prior to the start of reconstruction, the two census tracts that include Regent Park were home to 11,000 people; the housing project itself was home to 7,500 (TCHC 2006). As of 2006, almost 70 percent of the population in this area lived below the low-income cutoff for families. The population is much younger and less well educated than the citywide average. The vast majority of Regent Park residents are both visible minority and foreign-born. The area includes significant populations of more than a dozen minority groups, with the largest groups being South Asian, black, and Chinese (City of Toronto 2008b).

Regent Park housing has long been in disrepair, with estimated repair costs as of 2002 topping $400 million (PI). The area has a history of resident mobilization for reconstruction. In the late 1980s, some longtime residents formed the North East Regent Park Redevelopment Working Committee and spearheaded a campaign to reconstruct part of the complex. The attempt fell apart when the provincial government—which owned the housing project—refused to commit resources (Meagher and Boston 2003, 89). A resident survey found that many blamed Regent Park's built form for fostering criminal behavior and creating unsafe spaces and complained about the lack of commercial amenities in the complex (Meagher and Boston 2003). In early 2002 TCHC commissioned a study that found that tearing down and rebuilding the housing project would cost only about 20 percent more than conducting necessary repairs (PI). Since it is located near the central business district and next to one of Toronto's most desirable gentrified neighborhoods, Cabbagetown, the Regent Park site has strong market potential. Inspired by recent experiences of mixed-income revitalization in the United States (PI), TCHC officials decided to leverage the market potential of the site and rebuild Regent Park as a mixed-income neighborhood.

TCHC began its revitalization planning with a resident engagement process (PI; Meagher and Boston 2003). Regent Park residents were hired as "community animators" to run a series of consultations in each of Regent

Park's twelve major linguistic and cultural communities (Meagher and Boston 2003, 11–18). About two thousand residents, or 30 percent of the total adult population of Regent Park, participated (Meagher and Boston 2003, 5). A remarkable degree of cohesion concerning neighborhood problems and priorities among Regent Park's various ethnic and cultural communities was evident. Residents supported a phased rebuilding that would create a mixed-income community. They felt strongly that they should be assured replacement accommodation during the rebuild and have the right to return to a new social-housing unit in Regent Park. They wanted a new Regent Park to have ample commercial and community service space and through streets that connected it to surrounding communities. Furthermore, there was a strong feeling that redevelopment should also involve comprehensive planning for social services and recreational facilities (Meagher and Boston 2003).

In December 2002 TCHC released a $1 billion[7] draft redevelopment plan that reflected these priorities and that received "overwhelming approval" from residents (Meagher and Boston 2003, 51; PI). The plan involved replacing all the 2,100 existing units of social housing with 2,800 units, and adding 3,310 units of market-rate housing (TCHC 2006), more than doubling the density of the site. The $450 million cost of the social-housing component would be covered by borrowing, deferred maintenance costs on the old housing, and profits from the market-housing component (PI). A gradual approach to redevelopment, which would spread the project over fifteen years and several phases, would help to ensure sufficient demand for emerging market housing and make the temporary relocation of existing residents more feasible (PI). In 2004, over the protests of some social-housing advocates (J. Sewell 2005), TCHC altered its original plan to rebuild all the existing social housing on-site and chose instead to build about one-quarter of this housing in nearby locations, in order to enhance the site's market appeal (TCHC 2004, 5; PI).

The 2003 municipal election brought Mayor David Miller and a left-of-center council into power, riding on a wave of support among downtown Toronto residents. This change solidified political support for the Regent Park plan, which had been quite attractive to local politicians from the outset, since almost no new city money was required. In March 2006 TCHC established a public-private partnership to construct Phase I (out of a total of five phases). There were fears in late 2008 that the recession would slow or even stall the project. However, the housing market recovered quickly and Phase I was complete by April 2010. The project also benefited from the 2003 Canada-Ontario Affordable Housing Agreement, which contributed $23.5 million to the approximately $170 million cost of Phase I (TCHC 2010b). In April 2009 TCHC launched Phase II. There have been some difficulties in the resident relocation process, and residents express some anxiety about their right of return, but for the most part it appears that resident support remains solid (PI).

Although the physical redevelopment process has gone remarkably smoothly in Regent Park, other aspects of the project have faced some difficulties. The core funding model includes no provision for social infrastructure such as recreational spaces, community meeting spaces, and parks. TCHC officials from the outset recognized a need for at least $50 million in government funding for such spaces. In order to shore up political support, TCHC decided not to seek this funding up front but rather to secure it on an as-needed basis (PI). In 2005 City officials pushed to secure funding for social infrastructure from the provincial and federal governments as part of a trilevel Urban Development Agreement. This effort failed after the election of a conservative federal government in January 2006. Funding has nonetheless materialized for some pieces of community infrastructure, including an $11 million indoor pool and a $24 million arts and cultural center (PI; Javed 2009). While these investments are significant, neither was a top priority for TCHC planners, and the political need to realize them quickly required TCHC to revise its revitalization plans (PI). One local social agency respondent somewhat bitterly suggested, "It's not like the politicians suddenly opened their hearts and wallets to the downtrodden. In fifteen years this place will be teeming with yuppies and property values will be way up. That's why we've got this funding" (PI).

From the outset TCHC insisted that revitalization was about "more than just bricks and mortar" and needed to include provisions for enhanced resident services. However, developing a strategy for resident services proved to be complicated (PI). Regent Park is served by an array of vibrant local social-service agencies, which are significant agents in the community. However, there is more conflict than cooperation among these agencies, and many of them see the revitalization scheme as threatening to marginalize their client base as wealthier residents move into the neighborhood (PI). In 2004 TCHC and the City of Toronto launched a "social development planning" process that aimed to involve residents and social agencies in defining priorities for future community services. Resident interest in the lengthy three-year process proved difficult to sustain. And agency representatives took the process as "an opportunity to stake their specific, narrow claims on priorities and resources in the future Regent Park" (PI). The resulting Social Development Plan provides a long laundry list of some seventy priorities, "lacks a clear vision" (PI), and has had no stable funding for implementation. The future development of resident services in Regent Park remains very much an open question (PI).

Such challenges notwithstanding, TCHC is now aiming to replicate the Regent Park model of revitalization in other social-housing complexes (TCHC 2008). A much smaller (four-hundred-unit) project using this model has already been completed in Don Mount Court, a social-housing complex close to Regent Park. Others are now under way or being planned in five more social-housing complexes. However, only some of these locations have strong market appeal, and it is hard to envision how the Regent Park approach can succeed in locations with low market appeal without either significant additional government investment or an overwhelming bias toward market housing. Most suburban TCHC sites are far removed from wealthy and/or gentrifying areas and have limited market potential. Ironically, the market-linked character of TCHC's revitalization strategy may make it very difficult to implement precisely in those areas where poverty has grown most rapidly.

The Strong Neighborhoods Strategy

During the early years after amalgamation, neighborhood revitalization was very much off the citywide policy agenda. Yet by doing away with the old two-tier system, amalgamation had opened up the possibility that issues of spatially concentrated disadvantage might be tackled by a local government system that joined the commercial tax base and "progressive" political inclinations of the downtown core to suburban areas of social distress. Aware of this possibility, the City administration's Social Policy Analysis and Research unit (SPAR) was, in the words of one informant, "quietly working away" to develop a citywide spatial perspective on poverty.

Shortly after amalgamation, SPAR developed a system of 140 "social planning neighborhoods" to aid in geographically based data collection and issue identification. These social planning neighborhoods were defined through a purely administrative process and largely without reference to local understandings of neighborhood boundaries. According to an administrator involved in this process, "we tried to design the social planning neighborhoods to include diverse communities, even though this wasn't always possible. We wanted to avoid creating units that isolated poverty" (PI).[8] Using the social planning neighborhoods, City administrators then developed a database of neighborhood-level social indicators (PI).

The issue of spatially concentrated poverty in Toronto gained public attention in 2003, when the Toronto City Summit Alliance, a civic coalition of prominent business and community leaders, published a report titled *Enough Talk: An Action Plan for the Toronto Region*. The report highlighted rising neighborhood distress in the postwar suburbs and called for a coordinated intergovernmental response to enhancing community services there (Toronto City Summit Alliance 2003, 24–25). Yet the focusing event that really brought attention to poor suburban neighborhoods was a series of highly publicized gun murders in the summer and fall of 2003, the majority of which involved young black men from poor inner-suburban neighborhoods (Fowlie 2004). Even though Toronto murder rates remain very low in comparative perspective[9] and the city had only three more murders in 2003 than in 2002 (Fowlie 2004, 31, 28), the concentration of violence among black youth in a handful of postwar suburbs and the deteriorating social conditions in those same areas were quickly linked in popular and political discourse. The rise in gun violence thus came to be viewed as a problem of "neighborhood distress" that required a place-based policy solution.

The call for a response was soon taken up by Mayor Miller, who proposed a Community Safety Plan (CSP) that garnered enthusiastic support from City council. While the CSP was rather short on specifics and funding commitments, it nonetheless marked the beginning of a paradigm shift in Toronto political discourse, one in which the spatial dimension of social distress moved from being largely invisible to having a central role in the causal narrative of distress. The CSP highlighted the spatial dimension of violence in the city and identified four postwar suburban neighborhoods —Malvern, Jamestown, Kingston-Galloway, and Jane-Finch—as "at-risk" neighborhoods that required new public investment. In substantive terms, the CSP combined two very different understandings of the policy problem. On the one hand, since the trigger for the plan was violence, the immediate problem was social disorder and the need to prevent its escalation. On the other hand, the City's social administrators, the left-leaning Miller, and some councilors saw violence as a symptom of underlying structural problems: limited social opportunity and disempowerment among young people in some neighborhoods (PI). As a result, the CSP proposed "a package of prevention initiatives that will act as a catalyst for civic action to improve public safety and will build on existing strengths in our communities" by developing "an effective blend of programs and services—particularly for youth who live in at-risk neighborhoods" (City of Toronto 2004, 5). Given the fiscal constraints facing the City, the CSP also established a Community Safety Panel composed of prominent civic and business leaders to leverage private-sector resources. As one administrator interviewed for this research noted, the framing of the CSP allowed councilors to appear to be "tough on crime" while in fact opening the door to the development of spatially targeted social and community programming. Yet the goals of crime reduction and community development in poor neighborhoods remained in uneasy juxtaposition with each other.

The creation of the CSP encouraged the formulation of larger-scale policy initiatives at a time when the prospects for intergovernmental support of urban policy seemed on the rise. At the end of 2003, Paul Martin, who had endorsed a "New Deal for cities" as part of his bid for the leadership of the federal Liberal Party, assumed the post of prime minister. At the provincial level, Dalton McGuinty's Liberal Party defeated the Conservatives in the October 2003 election and also promised more support for urban-policy concerns (Horak 2008). These developments encouraged a flurry of policy advocacy on the part of local actors. In the spring of 2004, just after Council adopted the CSP, the United Way of Greater Toronto released its *Poverty by Postal Code* report, which linked social inequality to the dearth of social and community services in certain postwar suburban neighborhoods. This added considerably to the momentum of the emerging focus on the neighborhood dimensions of poverty. In May 2004 the United Way teamed up with the Toronto City Summit Alliance and the City of Toronto to launch the Strong Neighborhoods Task Force (SNTF), a high-profile effort to develop a strategy for Toronto's distressed neighborhoods. The SNTF also included some local social-service organization representatives. In addition, taking advantage of a new openness to multilevel policy dialogue at the provincial and federal levels, the SNTF included representatives from both of these levels of government.

The SNTF issued its final report in June 2005. It identified nine postwar suburban neighborhoods as "priority neighborhoods" for investment. For the most part, these were *not* the same neighborhoods named in the CSP. Whereas the CSP targeted high-violence areas, the SNTF neighborhoods reflected the emerging understanding among many in Toronto's social-policy community—including both United Way and City officials—that neighborhood distress was in part the product of long-term lack of access to social and community services. The selection methodology thus combined indicators of socioeconomic distress with an assessment of the accessibility of key services, such as libraries, schools, health centers, and youth services (SNTF 2005, 18–24).[10] In addition to identifying priority neighborhoods, the report called for a large-scale, five-year investment agreement among all three levels of government to channel public money into the priority neighborhoods.[11] Further, the SNTF recommended that a "Local Neighborhood Investment Partnership" be created in each priority neighborhood to develop, in dialogue with local residents, neighborhood-specific investment priorities and that an intergovernmental coordinating body be set up to commit and coordinate major new public resources to meet these locally defined priorities (SNTF 2005, 28–29).

The recommended investment agreement never materialized. In the spring of 2005 Toronto was working on an Urban Development Agreement with other levels of government, focusing on the Regent Park revitalization. After the publication of the SNTF report, these negotiations were expanded to include all thirteen of the priority neighborhoods. However, it soon became clear that no level of government was willing to commit resources on a scale envisioned by the SNTF. Focus thus shifted to negotiating a "framework agreement" for investment, without immediate financial commitments (PI). However, in January 2006 the federal Liberal government was defeated and its Conservative successor rejected the practice of trilevel agreements, effectively killing the initiative. Along with it died the prospect that Toronto would develop overarching institutional arrangements capable of comprehensively planning and funding a citywide neighborhood revitalization strategy.

Notwithstanding the failure of intergovernmental institution building, the SNTF report had a major impact on the evolution of neighborhood revitalization in Toronto. Immediately after the report came out, administrators in Toronto's SPAR unit proposed that the CSP priority neighborhoods and the SNTF priority neighborhoods both be included in a citywide Strong Neighborhoods Strategy (SNS) that would target thirteen priority neighborhoods in total. As if to underline the urgency of action, the summer of 2005 once again brought a spate of gun violence among poor (primarily black) youth. This time, the violence was considerably worse, with fifty-two gun murders in the year. As one City administrator respondent put it, "We all just went: holy s——! We need to do something about this!" In October 2005 City council approved an SNS that identified thirteen priority neighborhoods (City of Toronto 2005b). One administrator interviewed for this project commented that this was "a miracle. Here were twenty councilors saying, 'We don't need more money in our wards.' It probably wouldn't have happened without the violence." Given intense media coverage of the violence, the provincial and federal governments also felt pressure to act, and they also accepted the thirteen neighborhoods as priority areas for their own spatially targeted investments (PI).

Due to negotiation among councilors seeking funding for their wards, the areas identified for priority investment under the SNS were considerably larger than those proposed in the earlier reports. The result was a framework of thirteen very large "priority neighborhoods" (PNs), which were often not recognized as "neighborhoods" by residents. The population of each PN averages more than 37,000, and each typically includes multiple, demographically diverse local communities. Together, the thirteen PNs are home to some 482,000 people (calculated from City of Toronto 2008b)—nearly 20 percent of the City of Toronto's population. In addition, the boundaries of PNs do not fit ward boundaries. This both reflects and reinforces the long-standing political disconnect between representation and local social policy in Toronto. Neither City administrators nor United Way officials saw much positive potential in aligning PN boundaries with ward boundaries, since, in the words of one City administrator, "political support for [the PNs framework] is broad but very shallow." Indeed, actors committed to neighborhood-focused social policy in Toronto have tended to see councilors, most of whom focus heavily on the concerns of their property-owning constituents, as hindrances rather than as allies. One City administrator we interviewed went so far as to say that "the minute Councilor X comes out of his office to yell at me about neighborhood revitalization, that's when I know we're doing good work."

The Strong Neighborhoods Strategy in Practice: A Proliferation of Initiatives

The SNS marked a shift in which the spatial contours of poverty suddenly took center stage. Starting in 2005, the SNS provided a framework used by all three levels of government, as well as the United Way of Greater Toronto, to develop spatially targeted programs focusing on the thirteen PNs. The programs have had a wide variety of substantive foci, ranging from community social planning and capacity building to the provision of youth services, social and recreational infrastructure, and targeted policing services. Yet this move in policy orientation was not accompanied by a corresponding shift in the institutional landscape, and this has had significant implications for the way in which the SNS framework has been translated into practice. Because the hoped-for trilevel investment and coordination did not materialize, investment in Toronto's PNs has taken the form of multiple, loosely coordinated programs, often short in duration, launched by a variety of actors who pursue sometimes-incommensurable goals and methods.

The federal government's involvement in PN programming has been very limited. The only significant federal initiative is Action for Neighborhood Change (ANC), a modest capacity-building program that ran between 2005 and 2007 in six distressed neighborhoods in six Canadian cities, including the Toronto PN of Scarborough Village. Although the ANC was by all accounts well received (PI), the Conservative federal government that was elected in 2006 chose not to renew it, and the program was taken over by the United Way of Greater Toronto.

The provincial government has been more heavily involved than the federal government. Its two most significant funding commitments in the priority neighborhoods have been to the Toronto Anti-violence Intervention Strategy (TAVIS) and the Youth Challenge Fund (YCF). TAVIS was launched in the fall of 2005 by the Toronto Police Service. TAVIS aims to reduce gang activity and gun violence by deploying eighteen-member "Rapid Response Teams" in high-violence neighborhoods. This is complemented by a "community mobilization" program that aims to encourage local residents to work with police. As of 2008, the Ontario provincial government had provided over $20 million in funding for TAVIS (Ontario Ministry of Community Safety and Correctional Services 2008), and the program is still in place as of late 2013.

The other major provincially funded program was the YCF. Initiated in the summer of 2006, the program had a three-year life span. The YCF provided grants to youth-led initiatives in the thirteen PNs in areas such as arts, safety, peer support, and skills training. Altogether, the YCF funded 111 projects and leveraged $30 million in provincial funding into $46.6 million in total funding (Youth Challenge Fund 2010). The fund was exclusively focused on black youth, who are, according to a senior YCF employee, "out of school and in and out of the justice system—or on the verge" (PI).

The United Way has also developed some significant programs of its own in the PNs. The largest of these involves the construction of multipurpose community hubs that provide space for health, recreational, and social services. Supported in part by funding from the Provincial Ministry of Health and the City of Toronto (through the POL fund, discussed below), the United Way has built and opened seven such hubs as of 2013, at a total cost of more than $9 million (United Way of Greater Toronto 2013).

Ironically, although the SNS is officially a City of Toronto initiative, new City investment in the PNs has been limited, and even the geographical reallocation of existing City funds has been difficult (PI). A review of the sparse attention paid to the SNS in official City documents and at council meetings since 2005 supports the assertion (noted above) of "broad but very shallow" political support for SNS programs. That said, there have been some City programs related to the SNS. The Community Safety Panel, which operated until the end of David Miller's tenure as mayor in October 2010, leveraged some modest private-sector investment into youth employment and engagement programs. The City's Social Development, Finance and Administration Division also developed Neighborhood Action Teams (NATs) within each of the thirteen PNs. The NATs bring together administrators from various City divisions in order to "silo-bust" (PI) and coordinate the provision of City services and programming at the neighborhood level. In several neighborhoods, the NATs have been turned into Neighborhood Action Partnerships (NAPs), which bring City administrators, local residents, and service agency representatives together to identify neighborhood priorities. Finally, between 2006 and 2009 the City funded the Partnership Opportunities Legacy Fund, which leveraged $13 million of City funding into $37 million in total funding, dedicated to the construction of social and recreational infrastructure in the PNs (City of Toronto 2009).

Given the broad array of organizations and programs investing in Toronto's SNS neighborhoods, it is very difficult to determine exactly how much new money has flowed into these areas since 2005. A rough estimate arrived at by combining totals from the programs discussed above suggests that somewhere in the neighborhood of $190 million in new money had come into the thirteen PNs as of the end of 2012. This scale of investment—while not insignificant—is rather modest in view of the fact that the thirteen PNs together have a population of nearly 500,000, whereas Regent Park, with 7,500 inhabitants, is undergoing a $1 billion revitalization program. Perhaps more important than the actual funding invested is the role that the SNS played in introducing a neighborhood focus into the discourse about social policy in a political environment where this has been largely absent. Almost all the citywide actors interviewed for this project emphasized that the SNS, in the words of one, "change[d] the way government thinks about what it does at the local level." Yet when we examine the implementation of SNS programs in one PN between 2005 and 2010 (the year that the primary research for this project was completed), we see a fundamental lack of coherence and integration that does not augur well for the sustainability of this shift in policy orientation.

Implementing the Strong Neighborhoods Strategy in Jane-Finch

With a population of more than eighty thousand, Jane-Finch, located in the former municipality of North York, is the largest of Toronto's PNs. The area is both poorer and more heavily populated by immigrants and visible minority groups than Toronto as a whole. Yet this "neighborhood" is actually a sprawling, eight-square-mile area that includes many distinct demographics. It features at least ten significant concentrations of TCHC housing. It is in these areas that gang-related violence among black youth has repeatedly spiked in recent years (City of Toronto 2008a). Jane-Finch also includes numerous areas of middle-class single-family housing, populated mainly by second-generation Italian Canadians. The PN, which covers parts of three wards, is represented locally by three councilors, who are all of Italian descent and who respond mainly to the needs of the Italian Canadian home-owning population. Several respondents noted that much of the Italian Canadian population actively dislikes the poor immigrant population, who are seen by many as "those damn black immigrants." Overall, the area's largest visible minority group is black, although there are also large populations of South Asians, Latin Americans, and Southeast Asians.

Jane-Finch is home to a small but diverse base of social organizations. Respondents divided these organizations into two categories: "mainstream agencies," which have a professional staff and rely on United Way, government funding, or both, and "resident groups," which are voluntary and largely unfunded. There are a handful of mainstream agencies in Jane-Finch, including the Jane-Finch Community and Family Centre, the Jamaican Canadian Association, and the Delta Family Resource Centre, each of which offers a range of community social programming. There are also a number of small resident-led groups that have a variety of very specific, targeted goals, ranging from youth mentoring and support for single mothers to antiracism education. Until the emergence of the SNS, most of these resident groups had little interaction with government officials and survived largely without external funding (PI).

Just as in the rest of the city, neighborhood-level groups in Jane-Finch were not significantly involved in the development of the SNS framework. However, many of the programs subsequently developed under that framework involved neighborhood groups in various capacities. Representatives of local groups (both "mainstream" and "resident-led") viewed social-planning and capacity-building projects positively. The city's NAP initiative was seen as particularly successful, due both to the work of the City's capable community development officer for the area and to the broad representation of neighborhood agents at the table. Although it had no dedicated funding to disburse, the NAP successfully linked local agents to resources provided by a variety of programs, especially those run by the City itself. For example, the NAP process in Jane-Finch resulted in the identification of local needs for community space, several of which were then met using funding from the City's Partnership Opportunities Legacy Fund (PI).

The United Way's community capacity-building project, the ANC, was likewise assessed positively. Yet some neighborhood actors also noted a mismatch between the long-term goals of the ANC and the short-term availability of funding. As one respondent put it: "The ANC project front-loaded money towards developing the local planning and advocacy capacity of residents, but by the time they had plans and groups in place, there was no more ANC money, and other funds have been drying up too. So you build up expectations in the community without adequate follow-through." In addition, some respondents noted that there was a rivalry of sorts between the City-led NAT process and the United Way's ANC, both of which pursued similar goals and involved distinct but overlapping sets of neighborhood actors.

According to several respondents, the province's YCF was also prone to problems generated by the short-term duration of available funding. Some praised the innovative youth programming funded by the YCF. But others called it "a joke" and "a waste of $45 million.". In part, such vitriolic assessments may stem from the fact that the YCF self-consciously disbursed money directly to new grassroots youth initiatives, bypassing many of the preexisting groups in the neighborhood. However, even respondents with a stake in YCF programs were critical. One noted: "The approach was to throw buckets of money at the neighborhood without making sure the infrastructure was in place to use it properly. And pretty much as soon as these youth groups were on their feet, oops, the money's gone, sorry guys. . . . So now most of the YCF-funded programs are dying a quick, horrible death. So much for empowerment." The Toronto Police Service's provincially funded TAVIS program got the most uniformly negative reception. Neighborhood actors saw its focus on targeted crime reduction through rapid-response teams as fundamentally opposed to the goals of support for and empowerment of youth espoused by many other SNS programs. Respondents used phrases like "a disaster" and "totally counterproductive" to describe TAVIS. One noted that "recently TAVIS has been getting a bit better; they've realized they have to focus on the community piece of the puzzle too. But there are still problems. When youth feel they're being targeted and harassed, they won't respond to initiatives. You have to deal with the issue of trust before you can make much headway."

Overall, then, from the point of view of neighborhood organizations, between 2005 and 2010 the SNS brought some positive change to Jane-

Finch, but serious problems also emerged. First, despite the coordinating efforts of the NAPs and the ANC, there was no overarching coordination for various SNS programs, which as a result espoused distinct and sometimes-conflicting goals and methodologies. Second, while neighborhood actors value "sustained engagement and long-term solutions" (PI), much of the money made available through SNS programs was short-term project funding. Third, all the SNS programs were disconnected from local political representation mechanisms. Significantly, some respondents noted that they tried to avoid involving local councilors in neighborhood revitalization activity, since "their interest is political—I mean, it's about what gets them reelected—and that's not the kind of interest we need." These problems speak of the broader lack of integration of neighborhood social policy into the institutional and political fabric of Toronto and are symptomatic of the precarious position of the neighborhood revitalization agenda in the City.

The Precarious Place of Neighborhood Revitalization in Toronto

The American literature on neighborhood politics offers competing interpretations of the potential and the limits of neighborhood social policy (Horak and Blokland 2012). One strand of argument, which stretches from Kotler (1969) to von Hoffman (2003), suggests that the neighborhood, as the smallest spatial building block of social life and social mobilization in a city, is a powerful and effective unit for articulating and addressing social-equity concerns. A contrasting strand of argument, represented by writers such as Stone (1976), Katznelson (1981), and Goetz and Sidney (1994), suggests that the structure of urban political economies systematically privileges the politics of property development, and that the redistributive potential of neighborhood politics and policy is limited. There is powerful empirical evidence in both the United States and Canada to support the latter argument. The politics of property remains crucially important in the postindustrial city, yet—as we argue in the opening chapter of this volume—a new confluence of political and economic factors can also open up new spaces for policy attention to neighborhood distress. In Toronto, the confluence of institutional change, political change, and increasing sociospatial inequality brought revitalization onto the agenda. But the underlying structure of local politics did not change, and the possibilities for realizing comprehensive revitalization initiatives have remained accordingly constrained, with initiatives that tie into property development proving easier to realize.

Toronto has been characterized by some American scholars as a "social-centered" city, one in which local politics affords redistributive concerns a larger place than they are afforded in most American cities (Savitch and Kantor 2002). Social-equity concerns have indeed been prominent in Toronto politics, at least from time to time. The emergence of neighborhood revitalization initiatives over the last few years builds on a history of Toronto social policy that includes both the provincially led construction of public housing in the 1960s and the local progressive politics of downtown Toronto in the 1970s and 1980s. Furthermore, during David Miller's second term as mayor (2006–10), neighborhood revitalization formed part of a broader municipal strategy aimed at combating the concentration of poverty in the postwar suburbs. In early 2007 the Toronto Transit Commission, with Miller's enthusiastic support, published an ambitious transit expansion plan called "Transit City," which aimed to build over a hundred kilometers of light-rail lines in the postwar suburbs, which are poorly served by rapid transit (Kalinowski and Spears 2007). In 2009 the provincial government committed $7.2 billion in funding to this project (Ontario Ministry of Transportation 2009). In 2008 Miller unveiled another initiative, called "Mayor's Tower Renewal," a proposed retrofit program for Toronto's one thousand concrete-frame residential high-rise buildings, which house many of the city's poorest residents (Miller 2008).

Yet the history of progressive social policy in Toronto is a limited and episodic one, a pattern confirmed by recent developments. Since 2010, Toronto's inner-suburban social agenda has fallen on hard political times. The fall 2010 municipal election saw Miller (who did not run for reelection) replaced by Rob Ford, a plainspoken populist running on a platform of spending cuts. Ford, elected with strong support from homeowners in Toronto's inner suburbs and supported by a shift to the political right on council, quickly repudiated virtually all elements of Miller's social agenda (Paperny 2010). Early on in Ford's term, the SNS seemed unlikely to survive the political shift. But by 2012, Ford's council support had dramatically weakened as the mayor dealt with a host of personal scandals that made him the object of international notoriety. In this context, the United Way and City administrators developed an updated framework, the "SNS 2020." The new framework renamed priority neighborhoods "Neighborhood Improvement Areas" (NIAs), presented a new methodology for identifying NIAs, and proposed stronger mechanisms to monitor progress on key social and economic indicators (City of Toronto 2012). SNS 2020 was approved by council in 2012, and thirty-one NIAs were selected in April 2014. However, as of late 2014, no new municipal resources had been allocated. The new mayor, John Tory, a moderate conservative who overcame a strong challenge from Rob Ford's brother Doug in the October municipal elections, has thus far given little indication that he will bring a renewed focus on disadvantaged neighborhoods. That said, in contrast to the SNS the TCHC's strategy of mixed-income revitalization of Regent Park and other social-housing projects has forged ahead in recent years, building (literally) on the strong market development potential of many TCHC housing complexes.

In an important recent book, *Reforms at Risk*, Eric Patashnik argues that "what is required to *initiate* policy reform should not be confused with what is required to *sustain* it" (2008, 155, italics in original). A combination of factors in Toronto produced a paradigm shift in policy discourse toward a neighborhood-level spatial approach to fighting poverty. Yet, as Patashnik argues, in order to be sustained in the longer term, policy reforms must alter the institutional landscape into which they are introduced, such that new institutional capacities, political opportunity structures, and incentives entrench the new policy goals in the fabric of political life. In Toronto, a shift in policy thinking was neither accompanied nor followed by major institutional change. Instead, the preexisting institutional system has remained intact, and its features have in turn shaped and constrained neighborhood revitalization policies. These institutional features include the insulation of neighborhood social concerns from ward-based political representation, the absence of an overarching coordinating authority for place-based social intervention, and the limited, fragmented, and short-term availability of financing for neighborhood revitalization. Under these structural conditions, Toronto's policymakers have been able to implement revitalization as planned only in instances where they have chosen to harness the forces of the real estate market in pursuit of physical reconstruction.

The contrast between the SNS and the TCHC's program of social housing reconstruction is instructive. Absent either local or intergovernmental institutional change, the implementation of the SNS in Toronto has been hampered by a lack of coordination and fiscal capacity, resulting in a proliferation of disparate initiatives. While several of these have been significant, and some have been well received at the neighborhood level, the whole remains rather less than the sum of its parts. In comparison, the TCHC has been able to use its institutional clout and to harness market forces in pursuit of regeneration initiatives that have been far more intensive than any produced within the SNS framework. But even here, the redistributive potential of revitalization is limited to parts of the City with strong market-housing appeal, like Regent Park.

One of the most interesting aspects of Toronto's trajectory on neighborhood revitalization is that past successes in tackling poverty may well be contributing to the city's inability to address the concerns of poor neighborhoods today. Metro Toronto's past success in dispersing social housing throughout the city, coupled with the emergence of low-rent market housing in compact high-rise communities, has led to scattered pockets of significant poverty in the city. "Neighborhoods" like Jane-Finch are not vast swaths of low-income housing but middle-income suburbs pierced with concentrated extreme poverty. This geography, along with the ethnoracial diversity of poor communities, further hinders their access to a local political system long dominated by the concerns of property owners.

In a few short years, Toronto has achieved quite a lot in the field of neighborhood revitalization. Yet developing a sustained, large-scale set of neighborhood-focused social policies, with significant redistributive implications, would require both a fundamental opening of local politics to the interests of the poor and an institutional reordering of both local governmental and intergovernmental resources to support sustained policy action. At this time, neither of these shifts seems likely. As a result, Toronto may see further redevelopment of public housing into mixed-income neighborhoods in the near future, but broader neighborhood revitalization efforts focused on the increasingly distressed inner suburbs are likely to remain below the political radar until the next triggering event.

Notes

1. We use the term "City" (capitalized) to denote the municipality of Toronto and to distinguish it from the "city" as an urban form.
2. The provincial government financed much of the cost of mandated social-service programs, but a significant minority share of costs was also loaded onto the local property tax base.
3. "PI" stands for "personal interview." Twenty-three individuals from governmental and societal organizations were interviewed for this research. All interviews were confidential.
4. This trend resumed quickly after a brief dip in housing prices associated with the recession in 2008–9.
5. The term "social housing" gradually replaced "public housing" in Canadian policy discourse at this time, reflecting a change in federal and provincial policy from funding publicly built and owned housing to subsidizing the construction, operation, or both of a variety of other forms of assisted housing.

6. The report classifies census tracts with double to triple the national average family poverty rate (which dropped marginally in these twenty years, from 13 to 12.8 percent) as "poor" and those with more than triple the national rate as "very poor" (United Way of Greater Toronto 2004, 10).

7. This figure includes planned TCHC investment in new social housing ($450 million), private investment in market housing ($500 million), and anticipated government investment in infrastructure and community facilities ($50 million).

8. The logic behind this statement is not entirely clear given that the purpose of social planning neighborhoods was precisely to define geographical areas with particular social needs. This apparent confusion may reflect what several interviews conducted for this work revealed—an enduring ambivalence among many actors about whether place-based approaches should indeed replace the more people-based social-policy strategies of the past in Toronto.

9. For example, Baltimore's homicide rate in 2006 was twenty-four times as high as Toronto's (Topping 2008).

10. According to several individuals interviewed, the "accessibility of services" criterion is the reason that Regent Park was excluded from the priority neighborhoods list, since the history of Regent Park as part of the preamalgamation City of Toronto helped to ensure that "its service coverage is among the best in the city" (PI). This rationale was not accepted by local community-based organizations in Regent Park, which were outraged that the neighborhood did not make the priority list (PI).

11. In doing so, the SNTF report drew upon the smaller-scale precedents of trilevel Urban Development Agreements that had recently been signed in Vancouver and Winnipeg as vehicles for coordinating public investment in the poorest neighborhood in each of those cities.

NINE

Contending with Structural Inequality in a New Era

ROBERT P. STOKER, CLARENCE N. STONE, AND MARTIN HORAK

A new era surrounds the politics of distressed neighborhoods. New players and ideas, fresh policy tools, and a different context separate the current scene from the redevelopment period that followed World War II. That time left deep scars. Bulldozers rolled, expressways cut through long-established communities, and red lines spelled a fate of relentless decline for large swaths of America's cities. Few localities or their states made plans to respond constructively to vast shifts in demography. In short, aging neighborhoods suffered from disruption and neglect. But times have changed; today many of the old practices have been modified or ended, and some cities have reentered a period of growth.

Still, despite such reasons for optimism, distressed neighborhoods face new challenges and an uncertain future. While neighborhood revitalization efforts are evident across the urban landscape, and vibrant communities and sparks of renewal can be found in places once written off as dead or dying, disinvestment still plagues many areas. What, then, does our study tell us about the place of distressed neighborhoods in today's urban politics? When all is said and done, is our research merely another chapter in a long-running narrative of urban failure or can a counternarrative be discerned amid the crosscurrents of a still-evolving neighborhood politics? Does the new era hold the *possibility* of more beneficent treatment of distressed neighborhoods?

Some observers may think answers to these questions are dictated by inexorable market forces with little or no room for political agency. An always-present danger is that the capacity to act on wide-ranging, interwoven needs will be undercut by larger systemic forces. In the present era such forces are quite evident; global economic competition, the complexities of cross-domain policymaking, resource constraints, and persistent structural inequality are all at work in distressed neighborhoods. Yet political agency remains a factor. If we look back at the postwar redevelopment years, it is hard to overlook the part that selected elites played. At that time coalitions of strategically located actors shaped the paths that policy followed, largely determining which courses of action would be advanced and which not.

This book opened with a sympathetic embrace of Michael Katz's call for an alternative to the "urban narrative of failure" (2011). With the experiences of six study cities in consideration, is there ground for maintaining this embrace? We affirm in this concluding chapter that there is. We have seen progress. And we see in an unfolding new era the possibility of additional positive change. We conclude this book by looking back at the six study cities to identify the key elements of the emergent new era of neighborhood politics and by looking ahead to suggest ways to further advance the possibilities the new era holds.

The New Era of Neighborhood Politics

Governing the postindustrial city involves no mere extension of past patterns and practices. The six narrative chapters point to noteworthy shifts in how cities view and handle neighborhood policy. In contrast to the postwar redevelopment period, economic and community development efforts now intermingle. A narrowly economic understanding of development policy, privileged and shielded from other considerations, has yielded to a more flexible understanding and a more open approach. A closed form of elite convergence no longer holds. We do not find today the kind of big agenda-setting mobilizations of elites that Robert Salisbury (1964) brought to attention a half century ago. The overarching condition is that governing capacity no longer rests with a cohesive body of elites in command of an array of resources responding single-mindedly to the decline of the city's economic core. Governing power is now less concentrated, and today's urban movers and shakers are less single-minded about the city's business core and find themselves thinking more about how to reconcile bundles of social and economic challenges. The way forward is at once cloudier than it once seemed to be and more open to a variety of possible trajectories.

The postindustrial time poses anew the trial of coping with social and economic change and determining how the costs and benefits of such change are to be allocated. What does it mean politically to confront this test in today's setting of diffuse power relationships and weaker elite consensus? In its particulars, the postindustrial period is quite different from the redevelopment period. Intensified globalization has unsettled a once-established pattern, pulling some players away from heavy engagement with the city and helping bring new players and understandings into the picture. Hence, it is important to consider who today's key players are, what motivates them, what ideas and understandings guide them, and which policy tools they use.

As the influence of collective business groups has waned, foundations and ed & med institutions have become growing participants in neighborhood policymaking. At the same time many neighborhood actors have moved beyond an oppositional stance to try instead to shape the terms on which change impinges on their communities. These shifts have made new relationships possible. During the redevelopment period many neighborhood groups sought to block an economic-development agenda that endangered their quality of life. For their part, progrowth coalitions sought to exclude neighborhoods from policymaking. In the new era, neighborhoods are sometimes enlisted as coproducers in growth efforts. On occasion, elites pursue alliances with neighborhood participants. Although the neighborhood role is not necessarily very large or very stable, investment elites can even be motivated to support community development as a means to advance their agenda. Community-based groups that once contended against powerful business–city hall alliances now seek benefits in often highly complex initiatives.

Although the new era arrived piecemeal as various actors on the urban stage awakened to new conditions initially seen as, at most, loosely connected, the ensuing responses have coalesced into a new political order for postindustrial cities. Present-day arrangements for governing are not highly cohesive, nor do they rest on a single overriding factor or set of actors.[1] Instead, they are constituted by a body of interacting factors and agents that vary over time and across cases in terms of their particulars. We summarize the shift to a new governing order in table 9.1.

The table shows that the context for governing in the postindustrial city is quite different from the redevelopment period. The urban condition itself has shifted in important ways. Elite preoccupation with rescuing the central business core has given way to a more assorted body of concerns. Concurrently, the movers and shakers have become a more diverse lot. New players with fresh ideas can alter the power balance to the benefit of distressed neighborhoods. For example, foundations may have striking differences with other elites, as was true in Baltimore when the Annie E. Casey Foundation required a "paradigm shift" to give greater weight to residents' concerns as a condition of its participation in the East Baltimore redevelop-

Table 9.1 Comparing the redevelopment period and the new era

The redevelopment period	The new era
Local politics often featured a cohesive local governing coalition composed of city government and major businesses collectively organized for policy action.	Local politics features a more open, fragmented governing circle composed of city government, foundations, and the ed & med sector, with a less active role for *collectively* organized corporate business.
Governing coalitions in cities gave priority to an agenda of physical redevelopment in order to fend off downtown decay and promote economic growth.	Although the city has a stake in the interrelated issues of economic growth, human capital development, and crime control, no broad agenda has taken shape to pursue these issues, and a stable, integrated governing priority has not been clearly established.
Cities were a focus in national political campaigns, and ample federal resources were available to support a physical remake of the city (particularly through expressway construction and urban renewal).	Urban issues receive less attention nationally, and support at the national level for addressing city problems is sporadic and on a downward track.
Typically, the city's governing coalition enjoyed a strong capacity to advance its agenda; redevelopment was often politically insulated, and distressed and at-risk neighborhoods found themselves marginalized.	Creating capacity in a fragmented political context in which resources are scarce is the ongoing struggle at the center of city politics; economic development is no longer an insulated policy domain; the local agenda is more open-ended, and more attention goes to the ways in which policy domains intersect one another.
Much urban political analysis emphasized the tension between the redevelopment agenda and the need to address concerns in distressed neighborhoods; the relationship was often seen as negative-sum.	The new era reveals the possibility of complementary (positive-sum) relationships between pursuing economic growth and addressing concerns in distressed neighborhoods.

ment initiative. Resource-rich and strategically placed players are no longer tightly drawn together. While private investment continues to be a prime consideration, business interests have become more selectively engaged—with some less focused on the central city. Social problems have multiplied and grown at a time when governing power has become more diffuse.

As resources for neighborhood revitalization have come to be exceedingly scarce, bringing resources together increasingly involves identifying intersections between neighborhood revitalization and other policy aims, especially economic development and transportation. Anticrime and public-safety concerns can also play a significant role, as they have done, for example, in Toronto and Phoenix. In the United States, a major missed opportunity is urban-school reform. Top-down preoccupation with test score accountability is an uncongenial partner to neighborhood concerns, even though a case can be made for linking educational improvement with community development.[2]

A shift in the local governing pattern does not mean that neighborhoods have entered a golden age. Quite the contrary—beyond the challenges of coping with the emerging postindustrial era, trends in both the United States and Canada have hampered local efforts to address the needs of distressed neighborhoods. During the redevelopment period, relatively generous intergovernmental funding was available to enhance local capacity to plan and pursue an aggressive redevelopment program. In the new era, austere national budgets pose perhaps the single most serious constraint that local governance must overcome. Ironically, as the push for neighborhood concerns to be addressed locally has expanded, national policymakers have failed to develop a sustained and constructive neighborhood agenda. Particularly for neighborhood-related initiatives, cities find themselves in search of resources wherever they can be found—through state- or province-funded programs, by federally financed channels in overlapping and intersecting policy domains, from foundation grants, by partnership arrangements with ed & med institutions, or, as is often the case, by cobbling together support from multiple sources.

For a telling glimpse of this emerging future, consider Baltimore's experience with the area adjoining the medical campus of Johns Hopkins University and Denver's experience in moving beyond its distributional approach to neighborhood improvement. In both an older city with a fading industrial past and a younger city with boom-bust cycles, complexity asserts itself in policy design and finance, and it does so by showing the inadequacy of acting in small, disconnected moves. Developing the capacity to address wide-ranging and interwoven needs across policy domains has become the latest test that cities and their neighborhoods face.

In addition, today's diffuse pattern of power is still marked by substantial structural inequality. Starting with tightly limited resources and typically facing negative stereotyping as well, distressed neighborhoods are handicapped in multiple ways. Even when supported by external funds, neighborhood action is usually quite limited and may carry the stigma of "special treatment" (Hero 1992; Schneider and Ingram 1993). Neighborhoods of well-off residents, by contrast, are almost never viewed as receiving extraordinary financial benefits because much of the subsidy they receive is indirect. For example, benefits in the United States are distributed in the form of deductions from federal taxes for interest on home mortgages and property taxes—deductions that rise in value as incomes go up. The regressive policy bias is largely hidden by the low-visibility, complex federal tax code.

While structural inequality is a constant, policymaking in the new era no longer segregates neighborhood concerns from an insulated priority agenda for economic growth. Intermingled policies have come to be the raw material of neighborhood politics.[3] Positive-sum scenarios are now more readily imagined, and tools such as community benefits agreements (CBAs), transit-oriented development, Comprehensive Community Initiatives, and mixed-use and mixed-income housing developments provide means for converting imagination into concrete plans.

Of course, that positive-sum scenarios can be imagined and planned does not mean that zero-sum calculations have disappeared. Grounds for conflict remain. As the city studies demonstrate, some clashes derive from racial or class differences within neighborhoods, while other considerations can pit distressed neighborhoods against elites. Policy elites and neighborhood actors are very differently situated in the broader system of urban power relations, and a wide chasm often separates their perceptions of each other. Other differences can widen the gap even further. The amount and terms of resident displacement are obvious flashpoints, but another source of tension is the scope of revitalization efforts. Unlike neighborhood residents, many elites are inclined to think about neighborhood policy mainly in terms of property. For residents revitalization involves more than the value of real estate—residents in distressed neighborhoods concern themselves with a variety of issues and services, from crime control to parks and open space, from youth programs to expanded employment opportunities. Neighborhood issues thus do not form a tightly circumscribed policy arena.

To be sure, the spatial dimension of neighborhood politics remains important. Conflicts arise over highly particular sites—LULUs (locally undesirable land uses), for instance. And, of far-reaching concern, the spatial dimension brings about the intersection of neighborhood policy with both transportation and economic development. Thus, community-based actors find themselves engaged with elite players who are often focused on issues other than the quality of neighborhood life. Neighborhood politics thus inescapably involves interaction between players with divergent preferences and highly unequal power.

What can be made of a situation in which one side possesses resources and a solid power base while the other has a weak power base and scant resources, scant particularly in relation to the scope of problems it confronts? Oppositional tactics play a part, as in resistance to an initiative put forward by actors who are institutionally well positioned. But to gain effectiveness, such an approach needs to be accompanied by an understanding of the situation that puts the cause of the marginal side in a positive-sum light. Simply thinking in terms of redistribution, as Toronto so clearly illustrates, is unlikely to go very far as a fulcrum for the revitalization of distressed neighborhoods.

With elite cohesion often lacking, the capacity to govern in the new era has become more an ongoing process of fragmentary mobilization. For distressed neighborhoods the current power challenge is primarily one of constructing anew, not contending with a tight-knit band of elites. As Denver shows, a process that at one time consisted mostly of allocating government appropriations has given way to a "politics of construction," an ongoing task of putting together resource-yielding arrangements.

Cross-City Observations

As shown in chapter 2, the six study cities vary widely in socioeconomic features. Yet all display clear signs of movement into a new, postindustrial era. Since several factors have played a part, there is room for variation in how the shift has manifested itself. There is no simple pattern.

In cities as different as Baltimore and Phoenix, electoral outcomes mark especially clear turning points. However, the shift to a new era follows no neatly linear electoral path. For instance, after Harold Washington's election as Chicago's mayor, his elevation of the city's neighborhoods to a new position of political prominence faltered when a fatal heart attack brought his leadership to an end in only four years. Later elections moved quite different policy leadership to the mayor's office. Denver has also seen a far from linear electoral path, but in both Chicago and Denver an actively engaged philanthropic sector has played a key role in visibly heightening attention to the needs of less-well-off neighborhoods. Toronto's United Way played a similar role, especially in the promotion of the Strong Neighborhoods Strategy. As a highly fragmented polity, Los Angeles has taken no single giant step to mark a shift, and its new city charter is more a sign of an unfulfilled potential than a prominent move. But the creation of the Los Angeles Alliance for a New Economy (LAANE) and its backing in obtaining a landmark CBA for the Staples Center area are nevertheless an especially notable departure from that city's earlier development policy and practice.

In some instances the philanthropic sector has also been an important force in selectively strengthening neighborhood capacity, either directly, as in the Pacoima neighborhood of Los Angeles, or indirectly by strengthening community-based alliances, as in the case of LAANE. Yet philanthropic foundations have little presence in the political life of Phoenix's neighborhoods. In a globally marginal city like Baltimore, the ed & med sector is immensely important. Yet it has a barely visible role in contributing to the neighborhood agenda in Phoenix, which also is lacking a substantial global presence but has a highly regarded municipal administration. Toronto is very much a global city and, like Phoenix, has a well-regarded corps of professional managers in city government, but Toronto's United Way has played a major role in promoting the city's neighborhood agenda. On that score, another key Toronto player is the Toronto Community Housing Corporation, a very large public-housing agency that controls and can leverage substantial property in areas of the city with strong market potential. Worthy of note as well, Toronto's affluent inner-core communities, despite their historical reputation as a progressive force, have played no visible role of support for the city's "inner-suburban" ring of distressed neighborhoods. The parts of a city's politics rarely move in a synchronized fashion.

While a host of factors bring neighborhood distress into civic awareness and various entities play parts in addressing conditions of distress, we find that the dynamics of the politics of neighborhood revitalization is best understood in these broad terms: the need for resources and how they are obtained, the degree to which and ways in which neighborhood voices are institutionalized, and how these two factors interact. Structural disadvantage is always in the background, but political agency is in the foreground, with its impact tied to the way institutionalized relationships operate.

If revitalization means taking on multifaceted problems, then seeking and assembling resources are at the heart of the process. This is a tall order in times of austere national budgets. Choices about how to pursue this process are typically made by happenstance that reflects the availability of resources (often with a major part played by nongovernmental actors) rather than by city-level strategic planning. Opportunities and constraints vary by city, and even at the neighborhood level, no uniform pattern is evident. Ad hoc decision-making easily becomes the default process; calls for a more systematic approach are made but seldom fully heeded. Yet outcomes are not predestined. Local institutions can either mitigate the ad hoc tendencies of new-era policymaking (creating more systematic, strategic policymaking) or aggravate them (bringing about more fragmented, disjointed initiatives). Thus, a key question is to what extent and how neighborhood policymaking is institutionalized locally. How do players in and within various sectors relate to one another? Are there strategic relationships that hold over time and span issue concerns?

Among our study cities Phoenix stands out as the clearest case of a sustained, systematic approach to neighborhood policymaking. In Phoenix an electorally achieved political change was a crucial first step, followed by a policy embraced by the city's highly professional and well-regarded management team. Moreover, compared with many older cities, Phoenix had only a limited expanse (at least, prior to the foreclosure crisis) of residential disinvestment. Phoenix's highly professionalized approach occurred within a city-manager structure, though political developments, including a newly elected mayor, opened the way to greater attention to neighborhoods. In this case electoral politics and a widely recognized managerial capacity converged to reveal a substantial potential to institutionalize neighborhood concerns within city government, an arrangement that can bring stability and an important resource-seeking capacity into play. Although Phoenix started small, the city established a Neighborhood Services Department and staffed it with policy-minded professionals—a step that actors in Baltimore and Los Angeles contemplated but never brought about, that Chicago's city council undid after the death of Mayor Washington, and that Denver fell far short of with its decision to embed neighborhood policy in the mayor's Office of Economic Development. Phoenix's neighborhood program stands out for its stable institutional foundation, with professional staff not only adept at using city money strategically but also capable of maintaining an ongoing search for additional resources to put in place complementary initiatives.

Toronto contrasts with Phoenix by showing the consequences of a disjointed follow-through to an awakened neighborhood moment. Our Canadian study city was brought to the brink of a comprehensive and systematic approach by an initiative supported by the Toronto United Way. The launch of the Strong Neighborhoods Strategy was initially backed by intergovernmental funding, but when that funding proved to be unreliable and was taken away, frail local institutionalization left only a skeleton of the initiative in place. Although Toronto (like Phoenix) brings policy and managerial professionalism to its engagement with issues of neighborhood distress, it also brought a complex legacy of governmental restructuring and a fickle stream of intergovernmental support to its effort. Toronto's situation was complicated by its sparse experience with territorially oriented social policy, and in 2010 conditions for neighborhood action took an even less favorable turn with the election of an antigovernment and self-identified populist mayor who was not interested in leading on such issues.

Together, Phoenix and Toronto show how complicated navigating the public sector can be, even when a tradition of patronage politics (as per Baltimore and Chicago) is missing and the hyperfragmentation that characterizes Los Angeles is absent as well. The central point is that institutionalizing neighborhood policy in a city government department is not a simple do-or-don't decision. *Effective institutionalization involves integrating neighborhood policy with the political fabric of a city and giving it the kind of depth and centrality that can make it a robust factor in the governing process.* In the inset, Seattle illustrates the point further.

With its machine politics tradition, Chicago followed a much different path. Despite a surge in neighborhood empowerment during the brief mayoralty of Harold Washington, Chicago saw its participatory planning for a federally funded Empowerment Zone disregarded when a patronage mentality took over during implementation. It fell to institutions outside city government, the MacArthur Foundation and its reliance on the Local Initiatives Support Corporation (LISC), to try to put neighborhood revitalization on track through the New Communities Program (NCP). Moreover, as noted in chapter 4, it was hoped that the NCP would pioneer a new approach to community development and alter the ways the relevant players aligned (Chaskin and Karlstrom 2012, 22). However, this hope was in vain, as the NCP failed to target system-level change and focused instead on individual neighborhood initiatives. The city council's orientation toward particular ward-based benefits thus continued to be an unhelpful backdrop to community engagement.

Limited and Uneven Change

Elsewhere, Baltimore's Sandtown-Winchester initiative, once thought to offer a national model, went astray when foundation-funded professionals resisted the case made by BUILD for community engagement as a first step. In light of Baltimore's patronage-laden tradition, this city's movers and shakers have favored reliance on quasi-governmental, public-private partnerships. While reassuring to Baltimore's business and civic elites, which is important because otherwise they would be reluctant to contribute resources and expertise to neighborhood improvement efforts, this organizational form can also limit the voice of neighborhood residents and magnify the tendency toward ad hoc policymaking. In 1999 Baltimore neighborhoods brought off an impressive two-day Neighborhood Congress, identifying a citywide agenda, but the Citizens Planning and Housing Association, the nonprofit sponsoring the event, declined to support its

SEATTLE AS AN EXEMPLAR

To underscore the broad scope and multilayered character that a neighborhood policy could encompass, consider Seattle's program as an exemplar.[1] Though Seattle is a city outside the half dozen we studied, it highlights the value of institutionalization even while differing from our six study cities in a crucial way. In 1987, against a background of struggle over growth management, Mayor Charles Boyer assembled support for moving from talk about neighborhood planning to creation of an Office of Neighborhoods. The office gained firmer institutionalization in 1990 when, under newly elected mayor Norm Rice, it became a full-fledged municipal department and enjoyed city funding commensurate with this standing.[2]

Although Seattle's neighborhood program *was created to serve all neighborhoods, not just those in* distress—and hence, its political foundation and policy challenge differ in notable ways from the efforts undertaken in our study cities—Seattle's experience illustrates what a robust policy can do. It shows that neighborhood policy need not be a succession of disconnected initiatives.

In Seattle, neighborhoods have gained an insider voice; city resources have been made available for ongoing revitalization activities; neighborhoods have been encouraged to organize; and they have enjoyed an enhanced capacity as active participants in politics and policy processes. Further, Seattle's neighborhoods are a *collective* force in city politics.

Seattle's program consists of multiple components aimed at building and maintaining wide support. The neighborhood program has a substantial staff

1. For this cameo, we have drawn on a recently completed study (Sirianni 2009), complemented by an account of the program by its founding director of thirteen years (Diers 2004). Another city with an ambitious neighborhood program is Minneapolis (Fagotto and Fung 2006). The Minneapolis program struggled with an internal division between homeowners and advocates of affordable housing (Goetz and Sidney 1994, 1997). The launch of the program called for two successive ten-year plans. Funding was allocated for the initial ten-year plan; the second was to be funded by Tax Increment Financing derived from the initial plan. This proved to be overly optimistic, with the result that the second ten-year plan was sparsely funded, and the program was eventually replaced. Hampton, Virginia, also launched a substantial neighborhood program, but it also was less ambitious than Seattle's and was somewhat overshadowed on the city's agenda by the city's youth program (Sirianni 2009; Stone and Worgs 2004).

2. With sustained city hall backing, the department got off to a strong start covering multiple bases. When the program underwent major cuts in 2002–3 in response to a drop in tax revenue, it was by then well established as part of city government (Sirianni 2009, 109).

capacity for reaching out to communities insufficiently represented through political channels and, like Phoenix, a strong ability to work internally among government agencies to overcome silo tendencies and secure inter-departmental cooperation. For neighborhoods lacking a strong voice, the department launched a leadership development program and operated under the assumption that "the communities with the greatest needs are the communities that are least organized" (Diers 2004, 32). Hence, outreach and the development of community capacity were integral parts of the department's mandate.[3] Even after staff cutbacks, the department worked with the city's Department of Planning and Development to conduct some fifty meetings with groups across various parts of the city (Sirianni 2009, 113).[4] Until 2002–3, the department relied extensively on program development managers not only to supply and provide access to technical assistance but also to serve as mediators for intraneighborhood disputes.

The program also featured neighborhood service centers (successors to "little city halls") to facilitate work with community groups. In addition, in Seattle's thirteen districts the city formed independent community councils to give recognition to, and provide staff support for, various civic groups in order to bring them into the neighborhood network. One task of the departmental staffers who serve as district coordinators is "to facilitate collaborative work among community councils and other civic groups" (Sirianni 2009, 78). The neighborhood service centers also provide individualized help to residents.

As an incentive to engage in neighborhood improvement, Seattle established and still maintains a neighborhood *matching* fund. The neighborhood contribution can be in cash, in the form of an in-kind contribution of labor, or a combination of the two. In meeting their contribution neighborhoods can develop partnerships with civic groups and others. Applications go through a review process and approved projects are subject to oversight, which includes compatibility with the city's comprehensive plan. An advisory committee of neighborhood residents from the district councils is part of the overall effort to foster close contact between staff and the neighborhoods.

3. The department's founding director, Jim Diers, quoted a mentor: "Organizers organize organizations" (2004, 26). Diers thus understood institutionalization as a central part of his charge in directing a department.

4. For its part, Phoenix recruited a senior staff member experienced in promoting community engagement.

Even in this cursory overview, we can see that Seattle has developed an intricate arrangement to pursue neighborhood improvement, and that the effort involves residents in a way that broadens their understanding of the policy process and of the challenges the city faces. Politically, the process draws support citywide from all sectors of the population, but with an understanding that special efforts are needed to bring in the sectors of the city that are least advantaged. As city revenue declined, Seattle did not maintain its *initial* high level of staffing for neighborhood improvement. However, in order to maintain neighborhood involvement, the city's Department of Planning and Development conducted some fifty meetings with groups across the city (Sirianni 2009, 113). In the overall picture varied activities have had a mutually reinforcing effect.

Three things stand out about Seattle's experience: (1) from early on, reflecting the initial department director's background in community organizing, the department has made a special effort to include the city's distressed neighborhoods and, where neighborhood capacity was weak, has committed resources to leadership development and organized capacity (also, it has assigned staff to mediate intracommunity conflicts, a practice also used by LISC in Chicago); (2) the department's mode of operation encourages neighborhood representatives to think broadly about community needs and wants in relation to the city; and (3) neighborhood representatives are brought into deliberations about the city's budget and therefore into city governance.

continuation and the effort quickly faded. Various calls to create a policy-oriented department of neighborhoods in Baltimore have come to naught despite a range of supporters behind the idea.

In highly fragmented Los Angeles, substantial variation is evident in community capacity, and communities must take the initiative to gain the attention of policymakers. Los Angeles also reminds us that surface alterations in governmental form may penetrate the policy process only to a very limited extent. The adoption of a new city charter in Los Angeles and its creation of a neighborhood advisory system proved to be a reflection of, not a remedy for, the city's political/governmental fragmentation. A city council tendency to protect individual "turfdoms" is a barrier to a more comprehensive and integrated approach to neighborhood distress.

In this context, neighborhood-level institutions and the particular connections they have to elite patrons can be critically important to the prospects for neighborhood improvement. For example, a labor-community-environmental organization, LAANE, helped to bring about an impressive multipart CBA in the important Staples Center area of the city. LAANE's success came about because the organization fostered wide-ranging coalitions that encompassed labor and environmentalists as well as community and immigrant activists. While LAANE has not proved to be, in neighborhood issues, a citywide force,[4] the extent of its impact in the vital Staples Center area was made possible by foundation backing that has given it an in-depth capacity for planning, analysis, and advocacy.

The East Baltimore revitalization effort involves much the same scope of issues as the Staples Center CBA in Los Angeles: affordable housing, strengthened services, environmental issues (in the clearing and rebuilding process), and labor advocacy for expanded employment opportunities. But in comparative perspective East Baltimore falls far short in impact because it lacks a broad and stable coalition supported by a professional capacity for analysis and action. The community-based Save Middle East Action Coalition was too little and too late, and it did not survive. The Maryland Minority Contractors Association got the attention of the two city council members who represent East Baltimore, but this association's focus is narrow. From a community vantage point, oversight of the East Baltimore redevelopment effort is fragmented and insufficiently represents residents.

City-county consolidation has given Denver a far less fragmented government system than that of Los Angeles, but strong mayoral leadership in development matters has yielded no comprehensive plan of neighborhood improvement. As the city moved to join neighborhood concerns and development policy, the city's neighborhood subsystem centered on Community Development Block Grants (CDBGs) was dismantled, and in something of a throwback to an earlier mind-set, neighborhood policymaking through city hall found itself subordinated to economic-growth aspirations. Along with targeting selected neighborhoods for more intensive improvement efforts, city hall designed larger development districts that are not aligned with the city's traditional neighborhoods, thereby diminishing their municipal voice. While elected officials can be a leverage point for political change, the meaning of electoral politics depends on a wider arrangement of political relationships. The Denver picture is complicated. Community concerns have received considerable attention from varied sources in the philanthropic and broader nonprofit sector. In the aggregate neighborhood policy is far-reaching and encompasses aspects of regional transportation development, but its institutionalization suffers from significant disconnections. And neighborhood voices are muffled accordingly.

Ad hoc initiatives, disjoined parts, and sporadic mobilizations characterize the policy process.

In Denver, as in East Baltimore, the evolution of neighborhood policy and politics strongly suggests that the emerging challenge is not simply to organize and give voice to community concerns. The looming task is that of how to help neighborhoods cope with large and complicated initiatives. In today's world with its interwoven problems, effective community engagement calls for something more than public hearings, focus groups, charettes, and "customer" surveys. Furthermore, forming more community development corporations is not the answer. The nature of struggle has changed. In the redevelopment period, a highly cohesive and aggressive business–city hall alliance was the object of struggle. Today, the force to struggle against has become more impersonal and elusive. The challenge is finding a voice in a world increasingly populated by large-scale and complex projects.

Even with ad hoc policymaking, gains for neighborhoods have accrued. Compared with the initial years of postwar redevelopment, residents of distressed neighborhoods today can see that some of their problems have been mitigated. Advances span a variety of areas. Despite continuing tensions and uneven progress, police-community relations have moved beyond the days of deep and pervasive hostility that so openly marred the 1960s. Note, for example, in Los Angeles how Watts has turned from a case of an urban tinderbox into an instance of police-community consultation and cooperation.[5] Failing urban school systems have yet to be transformed in scale, and a community development approach has only a scattered presence. After-school and youth programs are in greater abundance than before, and they, along with job training and workforce development programs, are targets of CBAs in several places. Affordable-housing projects and programs of home improvement for the nonaffluent can be found across the six cities studied here. In housing, the poorest of the poor still tend to get the short straw, but policy has moved away from embracing the huge concentrations of the very poor (de facto warehousing) that once held sway in many cities.[6] Funding for neighborhood-based services has always been in short supply, but the ed & med sector has come through with many significant additions to alleviate some of the shortfall. East Baltimore's early-childhood center is a telling example. While gentrification can push housing costs beyond the means of longtime residents, special provisions can be made to protect and provide affordability (e.g., as in Denver).

While we observe that a new day in neighborhood politics and policymaking is emerging, we also note that city experiences show few signs of momentum building behind a broad agenda of social reconstruction and community development. Across the six cities we find a variety of neighborhood improvement efforts, but typically they do not cohere into a broad and coordinated approach nor bring together major actors to plan and pursue a joint strategy. Neighborhood activities tend to occur in fragments—a project here and disconnected efforts there and elsewhere. While there is a shared dynamic around the pursuit of resources, distinct experiences set off one city from another and sometimes even one neighborhood from another. Fundamentally, however, fragmentation runs deep and does not affect all players equally.

Fragmentation and Pluralism

On the surface, today's fragmented governing capacity may resemble Robert Dahl's (1961) conception of pluralism. Yet structural inequality separates Dahl's pluralism from the governance we see in today's postindustrial city. In *Who Governs?* (1961) structural inequality is largely a matter of the distant past, transcended by universal suffrage and a shift to interest-group politics. Dahl accords one-person, one-vote a key part in preventing concentrated power and emphasizes that modern society has moved from a few basic divisions into a complex body of social and economic roles, organized politically into groups around highly varied interests.[7]

Accordingly, people are thought to care little about most specialized issues that animate politics in an essentially splintered way. Basically, Dahl (1961, 197) argues, people have no sustained or far-reaching interest in politics. Consequently "control over any given issue-area gravitates to a small group which happens to have the greatest interest in it" (1961, 191). Varying intensities of concern and preference give rise to an arrangement in which power is dispersed; in Dahl's influential phrase, "minorities rule" (1956, 132).[8]

Dahl's (1961, 101) pluralism treats local politics as an electorally centered contest to gain control of public office and the resources found there. However, as he sees it, government "is only a fragment of social life" and politics "a sideshow in the great circus of life" (1961, 305). For Dahl (1961, 191, 197–98, 224–25), the basic structure of political action follows a division between a political stratum of political and policy professionals and an apolitical stratum of actors engaged only sporadically when they mobilize because they have a keen interest in a particular issue.[9]

Spanning the redevelopment and postindustrial periods, electoral politics has shown itself to be an instrument significant for both change and resistance. As the redevelopment experience reveals, however, universal suffrage is not the barrier to power cumulation that Dahl assumed. *Urban Neighborhoods in a New Era* builds from a different understanding of power, drawn from Clarence Stone's social-production model of power, with its emphasis on a contingent ability to act: "gaining and fusing a capacity to act—*power to* not *power over*" (1989, 229, italics in original). In such a process intensity of preference does not necessarily override inequalities in resources and connections.[10] Preemptive power can work against openness and accessibility (Stone 1989, 242). For the postindustrial city the prevailing condition is a diffusion of power, but that very diffusion stands in the way of a widely dispersed ability to influence matters of special concern. Thus, diffuse power does not bring about accessibility, not even in selected matters of heightened concern. For actors with highly limited resources, the quest for a capacity to register policy gains often calls for alliance with or backing from players who enjoy a substantial resource base. Thus, in the postindustrial city, the aphorism "minorities rule" is misplaced in application to marginal groups such as distressed neighborhoods.

The limitations of *Who Governs?* when applied to the new era are embedded in assumptions that were widely held in the 1950s but proved increasingly questionable once the turbulent 1960s and 1970s came to dominate the urban terrain.[11] For the time leading up to his New Haven study, Dahl saw a prevailing consensus on the fundamentals of society, its economy, and its mode of politics.[12] With prosperity seemingly paving the way for an ever-increasing middle class, Dahl (1961, 33, 59) saw assimilation as gradually overriding divisions of race, class, and social identity. Yet as the twentieth century moved from its midpoint to its closing decades, events and scholarly research exposed a society deeply rent by divisions of class, race, and religion (culture).[13] The black political mobilization against discrimination and exclusion brought a politics of racial and class conflict to the surface in a way that could no longer be ignored. Consensus as a political foundation turned out to be illusory, and interest-group politics proved not to provide the basic building block of politics after all.

Dahl's emphasis on a division between an apolitical stratum and a stratum of largely full-time governmental and political actors downplays the power consequences of the system of social stratification (Stone 1980). In his strong inclination to underscore the importance of political leadership, Dahl did not delve deeply into a structured body of relationships and how those relationships form a central part in the governance of a city. Thus, he makes little of a telling quote from Mayor Lee, explaining who was enlisted to serve on New Haven's redevelopment-related Citizens Action Commission:

> We've got the biggest muscles, the biggest set of muscles in New Haven on the top C.A.C. [Citizens Action Commission] . . . They're muscular because they control wealth, they're muscular because they control industries, represent banks. They're muscular because they head up labor. They're muscular because they represent the intellectual portions of the community. They're muscular because they are articulate, because they're respectable, because of financial power, and because of the accumulation of prestige which they have built up over the years as individuals in all kinds of causes, whether United Fund, Red Cross or whatever. (1961, 130)[14]

Because its members were little engaged in concrete decisions, Dahl treated the Citizens Action Commission as, in his words, an exercise in "democratic ritual" (1961, 130). Yet he was too astute an observer to reduce New Haven redevelopment to an aggregate of discrete policy decisions. In taking up the executive-centered coalition of Mayor Lee, Dahl observed that for redevelopment to move forward "the political order itself would have to be changed" (1961, 199). His scorecard of decisional initiatives and vetoes does not encompass matters of this range, that is, the power to alter an in-place system of governance. Yet his examination of New Haven's executive-centered coalition is quite wide in scope.[15]

Talk of changing the political order takes us well beyond a city's political stratum and a detached stratum of apolitical entities. Once attention fastens on the fate of a priority agenda and the arrangements needed to pursue it, then political analysis ceases to be about mobilization between long episodes of inaction by various disconnected, apolitical agents. As illustrated in Stone's (1989) analysis of regime arrangements in Atlanta, elements of a city (in Atlanta's case, the white business elite and a mobilized black community) can unite in a governing coalition around a broad agenda encompassing multiple issues. Other elements (whites not linked to the city's civic elite) found themselves excluded and turned to an exit strategy in reaction (Kruse 2005). As in our study of neighborhood policy and politics, the important consideration is to construct or alter a body of relationships. Pluralism's hidden hand of mutual adjustment through mobilization and countermobilization falls short as a compelling way to understand this level of politics and policymaking.

The coming together and falling apart of various relationships does not reduce to a simple matter of those with the greatest stake at issue securing a slot in the city's governing arrangements. Nor is it a matter of no one having a capacity to advance policy aims. Resources and connections still enter in a significant way, and they reflect structural inequality. Whereas Dahl argues that players "best off in one resource are often badly off with respect to many others" (1961, 228), the implied balance in such a statement does not hold up when the inverse proposition is considered. Players badly off in some regards enjoy no necessary compensation in other regards. Hence, cumulative disadvantage has no built-in limitation.

Thus, various disadvantaged interests may lack footing even in their narrow corner of policy turf. Here is a point at which in practice Dahl's idea of dispersed inequalities falls short of pluralist results. Mary Pattillo captures the point well when she talks about the unequal standing among players in lakeshore Chicago's remake: "Public housing residents did not have access to powerful networks. They were unable to hold institutions accountable. They could not define the terms of the debate. And because of their poverty, their claim in cultural, moral, or civic legitimacy was constantly called into question" (2007, 225).

In Chicago's lakeshore the poor and disadvantaged mobilized. At times they acquired short-term allies, but they were not able to penetrate actual policymaking in a manner that accords with classic pluralism. The concessions they seemingly extracted proved to be illusive. Pattillo points out that "promises are political acts. Over time, they are pronounced, manipulated, retracted, and denied within a context of unequal abilities to define the situation" (2007, 256).

For new-era politics a major question is to what extent the claims of distressed neighborhoods and their allies can be accorded a place in the governing order of cities. While fragmentation does not equal pluralism, it does leave open the possibility that the systemic bias of structural inequality can be countered in important ways. However, this can be accomplished only if multiple players come together on a basis different from the usual flow of events. To find a promising path to real change we must examine the neighborhood policy milieu.

The Neighborhood Policy Milieu

For distressed communities there is inevitably a strong pull toward tackling immediate problems because they are so pressing. In light of significant distress, neighborhood policymaking might seem to call for a version of incrementalism—immediate responses to particular problems guided by measures of progress. Although this approach may appear sound and seem realistic, the big picture of social change suggests an alternative view.[16] Consider how neighborhood-minded actors might invest their limited energy and resources. Is it better to respond to immediate needs or seek to alter the overall milieu within which resources are allocated and policy decisions are made? Should actors respond to particular problems or work to strengthen the neighborhood voice in the city's policy deliberations, civic and governmental?

Given an overall context of structural inequality, efforts to address particular problems gain little traction, seldom build momentum, and have little capacity to counter the force of structural inequality. It follows that there is reason to stretch beyond initiatives that address immediate problems to consider the features of the neighborhood policy milieu and their implications for shaping revitalization measures. Efforts can be made to provide a more supportive civic and political environment for addressing neighborhood concerns. Who is involved, what connections and alliances are possible, on which terms can efforts be joined, and what kinds of supports can be brought to bear? In short, how can support for neighborhood improvement be built and sustained? The reform perspective we put forward calls for a shift from a succession of battles to mitigate pressing concerns toward greater attention to the context within which neighborhood decisions take shape.[17]

Consider the character of the present milieu surrounding neighborhoods. It is one in which distressed neighborhoods are marginal players, short on material resources while also suffering from negative stereotyping. What kind of political agency is possible for those who are structurally disadvantaged? Striving to find a "way out of no way" brings dual considerations into play. The first is the core strength of the marginal group. This turns largely on what Cathy Cohen (1999) calls intracommunity features—such things as level of organization, cohesion and strength of shared identity, scope and quality of information possessed, capacity for communication within the group, leadership and civic skills, and ability to use legal challenges and other advocacy channels.[18] These internal features determine how formidable marginal groups might be as opponents and how effective they might be as allies. Consider how the residents of East Baltimore are handicapped, not by the total absence of community-based organizations, but by the sporadic character of such organizations. East Baltimore has a revolving door through which new entities appear only to exit a few years later, to be replaced by another short-term organization, as the cycle goes on. East Baltimore has had a succession of advocacy bodies but little continuity to provide the chance to learn, build strength, and form durable allies. Restarting time after time means that the transaction costs of both advocacy and cooperation are multiplied, and the situation is ripe for fatalistic cynicism. By contrast, sustained effort can energize. For example, with help from the philanthropic sector, the Pacoima neighborhood in Los Angeles has enjoyed organizational continuity and shown a significant capacity to engage, including an ability to resolve intracommunity conflict.

The second consideration is having a part in framing the understanding of the situation and how to act on it. This means an insider role—that is, a voice within the circle of actors who can identify a policy direction and take action accordingly. Such a role is the breakthrough that, in an earlier time, Atlanta's Citywide League of Neighborhoods came close to with the 1973 election of Maynard Jackson as mayor, but this insurgent group could not dislodge an entrenched, business-centered network that eventually brought the mayor's office back into its orbit. The Citywide League lost its inside position before it could be made secure (Stone 1989). With shallow institutionalization of the neighborhood political position, head-to-head conflict yielded a disappointing result. Thus, while Atlanta's 1973 city charter provided a formal niche for neighborhood advocacy, this advocacy lacked access to the well-entrenched civic network that the city's business elite had built over time as an integral feature of the governing coalition.

Like Seattle's neighborhoods, Atlanta's communities that made up the Citywide League encompassed significant middle-class population. Even with a newly formed body of Neighborhood Planning Units, the neighborhood position proved tenuous in the absence of a place in the city's informal governing arrangement. With departmental standing backed by city hall in a strong-mayor system, Seattle provided its neighborhoods an insider position. Atlanta's Neighborhood Planning units enjoyed broad backing in their initial stage, but the Citywide League was subject to strong centrifugal forces that splintered political energy along individual neighborhood lines. Building interneighborhood cohesion never crossed the needed threshold in Atlanta. In Phoenix the electoral coalition that brought district elections to the city has not become a durable, institutionalized force, but the highly regarded city-manager structure has provided a lasting foundation of support for those seeking resources and pursuing policy opportunities to improve neighborhoods.

Insider positions are hardly commonplace, but when they exist, they provide a way for limited-resource players and their advocates to make gains that otherwise would be unexpected in conditions of structural inequality. Large structural forces have effects, but action comes through mul-

tiple reactions to particular circumstances, allowing the operation of intermediate factors (such as organization, mobilization, institutionalization,
and processes or other experiences that can empower marginal groups).[19]
Since multiple structural forces are often at work, agency can operate in
devising the terms on which they are reconciled (W. Sewell 2005).

We do not see now or foresee for the future a wonderworld filled with
visionary thinking, long-term planning, and unquestioned priority for
neighborhood improvement, but neither do we see reasons for bleak pessimism. While we make no present claim even of the glass of neighborhood improvement being as much as half full, we do see a metaphoric
glass one-quarter full. Progress has been made and more progress is possible. Nevertheless, inequality persists, and the new era by no means guarantees a substantial level of social equity or even a strong effort in that
direction. The harsh reality is that many pockets of distress linger on and
some grow. Gentrification can pose a threat to residents who are less well-
off. Moreover, the redevelopment period left in its wake much social damage and large areas of neglect, which have yet to be addressed fully. A far-
from-finished task of social reconstruction can be readily identified, and
community problems are at the core of this challenge. How, then, to think
about the uncertain future of neighborhood policy?

Although resources are severely constrained, simply providing additional resources may do little to alter the basic situation.[20] Robert Halpern
observes how the market system plays a part, not merely in such matters
as the flow of investment, but also in stereotyping—in assessing the very
worth attributed to various segments of the population. He observes: "the
primacy of the marketplace in defining people's worth and entitlement"
defines boundaries of social obligation (1995, 228).[21] Promotion of a
policy agenda that is at odds with this view must overcome a bias against
those perceived as dependent or as making a special claim for assistance.[22]
Residents of distressed neighborhoods are at risk of being seen as beyond
the bounds of common concern and social obligation, as entitled to only
token gestures at most.

Here we can see the crux of the matter: residents in distressed neighborhoods not only have severely limited material resources but also may
be dismissed, by elites and members of the public, as entitled to nothing
more than minimal consideration. Efforts to address specific problems do
not alter this fundamental feature of neighborhood politics. A promising
path to reform lies in the reconstruction of the neighborhood policy milieu in such a way as to bring to the fore a less dismissive view of residents
in distressed neighborhoods.

Toward a Reform Program

In the redevelopment era the neighborhood struggle seemed clear—and disheartening. A well-resourced alliance (Salisbury's "convergence of power") ran roughshod over nonaffluent residents in aging city neighborhoods. The stark imbalance of power was the main plotline in the urban narrative. For the present time what is the plotline that faces residents in distressed communities? From outward appearances, it seems that power is now more diffuse, but distressed neighborhoods have no obvious road to empowerment and inclusion in the governing process. Institutionalization along the lines of the neighborhood departments in Phoenix and Seattle are one possibility, but judging from our observations, this is a move that rests on a complex set of conditions.[23] More broadly, then, how might the position of distressed neighborhoods be bolstered?

If one thinks of structural disadvantage not as a monolithic force but as a prevailing wind (as we suggested in chapter 1), then the challenge becomes one akin to constructing shelters and planting windbreaks. The aim is to create a milieu within which the needs and concerns of distressed neighborhoods can be attended to at a level greater than at present. Such a reform is not a summons to bring about a grand transformation; past successes in controlling the course of change at such a level are hard to find. The strategy we advocate is more pragmatic, reflecting the experiences of the cities we have studied, guided by feasibility more than grand design.

If the glass of neighborhood improvement is one-quarter full, how might it increase in measure? The six city cases contain instances of modest successes but also of disappointment over missed opportunities and partial steps. The weaknesses are easy to spot. However, if the marginal status of distressed neighborhoods is a barrier to the pursuit of their revitalization, then the called-for response is to strengthen their position. But how?

If proximate context and intermediate factors can mitigate structural forces, reforms should aim to enrich the neighborhood policymaking milieu with practices that alter the overall power picture—strengthening the intracommunity connections among marginal players and opening up channels of constructive interaction between marginal actors and others, particularly the city's movers and shakers. In short, reform efforts should aim to alter the local context within which policy is shaped. Admittedly, the new era does not provide abundant examples of a milieu-changing approach in operation. It is better at displaying the shortcomings of particularized and disconnected efforts, with their lack of staying power and failure to build momentum.

What might yield an improved neighborhood policy milieu?[24] As guideposts, we offer four considerations, each with a basis in new-era experiences: (1) ensuring the presence of a stable and substantial entity centered on neighborhood policy work; (2) giving major attention to building neighborhood capacity, particularly where capacity is weakest; (3) establishing a neighborhood constituency network and elevating its prominence in the city's civic and political life; and (4) encouraging cross-strata communication that respects and responds to the experiences of less-well-off neighborhoods, including recognition of long-established resentments they may hold. Although the reforms presented below are ambitious, they are not pie-in-the-sky hopes; each has some basis in existing practice.

A Stable Center

The neighborhood policy milieu is typically highly fragmented, producing ad hoc initiatives and a dearth of strategic thinking. A less fractured milieu can be brought about by establishing a stable center for neighborhood policy work, including strategic thinking and planning, gathering and analyzing data about neighborhood conditions, aggregating relevant expertise, providing for ongoing connections to and involvement of a neighborhood constituency, accumulating experience in searching for resources and enlisting support, and fostering the credibility of neighborhood-level organizations as policy actors and conveners.[25] Seattle is an exemplar, and among our study cities, Phoenix addressed this need most effectively by creating a policy-oriented department of neighborhood affairs. However, other entities could contribute to an improved milieu as well.

Nongovernmental entities also can create a stable center from which to study and advocate for neighborhood concerns. The MacArthur Foundation tried to encourage such efforts through LISC in Chicago. With its durable focus on Denver's poverty problems, the Piton Foundation is an example of a nongovernmental center capable of neighborhood policy work. Baltimore took initial steps in this direction with its short-lived Neighborhood Congress and a preliminary but unsustained move to create a Community Development Alliance. Parallels can also be found in other policy arenas in other cities; for instance, the El Paso Collaborative for Academic Excellence works for education reform and is housed on the campus of the University of Texas at El Paso and supported by the university's administration (Stone 2005).

Capacity Building

Building long-term capacity in neighborhood policymaking is no simple matter of a tweak here and there. Phoenix's Neighborhood Services Department was not a mere tweak.[26] The city's management team had the crucial understanding that professionalism by itself was not enough to effectively address neighborhood concerns. Residents needed to be engaged, and the existing management team recruited additional staff accordingly. Revitalization efforts thus included advancement of neighborhood capacity for engagement. Absent a neighborhood department, a city's planning or community development department could provide such an effort, especially if it were reinforced by foundation support.

Professionals have valuable skills; they know how to attract resources, design problem-solving strategies, manage complex initiatives, and monitor progress toward goals. Although this sort of professionalism appeals to many resource-rich elites, by itself it does little to alter the neighborhood policy milieu. However, it is not necessary to sacrifice effective problem solving to create community capacity. Needed is a long-term view of problem solving that includes community engagement. If residents in distressed neighborhoods are to have a voice in the policies that affect them and enjoy a place in the public lives of their cities, they need to actively participate in the policy process. Problem solving should occur in conjunction with capacity building; that is, problem solving should be seen as including an opportunity to build a capable community presence in the policy process. This is a long, hard road; building community capacity is costly and time-consuming and must be institutionalized in a way that decouples it from short-term and unstable political attention to neighborhood concerns, a problem that has hampered sustained capacity building in a number of our study cities, including such diverse places as Toronto and Baltimore. With a stable center for attention to neighborhood concerns in place (as discussed above), neighborhood capacity can be developed through the sustained experience of neighborhood actors working alongside policy professionals. By involving residents and community-based organizations in policy planning and implementation, a lasting legacy of constructive community activism can be created (Fung 2004).[27]

Despite urging from the city's Industrial Areas Foundation affiliate, BUILD, Baltimore's Sandtown-Winchester initiative failed to follow through on planned efforts to build community capacity. Problems ensued as capacity building was downplayed by foundation-funded professionals in their effort to make visible progress (Brown, Butler, and Hamilton 2001). In contrast, Pacoima in Los Angeles benefited from a foundation-funded process of capacity building, and the community was able to weather a division over the redevelopment of a former manufacturing site. LISC in Chicago has made some moves in this direction, but not to the extent of the efforts evident in Phoenix and Seattle. Building community capacity appears to get periodic recognition and occasional funding support, but it can be easily pushed aside if attention focuses on quick, visible results.

A Neighborhood Constituency Network

In line with Cohen's emphasis on intracommunity relationships, a key milieu-enhancing reform is to establish a neighborhood constituency network and heighten its prominence in the city's political and civic life. A useful first step is to develop a dynamic, composite picture of the city's less-well-off residents, the neighborhoods where they live, and ways in which the city could be socially reconstructed to meet their needs (this work could be undertaken in the city's stable center for neighborhood policy-making). For example, in Denver, the Piton Foundation tracks the situation of the city's poor residents and backs policies to address their needs. Periodic reports on conditions and trends can encourage informed advocacy rooted in an accurate picture of neighborhood distress.

The systematic collection of neighborhood-level information has a national advocate in the National Neighborhood Indicators Partnership, housed at the Urban Institute. Denver, Chicago, and Baltimore are among its local members.[28] In November 2012 the partnership sponsored a Community Indicators Consortium with such panel topics as "Using Data to Impact Community Change" and "Driving Change through Small Area Data." Local practice, however, reflects no comparable level of activism. For example, the Baltimore member of the national partnership, the Baltimore Neighborhood Indicators Alliance (BNIA), has not moved so far as to take up advocacy. BNIA was launched with backing from the Annie E. Casey Foundation, but now it is housed at the University of Baltimore, and in its location there, it has remained a passive source of information. BNIA has not held a consortium to encourage using its data to advocate for social change (though BNIA data were used by a neighborhood representative to prompt then mayor O'Malley to launch a revitalization plan for the city's Park Heights community).

To enhance the local connection between systematic data collection and informed activism, Cohen holds up horizontal (i.e., intracommunity) communication as a means to increase the power of marginal groups. In that vein, the foundation-funded Consortium on Chicago School Research is a model of how to connect expert research to community actors and inform city residents by feeding material to the news media (Shipps 2009, 132–35). Chicago foundations have also funded a newsmagazine devoted to covering school issues (Shipps 2009, 136). A parallel effort to enrich the neighborhood content in a city's policymaking milieu could establish or strengthen entities that promote the flow of information and encourage action.[29] Baltimore's Citizens Planning and Housing Association newsletter is partway down this path at the present time. Notably then, developing and disseminating information is a move already partially under way in some cities.

Cross-Strata Communication

Distressed neighborhoods and elite actors bring radically different experiences to the policymaking process, and it can be difficult to bridge the gaps that separate them.[30] Present practice mostly skates around this challenge. Elite policy actors and the staff who work for them are busy people with many demands on their time and energy. Predictably, they want to minimize those demands and operate within their own culture. For example, foundation officers and staff would rather work with organizations and groups that have professional staff and efficient management processes. They seemingly prefer serving on boards and task forces in which reinventing a professional mode of operation is unnecessary. A manifestation of this pattern is foundations' practice of running workshops for those who intend to apply for grants. In brief, such workshops amount to acculturation into the foundation world, leaving little apparent room for communication and interactions that are unfiltered by professionalism.

To change the policy milieu a different starting point may be in order. Consider the Johns Hopkins Urban Health Institute as it sought to move ahead with a neighborhood health assessment. The community-based advisory committee balked and complained of a tendency among Hopkins staff toward "assumed advantage" and "arrogance." Outside mediation proved necessary to move beyond that point, and the two groups ultimately came together to create TAP (The Access Partnership). Along with its willingness to bring in consultants skilled in bridging gaps, the Urban Health Institute has sought to level the communication field between medical professionals and community groups by sponsoring a "Reverse Research Day," in which community organizations present their needs and ideas for research.

Other unconventional steps also could be taken. Foundation staffers, city planners, and other professionals might, for example, do guided role-playing exercises or undergo other forms of training in how to see the world through the eyes of marginal players in small, un-, or understaffed organizations who are trying to represent a membership with multiple needs and limited experience in the professional world.[31] The lesson is that a difference in how power and privilege are experienced affects personal interactions and can form barriers to working together even when (or maybe especially when) upper-strata actors see themselves as persons of goodwill and beneficent intent.

The Role of Major Institutions

Our aim in proposing reforms is to look beyond the hurly-burly of everyday events to suggest how neighborhood revitalization might be placed in a context more favorable to sustained and connected actions in which distressed communities enjoy a significant voice in shaping their fate. However, to provide the full picture of new-era politics, we must include not only directions and possibilities for reform; we must also acknowledge the strengths and limitations of various potential agents of reform. Let us, then, look more closely at the major institutional sectors in the new-era milieu for shaping neighborhood policy.

The Government Sector

The government sector has features that can counteract some of the structural inequality facing distressed neighborhoods.[32] Government commands a greater potential resource base than any other participant in the policymaking process. In addition, government is an appropriate institutional setting to bring together a citywide program for neighborhood improvement. Finally, government carries with it an expectation of both equity and transparency, and this means representing and being responsive to the full public.[33] Although embedding responsibility for neighborhood policy in city government is no panacea, foundations, civic organizations, and state and federal governments could all make a positive contribution by pushing to upgrade city government capacity.[34] Phoenix is instructive on this point.

While government has a positive role to play, government action is not always constructive. Rather than making strategic investments, governments sometimes emphasize distributive politics in the form of "something for everyone." Denver's Mayor Peña brought all eligible neighborhoods under a policy of distributing federally provided CDBG funds so that all received something. However, this approach dilutes scarce resources and makes it harder to justify continuing attention to neighborhood distress, as government's efforts may seem fruitless, especially in the thin form often characteristic of CDBG funding. In its abusive form, distributive politics degenerates into patronage and favoritism. Early on, Phoenix managed to cleanse itself of this form of politics. With no comparable struggle ever waged in Baltimore and Chicago, these cities continue to be hampered by their reputation for unreformed politics. Hence, in both cities significant major policy efforts are housed outside the main channels of city government as a bulwark against patronage and political favoritism.

The Ed & Med Sector

With its resources, prestige, and an implicit obligation to do good, the ed & med sector is a likely candidate for a leadership role in city affairs, including as allies of marginal populations. In all five US study cities, ed & med institutions to varying degrees have had a role in initiatives that included neighborhood improvement efforts. For a onetime industrial city like Baltimore, ed & med institutions have special prominence and help fill a civic vacuum left by the diminishing role for corporate business.

As eleemosynary institutions, universities, hospitals, and medical schools have an assumed obligation to serve the public good. Moreover, most have huge sunk investments in a particular place, as well as an identity that is attached to a particular location. Nevertheless, ed & med ties to the surrounding residential community are often complicated. Many universities have friction-laden histories with nearby neighborhoods and their development agendas are often a source of tensions. For example, in Chicago's Pilsen and Woodlawn neighborhoods, the University of Illinois at Chicago and the University of Chicago acquired property for expansion, displacing existing residents and encouraging gentrification. Typically, ed & med institutions want to be surrounded by a low-poverty, low-crime area, lacking in signs of social disorder. Cities, however, have undergone changes that have brought persisting distress to many close-in locations. University administrators have now had many years to awaken to this enduring reality and ponder how to respond. Expansion needs often remain a factor and a source of tension, but universities are not monolithic and their leadership may see that they need to relate to the community in multiple ways.

Segments of complex ed & med organizations may be impelled to seek a constructive relationship with the community. In some cities universities have taken over the operation of previously low-performing schools. They may run medical clinics oriented to the neighboring population, or university units may form partnerships with community residents and their organizations (Nyden et al. 1997). Hence, though there are points of divergent interests, the university-community relationship does not reduce to zero-sum.

Still, despite the rich array of ed & med entities evident in the new era, they are not actors that occupy the same civic position as downtown business associations did in the redevelopment period. In our study cities the ed & med sector displayed little of the kind of collective citywide leadership that was characteristic of business participation during the redevelopment period. The Greater Baltimore Committee, for instance, not only was a major voice in setting Baltimore's redevelopment agenda but also took on a significant role in such issues as peaceful school desegregation (Orr 1999; Baum 2010). By contrast, Baltimore's ed & med sector has no collective voice and thus far is not organized to be a participant in setting a citywide agenda. Each institution tends to focus on its nearby community.

Despite this limitation, two lines of development could make the ed & med sector a greater contributor to milieu change. One is direct investment in and constructive engagement with the surrounding residential area around an explicit community development aim, as was done by the University of Pennsylvania.[35] The second is for the ed & med sector to form an intentional collective presence as part of an inclusive form of planning for the city's future. Rhetoric sometimes surfaces about the joined fate of the city and its neighborhoods with local institutions of higher education, but visible action along this line remains quite limited.[36] There is, however, evidence of growing attention to university-city relationships larger than the traditional town-and-gown version (Maurrasse 2001; Perry and Wiewel 2005; Rodin 2007; Etienne 2012; R. Hodges and Dubb 2012).

The Philanthropic Sector

The philanthropic sector is in many ways particularly well suited to promote milieu change. The donor community often plays a key role in agenda setting because it has both convening power and a capacity to contribute.[37] However, with the exception of the Chicago case, our study shows little evidence that foundations have put forward system-level change as a means to enhance the political standing of distressed neighborhoods.[38] On the other hand, foundations have been particularly important to neighborhood policymaking in Baltimore and Chicago, have given significant balance to spatially targeted social programs in Denver, and have supported important interventions in selected neighborhoods in Los Angeles.[39] In Canada, where foundations have no major role, the Toronto United Way helped to put the revitalization of declining neighborhoods on the city's agenda. Donor organizations unquestionably have a capacity to engender policy action where otherwise little or nothing might happen, but in the overall scheme of things their ability to fund is quite limited.[40]

Even when acting collectively, donors do not possess the deep pockets that are required for direct and sustained support for a citywide revitalization agenda. Still, our study cities suggest that the extensive involvement of philanthropic organizations in neighborhood issues has significant effects on where and how neighborhood intervention is pursued. With no electoral concerns, philanthropic organizations can target neighborhoods that would not be chosen through political processes. Toronto's United Way, for example, selected priority neighborhoods for intervention based on indicators of economic distress and service need; "opportunity" variables such as the economic-development potential of particular neighborhoods were not United Way's guiding consideration. In Chicago's New Communities Program, LISC relied on no fixed metric but instead used a combination of need and existing institutional capacity.

Philanthropic organizations are sometimes capable of leading neighborhood-specific initiatives without significant local government support or engagement, as in the Los Angeles neighborhood of Pacoima, where philanthropic organizations have targeted investments particularly around neighborhood schools. A number of funders have supported parent centers at Pacoima schools that aim to connect community members with neighborhood resources and services; more recently, philanthropic organizations have backed initiatives led by nonprofit organizations to address the high dropout rate at Pacoima area high schools. More ambitious multi-neighborhood initiatives, however, cannot be sustained without government support.

Though they initiate considerable activity, philanthropic organizations sometimes display behaviors that limit their potential as leaders of broad and sustained neighborhood revitalization efforts. Often foundations look less to creating neighborhood capacity than to supporting individual projects that can yield short-term measurable results. Recipients, however, often complain about the short-term character of grants. There are exceptions,[41] but the general understanding runs along the line of "three years and no continuing support." This version of the grant process reinforces the ad hoc character of neighborhood revitalization efforts. Foundations incline toward short-term support in part because they see themselves as sources of innovation, not as ongoing service providers. Innovation seemingly offers the "biggest bang for the buck." Structurally, foundations are driven by an inner dynamic in which the reality is that they do not in fact have the kind of deep pockets needed to underwrite long-term, service-providing support.[42] Lacking significant ongoing program responsibilities, foundations can pick up on the latest wave of ideas. Hence, the philanthropic sector is drawn toward innovation. By the same token, the sector is sometimes criticized for "faddism" and for dropping initiatives after a few years instead of providing long-term support to work through rough spots in implementation. To the extent that they adopt a near-term focus, foundations may forgo the alternative of building community capacity—an activity with less easily measured results, especially in the short run.[43]

At present, many foundations are caught up in the mentality that they must show value for their grants by demonstrating measurable gains in solving substantive problems. But, given limited funds for large and complicated problems, donors tend to narrow the scope of the problems they tackle, and they are drawn to problems or areas where significant community capacity already exists. Following disenchantment with the Sandtown initiative, Baltimore's foundation community turned to a Healthy Neighborhoods Initiative, a triage approach of upgrading neighborhoods with existing organizational capacity and with market appeal. Our point is not that triage is intrinsically a bad idea; it is that a quick abandonment of one approach for another can be largely opportunistic, based on scant consideration of long-term priorities. Though exceptions can be found,[44] a concern for short-term results often overrides long-term thinking—as was the case in Baltimore's Sandtown-Winchester initiative.

Although a milieu-changing approach is long term and offers no certain outcome, it fits the philanthropic sector well in the following way. As beneficiaries of tax-free status in return for social benefit, foundations are appropriate bodies for risk taking. As nonelected bodies, they are not tied to an election cycle and thus are better positioned to take a long-term view. However, as nonelected bodies, they are vulnerable to the charge that their money enables them to displace the public's judgment about the direction policy should take. For instance, foundations established by billionaires have been criticized for promoting a top-down, corporate model of school reform in circumstances where they have little experience or understanding (Ravitch 2010).[45] A donor focus on process and milieu is less vulnerable to such criticism. Thus, the philanthropic sector is well positioned to give special attention to those less well-off, and milieu change can be defended as facilitating (not displacing) the voice of those rarely heard in circles dominated by actors who are highly advantaged.

The Private Sector

The general trend we observe is for the business sector to become less engaged on a collective and strategic citywide basis.[46] This is not to suggest, however, that the business sector has become an inconsequential force. Whether guided by collective strategic planning or not, private investment remains important. There is ample reason, then, for neighborhood advocates and their allies to promote understanding among business executives about the importance of neighborhoods in the life and well-being of the city, and especially to heighten awareness of CBAs and their potential as contributors to positive-sum undertakings.

However, it is worth bearing in mind that in such arrangements there is always a potential for co-optation; the line between benefits of genuine and lasting value to the community and veiled co-optation can be hard to discern. The challenge surrounding the possibility of co-optation underscores an important role that can be played by entities such as LAANE, which is free of dependence on business funding and thus possesses independent analytical skills. When distrust based in past experience is not far below the surface, an independent player holds an especially significant position.

Looking at the Wider Context

The power challenge for distressed urban neighborhoods in the new era is one of constantly constructing and reconstructing the capacity to address issues, not one of confronting and overcoming a tight-knit business–city hall alliance. But construction nonetheless faces a context characterized by structural inequality. Our suggestions to reform the local civic and policy-making milieu have the potential to mitigate some features of structural disadvantage. A vast gulf in power and resources between elite actors and distressed neighborhoods still remains, however. A large part of the work of milieu reconstruction involves confronting this gulf. This means working toward enabling distressed neighborhoods to claim a place at the table and establishing a working level of trust between neighborhood actors and elite participants. The question ultimately posed by the new era is that of whether a changed composition of the upper strata of city actors can be combined with new neighborhood-based approaches to make a difference. As views about the urban core have altered, new thinking has taken hold— indeed, has taken hold in a way that brings about new relationships.

In offering an explicit reform strategy, we embrace an approach that differs from many other works in the urban field by focusing on the political and civic *milieu* in which policy is made rather than the *substance* of policy.[47] We have identified steps to place neighborhood revitalization efforts on a more durable path of policy action, more durable because the proposed path would relate actors in a fresh way. Present tendencies toward narrow and ad hoc initiatives rest in part on long-standing practices among advantaged participants. What, then, might encourage a fresh approach? We believe that new actors, changing conditions, and accumulating experiences expand possibility.

Our study is intended to make a case for strategic thinking about an evolving urban condition. Our hope is that by presenting the big picture of neighborhood policy and politics we can highlight shortcomings of the status quo and prompt a change in thinking among movers and shakers as well as neighborhood advocates. Strategic thinking comes more easily when players stand back from immediate pressures and look at the wider context. Neighborhood players and those sympathetic to ameliorating the problems of neighborhood distress should begin with the challenging question about how the status quo is working. We think the likely response in most places would be "not so well."

Too often those engaged in making neighborhood policy seem caught up in seeing only what is close up and immediate, as if they suffer from a form of policy myopia. While there is much rhetoric about measuring impact, some actors cannot see the forest of performance for worrying about measuring the growth of individual trees. As an alternative, we encourage standing back from immediate problems, looking at the big picture, and asking how in a large sense revitalization is working out as an ongoing effort. Is society getting value for the energy and resources expended? What would it take to achieve a multiplier effect? In the face of structural inequality, what is possible?

In rethinking the usefulness of continuing initiatives taken in isolation from one another, some foundation actors have embraced the concept of "collective impact" (Kania and Kramer 2011). The basic idea is to foster mutually reinforcing activities by a variety of stakeholders who are committed to a common agenda backed by a "backbone organization." A risk, however, is that such an undertaking may consist of little more than token inclusion for representatives of distressed neighborhoods, though in an effort wider than those taken in the past. Rather than adding a new action agent, we would emphasize changing relationships to put the policy process in an altered context. Is such a move feasible?

The urban condition has changed and therein lies opportunity. In the redevelopment period, a highly cohesive and aggressive business–city hall alliance was the object of struggle. At present the challenge is finding a voice in a world increasingly populated by large-scale and complex projects that cross policy domains. Political and policy alignments have become more fluid, and new opportunities for neighborhood improvement are within reach. But strategic thinking has to be adapted to particular times, places, and circumstances. In today's world, effective community engagement calls for something more than such practices as public hearings and closed-door sessions with a select few neighborhood voices. A change in the status of distressed neighborhoods within the policy process is what is needed.

Despite their many disadvantages, distressed neighborhoods have agency, and that is not to be overlooked in a reform agenda. It is important therefore not only that *distressed neighborhoods be able to come together as a collective force in a city's politics, but also that elite actors recognize that distressed neighborhoods have a capacity to voice their concerns and a legitimate right to do so.* In this vein we believe that disadvantaged communities must be brought into the civic discourse, not as squeaky wheels, but as voices in governing the city.

Representatives of distressed neighborhoods also need to take a wider view that looks beyond immediate problems toward a broader role in the policy process. Including residents in policymaking broadens the agenda and gives voice to neighborhood concerns. A wide-ranging, multipart agenda is a means for bridging some of the fractures that exist among city constituencies.[48] It is important, however, that attention be kept on the overarching policies and that interracial, interethnic competition not eclipse the possibility of policy change (Clarke et al. 2006). Black-Latino tensions sometimes run high, but such groups can also join efforts to address matters of common concern. Making systematic information available can blunt competition between racial and ethnic groups by showing the common problems that exist across distressed urban areas. Though incompletely connected to some of its city's widely dispersed neighborhood-based actors, LAANE represents a move toward multipart action with backing from labor, immigrant, and environmental groups and with community organizing as part of its approach (Milkman, Bloom, and Narro 2010; Meyerson 2013).[49] Coalition building is thus an important adjunct to achieving a neighborhood voice in governing the city. The caution that should surround such efforts is that those least well-off frequently get the slightest attention. In order to move beyond narrow, ad hoc policymaking, change-oriented coalitions need to be class inclusive as well as multiethnic and multi-issue. Austerity policies at the national level are a constricting factor, but the philanthropic sector has shown heightened interest in civic capacity, and it also has spurred new thinking about local and regional relationships (Briggs 2008; B. Katz and Bradley 2013).

By viewing the place of distressed neighborhoods in a long trajectory, we can see that their political development has undergone significant changes. For those willing to look with care at the big picture of an evolving neighborhood experience, the case for a new approach is compelling. Those on the local scene who would address the social reconstruction of the postindustrial city through neighborhood improvements lack the position and power of Salisbury's "new convergence," but strategic moves could make a difference. For too long, theorizing about urban politics has occurred in the shadow of the redevelopment period, the onetime massive physical redevelopment of the city core. In the new era, it is time for a fresh round of thinking about neighborhood politics. The marginal position of distressed neighborhoods should be, not a barrier to that effort, but an integral part of both theory and practice. Reforms with the right emphasis could set the politics in postindustrial cities on a path conducive to a larger and more sustained opening of political and policy space for neighborhood concerns.

Notes

1. Our argument parallels the political development approach of Orren and Skowronek (2004).
2. See especially the emphasis on severely disadvantaged neighborhoods in Bryk et al. 2010 and Payne 2010. Note also the launching of a nongovernmental initiative by President Obama, My Brother's Keeper, as an effort to bring cities, businesses, philanthropies, and others together around locally targeted programs to enhance opportunities for boys and young men of color.
3. While the Model Cities program of Great Society days sought to coordinate social services, it did not break down the differentiation and insulation of economic development from social policy. See, for example, the experience with the Port of Oakland when black insurgency challenged the port authority's insulation from agenda setting by the city (May 1971; Self 2003).
4. LAANE is a significant advocate on concerns involving labor, the environment, and transportation.
5. Watts is offered, not as a typical situation, but as an indication of the kind of turnaround that is possible.

6. Along with areas of improvement, it is important to acknowledge losses. The supply of standard, low-rent housing has declined (Briggs, Popkin, and Goering 2010). However, as Derek Hyra (2008) has shown, cities vary politically in the protection they offer to affordable housing.

7. Referring to political development in New Haven, Dahl observes that if the city's "Notables" were to put forward a policy agenda antagonistic to the populace generally, "judging from the fate of the patricians, politics would lead in the end to the triumph of numbers over notability" (1961, 84). In a similar vein Dahl argues that "the natural incentives of politicians to secure their own election" is sure to lead to "policies designed to appeal to numbers rather than wealth" (83). Concretely, Dahl says of New Haven's top elected official: "The preferences of any group that could swing weight at election time—teachers, citizens of the Hill, Negroes on Dixwell Avenue or Notables—would weigh heavily in the calculations of the Mayor" (214). Dahl (163) also sees critical elections as of great policy import. Thus, universal suffrage for Dahl is a central factor in the operation of city politics.

8. The importance of variations in intensity or preference was first laid out by Dahl in *A Preface to Democratic Theory* (1956). In his New Haven add-on, Nelson Polsby put the point this way: "If a man's life work is banking, the pluralist presumes he will spend his time at the bank, and not in manipulating community decisions" (1980, 117). For his part, Dahl comments on the reluctance of New Haven's Economic Notables "to give time to public affairs" (1961, 71).

9. A telling counterweight to Dahl's interpretation of New Haven politics is found in Domhoff 1978 (updated in Domhoff 2014). Rae (2003) provides a valuable link between Dahl's and Domhoff's competing interpretations.

10. Dahl gives special attention to majority rule versus rule by widely scattered small groups, each with a different, largely nonoverlapping focus. He sees the system this way: "the making of governmental decisions is not a majestic march of great majorities united upon certain matters of basic policy. It is the steady appeasement of relatively small groups" (1956, 146).

11. Although particulars of *Who Governs?* appear dated, especially its celebratory treatment of the mayoralty of Richard Lee, the book has durable strengths. It covers a very long trajectory of political development, and it offers a broad and multifaceted look at city politics, covering both elite and mass levels, as well as spanning multiple issue domains.

12. Dahl's *Who Governs?* describes New Haven as lacking "great cleavages" (1961, 198) and its government as run by a political stratum embodying "many of the most widely shared values and goals in the society" (91). In commenting on New Haven's then dominant pattern of two-party competition, Dahl adds: "Because the policies acceptable to the many as well as to the wealthy few generally do not diverge very much on the local level, the differences between the leaders in the two parties are never very great" (244). "Widespread consensus on the American creed of democracy and equality" comes in for major attention (76, 84, 310, 316–18, 324–25). The consensus theme in *Who Governs?* was anticipated in Dahl's *A Preface to Democratic Theory*: "Prior to politics, beneath it, enveloping it, restricting it, conditioning it, is the underlying consensus on policy that usually exists in the society among a predominant portion of the politically active members" (1956, 132). Written from the hindsight of a later time, treatments of New Haven politics in the era of Mayor Richard Lee that contrast with Dahl's can be found in Y. Williams 2008 and Jackson 2008. These latter authors find a deep racial cleavage.

13. Leading examples include Sugrue 1996; O'Connor 1993; Podair 2002; Self 2003; Kruse 2005; Lassiter 2006; Freund 2007; and Satter 2009.

14. A 1960s study of urban renewal, encompassing New Haven's experience, contained this observation of New Haven's Citizens Action Commission: "the Commission is composed primarily of the community's business leaders" (Note 1966, 526).

15. Dahl acknowledges the need for a wide-ranging examination when he observes: "Rapid comprehensive change in the physical pattern of a city is a minor revolution" (1961, 201).

16. It is significant that within philanthropic circles recent attention has turned to the concept of "collective impact." Kania and Kramer explain that such initiatives call for "a long-term process of social change without identifying any particular solution in advance" (2011, 41). The recommended strategy reflects the idea that it is "no longer enough to fund an innovative solution created by a single nonprofit or to build that organization's capacity. Instead, funders must help create and sustain the collective processes, measurement reporting systems, and community leadership that enable cross-sector coalitions to arise and thrive."

17. Our argument here reflects the emphasis that the MacArthur Foundation placed on system-level change in Chicago's New Communities Program. Beyond this, focusing on the policy milieu is paralleled in a recent Open Places Initiative by the Open Society Foundations. In selecting its final three places for grants, the Open Society Foundations (2013) issued a call for implementation proposals. The focus in this call was for a place-based program for building civic capacity. On this strategy, see Briggs 2008. He explains "the logic of empowerment" as one that "emphasizes changing political relationships and access to influence" and that calls for disadvantaged groups to undertake "the work of institutionalizing their influence in 'viable forms of cooperation' that sustain change over time" (12, 14).

18. The evaluation of the efforts to facilitate system-level change in Chicago's New Communities Program identified the need to create a mechanism with a dedicated staff to identify and prioritize cross-site issues (including data analysis) and to facilitate cross-site communication (see Chaskin and Karlstrom 2012, 79–80). Similar specifics in the Open Society Foundations document (2013) include creation of an institutional home for the local initiative, an expanded presence of social justice–minded organizations, communication hubs, data collection and analysis, grassroots organizing and mobilization of constituencies, convening diverse constituencies, and a collaborative relation with public officials. The various moves have as an eventual aim cross-sector cooperation (government, business, and nonprofit service providers and advocacy groups). The overlap with LAANE in Los Angeles and the Front Range Economic Strategy Center in Colorado is also noteworthy.

19. In addition to work by Cohen (1999) and Small (2004), there is kinship between the reasoning here and the argument that Pressman and Wildavsky (1984) used to show how policies that enjoyed broad support as a general aim could still falter when going through the many detailed steps that implementation entails. That intermediate factors have a potential impact is a necessary condition for structural determinism to give way analytically to the middle ground of structure-agency.

20. Baltimore's Sandtown-Winchester project illustrates the point.

21. "The most basic reasons for the prevalence and concentration of social problems in the inner city are not found in the lack of good human services, lack of neighborhood social organization, nor even in the condition of housing stock. They are found in the primacy of the marketplace in defining people's worth and entitle-

ments and in shaping social relations" (Halpern 1995, 228). This quotation shows how Small's conditional approach differs from a structural explanation. Halpern posits an overriding structural factor (the market system), which no doubt explains much—but not all. By contrast, Mario Small (2004) allows for variation by positing that multiple factors may be at work, and the same broad structural condition may be responded to differently depending on the frame of reference of individuals and their immediate circumstance. Consider, for example, the Toronto Community Housing Corporation. It is market responsive in redeveloping Regent Park but also accommodates tenant concerns. Its assets and operational autonomy enable it to set its own balance between market-rate housing and housing affordable to less-well-off tenants. Redevelopment of public housing in the Watts community of Los Angeles faces a much different situation, though it has significant backing from Congresswoman Maxine Waters, who can be counted on to give consideration to lower-income residents.

22. As pointed out in a recent study of education reform in Philadelphia, in a market-oriented understanding of citizenship, entitlement to social benefits rests on perceived contribution to society (Cucchiara 2013, 13–15).

23. Bear in mind that Chicago mayor Harold Washington established a neighborhood department as part of his effort to enhance the attention city government paid to neighborhoods; but after his death, this department was dissolved.

24. We do not preclude a resource-providing national policy as a possibility, but at this point we do not see its likelihood as very great in either the United States or Canada.

25. Note that Toronto's initial expertise in social distress lacked a territorial dimension, and its police force seemed inept at responding to a community's social needs.

26. Though Seattle's Office of Neighborhoods did not focus on distressed neighborhoods, it did include in its responsibility an outreach capacity for enhancing the strength of organizationally weak neighborhoods.

27. Rich and Stoker (2014) report that including the community in policy design and implementation was a key factor that distinguished effective from ineffective local Empowerment Zone programs. Effective local zones worked with the community to combat neighborhood distress.

28. The Piton Foundation is Denver's local affiliate.

29. Our assumption is that negative stereotyping has its most damaging impact when it is unchallenged by assertions of the possibility and worth of actions to bring about neighborhood improvement.

30. It is noteworthy that research shows that political isolation is especially strong in areas of concentrated poverty (Cohen and Dawson 1993).

31. Significant experience and relevant materials have accumulated to give civic elites exposure to a bottom-up perspective, especially concerning poverty issues. See, for example, materials at the website for Step Up Savannah: http://stepupsavannah.org/get-involved/poverty-simulations. The continuing work of this kind in Savannah comes out of an earlier grant from the Annie E. Casey Foundation's New Futures Program. This example underscores the point that although the gains in such matters as social change can be long-lasting, they may not fully reveal themselves for many years. On New Futures and the virtue of a long-term view, see Annie E. Casey Foundation 1995; Walsh, n.d.

32. An unfortunate aspect of the current national deadlock in US politics is that the Right maintains a steady drumbeat of antigovernment rhetoric, equating freedom

with the absence of government and forgoing pursuit of possible ways in which government could be a channel for constructive problem solving. Obscured is the tyranny of inaction, as well as the positive freedom of people coming together to address shared concerns.

33. In Baltimore, the partnership form of East Baltimore Development Inc. has kept elected officials at some distance from the workings of the organization, but city council members have been attentive to the organization's agreement to provide contract opportunities to small businesses owned and managed by women and minorities. Note also that in the tension between marketing and equitable school reform in Philadelphia, elected officials have come down on the side of greater attention to equity, whereas the Center City business improvement district has championed marketing (Cucchiara 2013).

34. Note, for example, the argument made by Archon Fung (2004) for the contribution that professional management can make to community engagement.

35. In the early stages of East Baltimore Development Inc., some of its architects saw the University of Pennsylvania's community development plan as a model to be followed. However, the mix of purposes sought in East Baltimore fitted the Pennsylvania model poorly.

36. A significant step in the direction of a strategic collaboration for a large multineighborhood area is the Central Baltimore Partnership, which includes Johns Hopkins University, the Maryland Institute College of Art, and the University of Baltimore as key partners in a wider coalition seeking to revitalize what some major players regard as the central corridor of the city.

37. Although the role of this sector varies from city to city, it is noteworthy that all five of our US study cities are part of the Living Cities initiative, which is an effort by the donor community to advance the revitalization of cities and their neighborhoods.

38. As noted in chapter 4, the efforts by Chicago foundations to implement system-level change achieved limited success.

39. The California Endowment is an example of foundation support for capacity building.

40. In a study of the role of foundations in big-city school reform, Sarah Reckhow (2013) spotlights the nondemocratic impact foundations can have on both the geographic distribution of reform and the substantive character of reforms. Particularly with their tilt toward charter schools, foundations have played a large part in weakening the position of neighborhood schools.

41. Chicago's New Communities Program intentionally runs against the grain of short-term funding by, first of all, being built on an earlier pilot program and, second, by being, on its own, scheduled as a ten-year program. Even so, some actors wonder what will happen when the ten-year period is over. Time span may have emerged as a matter of increasing concern. Outside our study cities, the Open Places Initiative is another example of a foundation taking a ten-year approach.

42. For instance, a study of education reform in Chicago (an especially prominent recipient of large and varied philanthropic support for education) estimated that the city had received $200 million from foundations for school improvement between 1988 and 2008. This was 0.25 percent of the $80 billion spent by the Chicago public schools in that same twenty-year period (Menefee-Libey 2010).

43. From time to time, foundations in Baltimore have taken a wide view of capacity building for neighborhoods, but they have not come together or partnered with the city for a sustained effort. The collapse of an initial move to form a proposed

Community Development Alliance illustrates how easily such an idea founders on distrust across sectors and on reluctance to devote resources to a collectively determined agenda.

44. The Annie E. Casey Foundation is noteworthy for its efforts to take stock of its experiences. See, e.g., Walsh, n.d.; Annie E. Casey Foundation 1997; Brown, Butler, and Hamilton 2001; Hyman 2002.

45. For a contrasting approach to corporate school reform, see Bryk et al. 2010; Payne 2010.

46. Erie, Kogan, and MacKenzie (2011) report a pronounced trend in this direction for San Diego.

47. A related point can be found in Rich and Stoker 2014. They argue that what distinguished well-performing from poorly performing local Empowerment Zone initiatives was the quality of the local governance process.

48. Phillip Thompson offers this observation: "The problem of substantive political and economic reform is not so much about fighting a wealthy elite—whether majority or minority—as it is about developing the capacity of blacks and white nonelites to unite democratically without asserting the primacy and infallibility of their own perspectives" (2006, 250).

49. It should be noted that labor was part of the coalition that brought change to the city council in Phoenix.

REFERENCES

Abrams, Philip. 1982. *Historical Sociology*. Ithaca, NY: Cornell University Press.

Altshuler, Alan A. 1965. *The City Planning Process*. Ithaca, NY: Cornell University Press.

Anderson, J. Craig, Ryan Konig, and Matthew Dempsey. 2011. "Phoenix-Area Home Prices Remain Too Cheap." *Arizona Republic*, October 8. Accessed November 7, 2013. http://www.azcentral.com/business/realestate/articles/2011/10/08/20111008phoenix -real-estate-improved-fundamentals.html.

Angotti, Tom. 2008. *New York for Sale*. Cambridge: MIT Press.

Annie E. Casey Foundation. 1995. *The Path of Most Resistance*. Baltimore, MD: Annie E. Casey Foundation.

———. 1997. "Evaluating Comprehensive Community Change." Baltimore, MD: Annie E. Casey Foundation.

———. 2008. "Responsible Redevelopment: Relocation Road Map 1.0." Baltimore, MD: Annie E. Casey Foundation. http://www.aecf.org/m/blogdoc/aecf-Responsible RedevelopmentRelocationRoadMap-2008.pdf.

———. 2014. "The Annie E. Casey Foundation's Role in the East Baltimore Revitalization Initiative." Baltimore, MD: Annie E. Casey Foundation. http://www .eastbaltimorerevitalization.org/casey-east-baltimore/.

Argersinger, Jo Ann E. 1988. *Toward a New Deal in Baltimore*. Chapel Hill: University of North Carolina Press.

Armbruster, Timothy D. 2011. "Vision Needed for Baltimore's Neighborhoods." *Baltimore Sun*, August 29.

Arnold, Joseph L. 1976. "The Last of the Good Old Days: Politics in Baltimore, 1920–1950." *Maryland Historical Magazine* 71 (Fall): 443–48.

Artigiani, Erin. 1996. *Revitalizing Baltimore's Neighborhoods: The Community Association's Guide to Civil Legal Remedies*. Baltimore, MD: Community Law Center.

Bartik, Timothy J., and George Erickcek. 2008. "'Eds and Meds' and Metropolitan Economic Development." In *Urban and Regional Policy and Its Effects*, edited by Margery Turner, Howard Wial, and Harold Wolman, 21–51. Washington, DC: Brookings Institution Press.

Baum, Howell S. 2010. *"Brown" in Baltimore*. Ithaca, NY: Cornell University Press.

Been, V. 2010. "Community Benefits Agreements: A New Local Government Tool or Another Variation on the Exactions Theme?" *University of Chicago Law Review* 77 (1): 5–35.

Behavioral Research Center. 2010. "Community Attitude Survey: Volume I—Analysis." City of Phoenix (December), 5. http://phoenix.gov/webcms/groups/internet/@inter/@citygov/@facts/@mgrrept/documents/web_content/2010attsurvey.pdf.

Beilenson, Peter L., and Patrick A. McGuire. 2012. *Tapping into "The Wire": The Real Urban Crisis*. Baltimore, MD: Johns Hopkins University Press.

Bellamy, Denise E. 2005. *Toronto Computer Leasing Inquiry / Toronto External Contract Inquiry Report*. 4 vols. Toronto: City of Toronto.

Bennett, Larry. 2010. *The Third City: Chicago and American Urbanism*. Chicago: University of Chicago Press.

Berrien, Jenny, and Christopher Winship. 2002. "An Umbrella of Legitimacy: Boston's Police Department—Ten Point Collaboration." In *Securing Our Children's Future: New Approaches to Juvenile Justice and Youth Violence*, edited by Gary S. Katzmann, 200–228. Washington, DC: Brookings Institution Press.

Betancur, John J., Deborah E. Bennett, and Patricia A. Wright. 1991. "Effective Strategies for Community Economic Development." In *Challenging Uneven Development: An Urban Agenda for the 1990s*, edited by Philip W. Nyden and Wim Wiewel, 198–224. New Brunswick, NJ: Rutgers University Press.

Betancur, John, with Lee Smith. 1988. *Linked Development in U.S. Cities*. Report prepared for the Chicago Rehab Network, Center for Urban Economic Development, University of Illinois at Chicago.

Biondi, Martha. 2003. *To Stand and Fight*. Cambridge, MA: Harvard University Press.

Blumenberg, Anne, Brenda Blom, and Erin Artigiani. 1998. "A Co-production Model of Code Enforcement and Nuisance Abatement." *Crime Prevention Studies* 9:261–90.

Boehlke, David. 2001. *Great Neighborhoods, Great City: Revitalizing Baltimore through the Healthy Neighborhoods Approach*. Baltimore, MD: Goldseker Foundation.

Bommersbach, Jana. 2009. "When You're an All-American City, 'Jana's View.'" *Phoenix Magazine*, July. Accessed November 7, 2013. http://www.janabommersbach.com/phx-mag-july09.php.

Box, Richard C., and Juliet A. Musso. 2004. "Experiments with Local Federalism: Secession and the Neighborhood Council Movement in Los Angeles." *American Review of Public Administration* 34 (3): 259–76.

Braga, Anthony A., and Christopher Winship. 2006. "Partnership, Accountability, and Innovation." In *Police Innovation*, edited by David Weisburd and Anthony A. Braga, 171–87. New York: Cambridge University Press.

Bridges, Amy. 1997. *Morning Glories: Municipal Reform in the Southwest*. Princeton, NJ: Princeton University Press.

———. 2011. "The Sun also Rises in the West." In *The City Revisited*, edited by Dennis Judd and Dick Simpson, 79–103. Minneapolis: University of Minnesota Press.

Briggs, Xavier de Sousa. 2008. *Democracy as Problem Solving*. Cambridge, MA: MIT Press.

Briggs, Xavier de Sousa, Susan Popkin, and John Goering. 2010. *Moving to Opportunity*. New York: Oxford University Press

Brodkin, K. 2007. *Making Democracy Matter: Identity and Activism in Los Angeles*. New Brunswick, NJ: Rutgers University Press.

Brown, Prudence, Benjamin Butler, and Ralph Hamilton. 2001. "The Sandtown-Winchester Neighborhood Transformation Initiative: Lessons Learned about Community Building and Implementation." Columbia, MD: Enterprise Foundation.

Brown, Prudence, and Leila Fiester. 2007. "Hard Lessons about Philanthropy and Community Change from the Neighborhood Improvement Initiative." Chicago: Chapin Hall at the University of Chicago.

Bryk, Anthony S., Penny Bender Sebring, Elaine Allensworth, Stuart Luppescu, and John Q. Easton. 2010. *Organizing Schools for Improvement*. Chicago: University of Chicago Press.

Bui, Lynh. 2012. "Phoenix Mayor Stanton's First 100 Days Marked by Change: 'New Energy' Marks Greg Stanton's 3 Months on the Job in Phoenix, Say Colleagues, Citizens." *Arizona Republic*, April 7. Accessed November 7, 2013. http://www.azcentral.com/arizonarepublic/local/articles/20120402phoenix-stanton-first-days-mayor.html.

Callcott, George H. 1985. *Maryland and America, 1940–1980*. Baltimore, MD: Johns Hopkins University Press.

Camou, Michelle. 2014. "Labor Community Coalitions." *Urban Affairs Review* 50 (5): 623–47.

Carey, Eleanor M., Nina Harper, Shale D. Stiller, and Kenneth L. Thompson. 2010. "Mayor Stephanie Rawlings-Blake: Transition Team Report." March 19. City of Baltimore, MD.

Carmon, N. 1997. "Neighborhood Regeneration: The State of the Art." *Journal of Planning Education and Research 17* (2): 131–44.

Carroll, Barbara. 2002. "Housing Policy in the New Millennium: The Uncompassionate Landscape." In *Urban Canada: Sociological Perspectives, edited by Harry H. Hiller*, 69–89. Don Mills, ON: Oxford University Press.

Chaskin, Robert J., and Mikael Karlstrom. 2012. "Beyond the Neighborhood: Policy Engagement and Systems Change in the New Communities Program." June. New York: Manpower Development Research Corp.

Cisneros, Henry. 2009. "A New Moment for People and Cities." In *From Despair to Hope*, edited by Henry Cisneros and Lora Engdahl, 3–13. Washington, DC: Brookings Institution Press.

Cisneros, Henry G., and Lora Engdahl, eds. 2009. *From Despair to Hope*. Washington, DC: Brookings Institution Press.

City and County of Denver. 2006. *Lincoln Park Neighborhood Assessment*. https://www.denvergov.org/Portals/646/documents/planning/Plans/plans_pre_2013/lalp/LaAlmaLincolnParkAssessment.pdf.

———. 2010. *Mayor's 2010 Budget Summary*. http://www.denvergov.org/Portals/9/documents/2010Final_Budget_Summary_Book.pdf.

———. 2012. *2013–2017 Consolidated Plan (Draft)*. http://www.denvergov.org/Portals/690/documents/New/Con-PlanDraft2013wAppen.pdf.

———. 2014. "Transit Oriented Development: Transit Oriented Development Strategic Plan 2014." http://www.denvergov.org/Portals/193/documents/DLP/TOD_Plan/TOD_Strategic_Plan_FINAL.pdf.

City and County of Denver, Office of Economic Development (OED). 2007. *2008–2012 Consolidated Plan*. http://www.denvergov.org/Portals/690/documents/ConsolidatedPlan2008-2012.pdf.

———. 2012. *JumpStart 2012: Revving Up Denver's Economic Engine*. http://www.denvergov.org/Portals/690/documents/JumpStart%202012%20-%20OED%20Strategic%20Plan%202012%20(lr).pdf.

———. 2013. *JumpStart 2013*. 2013 Strategic Plan. http://www.denvergov.org/Portals/690/documents/New/OED%20JumpStart%202013%20for%20web.pdf.

City of Denver, Department of Community Planning and Development (CPD). 2010. *La Alma / Lincoln Park Neighborhood Plan*. http://www.denvergov.org/Portals/646/documents/LALP%20Public%20Review%20Draft.pdf.

City of Phoenix. 1999. *Garfield Redevelopment Plan.* Produced by the City of Phoenix, Arizona, adopted by the City Council on March 17, 1999. Accessed November 6, 2013. http://phoenix.gov/webcms/ groups/internet/@inter/@dept/@dsd/documents/web_content/pdd_pz_pdf_00054.pdf.

———. 2010. *Consolidated Action Plan, 2010–2015, and 2010–2011 Annual Action Plan* Accessed November 5, 2013. http://phoenix.gov/webcms/groups/internet/@inter/@dept/@nsd/documents/web_content/nsd_rp_conplan.pdf.

City of Phoenix, Neighborhood Services Department. 2006. *Code Enforcement Policy Effective June 29, 2006.* Accessed November 7, 2013. http://phoenix.gov/webcms/groups/internet/@inter/@dept/@nsd/@preservation/ documents/web_content/nsd_np_policy.pdf.

City of Phoenix, Planning Department. 1992. *Garfield Neighborhood Plan.* Accessed November 5, 2013. http://phoenix.gov/webcms/groups/internet/@inter/@dept/@dsd/documents/web_content/pdd_pz_pdf_00053.pdf.

———. 2001. *South Phoenix Village: Redevelopment Area Plan.* Accessed November 5, 2013. http://phoenix.gov/webcms /groups/internet/@inter/@dept/@dsd/documents/ web_content/pdd_pz_pdf_00148.pdf.

City of Toronto. 2004. "Community Safety Plan and Malvern Youth Employment Initiative." Clause 2 in Report 2 to Policy and Finance Committee.

———. 2005a. *"City of Toronto Long Term Fiscal Plan."* Report from deputy city manager and chief financial officer. Unpublished paper.

———. 2005b. "Toronto Strong Neighborhoods Strategy." Report to Policy and Finance Committee, October. http://www.toronto.ca/demographics/sntf/city_sntf_staff_report.pdf.

———. 2008a. "Crime Shootings Density, 2005–06." http://www.toronto.ca/demographics/pdf/firearms_incidents2006–2006d.pdf.

———. 2008b. *Toronto Social Atlas, 2006.* http://www.toronto.ca/demographics/atlas_2006.htm#3.

———. 2009. "2009 Budget Briefing Note: Meeting the City's Commitment to Priority Neighbourhoods; The Partnership Opportunities Legacy (POL) Fund." http://www.toronto.ca/budget2009/pdf/cap_budget_pdfs/BN_POL_%20Fund.pdf.

———. 2011. "Toronto Demographics." http://www.toronto.ca/invest-in-toronto/immigration_char.htm.

———. 2012. "Strong Neighbourhoods, 2020." Staff report to Council. http://www.toronto.ca/legdocs/mmis/2012/cd/bgrd/backgroundfile-45143.pdf.

Clark, Kenneth. 1965. *Dark Ghetto.* New York: Harper and Row.

Clarke, Susan E., Rodney Hero, Mara Sidney, Luis Fraga, and Bari Erlichson. 2006. *Multiethnic Moments.* Philadelphia: Temple University Press.

Clarke, Susan E., and Martin Saiz. 2002. "From Waterhole to World City: Place Luck and Public Agendas in Denver." In *The Infrastructure of Urban Tourism,* edited by Dennis Judd and Alan Artibise, 168–201. New York: M. E. Sharpe.

Clavel, Pierre. 2010. *Activists in City Hall.* Ithaca, NY: Cornell University Press.

Cohen, Cathy J. 1999. *The Boundaries of Blackness: AIDS and the Breakdown of Black Politics.* Chicago: University of Chicago Press.

Cohen, Cathy J., and Michael Dawson. 1993. "Neighborhood Poverty and African American Politics." *American Political Science Review* 87 (June): 286–302.

Committee for Economic Development. 1995. *Rebuilding Inner-City Communities: A New Approach to the Nation's Urban Crisis; A Statement by the Research and Policy Commit-*

tee of the Committee for Economic Development. New York: Committee for Economic Development.

Community Redevelopment Agency of Los Angeles. 2010. *South Los Angeles Fiscal Year 2010 Budget.* Accessed November 16, 2010. http://www.crala.lacity.org/upload/budget/budget10/South%20LA.pdf.

Cone Sexton, Connie. 2012. "Stanton Creates Citywide Advisory Group: 29 Neighborhood Leaders to Meet Quarterly." *Arizona Republic, February 20.* Accessed November 7, 2013. http://www.azcentral.com/community/phoenix/articles/2012021 4stanton-creates -citywide-advisory-group.html.

Costigan, Patrick M. 1997. "Building Community Solutions." Unpublished paper.

Coulton, C. J. 1998. "Restoring Communities within the Context of the Metropolis: Neighborhood Revitalization at the Millennium." http://eric.ed.gov.

Crenson, Matthew A. 1983. *Neighborhood Politics.* Cambridge, MA: Harvard University Press.

Crowley, Sheila. 2009. "HOPE VI: What Went Wrong." In *From Despair to Hope,* edited by Henry Cisneros and Lora Engdahl, 229–47. Washington, DC: Brookings Institution Press.

Cucchiara, Maia B. 2013. *Marketing Schools, Marketing Cities.* Chicago: University of Chicago Press.

Dahl, Robert A. 1956. *A Preface to Democratic Theory.* Chicago: University of Chicago Press.

———. 1961. *Who Governs? Democracy and Power in an American City.* New Haven, CT: Yale University Press.

Dantico, Marilyn, Subhrajit Guhathakurta, and Alvin Mushkatel. 2007. "Housing Quality and Neighborhood Redevelopment: A Study of Neighborhood Initiatives in Phoenix, Arizona." *International Journal of Public Administration* http://www.informaworld.com/smpp/title~content=t713597261~db=all~tab=issueslist~branches=30 - v3030 (January): 23–45.

Denver City Council. 2007a. Minutes of Neighborhood, Community, and Business Revitalization committee meeting, February 27.

———. 2007b. Minutes of Neighborhood, Community, and Business Revitalization committee meeting, December 11.

———. 2008. Minutes of Neighborhood, Community, and Business Revitalization committee meeting, June 24.

Denver Post. 2008. "Seedco on the Right Path, but Vigilance Is Necessary." Editorial. December 19.

Diers, Jim. 2004. *Neighborhood Power: Building Community the Seattle Way.* Seattle: University of Washington Press.

Domhoff, G. William. 1978. *Who Really Rules?* New Brunswick, NJ: Transaction Books.

———. 2014. "Who Really Ruled in Dahl's New Haven?" Unpublished paper. http://whorulesamerica.net/local/new_haven.html.

Douzet, Frédéric. 2012. *The Color of Power.* Charlottesville: University of Virginia Press.

Dreier, Peter, John Mollenkopf, and Todd Swanstrom. 2004. *Place Matters.* 2nd ed. Lawrence: University Press of Kansas.

Dresser, Michael. 2010. "Red Line Would Bring Almost 10,000 Jobs, Study Contends." *Baltimore Sun,* January 7.

Durr, Kenneth D. 2003. *Behind the Backlash: White Working-Class Politics in Baltimore, 1940–1980.* Chapel Hill: University of North Carolina Press.

Ehrenhalt, Alan. 2013. *The Great Inversion and the Future of the American City*. New York: Vintage.

Elfenbein, Jessica I., Thomas Hollowak, and Elizabeth Nix, eds. 2011. *Baltimore '68*. Philadelphia: Temple University Press.

Engdahl, Lora. 2009. "New Holly, Seattle." In *From Despair to Hope*, edited by Henry Cisneros and Lora Engdahl, 93–119. Washington, DC: Brookings Institution Press.

Erie, Steven P. 1988. *Rainbow's End*. Berkeley: University of California Press.

———. 2004. *Globalizing LA*. Berkeley: University of California Press.

Erie, Steven P., Vladimir Kogan, and Scott MacKenzie. 2011. *Paradise Plundered*. Redwood City, CA: Stanford University Press.

Ethington, Philip J., William H. Frey, and Dowell Myers. 2001. "The Racial Resegregation of Los Angeles County, 1940–2000." Public Research Report no. 2001–04. Los Angeles: University of Southern California; Ann Arbor: University of Michigan. http://www.usc.edu/schools/price/research/popdynamics/pdf/2001_Ethington-Frey-Myers_Racial-Resegregation.pdf.

Etienne, Harley F. 2012. *Pushing Back the Gates*. Philadelphia: Temple University Press.

Fagotto, Elena, and Archon Fung. 2006. "Empowered Participation in Urban Governance." *International Journal of Urban and Regional Governance* 30 (September): 638–55.

Fanton, J. 2006. *The Power of Partnerships: Insights from Chicago's Plan for Transformation*. Chicago: Council of Large Public Housing Authorities Annual Meeting.

Ferman, Barbara. 1996. *Challenging the Growth Machine: Neighborhood Politics in Chicago and Pittsburgh*. Lawrence: University Press of Kansas.

Fogelson, R. 1967. *The Fragmented Metropolis: Los Angeles, 1850–1930*. Cambridge, MA: Harvard University Press.

Fowlie, Jonathan. 2004. "Most of Toronto's Gun Deaths Involve Gangs, Black Victims." *Globe and Mail*, January 7.

Freund, David M. 2007. *Colored Property*. Chicago: University of Chicago Press.

Friedland, Robert, and David Palmer. 1984. "Park Place and Main Street." *Annual Review of Sociology* 10:393–416.

Frisken, Frances. 2008. *The Public Metropolis: The Political Dynamics of Urban Expansion in the Toronto Region, 1924–2003*. Toronto: Canadian Scholars' Press.

Fung, Archon. 2004. *Empowered Participation*. Princeton, NJ: Princeton University Press.

Gaeke, M. A., and T. L. Cooper. 2002. "Organizing Neighborhood Councils in Los Angeles: Social Capital, Leadership, and Ethics." Paper presented at the American Society of Public Administration Annual Conference, Phoenix, AZ.

Gallagher, Leigh. 2013. *The End of the Suburbs: Where the American Dream Is Moving*. New York: Portfolio.

Galster, George C., Peter A. Tatian, Anna M. Santiago, Kathryn L. S. Pettit, and Robin E. Smith. 2003. *Why Not in My Backyard? Neighborhood Impacts of Deconcentrating Assisted Housing*. New Brunswick, NJ: Center for Urban Policy Research.

GAO (Government Accountability Office). 2006. "Empowerment Zone and Enterprise Community Program: Improvements Occurred in Communities, but Effect of the Program Is Unclear." Washington, DC: Government Accountability Office.

Gay, Christine. 2012. "Moving to Opportunity." *Urban Affairs Review* 42 (March): 147–79.

George, Hermon. 2004. "Community Development and the Politics of Deracialization: The Case of Denver, Colorado, 1991–2003." *ANNALS of the American Academy of Political and Social Science* 594:143–57.

Gettleman, Jeffrey. 2002. "Ashes and Tears in Lost Battle of Drug War." *New York Times*, October 18.

Gills, Doug. 1991. "Chicago Politics and Community Development: A Social Movement Perspective." In *Harold Washington and the Neighborhoods: Progressive City Government in Chicago, 1983–1987*, edited by Pierre Clavel and Wim Wiewel, 34–63. New Brunswick, NJ: Rutgers University Press.

Gills, Doug C., and Wanda J. White. 1997. "Chicago's Empowerment Zone and Citizen Participation." In *Building Community: Social Science in Action, edited by* P. Nyden, A. Figert, M. Shibley, and D. Burrows, 211–19. Thousand Oaks, CA: Pine Forge Press.

———. 1998. "Community Involvement in Chicago's Empowerment Zone." In *Empowerment in Chicago: Grassroots Participation in Economic Development and Poverty Alleviation*, edited by C. Herring, Michael Bennett, Doug Gills, and Noah Temaner Jenkins, 14–70. Chicago: Great Cities Institute; Urbana-Champaign: University of Illinois Press.

Glaeser, Edward L. 2011. *Triumph of the City*. New York: Penguin Press.

Glanton, O., W. Mullen, and D. Glanton. 2011. "Abandoned Homes Multiply in Englewood, and Crime Follows." *Chicago Tribune*, June 23. http://articles.chicagotribune.com/2011-06-23/news/ct-met-englewood-empty-houses-20110623_1_foreclosure-crisis-englewood-and-west-englewood-vacant-properties.

Goetz, Edward G. 1997. "Sandtown-Winchester, Baltimore: Housing as Community Development." In *Affordable Housing and Urban Redevelopment in the United States*, edited by Willem Van Vliet, 187–209. Thousand Oaks, CA: Sage.

———. 2003. *Clearing the Way*. Washington, DC: Urban Institute Press.

Goetz, Edward G., and Mara Sidney. 1994. "The Revenge of the Property Owners." *Journal of Urban Affairs* 16 (4): 319–34.

———. 1997. "Local Policy Subsystems and Issue Definition: An Analysis of Community Development Policy Change." *Urban Affairs Review* 32 (4): 490–512.

Goldseker Foundation. 2012. "Featured Initiatives: Central Baltimore Partnership." Accessed September 25, 2012. http://www.goldsekerfoundation.org/featured_initiatives/central_baltimore_partnership.

Gomez, Marisela B. 2013. *Race, Class, Power, and Organizing in East Baltimore*. Lanham, MD: Lexington Books.

Gottlieb, Robert, Mark Vallianatos, Regina M. Freer, and Peter Dreier. 2006. *The Next Los Angeles: The Struggle for a Livable City*. Los Angeles: University of California Press.

Greater Baltimore Committee. 1997. *One Region, One Future*. Baltimore, MD: Greater Baltimore Committee.

Greenberg, D., N. Verma, K. R. Dillman, and R. Chaskin. 2010. "Creating a Platform for Sustained Neighborhood Improvement: Interim Findings from Chicago's New Communities Program." New York: MDRC.

Grogan, Paul S., and T. Proscio. 2000. *Comeback Cities*. Boulder, CO: Westview Press.

Gross, J. 2005. "Community Benefits Agreements: Making Projects Accountable." Washington, DC: Good Jobs First and the California Partnership for Working Families.

Hacker, Jacob S., Suzanne Mettler, and Joe Soss. 2007. "The New Politics of Inequality." In *Remaking America*, edited by Joe Soss, Jacob S. Hacker, and Suzanne Mettler, 3–23. New York: Russell Sage Foundation.

Hall, John Stuart. 1983. "Fitting the Community Development Block Grant Program to Local Politics: Who Is the Tailor?" *Publius* 13 (3): 73–84.

Halpern, Robert. 1995. *Rebuilding the Inner City: A History of Neighborhood Initiatives to Address Poverty in the United States*. New York: Columbia University Press.

Hanchett, Thomas W. 1998. *Sorting Out the New South City*. Chapel Hill: University of North Carolina Press.

Hanlon, Bernadette, John Short, and Thomas Vicino. 2010. *Cities and Suburbs*. New York: Routledge.

Hanson, Royce, Hal Wolman, David Connolly, and Katherine Pearson. 2006. "Corporate Citizenship and Urban Problem Solving: The Changing Civic Role of Business Leaders in American Cities." Washington, DC: Brookings Institution, Metropolitan Politics Program.

Hare, Mary Gail. 2011. "E. Baltimore Residents Rally for Jobs at EBDI Development." *Baltimore Sun*, December 20. http://articles.baltimoresun.com/2011-12-20/news/bs-md-ebdi-protest-20111220_1_ebdi-construction-jobs-residents-rally.

Henderson, Lenneal J., Jr. 1996. "The Governance of Kurt Schmoke as Mayor of Baltimore." In *Race, Politics, and Governance in the United States*, edited by Huey L. Perry, 165–75. Gainesville: University of Press of Florida.

Henig, Jeffrey R., Richard Hula, Marion Orr, and Desiree Pedescleaux. 1999. *The Color of School Reform*. Lawrence: University Press of Kansas.

Herbert, Steve. 2006. *Citizens, Cops, and Power*. Chicago: University of Chicago Press.

Hermon, George. 2004. "Community Development and the Politics of Deradicalization: The Case of Denver, Colorado, 1991–2003." *Annals of the American Academy of Political and Social Sciences* 594:143–57.

Hero, Rodney E. 1992. *Latinos and the U.S. Political System*. Philadelphia: Temple University Press.

Hill, David. 2013. "Mile High on Rail." *Architect*, May 22. http://www.architectmagazine.com/transportation-projects/mile-high-on-rail.aspx.

Hirsch, Arnold R. 1983. *Making the Second Ghetto*. Cambridge: Cambridge University Press.

Hise, G. 2002. "Industry and the Landscapes of Social Reform." In *From Chicago to LA*, edited by M. J. Dear, 97–131. Thousand Oaks, CA: Sage.

Hochschild, Jennifer, Vesla Weaver, and Traci Burch. 2012. *Creating a New Racial Order*. Princeton, NJ: Princeton University Press.

Hodges, Arthur. 1994. "Denver's Planning Department Is Accused of Planning Obsolescence." *Westword*, May 11.

Hodges, Rita A., and Steve Dubb. 2012. *The Road Half Traveled*. East Lansing: Michigan State University Press.

Hopkins, E. 2005. *Collaborative Philanthropies: What Groups of Foundations Can Do That Individual Funders Cannot*. Lanham, MD: Lexington Books.

Horak, Martin. 1998. "The Power of Local Identity: C4LD and the Anti-amalgamation Mobilization in Toronto." Research Paper 195. Toronto: Centre for Urban and Community Studies.

———. 2008. "Governance Reform from Below: Multilevel Politics and Toronto's 'New Deal' Campaign." Global Dialogue Paper, series 4. Nairobi: UN-Habitat.

Horak, Martin, and Talja Blokland. 2012. "Neighborhoods and Civic Practice." In *Oxford Handbook of Urban Politics*, edited by Susan Clarke, Peter John, and Karen Mossberger, 254–72. Oxford: Oxford University Press.

Horan, Cynthia. 1997. "Coalition, Market, and State: Postwar Development Politics in Boston." In *Reconstructing Urban Regime Theory: Regulating Urban Politics in a Global Economy*, edited by Mickey Lauria, 149–70. Thousand Oaks, CA: Sage.

Horstman, Barry M. 1989. "Phoenix Rises as Example as S.D. Heads for District Races." *Los Angeles Times*, July 30. Accessed November 7, 2013. http://articles.latimes.com/1989-07-30/local/me-876_1_district-elections.

Hubbard, Burt. 2009. "Denver Gets Whiter; Suburbs More Diverse." *Denver Post*, March 29.

HUD (US Department of Housing and Urban Development). 2001. "Interim Assessment of the Empowerment Zones and Enterprise Communities (EZ/EC) Program: A Progress Report." Washington, DC: US Department of Housing and Urban Development.

———. 2012. "Court Approves Final Settlement in *Thompson v. HUD*." http://portal.hud .gov/hudportal/HUD?src=/press/press_releases_media_advisories/2012/HUDNo .12-174.

———. 2013. "Expenditure Reports, FY 2010-2011, Denver." Office of Community Planning and Development. http://portal.hud.gov/hudportal/HUD?src=/program _offices/comm_planning/communitydevelopment/budget/disbursementreport.

Hulchanski, David. 2010. "The Three Cities within Toronto: Income Polarization in Toronto's Neighborhoods, 1970-2005." Toronto: Cities Centre.

Hyman, James B. 2002. *Not Quite Chaos*. Baltimore, MD: Annie E. Casey Foundation.

Hyra, Derek S. 2008. *The New Urban Renewal: The Economic Transformation of Harlem and Bronzeville*. Chicago: University of Chicago Press.

———. 2011. "Community Inclusion and Conflict." Paper presented at the "Conference on Ethnography, Diversity and Urban Spaces," St. Annes College, Oxford University, September 27.

Ibbitson, John. 1997. *Promised Land: Inside the Mike Harris Revolution*. Scarborough, ON: Prentice Hall.

Jackson, Mandi I. 2008. *Model City Blues*. Philadelphia, PA: Temple University Press.

Jacobson, Joan, and Melody Simmons. 2011. "The Muddled Money Trail"; "Maryland Elected Officials Short on Financial Details." *Maryland Daily Record*, January 31.

Jargowsky, Paul. 2003. *Stunning Progress, Hidden Problems: The Dramatic Decline of Concentrated Poverty in the 1990s*. The Living Cities Census Series. Center on Urban and Metropolitan Policy. Washington, DC: Brookings Institution. Accessed November 16, 2010. http://www.brookings.edu/~/media/Files/rc/reports/2003/05 demographics_jargowsky/jargowskypoverty.pdf.

Javed, Noor. 2009. "Regent Park Gets Million for Arts Centre." *Toronto Star*, December 16.

Jones, Bryan D., Tracy Sulkin, and Heather A. Larsen. 2003. "Policy Punctuations in American Political Institutions." *American Political Science Review* 97:151-69.

Jones-Correa, M., ed. 2001a. *Governing American Cities: Inter-ethnic Coalitions, Competition, and Conflict*. New York: Russell Sage Foundation.

———. 2001b. "Structural Shifts and Institutional Capacity: Possibilities for Ethnic Cooperation and Conflict in Urban Settings." In *Governing American Cities: Inter-ethnic Coalitions, Competition, and Conflict, edited by M. Jones-Correa, 183-209*. New York: Russell Sage Foundation.

Joravsky, B., and M. Dumke. 2009. "The Shadow Budget." *Chicago Reader*, October 22.

Judd, Dennis. 1986. "From Cowtown to Sunbelt City." In *Restructuring the City: The Political Economy of Urban Redevelopment*, rev. ed., edited by Susan S. Fainstein, Norman I. Fainstein, Richard Child Hill, Dennis Judd, and Michael Peter Smith, 167-201. New York: Longman.

Judd, Dennis R., and Todd Swanstrom. 1998. *City Politics: Private Power and Public Policy*. 2nd ed. New York: Addison Wesley.

Kalinowski, Tess, and John Spears. 2007. "Success Driven by TTC: Miller." *Toronto Star*, June 17.

Kania, John, and Mark Kramer. 2011. "Collective Impact." *Stanford Social Innovation Review* 9 (Winter): 36-42.

Karnig, Albert. 1976. "Black Representation on City Councils: The Impact of District Elections and Socioeconomic Factors." *Urban Affairs Quarterly* 12:223–42.

Karnig, Albert, and Susan Welch. 1980. *Black Representation and Urban Policy*. Chicago: University of Chicago Press.

Katz, Bruce, and Jennifer Bradley. 2013. *The Metropolitan Revolution*. Washington, DC: Brookings Institution Press.

Katz, Michael B. 2011. *Why Don't American Cities Burn?* Philadelphia: University of Pennsylvania Press.

Katznelson, Ira. 1981. *City Trenches*. Chicago: University of Chicago Press

Kennedy, David M. 2002. "A Tale of One City." In *Securing Our Children's Future: New Approaches to Juvenile Justice and Youth Violence*, edited by Gary S. Katzmann, 229–61. Washington, DC: Brookings Institution Press.

Klemek, Christopher. 2011. *The Transatlantic Collapse of Urban Renewal*. Chicago: University of Chicago Press.

Kneebone, Elizabeth, and Alan Berube. 2013. *Confronting Urban Poverty in America*. Washington, DC: Brookings Institution Press.

Koschinsky, J., and T. Swanstrom. 2001. "Confronting Policy Fragmentation: A Political Approach to the Role of Housing Nonprofits." *Policy Studies Review* 18 (4): 111–27.

Kotler, Milton. 1969. *Neighborhood Government*. Indianapolis, IN: Bobbs-Merrill.

Kotlowitz, Alex. 1991. *There Are No Children Here*. New York: Anchor Press.

Kraus, N., and T. Swanstrom. 2005. "The Continuing Significance of Race: African American and Hispanic Mayors, 1968–2003." In *Contemporary Patterns of Politics, Praxis, and Culture*, edited by Georgia A. Persons, 54–70. National Political Science Review, vol. 10. Edison, NJ: Transaction.

Kraus, Neil. 2013. *Majoritarian Cities*. Ann Arbor: University of Michigan Press.

Kretzmann, John. 1991. "The Affirmative Information Policy: Opening Up a Closed City." In *Harold Washington and the Neighborhoods: Progressive City Government in Chicago, 1983–1987*, edited by Pierre Clavel and Wim Wiewel, 199–220. New Brunswick, NJ: Rutgers University Press.

Kretzmann, John P., and John McKnight. 1993. *Building Communities from the Inside Out*. Evanston, IL: Asset-Based Community Development Institute, Institute for Policy Research, Northwestern University; distributed by ACTA Publications.

Kruse, Kevin M. 2005. *White Flight*. Princeton, NJ: Princeton University Press.

Kubisch, Anne C., P. Auspos, P. Brown, R. Chaskin, K. F. Anderson, and R. Hamilton. 2002. *Voices from the Field II: Reflections on Comprehensive Community Change*. Washington, DC: Aspen Institute.

Kubisch, Anne C., P. Auspos, P. Brown, and T. Dewar. 2010. *Voices from the Field III: Lessons and Challenges from Two Decades of Community Change Efforts*. Washington, DC: Aspen Institute.

Laake, Deborah. 1990. "Terry Goddard." *Phoenix New Times*, October 3. Accessed November 20, 2014. http://www.phoenixnewtimes.com/1990-10-03/news/terry-goddard/full/.

Lassiter, Matthew D. 2006. *The Silent Majority*. Princeton, NJ: Princeton University Press.

Lejano, R., and A. Taufen Wessells. 2006. "Community and Economic Development: Seeking Common Ground in Discourse and in Practice." *Urban Studies* 43 (9): 1469–89.

Leonard, Stephen J., and Thomas J. Noel. 1990. *Denver: Mining Camp to Metropolis*. Boulder: University Press of Colorado.

Letts, C., and A. McCaffrey. 2003. *Los Angeles Urban Funders*. Harvard University Kennedy School of Government Case Study no. 1682. Boston, MA: Harvard Business Publishing.

Ley, David, and Heather Smith. 2000. "Relations between Deprivation and Immigrant Groups in Large Canadian Cities." *Urban Studies* 37 (1): 37–62.

———. 2007. "The Immigrant Experience of Poverty in Toronto Neighbourhoods of Concentrated Disadvantage." Workshop presentation at Ninth National Metropolis Conference, Toronto. http://ceris.metropolis.net/9thMetropolisConference/WorkshopPresentations/B11_Smith.pdf.

Lindblom, Charles E. 1977. *Politics and Markets*. New York: Basic Books.

LISC (Local Initiatives Support Corporation). 2011. "Our History." Accessed November 15, 2011. http://www.lisc.org/section/aboutus/history.

———. n.d.-a. "Centers for Working Families." Accessed March 18, 2012. http://www.lisc-chicago.org/Our-programs/Centers-for-Working-Families/index.html.

———. n.d.-b. "New Communities Program." Accessed March 13, 2011. http://www.newcommunities.org/whoweare/liscchicago.asp.

LISC (Local Initiatives Support Corporation) and Woodlawn Preservation and Investment Corporation. 2005. *Woodlawn: Rebuilding the Village; Quality of Life Plan*. Chicago: Local Initiatives Support Corp. and Woodlawn Preservation and Investment Corp.

Logan, John R., and Harvey L. Molotch. 1987. *Urban Fortunes*. Berkeley: University of California Press.

Lowe, Jeanne R. 1967. *Cities in a Race with Time*. New York: Random House.

Lukas, J. Anthony. 1984. "All in the Family." In *Boston, 1700–1980*, edited by R. P. Formisano and C. K. Burns, 241–57. Westport, CT: Greenwood Press.

Lyall, Katherine. 1982. "A Bicycle Built for Two: Public-Private Partnership in Baltimore." In *Public-Private Partnerships in American Cities*, edited by R. Scott Fosler and Renne A. Berger, 17–57. Lexington, MA: Lexington Books.

MacArthur Foundation. 2010. *A Comprehensive Approach to Transforming Communities*. http://www.macfound.org/site/c.lkLXJ8MQKrH/b.938145/k.FEC9/Domestic_Grantmaking__Community__Economic_Development.htm.

———. 2011. "Historical Timeline." Accessed November 15, 2011. http://www.macfound.org/site/c.lkLXJ8MQKrH/b.855245/k.588/About_the_Foundation.htm.

Magnusson, Warren. 1990. "Progressive Politics in Canadian Cities". In *Challenges to Local Government*, edited by Desmond S. King and Jon Pierre, 173–94. Newbury Park, CA: Sage.

Maida, C. 2008. *Pathways through Crisis: Urban Risk and Public Culture*. Lanham, MD: Altamira Press.

Markowitz, Gerald, and David Rosner. 1996. *Children, Race, and Power*. Charlottesville: University Press of Virginia.

Maurrassee, David J. 2001. *Beyond the Campus*. New York: Routledge.

May, Judith V. 1971. "Two Model Cities." *Politics and Society* 2 (1): 57–88.

McCarron, J. 2007. "Pilsen Comes Together to Preserve and Build: LISC Chicago's New Community Program/Pilsen (Lower West Side)." Chicago: Local Initiatives Support Corp.

McDonald, Joseph P. 2014. *American School Reform*. Chicago: University of Chicago Press.

McDougall, Harold A. 1993. *Black Baltimore*. Philadelphia: Temple University Press.

McLaughlin, Edmund M. 1975. "The Power Network in Phoenix: An Application of Smallest Space Analysis." *Critical Sociology* 5 (April): 185–95.

McNeely, Joseph B. 2012. "Homewood Community Partners Initiative, a Call to Action: Findings and Recommendations." Baltimore, MD: Homewood Community Initiative.

Meagher, Sean, and Tony Boston. 2003. *Community Engagement and the Regent Park Redevelopment*. Report to Toronto Community Housing Corporation. http://www.regentparkplan.ca/communityengagement.htm.

Medoff, Peter, and Holly Sklar. 1994. *Streets of Hope*. Cambridge, MA: South End Press.

Menefee-Libey, David. 2010. "Neoliberal School Reform in Chicago? Renaissance 2010, Portfolios of Schools, and Diverse Providers." In *Between Public and Private*, edited by Katrina E. Bulkley, Jeffrey R. Henig, and Henry M. Levin, 55–90. Cambridge, MA: Harvard Education Press.

Meyerson, H. 2013. "L.A. Story." *American Prospect, August 6.*

Milkman, Ruth. 2006. *L.A. Story: Immigrant Workers and the Future of the U.S. Labor Movement*. New York: Russell Sage Foundation.

Milkman, Ruth, Joshua Bloom, and Victor Narro. 2010. *Working for Justice*. Ithaca, NY: Cornell University Press.

Miller, David. 2008. "Mayor's Tower Renewal." Report to Executive Committee, August 19. http://www.towerrenewal.ca/MTR_execReport.pdf.

Modarres, A. 1999. "Los Angeles: Borders to Poverty—Empowerment Zones and Spatial Politics of Development." In *Rebuilding Urban Neighborhoods: Achievements, Opportunities, and Limits*, edited by W. D. Keating and N. Krumholz, 140–58. Thousand Oaks, CA: Sage.

Mohl, Raymond A. 2004. "Stop the Road." *Journal of Urban History* 30 (5): 674–706.

Mollenkopf, John. 1983. *The Contested City*. Princeton, NJ: Princeton University Press.

Molotch, Harvey. 1976. "The City as a Growth Machine." *American Journal of Sociology* 82 (September): 309–31.

———. 1993. "The Political Economy of Growth Machines." *Journal of Urban Affairs* 15 (1): 29–53.

Moore, Aaron Alexander. 2013. *Planning Politics in Toronto: The Ontario Municipal Board and Urban Development*.Toronto: University of Toronto Press.

Mossberger, Karen. 1999. "State-Federal Diffusion and Policy Learning in a Federal System: From Enterprise Zones to Empowerment Zones." *Publius: The Journal of Federalism* 29 (3): 31–50.

Moulton, Jennifer. 1999. "Ten Steps to a Living Downtown." Discussion Paper. Center on Urban and Metropolitan Policy, Brookings Institution, Washington, DC.

Mouritzen, Poul Erik, and James Svara. 2002. *Leadership at the Apex: Politicians and Administrators in Western Local Governments*. Pittsburgh, PA: University of Pittsburgh Press.

Munoz, Carlos, Jr., and Charles P. Henry. 1990. "Coalition Politics in San Antonio and Denver: The Cisneros and Peña Mayoral Campaigns." In *Racial Politics in American Cities*, edited by Rufus P. Browning, Dale R. Marshall, and David H. Tabb, 179–90. New York: Longman.

Mushkatel, Alvin, John Stuart Hall, Bruce Merrill, and L. A. Wilson II. 1984. "Municipal Reform in Phoenix: When and Why." In *Urban Villages / Council Districts: The Future or Frustration?*, edited by John Stuart Hall and Albert K. Karnig, 20–36. Tempe: Center for Public Affairs, Arizona State University.

Musso, Juliet A., and Christopher Weare. 2009. "Citizen and City: Institutional Reform and Self-Governance in Los Angeles." In *The Politics of Self-Governance*, edited by E. Sorensen and P. Triantafillou, 95–116. Burlington, VT: Ashgate.

Musso, Juliet A., C. Weare, T. Bryer, and T. L. Cooper. 2011. "Toward 'Strong Democracy' in Global Cities? Social Capital Building, Theory-Driven Reform, and the Los Angeles Neighborhood Council Experience." *Public Administration Review* 71 (1): 102–11.

Nast, Lenora, Laurence Krause, and R. C. Monk, eds. 1982. *Baltimore: A Living Renaissance.* Baltimore, MD: Historic Baltimore Society.

National Advisory Commission on Civil Disorders. 1968. *Report.* New York: Bantam Books.

National Commission on Excellence in Education. 1983. *A Nation at Risk.* Washington, DC: Government Printing Office.

Nelson, Douglas W., and Christopher Shea. 2010. "East Baltimore's Rebirth." *Baltimore Sun,* November 11.

New Communities Program. 2005. *Chicago Neighborhood Plans: Quality of Life Plan Summaries; New Communities Program.* Chicago: LISC.

Nicholls, Walter J., and Justin R. Beaumont. 2004. "The Urbanisation of Justice Movements? Possibilities and Constraints for the City as a Space of Contentious Struggle." *Space and Polity* 8 (2): 119–35.

Nilsen, Richard. 2011. "1980s Bring Change, Culture to Phoenix." *Arizona Republic, October 8.* Accessed November 5, 2013. *http://bit.ly/ypXTQf.*

Note. 1966. "Citizen Participation in Urban Renewal." *Columbia Law Review* 66 (3): 485–607.

Nyden, Philip, Anne Figert, Mark Shibley, and Darryl Burrows. 1997. *Building Community: Social Science in Action.* Thousand Oaks, CA: Pine Forge Press.

O'Connor, Thomas H. 1993. *Building a New Boston.* Lebanon, NH: Northeastern University Press.

Olivo, Antonio. 2012. "Questions Raised about Leon Finney Jr.'s Woodlawn Organization." *Chicago Tribune,* January 6. http://articles.chicagotribune.com/2012-01-06/news/ct-met-finney-woodlawn-20120106_1_property-management-federal-lawsuit-chief-financial-officer.

Olson, Sherry. 1976. *Baltimore.* Pensacola, FL: Ballinger.

———. 1980. *Baltimore: The Building of an American City.* Baltimore, MD: Johns Hopkins University Press.

Ontario Ministry of Community Safety and Correctional Services. 2008. "McGuinty Government Renews Toronto Anti-violence Intervention Strategy." Press release, June 24. http://ogov.newswire.ca/ontario/GPOE/2008/06/24/c7105.html?lmatch=&lang=e.html.

Ontario Ministry of Transportation. 2009. "Province Moving Transit Projects Forward." Press release, April 1. http://news.ontario.ca/mto/en/2009/04/province-moving-transit-projects-forward.html.

Open Society Foundations. 2013. "The Open Places Initiative Call for Implementation Proposals, Deadline: September 27, 2013."

Orfield, Gary, Genevieve Siegel-Hawley, and John Kucsera. 2011. *Divided We Fail: Segregation and Inequality in the Southland's Schools.* The Civil Rights Project / Proyecto Derechos Civiles. Los Angeles: University of California, Los Angeles.

Orr, Marion. 1992. "Urban Regimes and Human Capital Policies." *Journal of Urban Affairs* 14 (2): 173–87.

———. 1999. *Black Social Capital.* Lawrence: University Press of Kansas.

Orren, Karen, and Stephen Skowronek. 2004. *The Search for American Political Development.* New York: Cambridge University Press

Orser, W. Edward. 1994. *Blockbusting in Baltimore: The Edmondson Village Story.* Lexington: University of Kentucky Press.

Osborne, David, and Ted Gaebler. 1992. *Reinventing Government: How the Entrepreneurial Spirit Is Transforming Government."* Reading, MA: Addison-Wesley.

Osborne, David, and Peter Plastrik. 1997. *Banishing Bureaucracy: The Five Strategies for Reinventing Government.* Reading, MA: Addison-Wesley.

Paperny, Anna. 2010. "Future of Programs for Poor Neighborhoods in Question." *Globe and Mail*, December 15.

Pastor, Manuel, Jr., Chris Benner, and Martha Matsuoka. 2009. *This Could Be the Start of Something Big: How Social Movements for Regional Equity Are Reshaping Metropolitan America.* Ithaca, NY: Cornell University Press.

Patashnik, Eric M. 2008. *Reforms at Risk.* Princeton, NJ: Princeton University Press.

Pattillo, Mary. 2007. *Black on the Block: The Politics of Race and Class in the City.* Chicago: University of Chicago Press.

Payne, Charles M. 2010. *So Much Reform, So Little Change.* Cambridge, MA: Harvard Education Press.

Penglei, Ni, ed. 2012. *The Global Urban Competitiveness Report—2011.* Northhampton, MA: Edward Elgar.

Perry, David C., and Wim Wiewel, eds. 2005. *The University as Urban Developer.* Armonk, NY: M. E. Sharpe.

Peterson, Paul. 1981. *City Limits.* Chicago: University of Chicago Press.

Pierce, Neal R., and Carol F. Steinbach. 1987. *Corrective Capitalism. The Rise of America's Community Development Corporations.* New York: Ford Foundation.

Pierson, Paul. 2004. *Politics in Time.* Princeton, NJ: Princeton University Press.

Pietila, Antero. 2010. *Not in My Neighborhood.* Chicago: Ivan R. Dee

Piton Foundation. 2004. *Neighborhood Data Book.* Denver, CO: Piton.

———. 2011a. *Denver Children's Corridor.* http://www.denverchildrenscorridor.org.

———. 2011b. *Neighborhood Focus: Denver's Growth Slows, Diversity Unchanged.* Piton Foundation's 2010 Census Project. http://www.piton.org/census2010/.

Podair, Jerald E. 2002. *The Strike That Changed New York.* New Haven, CT: Yale University Press.

Pogge, Jean. 1992. "Reinvestments in Chicago Neighborhoods: A Twenty Year Struggle." In *From Redlining to Reinvestment*, edited by Gregory D. Squires, 133–48. Philadelphia: Temple University Press.

Pollock, Marcus, and Ed Rutkowski. 1998. "The Urban Transition Zone." Baltimore, MD: Patterson Park Community Development Corp.

Polsby, Nelson W. 1980. *Community Power and Political Theory.* 2nd ed. New Haven, CT: Yale University Press.

Popkin, Susan J., Bruce Katz, Mary Cunningham, and Margery Turner. 2004. *A Decade of HOPE VI: Research Findings and Policy Challenges.* Washington, DC: Urban Institute and the Brookings Institution.

Pressman, Jeffrey L., and Aaron Wildavsky. 1984. *Implementation.* 3rd ed. Berkeley: University of California Press.

PRRAC (Poverty and Race Research Action Council). 2005. "An Analysis of the *Thompson v. HUD* Decision." February.

Pryor, Beth Williams, Jennifer Blake, Henrique Caine, and Diana Meyer. 2000. *On the Ground with Comprehensive Community Initiatives.* Baltimore, MD: Enterprise Foundation.

Purcell, Mark. 2000. "Decline of the Political Consensus for Urban Growth: The Example of Los Angeles." *Journal of Urban Affairs* 22 (1): 85–100.

Rae, Douglas W. 2003. *City: Urbanism and Its End.* New Haven, CT: Yale University Press.

Ravitch, Diane. 2010. *The Death and Life of the Great American School System.* New York: Basic Books.

Reckhow, Sarah. 2013. *Follow the Money: How Foundation Dollars Change Public School Politics*. New York: Oxford University Press.

Reckhow, Sarah, and Margaret Weir. 2012. "Building a Resilient Social Safety Net." In *Urban and Regional Policy and Its Effects*, vol. 4, *Building Resilient Regions*, edited by Margaret Weir, Nancy Pindus, Howard Wial, and Harold Wolman, 275–324. Washington, DC: Brookings Institution Press.

Rich, Michael J., and Robert P. Stoker. 2010. "Rethinking Empowerment Zones." *Urban Affairs Review* 45 (6): 775–96.

———. 2014. *Collaborative Governance for Urban Revitalization*. Ithaca, NY: Cornell University Press.

Robbins, Liz. 2012. "In Brooklyn, Bracing for Hurricane Barclays." *New York Times*, September 21.

Robinson, Tony. 2000. "The Los Angelization of Denver." *Denver Post*, December 31.

———. 2005. *Missing the Target: How Denver's Inclusionary Housing Ordinance and Urban Renewal Policy Could Better Meet Denver's Housing Needs*. Denver, CO: Front Range Economic Strategy Center.

———. 2006. "Breaking New Ground at Gates." *Denver Post*, February 12, A1.

Rodin, Judith. 2007. *The University and Urban Revival*. Philadelphia: University of Pennsylvania Press.

Rose, Albert. 1980. *Canadian Housing Policies (1935–1980)*. Owen Sound, ON: Ginger Press.

Rubin, Herbert J. 2000. *Renewing Hope within Neighborhoods of Despair*. Albany: State University of New York Press

Rubin, Julia S., and Gregory M. Stankiewicz. 2001. "The Los Angeles Community Development Bank: The Possible Pitfalls of Public-Private Partnerships." *Journal of Urban Affairs* 23 (2): 133–53.

Ruble, Blair. 2010. *Washington's U Street*. Washington, DC: Johns Hopkins University Press / Woodrow Wilson Center.

Rusk, David. 1996. *Baltimore Unbound: A Strategy for Regional Renewal*. Baltimore, MD: Abell Foundation.

Ryan, James E. 2010. *Five Miles Away, a World Apart*. Oxford: Oxford University Press.

Saegert, Susan. 2006. "Building Civic Capacity in Urban Neighborhoods: An Empirically Grounded Anatomy." *Journal of Urban Affairs* 28 (3): 275–94.

Saito, Leland T. 2012. "How Low-Income Residents Can Benefit from Urban Development: The LA Live Community Benefits Agreement." *City and Community* 11 (2): 129–50.

Saiz, Martin. 1993. "Transforming Growth Politics: Denver during the Peña Administration." Paper presented at the Annual Meeting of the Western Political Science Association, Pasadena, CA.

Salisbury, Robert H. 1964. "Urban Politics: The New Convergence of Power." *Journal of Politics* 26 (November): 775–97.

Sampson, Robert J. 2012. *Great American City*. Chicago: University of Chicago Press.

Sassen, Saskia. 2001. *The Global City*. 2nd ed. Princeton, NJ: Princeton University Press.

Satter, Beryl. 2009. *Family Properties*. New York: Henry Holt.

Savitch, H. V., and Paul Kantor. 2002. *Cities in the International Marketplace*. Princeton, NJ: Princeton University Press.

Schachtel, Marsha. 2011. "The East Baltimore Revitalization Initiative: A Commitment to Economic Inclusion." Baltimore, MD: Annie E. Casey Foundation.

Schneider, Anne, and Helen Ingram. 1993. "Social Construction of Target Populations." *American Political Science Review* 87 (2): 334–47.

Self, Robert O. 2003. *American Babylon*. Princeton, NJ: Princeton University Press.

Seligman, Amanda I. 2005. *Block by Block*. Chicago: University of Chicago Press.

Sewell, John. 2005. "What to Do with Regent Park." *Eye Weekly*, January 20.

Sewell, William H., Jr. 2005. *Logics of History*. Chicago: University of Chicago Press.

Sharkey, Patrick. 2013. *Stuck in Place*. Chicago: University of Chicago Press.

Shefter, Martin. 1992. *Political Crisis / Fiscal Crisis*. New York: Columbia University Press.

Shipps, Dorothy. 2009. "Updating Tradition." In *When Mayors Take Charge: School Governance in the City, edited by* Joseph Viteritti, 117–47. Washington, DC: Brookings Institution.

Shorebank. 2005. "Community Development Finance Resources in Denver: Strategies and Roles for the City of Denver." Chicago: Shorebank Advisory Services.

Sides, Josh. 2003. *L.A. City Limits: African American Los Angeles from the Great Depression to the Present*. Berkeley: University of California Press.

Siegel, Fred. 1997. *The Future Once Happened Here: New York, D.C., L.A., and the Fate of America's Big Cities*. New York: Free Press.

Simmons, Melody. 2011a. "Minority Contractors Have Earned $64M from EBDI." *Maryland Daily Record*, February 8.

———. 2011b. "New EBDI Plan." *Maryland Daily Record*, August 1.

———. 2012. "Officials Blast EBDI Results." *Maryland Daily Record*, May 30.

Simmons, Melody, and Joan Jacobson. 2011. "A Dream Derailed." *Maryland Daily Record*, January 30, A1.

Simon, David, and Edward Burns. 1997. *The Corner*. New York: Broadway Books.

Simpson, Dick. 2001. *Rogues, Rebels, and Rubber Stamps: The Politics of the Chicago City Council from 1863 to the Present*. Boulder, CO: Westview Press.

Sirianni, Carmen. 2009. *Investing in Democracy*. Washington, DC: Brookings Institution Press.

Skloot, Rebecca. 2010. *The Immortal Life of Henrietta Lacks*. New York: Crown.

Skogan, Wesley G. 2006. "Community Policing: Advocate." In *Police Innovation, edited by* David Weisburd and Anthony Braga, 27–43. Cambridge: Cambridge University Press.

Small, Mario Luis. 2004. *Villa Victoria*. Chicago: University of Chicago Press.

Smith, C. Fraser. 1999. *William Donald Schaefer: A Political Biography*. Baltimore, MD: Johns Hopkins University Press.

Smith, Chris. 2011. "On the Block." *American Prospect* 22 (1): A6–A8.

SNTF (Strong Neighbourhoods Task Force). 2005. *A Call to Action: The Report of the Strong Neighbourhoods Task Force*. Toronto: United Way of Greater Toronto. http://www .unitedwaytoronto.com/document.doc?id=61.

Soja, Edward W. 2010. *Seeking Spatial Justice*. Minneapolis: University of Minnesota Press.

Sonenshein, Raphael J. 1994. "Los Angeles Coalition Politics." In *Los Angeles Riots: Lessons for the Urban Future, edited by* M. Baldassare, 47–72. Boulder, CO: Westview Press.

———. 2004. *The City at Stake: Secession, Reform, and the Battle for Los Angeles*. Princeton, NJ: Princeton University Press.

———. 2006. *Los Angeles: Structure of a City Government*. Los Angeles: League of Women Voters of Los Angeles.

Squires, Gregory D. 1989. *Unequal Partnerships*. New Brunswick, NJ: Rutgers University Press.

Stinchcombe, Arthur L. 1978. *Theoretical Methods in Social History*. Philadelphia: Academic Press.

Stoker, Robert P. 1987. "Baltimore: The Self Evaluating City." In *The Politics of Urban De-*

velopment, edited by Clarence N. Stone and Heywood T. Sanders, 244–66. Lawrence: University Press of Kansas.

Stoker, Robert P., and Michael J. Rich. 2006. *Lessons and Limits: Tax Incentives and Rebuilding the Gulf Coast after Katrina.* Washington, DC: Brookings Institution, Metropolitan Policy Program.

Stone, Clarence N. 1976. *Economic Growth and Neighborhood Discontent.* Chapel Hill: University of North Carolina Press.

———. 1980. "Systemic Power in Community Decision Making." *American Political Science Review* 74 (4): 978–90.

———. 1989. *Regime Politics: Governing Atlanta, 1946–1988.* Lawrence: University Press of Kansas.

———. 2005. "Civic Capacity What, Why, and from Whence." In *The Public Schools,* edited by Susan Fuhrman and Marvin Lazerson, 209–34. New York: Oxford University Press.

———. 2013. "The Empowerment Puzzle." Paper presented at the Annual Meeting of the American Political Science Association, August 29–September 1. Chicago.

Stone, Clarence, Marion Orr, and Donn Worgs. 2006. "The Fight of the Bumblebee: Why Reform Is Difficult but Not Impossible." *Perspectives on Politics* 4 (3: 529–46.

Stone, Clarence N., and Heywood T. Sanders, eds. 1987. *The Politics of Urban Development.* Lawrence: University Press of Kansas.

Stone, Clarence N., and Donn Worgs. 2004. "Community Building and a Human-Capital Agenda in Hampton, Virginia." Washington, DC: George Washington Institute of Public Policy, George Washington University.

Strom, Elizabeth. 2008. "Rethinking the Politics of Downtown Development." *Journal of Urban Affairs* 30 (1): 37–61.

Sugrue, Thomas J. 1996. *The Origins of the Urban Crisis.* Princeton, NJ: Princeton University Press.

Svara, James. 2008. *The Facilitative Leader in City Hall: Reexamining the Scope and Contributions.* Boca Raton, FL: CRC Press.

Tarrow, Sidney, 1994. *Power in Movement: Collective Action, Social Movements and Politics.* Cambridge: Cambridge University Press.

Taub, Richard P., Garth Taylor, and Jan Dunham. 1984. *Paths of Neighborhood Change.* Chicago: University of Chicago Press.

Taylor, Ralph B. 2001. *Breaking Away from Broken Windows.* Boulder, CO: Westview Press.

TCHC (Toronto Community Housing Corporation). 2004. "Regent Park Revitalization Initiative." Report from CEO to TCHC Board of Directors, December 15. http://www.torontohousing.ca/webfm_send/2779/1?#.

———. 2006. "Regent Park Revitalization Backgrounder." http://www.regentparkplan.ca/pdfs/about/regentpark_backgrounder.pdf.

———. 2008. "Real Estate Asset Investment Strategy." Report to TCHC Board of Directors. http://www.torontohousing.ca/webfm_send/6533.

———. 2010a. "Annual Review for 2009." http://www.torontohousing.ca/annual_review/2009.

———. 2010b. "Celebration Marks Official Opening of Four Buildings, Part of Regent Park Revitalization." Press release, April 23. www.torontohousing.ca/news.

Teaford, Jon C. 1990. *The Rough Road to Renaissance.* Baltimore, MD: Johns Hopkins University Press.

Thompson, J. Phillip. 2006. *Double Trouble: Black Mayors, Black Communities, and the Call for a Deep Democracy.* New York: Oxford University Press.

Topping, David. 2008. "A Tale of Sixty Cities." *Torontoist*, July 24. http://torontoist.com/2008/07/metrocide_a_tale_of_sixty_cities.php.

Toronto City Summit Alliance. 2003. *Enough Talk: An Action Plan for the Toronto Region.* http://www.torontoalliance.ca/docs/tcsa_report.pdf.

Trounstine, Jessica. 2008. *Political Monopolies in American Cities: The Rise and Fall of Bosses and Reformers.* Chicago: University of Chicago Press.

United Way of Greater Toronto. 2001. "Annual Report, 2001." http://www.unitedwaytoronto.com/downloads/aboutUs/AR2001/Full_Report_2001.pdf.

———. 2004. *Poverty by Postal Code: The Geography of Neighbourhood Poverty, 1981–2001.* http://www.unitedwaytoronto.com/whatWeDo/reports/povertyByPostalCode.php.

———. 2009. "Annual Report, 2009." http://www.unitedwaytoronto.com/downloads/aboutUs/AR2009/2009UWTannualReport.pdf.

———. 2013. "Community Hubs." http://www.unitedwaytoronto.com/whatWeDo/communityHubs.php.

Urban Health Institute. 2010. "Self-Study and External Evaluation." August 31. Johns Hopkins University.

Vale, Lawrence J., and Erin Graves. 2010. "The Chicago Housing Authority's Plan for Transformation: What Does the Research Show So Far?" Accessed March 20, 2012. http://www.mit.edu/dusp/dusp_extension_unsec/people/ faculty/ljv/vale_macarthur_2010.pdf.

Vasquez, Beverly. 1999. "Moulton Molds Denver." *Denver Business Journal*, July 11. http://www.bizjournals.com/denver/stories/1999/07/12/story3.html?s=print.

von Hoffman, Alexander. 1994. *Local Attachments.* Baltimore, MD: Johns Hopkins University Press.

———. 2003. *House by House, Block by Block.* Oxford: Oxford University Press.

Walsh, Joan. 1997. *Stories of Renewal.* New York: Rockefeller Foundation.

———. n.d. *The Eye of the Storm.* Baltimore, MD: Annie E. Casey Foundation.

Warren, Mark R., and Karen L. Mapp. 2011. *A Match on Dry Grass: Community Organizing as a Catalyst for School Reform.* Oxford: Oxford University Press.

Weir, Margaret. 2011. "Creating Justice for the Poor in the New Metropolis." In *Justice and the American Metropolis*, edited by Clarissa Hayward and Todd Swanstrom, 237–56. Minneapolis: University of Minnesota Press.

Weisburd, David, and Anthony Braga. 2006. *Police Innovation.* Cambridge: Cambridge University Press.

Wenger, Yvonne. 2012. "Hopkins President: University Has Moral Obligation to City." *Baltimore Sun*, February 23.

Weschler, Louis, N. Joseph Cayer, and Bernard Ronan. 1984. "Impacts of the District and Urban Village Systems on Government and Politics in Phoenix." In *Research Report: Urban Villages / Council Districts—the Future . . . or Frustration*, edited by John Stuart Hall and Albert K. Karnig, 102–15. Phoenix Together, Fourth Annual Phoenix Town Hall, November 15–16. Phoenix: Phoenix Together.

Williams, Ashlei. 2011. "Latino Population Shrinks in Some Chicago Neighborhoods, Grows in Others." May. Medill Reports Chicago. Accessed September 8, 2011. http://news.medill.northwestern.edu/chicago/news.aspx?id=193791.

Williams, Yohuru. 2008. *Black Politics / White Power.* Malden, MA: Blackwell.

Wilson, William J. 1987. *The Truly Disadvantaged.* Chicago: University of Chicago Press.

———. 1996. *When Work Disappears.* New York: Random House.

Wolf-Powers, L. 2010. "Community Benefits Agreements and Local Government: A Review of Recent Evidence." *Journal of the American Planning Association* 76 (2): 141–59.

Wong, Kenneth K. 1990. *City Choices*. Albany: State University of New York Press.

Wright, David J. 2001. *It Takes a Neighborhood: Strategies to Prevent Urban Decline*. Albany, NY: Rockefeller Institute of Government.

Yerak, B. 2010. "Chicago's Shorebank Fails, Is Bought by Investors." *Chicago Tribune*, August 20. Accessed November 8, 2013. http://articles.chicagotribune.com/2010-08-20/business/ct-biz-0821-shorebank-20100820_1_fdic-assets-david-vitale.

Youth Challenge Fund. 2010. "Funded Initiatives." http://youthchallengefund.org/index.php/groups/pg/.

Zhang, Y. 2011. "Boundaries of Power: Politics of Urban Preservation in Two Chicago Neighborhoods." *Urban Affairs Review* 47 (4): 511–40.

Zimring, Franklin E. 2012. *The City That Became Safe*. Oxford: Oxford University Press.

COAUTHORS

John Betancur is professor of urban planning and policy at the University of Illinois at Chicago. He is the editor of *The Collaborative City*.

Susan E. Clarke is professor of political science at the University of Colorado. She is a coauthor of *The Work of Cities* and *Multi-ethnic Moments: The Politics of Urban Education Reform* and is a coeditor of *The Oxford Handbook of Urban Politics*.

Marilyn Dantico is associate professor in the School of Politics and Global Studies at Arizona State University.

Martin Horak is associate professor of political science at the University of Western Ontario. He is the author of *Governing the Post-Communist City: Institutions and Democratic Development in Prague* and a coeditor of *Sites of Governance: Multilevel Governance and Policy Making in Canada's Big Cities*.

Karen Mossberger is professor and director, School of Public Affairs, at Arizona State University. She is the author of *The Politics of Ideas and the Spread of Enterprise Zones*, a coauthor of *Digital Cities* and *Digital Citizenship*, and a coeditor of *The Oxford Handbook of Urban Politics*.

Juliet Musso is associate professor and the Houston Flournoy Professor of State Government at the Sol Price School of Public Policy, University of Southern California.

Jefferey M. Sellers is associate professor of political science and public policy at the University of Southern California. He is the author of *Governing* *from Below* and of the forthcoming *Three Worlds of Multilevel Democracy*, a coauthor of *Metropolitanization and Political Change*, and a coeditor of *The Political Ecology of the Metropolis* and *Metropolitan Inequality and Governance in Global Perspective*.

Ellen Shiau is assistant professor of political science at California State University, Los Angeles.

Clarence N. Stone is research professor of political science and public policy at the George Washington University. He is an author or editor of several books, including *Regime Politics* and *Building Civic Capacity*.

Robert P. Stoker is professor of political science, public policy, and public administration at the George Washington University. His most recent book is *Collaborative Governance for Urban Revitalization*.

Harold Wolman is research professor, George Washington Institute of Public Policy, and professor emeritus of political science at George Washington University. He is a coauthor of *Urban Politics and Policy* and a coeditor of *Theories of Urban Politics* and *Urban and Regional Policy and Its Effects*.

Donn Worgs is associate professor of political science and director of African and African American studies at Towson University.

INDEX

The letter *t* following a page number denotes a table.

Abell Foundation, 59, 76n2

Access Partnership, The (TAP), in Baltimore, 64, 65, 78n28, 235

Action for Neighborhood Change (ANC), in Toronto, 199–200, 203, 204

Addams, Jane, 82

affordable housing, 223; in Baltimore, 59, 66, 67, 222; in Chicago, 82, 98, 101–2; in Denver, 155, 157, 171, 174, 175, 177–78, 181n24; exaction fees and, 30n2; in Los Angeles, 138, 141, 142, 143–44, 147; in Minneapolis, 219n1; in Toronto, 184, 185

Affordable Housing Trust Fund: in Baltimore, 67; in Los Angeles, 143–44

African American communities: Chicago's New Communities Program and, 94; in Denver, 156, 159; displacement in Washington, DC's Southwest area, 10; in Los Angeles, 134, 135; redevelopment and population displacement and, 8, 9; Schaefer's mayoralty in Baltimore and, 11; in South Phoenix Village, 118; ward politics in Chicago and, 84; in Woodlawn (Chicago), 99

African Americans: dispersion of, in Watts, 150; populations in US cities and suburbs, 2010, 41, 41t; social distress and spatial and social segregation of, 47

Alain Leroy Locke High School (Los Angeles), 138

aldermen in Chicago: Richard M. Daley administration and, 88, 89; neighborhood policymaking and, 103; patronage politics and EZ program and, 92; Pilsen neighborhood and prodevelopment stance of, 99; ward-based politics and, 81, 83–84; Washington's mayoralty and, 87

Alinsky, Saul, Chicago community organizing by, 82, 86, 100

alliance building, challenges of, xvii

AmeriCorps volunteers, in Garfield (Phoenix), 121

ANC. *See* Action for Neighborhood Change (ANC)

Andrews, Marvin, 114

Annie E. Casey Foundation, 50, 58, 61, 62, 65, 68, 76n2; in Baltimore, 72, 159, 211; BNIA launching and, 234; Making Connections Program, 173

Anschutz Entertainment Group, 133, 142

anti-expressway movement, 31n15

antiviolence campaigns, 7

Apostolic Church (Chicago), 100, 101, 107n16

Arizona Cardinals football stadium, 121

Arizona State University, 115, 121

Armbruster, Timothy, 69

Asian population, US cities and suburbs, 2010, 41t

Karlstrom, Mikael, 95

Katz, Bruce, HOPE VI and, 31n20

Katz, Michael, x, xvii, 14, 210

Katznelson, Ira, 204

Kemp, Jack, 17

Kerner Commission Report (1968), 14

KEYS (Knowledge, Education, Youth, and Society) Community Center (Phoenix), 122

King, Martin Luther, 26

King, Rodney, 14; South Los Angeles uprising (1992) and, 135

Kingston-Galloway neighborhood (Toronto), 196

Klemek, Christopher, 186

Kotler, Milton, 204

Kretzmann, John, 18

La Alma/Lincoln Park (Denver), 172–75; Consolidated Plan and revitalization in, 173; demographics in, 173; neighborhood assessment for, 174

LAANE. See Los Angeles Alliance for a New Economy (LAANE)

labor force participation rates, across cities, 1980–2010, 37–38, 37t

L.A. Bridges anti-gang program, 140, 143, 144

L.A. Live, 137

Lamm, Richard, 162

LAPD. See Los Angeles Police Department (LAPD)

Larsen, Heather A., 177

Lastman, Mel, 186; Toronto mayoralty of, 191

Latinos: Chicago's New Communities Program and, 94; in Denver, 155, 156, 159, 162, 164, 173; in-migration of, in Watts, 150, 151; in Los Angeles, 132, 134, 135, 141, 142, 146, 148; in Phoenix, 112, 118, 120; in Pilsen neighborhood (Chicago), 97. See also Hispanics; Mexican Americans

leadership, postindustrial period and fractured pattern of, 20

Lee, Richard, New Haven mayoralty of, 6, 10, 225, 226, 245n11, 245n12

Liberal Party (Canada), 197

linked development, 30n2

LISC. See Local Initiatives Support Corporation (LISC)

Livable Communities Program, in Los Angeles, 139

Living Cities Project, 54; grants, 18; launching of The National Community Development Initiative, 18

Local Initiatives Support Corporation (LISC): in Chicago, 88, 92, 93, 94, 95, 96, 100, 218, 221, 232, 234, 239; in Denver, 159, 161

locally undesirable land uses (LULUs), 214; noxious facilities 32n28

local politics, Dahl's pluralism and, 224

Logan, John, 12

Logan Square community (Chicago), New Communities Program and, 94

Los Angeles, 4, 217; black-white segregation in, 1990 and 2010, 44, 44t; Bradley mayoralty in, 138, 139; central-city educational attainment, 1990–2010, 36, 37t; charter reform in (1999), 137, 140, 145; city and suburban poverty rate in, 45, 45t; city manufacturing employment trends, 1980–2009, 36t; city population, 1950–2010, 39t; city population as percentage of metropolitan-area population, 1990–2010, 40t; city resident unemployment and labor force participation rates, 1980–2010, 37t, 38; community revitalization in, 152, 153; contextual trajectory of, brief profile, 48; deindustrialization in, 35, 35t; disinvestment patterns in, 134–35; EZ program and civil unrest in (1992), 91; foreign-born percentage of population in, 43t, 44; gang intervention activities in, 140; geographic, economic, and social fragmentation in, 133–35; as globalized city, 34, 48, 131, 134; global urban competitiveness rankings, 2011, 38, 38t; Hahn's mayoralty of, 143, 144; hyperfragmentation in, 131, 145, 151, 152, 153, 154, 215, 218, 221; institutional fragmentation in, 135–37; major outbreaks of civil violence in, 131, 135, 138, 150; metropolitan-area manufacturing employment trends, 1980–2009, 35, 35t; neighborhood connections and